What Every Woman
Needs to Know
About the Law

MARTHA POMROY

What Every Woman Needs to Know About the Law

Doubleday & Company, Inc.   Garden City, New York 1980

ISBN: 0-385-15121-7
Library of Congress Catalog Card Number 78–22818
Copyright © 1980 by Martha Pomroy
All Rights Reserved
Printed in the United States of America
First Edition

To Tessie and Bill Miller,
my parents, who paid for law school

ACKNOWLEDGMENTS

Amanda Ambrose of Applied Scholastics, Inc.
Sarah Berglund
Pat Burns of Narcanon, New York
Rudgely Calhoun of the Social Security Administration, New York
Elizabeth C. Clemmer of Continental Association of Funeral and Memorial Societies, Inc.
Hilary Condit
Joan Dioguardi
Egon Dumler, of Dumler and Giroux
Don Frank, of Erdheim, Shalleck, and Frank
Ron Haugen
Rex Hearn
Steve Herbert of Life Insurance Institute, New York
L. Ron Hubbard
Fred Inbau, Northwestern University School of Law
Raphael P. Jannone and Ronald Hillary of the Bowery Savings Bank
Jerry Lareau of Consumer Credit Counseling Service of New York
Bill Lewis
The Memorial Society of Riverside Church
Paul Miller
John Minehan, Kevin Murphy and Jerry Lillis of the Morgan Guaranty Trust Co.
Harvey Moldauer
Gilbert Stafford
Alta Mae Westgaard
Susan Wolfson
Jones Yorke of Bruns, Nordeman and Rea and Co.
Ellen Zinke

SPECIAL ACKNOWLEDGMENTS

Special thanks to Dale Westgaard, factotum extraordinaire.
Many thanks to Kristina Geiser Mañón, who did much research for this book.

CONTENTS

PART I FAMILY

PART II WORKING

PART III HOUSING

PART IV MONEY

PART V YOUR PERSON

PART VI DEALING WITH GOVERNMENTS

PART VII CONSUMERISM

PART VIII CRIME AND PUNISHMENT

PART IX ADVOCACY

*"You ain't dumb. If you don't understand
it, they didn't explain it right."**

INTRODUCTION

This book is about the law women need to know.

Picture this: You bought a bathing suit. After three swims, the chlorine in the YWCA pool has bleached it beyond recognition. You decide to return it to the store.

YOU: I only wore this swimsuit three times. Just look at it. It's a mess and I want another one.

CLERK: I'm sorry, miss. We never accept bathing suits for exchange.

If you didn't know a little law, you'd plunk down another twenty-five dollars for another swimsuit. But knowledge is power, so you know what to say.

YOU: According to the Uniform Commercial Code, goods have to be fit for their use. The fabric in this swimsuit bleaches out when exposed to chlorine. Therefore it is not fit for use, and you *have* to give me another swimsuit.

You win. This is the practical approach of *What Every Woman Needs to Know About the Law.*

The information in this book covers many of the joys and problems any normally upright female person is likely to encounter: working, marriage, buying a house, raising kids, rotten consumer goods, and so on. It's a book about life, and the law. The law governs how the elements of life work together.

Did you ever call a plumber to fix your washing machine? It wasn't getting any hot water. He turned a valve on the wall, and lo, hot water. One of the kids had turned it off. You probably laughed, and bravely paid the bill, but inside you felt like a real dumbhead. The next time

* My father.

there was no hot water, I'll bet that valve was the first thing you checked. This book is written so you can check valves, except our subject is law, not plumbing.

It's been tough for people to learn about the law. First, law is complicated, and *old*. Our legal history extends back to England, to the Roman Empire, even to Babylon. That means lawmakers have had millennia to make it complex. Second, the terminology is strange. Lawmakers have had the same millennia to develop their own language. American attorneys currently speak a patois made up of Latin, Middle English, and their local dialect. Lawyers don't really understand it either. And third, there is a *lot* of law. In the United States we have many different levels of government. Each one of them has the power to make law, from the U. S. Congress right down to the local zoning board. In our short history, these lawmaking bodies have consented to millions of laws, statutes, regulations, ordinances, decrees, bylaws, and orders. No wonder everybody is confused.

There *is* hope. In spite of odd language and too many laws, there are certain basic principles we can rely on. In this book, these principles are called RULES. The dictionary says rules are "established guides for action or conduct." That's the key to *What Every Woman Needs to Know About the Law,* because this is a book about doing. The rules are there to help you do, undo, and not do.

You've already seen one of the rules in action—returning the swimsuit. The rule is simple: "If you buy something that doesn't work, the guy who sold it to you has to take it back." This is a broad rule, and whether it's swimsuits or refrigerators, the rule is the same.

The law doesn't change much. That's one of the comforting things about it. A fifteenth-century English solicitor could easily close the deal on your house, though he'd be amazed at our system of title insurance. That's an extraordinary example, but you can expect that most of the information you glean from this book will last you a long time.

You will be reading about general principles. Many people have difficulty understanding advanced concepts just because they never learned the basics. Imagine trying to multiply if you've never learned to add. In this book, we've tried not to leave out the basics.

The basics will help you think about your problems in legal language. Individual states sometimes have exceptions to the RULES you will find here. If you know the basics, you will be able to easily find out what exceptions apply to you. So here is your starting place. This book won't make you into an attorney, but you will be a very sophisticated civilian.

Now we come to the bias of this book. Why write a book for women about the law? Isn't it the same for women as for men? In theory it is, but women do have many special rules. (Then there's survival. Too few people have been blessed with an education in taking care of themselves, but with women it's worse. Also, women tend to be interested in slightly different topics than men are.)

You will read about some funny and some unpleasant issues in these pages. Far too often I've talked to women who wailed, "But nobody told me *that* was the right thing to do." So we'll just have to talk about some difficult situations.

The more conservative reader may be interested in my particular degree of feminism. I have no interest in changing any woman's life, but I don't want anybody limiting my life, either. I would like it very much if all husbands were responsible for their families and all women lived in a paradise of responsibilities that they chose. Neither is true of life, or the law. Some men do abandon their families, as do some women. A number of women are ignorant of their own capabilities. But the one thing we can all count on is change. This book is here to help you if you choose to change your life, or if it is changed for you.

This law stuff is not hard. Probably nobody ever explained it right.

Part I
FAMILY

Chapter 1
I NOW PRONOUNCE YOU

Your marriage contract is more complicated than "love, honor, and cherish" implies. Whenever so many divergent interests are involved, such as children, business, inheritance, relationships, and love, things can get complex, as marriage often does. We tend to forget marriage is basically simple and try to create a wonderful elaborate game of it. The law treats marriage at a simple level, and leaves the elaborations to those of us who are doing it.

Normally the first step toward marriage is the engagement. But amidst June flowers, romance, parties, setting up the nest, invitations, gifts, shopping, and the rest of the preliminaries, lurks the law of the engagement ring.

> RULE: THE ENGAGEMENT RING
> BELONGS TO HIM.

Custom says it is good form to return the engagement ring if the engagement is broken. The law requires it. The law separates gifts between lovers into two categories: the gifts of pursuit and the gifts conditional on performance of the marriage.

If the man courting you feels he must shower you with flowers, monogrammed lingerie, or maybe even a mink coat before you've said you'll marry him, they're yours to keep. The courts consider these gifts to be an expression of your suitor's regard.

However, gifts you get from anyone from the time of your engagement up until you're married are considered yours only if the marriage happens. If the marriage isn't performed, you must give back everything from the shower gifts to the engagement ring.

> RULE: DON'T CONVERT THE WEDDING
> PRESENTS INTO CASH UNTIL
> YOU'RE ACTUALLY MARRIED.

When gifts arrive, you may be very tempted to return them to the stores, so you can use the cash to set up your household. This is not a good idea. You should take out a short-term loan instead.

A friend of mine sent out her wedding invitations. A business associate of her father's immediately sent her a six-hundred-dollar sterling-silver punch bowl from Tiffany's. Since she didn't have enough money for a security deposit and first month's rent for the apartment they had chosen, she returned the punch bowl for cash. This woman soon realized she should not marry her fiancé. In fact, their marriage was a shambles from the start and was finally annulled. But she went through with the ceremony anyway, since she couldn't give back the punch bowl. This story is improbable, but this woman swears she never would have married the guy if she hadn't cashed in the punch bowl.

When you've successfully weathered the engagement, marriage is sure to follow. In the old days on the frontier, preachers were hard to come by. Couples might even perform their own marriage ceremony, and that was valid for them. It was called a common-law marriage. The couple would cohabit over a long period and conduct themselves as husband and wife. That was sufficient as long as there weren't a lot of monetary benefits to wives, such as Workmen's Compensation and Social Security. Now, because so many institutions give widows money, we must be more organized. The state must be able to certify who's married to whom, who's responsible for which children, and who is entitled to rights of inheritance. So the days of affirming your relationship in a little sod hut on the prairie are gone for good.

> RULE: NEVER ASSUME COMMON-LAW MARRIAGE.

Common-law marriage has had a popular resurgence in recent years. Many individuals have heard a rumor that it exists, and have ignored a marriage ceremony. Thirty-six states refuse to recognize any form of common-law marriage. Fourteen states and the District of Columbia will recognize some form of it (Alabama, Colorado, Florida, Georgia, Idaho, Iowa, Kansas, Montana, Ohio, Oklahoma, Pennsylvania, Rhode Island, South Carolina, and Texas). However, even in these states, the person claiming a common-law marriage may have to sue or be sued before a court will rule whether her marriage is valid or not. There is also no automatic seven years, after which a common-law marriage becomes valid. This is a myth, promoted by wishful thinking.

The loss of benefits to the woman and the children is a great price to pay for the freedom which some people attribute to common-law marriages. But living together is not marriage. For persons to gain the benefits of marriage, they must follow the rules.

RULE: YOU MUST OBTAIN A MARRIAGE LICENSE.

Every state in the Union requires that you have a license. The waiting period between the time you get it and the time you may marry varies from twenty-four hours to five days. The normal waiting period is three days. The purpose of the waiting period is to prevent a marriage prompted by lust or drunkenness. However, there are locations where the strongly determined can get married almost immediately. On the East Coast, it's Elkton, Maryland. Las Vegas is popular in the West.

The person who issues marriage licenses is usually the county clerk. He can tell you how long the waiting period is and when the license will expire. Normally, you must use the license within thirty days of the date of issue, as the license may certify that the parties are free of disease and most states aren't willing to make this certification for longer than thirty days.

RULE: HANG ON TO THE LICENSE.

One of my dumber friends, who married on Halloween under bizarre circumstances, neglected this rule. She and her husband split up within two years. She never got a copy of the license, and isn't quite sure she was ever married. Now she doesn't know if she should get a divorce. When she finally decides to formally dissolve the relationship, she's going to have to write to the county clerk to see if her marriage was registered. If it was, she'll wait weeks for a reply. If it wasn't, she may have to pay transportation for her marriage witnesses to come to testify at the divorce. If you lose your marriage license, the clerk in the county in which you were married can issue you a copy, for a small fee.

There's a lovely Lithuanian custom that says the wife keeps the marriage license. In a Lithuanian home, you'll usually notice it hanging in a fancy frame. A Lithuanian woman would be unlikely to have my friend's problem.

RULE: YOU MUST HAVE BLOOD TESTS.

The basic purpose of blood tests is to ensure that the parties are free of venereal disease. Some states also require a physician's certificate stating that both parties are free of certain other physical illnesses, such as tuberculosis, epilepsy, and addictions to drugs or alcohol, but these requirements seem to be the exception rather than the rule.

There is an important medical reason for having a blood test. The mates may discover that they have incompatible blood types. About 10 per cent of the population is Rh-negative. If the mother is Rh-negative, and the father is Rh-positive, the couple can count on a number of miscarriages, unless the wife gets proper treatment.

Please ask your doctor if you and your fiancé have different Rh factors. The treatment is nothing more than an injection immediately following delivery of your first child. But if you don't know to ask for it, someone may slip up. You could be in and out of the hospital with miscarriages—just because you didn't have a shot.

RULE: YOU MUST BE OLD ENOUGH
TO GET MARRIED.

The age for a woman to marry ranges from 12 in Massachusetts to 16 in most other states. Before that age, a woman simply may not marry, whether she has her parents' consent or not. If a woman wishes to marry without her parents' consent, the states are almost equally divided on whether she's wise enough to do so at age 18 or at age 21. The marriage license bureau can tell you this.

Generally, a male has to be 18 before he can marry without his parents' consent. The exceptions are: Georgia (16), Hawaii (16), Maryland (16), Mississippi (17), Oregon (17), and Utah (16). Puerto Rico requires that a male be 21, but the Puerto Rican exception has a further exception. A male only needs to be 18 if his prospective wife has been seduced or is pregnant.

RULE: NOT EVERYONE CAN GET
A MARRIAGE LICENSE.

If you're in the process of divorce, but it's not yet final, the clerk in the marriage license bureau may refuse to issue you a license. If you have any prior marriages, you'd better take along your divorce papers or your former spouse's death certificate when you apply for the license.

RULE: BE SURE THE PERSON WHO
PERFORMS YOUR CEREMONY
HAS THE RIGHT TO DO IT.

Normally, justices of the peace and ministers have the right to perform wedding ceremonies. Sometimes they have to be licensed. You
may want to look at the license to see if it is up to date. One of my
cousins was married by another cousin whose license to marry had expired. By the time they discovered this embarrassing oversight, Eldon
and Florence were Presbyterian missionaries in China and the parents
of two children. They weren't married. The whole family had to float
downriver to Peking to redeem themselves from a life of sin.

Contrary to romantic literature, American sea captains have never
had the right to perform marriages. Despite research, legal scholars
have yet to determine how and where this rumor got started.

RULE: WHAT IS SAID AT THE
CEREMONY IS UP TO YOU.

All you and your spouse are required to do is declare in the presence
of a proper church or civil official that you take each other as husband
and wife. West Virginia requires that its justices of the peace follow a
particular ceremony. Many churches have set ceremonies, but that is a
requirement of the church—not the law.

Usually, you'll have two witnesses. They should be people about your
own age. The purpose of the witnesses is to have somebody who can
confirm that your marriage took place.

RULE: YOU MAY KEEP
YOUR OWN NAME.

A woman has never been required to take her husband's name. It
was a matter of etiquette, not law. You may keep your maiden name,
take his name in combination with yours (Fawcett-Majors), or make
the traditional choice and use his name. One couple I know thought
none of these solutions was fair. They chose a different last name which
both of them use.

Whatever name you use, make sure Social Security has an up-to-date
record of it. They need that to keep track of your payroll withholding.
They'll send you a name-change form if you decide to alter your name.

Theoretically, using your maiden name on joint income tax returns
should not create a problem. The front office of the IRS instructs taxpayers to put the husband's last name first, a slash, and then the wife's

last name (Majors/Fawcett). At the date of this writing, the IRS computer is still confused by this name structure. Needless to say, trying to maintain two names can lead to confusion, but there is nothing illegal about it.

After the marriage is performed, the next step is the honeymoon. Normally, marriages are consummated at this time. But not always. If it isn't, are you still married? There's some conflict about this in the legal mind. A few courts say it's got to be consummated, but most agree a ceremony and good intentions are enough.

Intercourse, as a problem of marriage, is discussed in the chapter on divorce.

There's been a lot of talk recently about reforming the structures of marriage so that a marriage with children has more stringent standards than a childless marriage. Many social thinkers and divorce attorneys agree that the standard should be different. However, judges and legislators are very conservative about marriage, and the likelihood of speedy alteration in this area is nonexistent.

Although the honeymoon has limited legal consequence, marriage is rife with legal significance. Judges have developed many rules to protect you and your children from the inconstancies of life. But sometimes judges tend to overprotect us. We'll get to that as well.

RULE: YOU HAVE SOME RIGHT
TO HIS PROPERTY.

In days gone by, when two people married, all of the woman's property became the property of her husband. In return, she got limited rights to his property. We no longer give up our property by virtue of marriage. But we still receive rights to his property because we contribute so much to the family unit. These property rights become important during divorce or if your spouse dies. This subject will be more fully discussed in the chapters on wills and divorce, but be aware that property rights are an integral part of marriage.

RULE: MAKE SURE YOU RETAIN YOUR
AMERICAN CITIZENSHIP IF YOU
ARE MARRYING A FOREIGNER.

Traditionally, the woman's citizenship became that of her husband's country. Today, she generally retains her own citizenship and acquires the right to travel on a passport from his country. But problems occur. Depending on the conventions the United States has with his country, she may lose the right to vote in U.S. elections. Also, there may be some unusual elements in the law of his country. For example, an American wife married to an Iranian may not leave Iran without her husband's consent, regardless of her citizenship. Your rights in your husband's country definitely should be investigated before you marry a foreign national. Write to your congressman or the U. S. State Department.

If you marry abroad, U.S. courts will recognize the marriage as legal no matter how bizarre the ceremony may be. The marriage simply has to be properly performed under the laws of that country. But whatever you do, save the local equivalent of the marriage license.

It is too often the case that a foreign national will marry a U.S. citizen merely to acquire U.S. immigration and work papers. If the guy who is courting you doesn't have a permanent residence status in the United States, be very wary. Your marriage may not last past the arrival of his residency papers.

RULE: YOUR HUSBAND CAN SUE IF YOU CAN'T HAVE INTERCOURSE.

Your husband's right to sue if you are injured and can't have intercourse is called the right to consortium. He doesn't sue you; he sues the person who injured you. Originally, this type of suit was just as barbaric as it sounds. If a man couldn't have his wife, he'd been damaged.

The thrust of the consortium suit has changed in recent years. Consortium is now brought to cover monetary damages to the family resulting from the wife's injury. The wife sues for her personal injuries, and the husband will sue for other damages.

This is how consortium works: A neighbor was having fuel delivered in the middle of winter. Her driveway was icy. Her two children were out playing and she couldn't find the four-year-old. As the fuel truck backed down her icy driveway, she feared the little boy might be too near the truck. She dashed behind the truck from the driver's blind side, slipped, and fell behind the truck. It rolled over her and broke her pelvis. In order to get the fuel company's insurance to pay off, they brought suit for three things: the woman's hospital bills, her pain and suffering, and consortium. The insurance company would have paid her hospital bills without question and probably would have paid damages. However, the family had baby-sitting fees and housekeeping expenses, and her husband had lost time at work. The only way to cover these expenses was for the husband to sue for consortium, since these damages were not to the woman herself but to her family.

There is a growing movement to give women the same right to consortium as their husbands. Twenty-eight states already do, and probably more will soon. Ask your attorney.

RULE: ANY AGREEMENT MODIFYING YOUR
MARRIAGE IS NOT REALLY BINDING.

Judges reason that the law is there to protect you, and they refuse to allow you to give up your protection. If you pledge to support the children, the judge may admire your spirit, but he'll still hold your husband responsible. That is the law. By the same token, a judge doesn't want to be bothered with a suit stemming from your special contract with your husband wherein he promises to hire a baby-sitter so you can work. By the law, it is your job to care for the children. If your salary doesn't pay for the sitter, you'd better find a cheaper sitter or a better job.

RULE: YOUR HUSBAND MUST SUPPORT YOU.

As my mother says about family finances, "What's his is mine and what's mine is mine." The law requires that the husband work and the wife take care of the house. This basic rule keeps a family running smoothly, but it won't apply to everybody. If you're a healthy young person with no responsibility for children, a judge is going to laugh at you when you say that your husband isn't supporting you. You may get some support, but it won't be worth the effort.

It is often the case that the basic rule and the outcome of a suit appear to conflict. This may seem odd to you, but the law has to start someplace. Lawmakers started with the basic rule that a man supports and a woman takes care of the house. In actual cases, judges look at the capacities of the individuals, then vary the outcome to suit the needs and capabilities of the people involved.

The father has an absolute duty to support his children. The mother has no duty to do so unless the father is incapable. We acquired this responsibility to support our children through the Family Expense Acts. A woman is now responsible for her children's care to the extent that their father is not able to provide for it.

RULE: YOU HAVE THE RIGHT TO
INHERIT FROM YOUR HUSBAND.

Under old English law a wife had a right to the use of one third of her husband's property after his death. This share was called the right of dower. The woman could use the property, but didn't actually own it. In most states the dower right has been replaced by a modern law. Widows now can get a true ownership of part of her husband's property. The man's ancient curtesy right of inheritance has also been reformed by new legislation.

Every state requires that a wife receive from one third to one half of the husband's estate. A husband gets the same share of his wife's estate. He may leave it to you outright or in the form of a trust. (You may do likewise.) If he leaves it to you outright, you merely take over complete control of your share. If he leaves it to you in trust, a bank or some other institution will hold the funds and make payments of the interest to you. Wills and inheritance will be fully covered later in the book.

RULE: MARRIED WOMEN CAN BUY, SELL, OR
BORROW MONEY ON THEIR OWN PROPERTY.

Under the Married Woman's Property Acts a woman can do anything with her own property that she pleases. No state absolutely requires her husband's permission if she buys, sells, or borrows. Some states recommend that she obtain her husband's consent. These states are Missouri, Nebraska, and Pennsylvania.

RULE: DON'T MAKE A CONTRACT
WITH YOUR HUSBAND.

For the most part, a woman's business contract with her husband will not be upheld by a court. Even if you have the same contract with him as his other employees, you may not win if you sue him to collect your salary. After all, the business is already providing you with your livelihood. If you are entering into any contractual relationship with your husband to buy or sell or work, seek a lawyer's advice.

RULE: DON'T MAKE FINANCIAL DEALS WITH
YOUR HUSBAND.

The most surprising and disappointing legal problem a married woman has is the financial deals that she makes with her husband. Women generally expect that they can deal with their husbands in a fair way. But when a woman tries to enforce payment on a contract, she may be shocked at the outcome. For example, if you sell him your house, there's some chance that you couldn't collect because you are living in the house too. By general agreement, this area of the law should be modified. If you could sell your house to somebody else, there's no reason in the world why your husband shouldn't pay you.

Courts recognize this problem and are generally changing. It's a good idea to check with your lawyer to find out if the contracts you make will be enforceable.

RULE: IT'S YOUR DEBT IF
IT'S IN YOUR NAME.

Under modern law, if your name is on the charge account or loan, you are held responsible for it. So if your husband runs up a big bill on your joint charge account, the creditor can garnishee your salary. Conversely, if you charge on your husband's name, the creditors can collect from him.

Creditors aren't naïve. They often require that both spouses sign a credit application. In this way, they can hold each responsible for the debt. This area of the law has been modified recently and is covered extensively in the chapter on credit.

RULE: YOU CAN BE SUED BY YOUR
HUSBAND'S CREDITORS.

His creditors can sue you if you allow your husband to borrow money using your property as security or if you co-sign the loan. Normally, his debts can only be collected against his property, and your debts can only be collected against your property. If you cosign his loan or allow him to use your house or anything else as collateral, you may lose it.

Short-term debts are probably safe, but for longer loans you should be cautious. For example, a husband took out a ten-year second mortgage on his wife's house. After a few years, the marriage disintegrated. Even though he used the money from the mortgage to start his own business, the wife was stuck with the rest of the mortgage payments. If it had been possible for the wife to draw up a contract with her husband at the time of the loan, she could have collected the loan from him, using his business as security. But, as you saw in the previous rule, such a contract would not necessarily have been enforceable.

For many women, this area of the law will never be a problem. For others of us who are self-employed or who finance our husband's business, it can be nasty. Wives want to help their husbands, but business relationships are usually more successful when the parties deal at arm's length. It's tough to be at arm's length from your husband.

RULE: NOTIFY THE CREDITORS TO
DISSOLVE YOUR RESPONSIBILITY
FOR YOUR HUSBAND'S DEBTS.

If you have a number of joint charge accounts with your husband, and he's turned out to be a spendthrift, your responsibility to your family and yourself may require that you dissolve your responsibility for any further debts he acquires. You may have to pay the debts he's already acquired.

You notify the creditors by *registered* letter that you will no longer be held responsible for any credit they extend to your husband. Don't call them. You'll have no proof that you notified them. In such a case it would be your word against theirs. Keep a carbon or photocopy of the letter and attach the postal service receipt to it. If you do that, they may try to get the money from you, but it's unlikely that they will succeed.

You're probably familiar with the newspaper notices disclaiming any responsibility for debt. This may be required under your local laws or statutes. You may speak with your attorney, or your union, or perhaps there is an office of the Consumer Credit Counseling Service in your city. Any one of these sources will tell you if you have to take any further action.

RULE: YOU MAY CHARGE NECESSITIES
WITHOUT YOUR HUSBAND'S CONSENT.

Women have a decided advantage here. If your husband hasn't been providing for you and your children up to your standard of living, you can charge your normal clothing, food, and other purchases without his permission. He will be held responsible for those debts whether he consented to the credit or not. This is called the doctrine of necessaries.

A needy woman may have difficulty finding a creditor who will give her credit under these circumstances. If a husband isn't giving her enough money for food and clothing, generally he either has run away or is stone broke. Merchants aren't entranced by either prospect.

RULE: EACH SPOUSE IS RESPONSIBLE
FOR THE ENTIRE TAX IF
THEY FILE A JOINT TAX RETURN.

If your husband refuses to pay his income taxes, the IRS can collect them from you if you filed a joint tax return for the year in question. If one of you doesn't declare all of your income, that's fraud and you both could be fined or go to jail.

As a practical matter, the IRS rarely sues a woman for her husband's tax debt, because she seldom has enough money to make it worthwhile. And on top of that, the family does have the right to keep certain possessions, such as the home, basic household furnishings, and perhaps one car. However, the IRS will blithely invade your savings account to recover your husband's tax bill.

While we're talking about unpleasant events, we may as well say a word here about abused women.

RULE: YOUR HUSBAND MAY NOT BEAT YOU.

Absolutely nothing in the law, American or English, has ever permitted a husband to beat his wife, though some states have ancient laws allowing him to spank her. But if a wife is beaten, her legal remedies are weak. Besides the insult of being beaten, the wife may not be able to sue her husband for damages. You'll find a chapter on abused women later in the book.

RULE: YOU CAN SUE YOUR HUSBAND, MAYBE.

Traditionally, wives were not allowed to sue their husbands for damages resulting from auto accidents, physical assaults, or other types of non-criminal injuries to her body or character. This lack of ability to sue prevented a woman from recovering damages if her husband beat her, if he injured her in an auto accident, or if he told lies about her.

Auto accidents were the most serious practical difficulty. If the husband and wife were in a one-car accident and she was badly injured, she could not sue their auto insurance company to pay her medical bills. (Since a wife couldn't sue her husband, she couldn't sue his insurance company either.)

More heartrending was the refusal of the courts to allow a woman to sue her husband if he beat her. She might be badly injured and would have no way to recover damages.

Fortunately, the situation has changed for the better. Twenty-eight states and the District of Columbia now allow a wife to sue her husband for injuries to her body or her character, or if he has been negligent (not ordinarily careful). These states are: Alabama, Alaska, Arizona, Arkansas, California, Colorado, Connecticut, Idaho, Indiana, Iowa, Kansas, Kentucky, Minnesota, Missouri, New Hampshire, New Jersey, New York, North Carolina, North Dakota, Ohio, Oklahoma, South Carolina, South Dakota, Texas, Vermont, Washington, West Virginia, and Wisconsin. The rest of the states have widely differing statutes. Delaware, Florida, Hawaii, Louisiana, and New Mexico allow no suit at all. Michigan, Oregon, Rhode Island, and Wyoming will not allow suits for negligence. Massachusetts will allow negligence suits only if they stem from auto accidents. Georgia, Illinois, Maine, Maryland, Mississippi, Montana, Nebraska, Pennsylvania, Tennessee, Utah, and Virginia will not allow a wife to sue her husband for torts. Torts would include physical assault, holding a wife against her will, and intentional mental cruelty. Nevada may not have a statute regarding a wife suing her husband, since a diligent search could not find one.

For years the courts would not hear suits between spouses since judges felt such suits would interfere with family relationships. If you are suing your husband to recover from his insurance company, the suit is merely a matter of form and may not disturb your relationship at all. If you have been the victim of a marital assault, your relationship is in big trouble. Your only course of safety is to move out and sue him.

RULE: YOU CHOOSE WHETHER YOU TESTIFY
AGAINST YOUR HUSBAND.

If your husband is being sued on a criminal matter, it is your privilege to refuse to testify. Even in civil suits, a wife's testimony in favor of her husband is not taken as seriously as the testimony of a less intimately related person.

By the same token, a husband and wife cannot be accused of conspiracy with each other. Their relationship is one which naturally requires intimate discussion and planning. So feel free to discuss with your husband anything of interest to either of you.

Much of this chapter has been grim and discouraging. You may be wondering what happened to all the nice aspects of marriage: the companionship, family picnics, your husband's enthusiasms, and first baby steps. Marriage does work. I know that, and I've seen it often. Unfortunately for the legal profession, successful relationships seldom sit across the desk. The law is superfluous when everybody's happy.

Chapter 2
AND THEY BEGAT

Your child is a ward of the state. The state has the job of seeing that your child physically reaches the age of 18. The state guards the body. It has no responsibility for the mind or the spirit.

RULE: YOUR CHILD BECOMES A WARD OF
THE STATE AT CONCEPTION.

Although a fetus can be aborted, the unborn child is considered a potential citizen, and is therefore entitled to protection. A pregnant woman will never be executed nor will the state allow the child's life to be harmed without cause. The banning of Thalidomide is an example of the state protecting children before birth. However, the most powerful protection the unborn had, the anti-abortion statutes, have been found unconstitutional.

The law became involved in the protection of the unborn in a rather surprising way. Ancient jurists thought it fair that a woman could sue for the negligent death or damage to her unborn child. Negligence, not abortion, was the starting point for protection of the unborn. Anti-abortion statutes were passed for the protection of the woman, not the child. In the nineteenth century, operating conditions were unsanitary. Infection and death were likely to follow abortion. So it was outlawed.

RULE: PREGNANCIES MAY
BE ABORTED.

As it stands now, during the first three months of pregnancy, the decision for abortion is between you and your doctor. The state may not

interfere. In the second three months, your state may require a special
procedure. Ask your doctor. There is no abortion possible during the
last three months of a pregnancy. The child could very possibly live
and the danger to the mother is overwhelming.

Abortion is not now an unhealthy procedure. Modern antiseptics and
drugs prevent infection. If the abortion is performed in the first three
months, the woman is unlikely to even be ill. These trimester guidelines
are fair. It gives you three months to decide what to do.

RULE: YOU CAN HAVE THE BABY
ANYWHERE YOU WANT.

There seems to be absolutely no law requiring you to have your baby
in any particular place using any particular method of delivery. But
hospitals make their own rules. Some still won't allow fathers in the delivery room or Le Boyer deliveries. Hospitals tend to get choleric when
patients assert their individuality and hospital personnel may present
policy as though it is the law.

RULE: YOUR CHILD'S BIRTHPLACE MAY
DETERMINE HER CITIZENSHIP.

There are two ways to become an American citizen at birth. A child
born of two American citizens abroad is automatically an American citizen. A child born on U.S. territory is a citizen regardless of the citizenship of his parents. In fact, that's how most of us got our citizenship. If
only one parent is an American and the child is born outside of this
country, the child has a choice of citizenship.

The saga of Gracie exemplifies these somewhat confusing principles.
Gracie's mother, Ann, was born in Pennsylvania of Lithuanian parents.
Ann's parents died when she was eight and she was sent back to
Lithuania to be raised by her two maiden aunts. Ann became a physician and married a Lithuanian. She had Gracie in Lithuania and then
the Second World War broke out. The family ended up in Austria,
where Gracie's brother, Al, was born. After the war Gracie's mother
reasserted her American citizenship so the family could come to the
United States without having to qualify for immigration quotas. Because Ann was a U.S. citizen, her husband, a Lithuanian citizen, had no
trouble entering the country. Gracie was already a U.S. citizen, since at
the time of her birth a child needed only one American parent in order
to automatically become a citizen, regardless of where the child was
born. Al was born after the law changed. Like other non-citizen children, he had to choose U.S. citizenship while in his teens. Ann practices
medicine, her husband has worked his way up from baker's helper to

bank president. Gracie is a dentist, and Al is an attorney. This whole success story might not have happened if Gracie's mother hadn't been lucky enough to be born in Pennsylvania.

RULE: CHILDREN HAVE SOME CIVIL RIGHTS.

Time was that children below the age of seven were considered incapable of committing a crime. If a child of six murdered four of his maiden aunts, the state would refuse to recognize the deed. If, when that child reached the age of eight he polished off the other three, the state would prosecute him as if he were an adult with full civil rights. Starting about 1900, the weight of adult court was removed and children began to appear before juvenile courts. Within the process of that change, children lost their civil rights. The child's civil rights were supposedly restored in 1967 with a decision which stated that children are entitled to the same rights in court as adults have. However, the juvenile courts have avoided this constitutional imperative whenever possible, according to Charles Silberman, author of the outstanding book *Criminal Violence, Criminal Justice*. Mr. Silberman cites some horrifying statistics. In 1974, between 780,000 and 1,030,000 children were locked up. Of the children arrested, only 77,500 were accused of violent crimes as defined by the FBI. A full 40 per cent were accused of the so-called "status" crimes—truancy, incorrigibility, running away, and sexual activity. One third of the children in detention centers are females; 75 per cent of these girls were charged with status crimes; white girls are more likely to be charged with premature sexual activity than girls of other racial groups.

These status crimes are one of the elements that distinguish juvenile justice from adult justice. In essence, charging a child with a status crime is no more than accusing him of unhappiness. The sanest theory of "incorrigibility" is that a child's acting up indicates there's something wrong at home or in school. Parents generally do the best job they know how to, but perhaps the parents don't know enough. The child may need an adult go-between to provide another point of view. The answer could be as simple as the parent consulting the child about the child's own welfare.

The child's school situation can be equally important. Amanda Ambrose is the president of Applied Scholastics, Inc., a nonprofit educational organization dedicated to excellence in education, using L. Ron Hubbard's study technology. Mrs. Ambrose asserts that crime is a direct result of poor education. She says, "Children do not go to school as criminals. They become criminals in school. They do go to school to become educated in how to make their dreams come true and to learn the ground rules of the game in life. It's asking a bit much of that person to be ethical and play by the rules, if he can't read them." Mrs. Ambrose's organization certainly knows whereof it speaks in the educational area. In a pilot program done in conjunction with the Los Angeles City Unified School District, the methods of Applied Scholastics raised the reading age of tenth-, eleventh-, and twelfth-grade students an average of 2.4 years in twenty-four hours of instructional sessions. One girl in the project went from a sixth-grade reading level to a twelfth-grade reading level. The experience of Applied Scholastics is that a child who is actively working toward his goals and dreams will rarely, if ever, fall into criminal activities. If juvenile homes and schools could successfully place the power of the written word within the grasp of their child inmates, there is no doubt that children would be better able to confront their own part of this world. Certainly the child's dreams could be more easily realized. (The results of Applied Scholastics, Inc., are startling in light of the seeming lack of success of so many other educational theories. There are twenty-five Applied Scholastics organizations in the United States and Mexico. If you would like more information on this remarkable organization, write: Applied Scholastics, Inc., 955 South Western, Los Angeles, California 90006.)

Another problem of the juvenile justice system is that innocent and lost children will probably be lumped into juvenile detention centers along with the violent children who comprise 10 per cent of the errant child population. Far more often than the authorities would like to admit, children are also dumped into adult jails, often "for their own good" or to "teach them a lesson." The world seems very lonely to child inmates. They sorely miss their families, no matter how idyllic the youth detention facility might be. Imagine the cruelty a child must confront in an adult jail.

The juvenile justice system itself was started to help children become better adults. Ideally, the system would operate to help the child. Help is less formal than justice, and much of the weight of the work has fallen on the shoulders of probation officers and social workers. A child can be incarcerated in most states on the word of these individuals alone. Only eighteen states require any hearing for the child at all. The child is therefore subject to the whim and personal prejudice of the social worker. Additionally, the child can be held incommunicado. Some institutions control children by refusing to allow them to call their parents.

An additional problem of juvenile justice is the hearing itself. These hearings are often held behind closed doors. Sometimes this helps the child, but it also has the effect of removing juvenile judges from general scrutiny. Transcripts of the hearings are rarely kept, and without a transcript, no appeal is possible. Indeed, juvenile appeals are rare. Many states do not even provide a way for a juvenile to appeal.

Juvenile court often assumes the aura of a kangaroo court. The child comes before the court accused with sleeping with her boy friend, not obeying his parents, or stealing a basketball. The judge has the right to order these children away from home for these very offenses.

Reform is too mild a term for the remedies needed in this area. A full discussion of juvenile justice is beyond the scope of this book, but I recommend that you read *Criminal Violence, Criminal Justice* by Charles Silberman (Random House, 1978). This fascinating book is exhaustively researched, but it is so shocking that you may have to work up your courage to read it.

RULE: CHILDREN HAVE A RIGHT
TO INHERITANCE.

Children born during wedlock must be remembered in the wills of both their mother and their father. If they are not, the courts consider it an oversight and will give the child a share. If you have a kid you wouldn't give a penny to, the only way to disinherit him is to mention him in the will, then cut him off. An individual child isn't always disinherited out of spite. Sometimes a parent will leave everything to one kid because he or she *needs* the assets and assistance much more than the other child.

If you die without a will, each of your children born in wedlock will receive part of your estate. What portion your children inherit will depend on the state in which you reside at the time of your death. There's much more to be said about this in the chapter on wills.

RULE: A PARENT MAY NOT
HARM HER CHILD.

Since the body of the child is under the protection of the state, the state can step in to protect a child from abuse. Even though the right of the state to do this is clear-cut, two practical problems arise. State child welfare workers balk at predicting which parent is likely to go too far in child discipline. Acts which one person considers strict punishment, another person considers abusive. King Solomon's problem was easy compared to the issues that welfare workers confront when endeavoring to remove a child from a possibly abusive home. The other problem is detection. A parent can abuse a child in ways not requiring medical care or hospitalization. Who would be likely to detect repeated cigarette burns on an infant's body?

The preschooler is the child most likely to be abused. He doesn't even have a teacher to notice when something is wrong. The difficulty here is not so much one of the law but one of finding abused children before their health and psychic well-being are affected.

If Mommy and Daddy aren't married when a child is born, the few rights of the child are modified. Illegitimate children have little or no legal standing, except that the state recognizes their existence. As adults, these kids are citizens, just like anybody else, but they may leap into the world as though they never had a mother or a father.

RULE: ILLEGITIMATE CHILDREN MAY NOT
BE ABLE TO INHERIT.

Under old English law, children born out of wedlock never inherited from the father and, depending on the era, were barred from inheriting from their mother. Modern statutes have changed this somewhat. In most states a bastard child can inherit from his mother without a will. But if the father leaves no will, the child is unlikely to inherit from him and the father's money will go to other members of the family no matter how distantly related.

Too few parents of illegitimate children consider the full implications of this problem. The parent may possess meager worldly possessions, but have substantial benefits at his or her job. For example, Workmen's Compensation, Social Security, and employee benefit plans all carry some death or pension benefits. Without a will, the child may be deprived of some or all of these. The dead parent's brothers and sisters or other relatives, no matter how distant, may end up with all or part of the money unless there is a will protecting the child.

Though not in line to inherit, a child born out of wedlock may receive dependent's benefits from Social Security. The child's parentage will have to be proven to the satisfaction of the Social Security Administration. That agency will explain the documentation needed.

RULE: THE ILLEGITIMATE CHILD
HAS A RIGHT TO SUPPORT.

Traditionally, the illegitimate child could expect support only from his mother. Most modern statutes have expanded support to hold the father responsible as well.

Before a man will be required to pay support, his paternity must be proved. The first step is medical testing, which can prove conclusively that a man is *not* the father of the child but cannot prove conclusively that he is. If the man could genetically be the father of the child in question, more proof is presented. The man's admission that he's the father is one favorable fact. If the mother and father were living together at the time of birth that will also weigh in favor of a support judgment. Each support and paternity case is unique. An attorney would be necessary to line up the proof for the mother and child.

RULE: AN ILLEGITIMATE CHILD CAN BE MADE LEGITIMATE.

There are two reasons for this: one legal and one social.

The legal reason is inheritance. Every state has a statute which allows the parent to protect the child's inheritance. Depending on the state, the requirements vary from public conduct, to acceptance of the child into the home, to a written statement made before a notary that the child is the offspring of the father. There's rarely any mystery about the mother's identity. These statutes may only govern inheritance from the parents. The law still varies substantially on whether a child born out of wedlock, regardless of the subsequent efforts of his parents, will be able to inherit from the relatives of the parents. There seems to be little need for so much stringency in this area.

The social reasons for legitimatizing a child vary from the clucks of fainthearted school registrars to name calling by the child's peers. Depending on the law of the state, the birth certificate may indicate— for all of the child's life—that he is a bastard. Regardless of the parents' convenience or social views, that's just plain inconsiderate.

If you are the parent of an illegitimate child, you may adopt your own child and thereby give your child full inheritance rights from you and your relatives. You can arrange an adoption through an attorney.

RULE: ADOPTED CHILDREN STAND IN THE SAME LEGAL POSITION AS YOUR NATURAL CHILDREN.

Adopted children have the same legal status as any child born into your family during a legal marriage. They have all the rights of inheritance from you and your husband and all the relatives on both sides. In certain cases they may also be able to inherit from their natural parents. They have a right to support from their adopted parents, but it's unlikely that their natural parents could be sued for support.

Sooner or later, your child is going to start doing things on her own. She may become a twelve-year-old wheeler-dealer and business tycoon. There are laws for these kids too.

RULE: CHILDREN MAY NOT WORK IN DANGEROUS OR UNHEALTHY CONDITIONS.

By 1920 the horrors of children deformed by opportunistic employers had ended. Now each state and the federal government strictly control children's work conditions and prohibit children from doing dangerous jobs. However, the government doesn't interfere when children work for their parents.

RULE: A CHILD MAY NEED A PERMIT IN ORDER TO WORK.

Child work permits exist to control school truancy and to notify the state that a child may be working under potentially harmful circumstances. Permits are usually required for any child of school age. Your child's potential employer or high school should be able to acquaint your child with the work permit requirements in your state. As a general rule, first get the job, then get the permit.

Private enterprises like baby-sitting and mowing lawns rarely require work permits. However, the work permit requirement may bar a child from a job in a butcher shop or a small factory.

RULE: CHILDREN MAY OWN PROPERTY.

Children may own property, either real estate or personal property, but they may not be able to hold it in their own name or sell this property until they reach 18 (in most states). At age 18 a child can normally make a contract, hold, buy, or sell real estate and personal property, use bank accounts, make a will, sue, or take out a loan. These are the exceptions, as of January 1, 1979:

Alabama   contracts at 19, wills of personal property at 18, wills of real estate at 19;

Colorado   age of majority is 21, but can contract, sue, draw will, and take possession of real estate at 18;

Georgia   full majority at 18, but can draw will at 14;

Hawaii   full majority at 18, but no will until 20;

Kansas   full majority at 18, but can make contracts, sue, and have full property rights at 16, no will until 18;

Louisiana   age of majority at 18, can draw will at 16;

Mississippi   full majority at 21, contracts for personal property and wills at 18.

Missouri   full majority at 21, contracts, wills, and real estate at 18;
Nebraska   full majority at 19;
Puerto Rico   full majority at 21, wills at 14;
Tennessee   full majority at 18, can sue to gain title to real estate at age
    16 to 18;
Virgin Islands   full majority at 18, except wills concerning real prop-
    erty at 21;
Wyoming   full majority at 19.
Many states allow minors to contract for insurance at 15 and educa-
tional loans at 16.

RULE: A CHILD MAY BE UNABLE
TO USE HIS PROPERTY.
FOR HIS OWN BENEFIT.

Because the minor child cannot sell property or hold a bank account
in her own name, she can have financial problems. There are at least
two ways to avoid this practical predicament. One way is to set up a
guardianship under court supervision. The guardian administers the
child's property for the benefit of the child. Any contracts the guardian
makes are binding on the child. The other method is much simpler.
Most states have adopted a law called the Uniform Gifts to Minors Act.
If you've ever opened a bank account for your child, you probably have
a nodding acquaintance with this act. It allows parents to make particular kinds of gifts to their child. A trustee, usually a close relative, is appointed at the time of the gift by the person who makes the gift. The
trustee can draw on the account. No court interference is necessary.

RULE: CHILDREN MAY MAKE CONTRACTS.

Children can make contracts, but they can throw them out the minute they reach age 18 (in most states). So, a child can make sure you
keep your part of the bargain, but he doesn't necessarily have to keep
his part. Suppose you sell a minor a motorcycle. He promises to pay
you for the motorcycle and you hand it over. He uses the motorcycle
gleefully for six months, at which point he wrecks it. You've gotten two
installments out of him and there's no motorcycle to take back. All he
has to do is wait until he's 18 and say, "I was a minor. I disaffirm my
motorcycle contract." You are out one motorcycle. You may, however,
keep the money you've already received.

There are only two ways to do business with a minor. Insist on cash
up front or have his parents co-sign the installment sale. Then you can
collect from the parents.

RULE: CHILDREN CAN'T WRITE WILLS.

Every state says that minors can't write wills. Most states set the will-drafting age at 18, but sometimes the age for wills affecting real estate is higher, as we've already seen. Any child can write a will disposing of insignificant personal possessions, but a will bequeathing dolls and baseball cards probably need not be probated.

Since children don't have the right to dispose of property through a will, property is rarely left to them before they reach age 18. Instead, the property they are to receive is placed in a trust until they reach the proper age. If the child dies before reaching that age, the money will go to other people, which the deceased determined in his own will.

RULE: CHILDREN CAN'T SUE.

Children are not entitled to bring lawsuits in their own behalf. It is often necessary that someone sue on behalf of the child if his property has been mismanaged, he has been injured, a consumer transaction has gone sour, etc. In this case, either the parent or a guardian can bring a suit for the child.

There is now a law clinic in San Francisco set up specifically to aid children. It is publicly funded, since children normally can't pay the price for legal help. This clinic handles some very serious problems, such as child abuse, rape, and abandonment. In this clinic the child retains the attorney, who handles the legal procedures.

RULE: CHILDREN ARE ENTITLED
TO THEIR OWN MONEY.

Children get money from three sources: they earn it, they inherit it, and they receive support checks. Whatever the source of the money, it must be used for the child's benefit.

The money a child earns can be spent only by the child himself. Ordinarily, this presents no problems for a child with a paper route or a summer job. Occasionally, a child will have a very lucrative profession such as modeling or acting. Some states have statutes specifically determining how the professional child's salary should be allocated between business expenses and saving for the future. If a child earns money, it in no way excuses the parent from his responsibility to support the young child. You have to do that regardless of how much your child makes. This rule lessens in importance as the child reaches the mid-teens, as we'll discuss later in this chapter.

Children also inherit money. For example, it's not unusal for a grandparent to set up a joint account with a grandchild. After the grandparent dies, the child has a trust account. Even though the parent may be a trustee, the principal in the account may never be used for the child's support, although the interest earned on the principal can.

Parents may receive payments to use for a child's support. These payments can come from Social Security, a father's child support, or a trust for the child's benefit. These payments may be spent for the child's support, but may not be used to support the family at large. For example, the fact that your child receives huge support payments, and you haven't got a penny, doesn't mean you can buy a mink coat for yourself with his money.

As a practical issue, it's pretty hard to separate support from the rest of the family finances. The courts will not interfere in your use of support payments as long as you keep your kid in good shape. They will interfere if the child's money is used outrageously.

Parents who are otherwise able to support their children tend to bank the support benefits to use either for the child's education or for the always changing future.

RULE: PARENTS ARE GUARDIANS
OF THEIR CHILDREN'S MONEY.

Like support, guardianship is part of being a parent. It happens automatically if a court hasn't already appointed a guardian. Parents are held to the same standards as court-appointed guardians.

Guardians must protect the principal of a child's assets. These assets may not be used for support purposes, although they may be spent for the child's benefit. However, expenditures of principal would be limited to things the parent might not otherwise be able to afford, such as medical school or straightening teeth.

Some expenditures for the child's benefit may be questionable, such as private schooling or trips to Europe. In such a case a court order may be necessary to release the money and to protect the parent. Since guardians are held financially responsible for unauthorized expenditures, the child, when she reaches age 18, could sue the parent to recover money spent without court authorization. So watch it.

Children are set loose on society in stages. Between the ages of 14 and 16 children are generally allowed to work in a factory or an office, if a proper work permit is secured. One usually acquires the right to vote at age 18, and one can marry between 16 and 18 with parental consent and at 18 without it. At 18, children are generally endowed with full adult responsibility for debts and contracts and may take ownership of property. However, if the child is still in school, he or she may still be entitled to full support. These rights and privileges can be modified to a certain degree by a legal concept called emancipation.

RULE: YOU ARE NOT RESPONSIBLE
FOR YOUR CHILD IF HE CAN
SUPPORT HIMSELF.

Under the doctrine of emancipation, if your minor child demonstrates the ability to take on the responsibility of support, independent choice of home, etc., you are no longer responsible. For example, when a boy joins the Army his parents are no longer under any obligation to support him. The same is true of any child who moves out of the home and begins to support himself. When your child reaches the age of 21, you have no obligation whatsoever. Emancipation could never occur in the case of a young child, but might become possible if the self-supporting child is in his mid to late teens.

Curiously, emancipation has become an issue in a class of our society where one might least expect it—the middle class. With inflation affecting both college tuition and the buying power of the parent's salary, emancipation of a college student may be necessary. Through emancipation the child is likely to be eligible for a scholarship based on need. Parents strapped for tuition will sit down with their child and draw up a plan. The child enters college, gets his own apartment, and starts to make his own living, usually just part-time work. Then, after a year or so, the child is emancipated. He can show his own financial independence and apply for a need scholarship. For example, a family earning $30,000 a year might be ineligible for scholarship aid, but an emancipated child of the same family earning $3,500 a year would certainly be eligible for a scholarship. Probably the financial-aid department of your child's university would have information on scholarship eligibility.

This use of emancipation is unattractive to many parents. It seems like cheating. But it may also be the only way to get their child an education.

Chapter 3
PUTTING ASUNDER

Divorce is a loss. It ranks with the death of a spouse as one of the more trying periods any individual will ever overcome. Divorce can have the effect of reactivating every loss the individual has ever experienced and can bring on personal problems which he or she did not have while married. It is not unusual for men to quit their jobs and drop out. Women may erratically change their pattern of sexual behavior. Many divorced persons blame these breakdowns on the legal process of divorce itself. The courts can be of little or no help to the couple, and may even force them to accuse one another. The legal process is guilty of ineptitude. However, the couple did create the situation which now must be resolved.

This chapter is much longer than the others because when people need help with divorce, they really need it.

There are two kinds of divorces: the ones that make sense and the ones that don't. Sometimes the individuals in a marriage are going off in diametrically opposed directions. At age twenty-one, Sarah and Abraham had the same goal—beautiful babies. At age thirty, Abraham is an airline pilot who wants a wife at home; Sarah owns a chain of franchise restaurants and doesn't want to give this up. They can't give each other what is wanted, and so they divorce. The divorce is really the best thing they could do for one another.

When divorce doesn't make sense, it really hurts. Heloise and Abelard have been married for a number of years; they both have been doing their part, and both want nearly the same things. Everything seems fine. Then Abelard becomes aloof and distant, starts criticizing

Heloise, and then demands a divorce. Heloise is mystified; she's not doing anything differently. She tries harder, and he gets more and more truculent. An ugly picture.

So what's Abelard's problem? It's probably something he did. As L. Ron Hubbard observes, "It is rather noble commentary on man that *when a person finds himself,* as he believes, *incapable of restraining himself from injuring a benefactor, he will defend the benefactor by leaving."* The injury Abelard thinks he perpetrated on Heloise might or might not be that serious. Heloise might be willing to forgive and forget. But Abelard can't bring himself to tell her about the paycheck he lost in a poker game, so this injury to his family churns around in his mind. He justifies his injury by making it Heloise's fault (My wife doesn't understand me,) and he leaves. (For further development of Hubbard's observations, read pp. 331–62: *The Volunteer Minister's Handbook,* by L. Ron Hubbard, © 1976, Church of Scientology Publications Organization United States; Los Angeles, California.)

Of course, it might have been solved, if Abelard had just *talked* to Heloise. Doubtless some angry words might have been exchanged, but there would have been some chance of recovery. Just talking can help a lot, which partially accounts for the success of the Catholic Church's highly effective marriage encounters. (The marriage encounters sponsored by the Catholic Church are open to persons of all faiths, and can even be helpful to a marriage that has just lost its spark.) If communications have totally broken down, you have a real problem.

RULE: WHEN YOU CAN'T TALK ANY MORE, GET HELP.

Couples have been known to solve the most awful problems. But they have to be able to talk to one another to reach a solution. One couple saved their marriage in an hour's talk with a minister. He gave them an unbiased outside view. Churches have been active in marriage counseling for a long time, and often have a lot of accumulated experience. Occasionally, a minister won't know how to help and may then be inclined to leave the solution to divine guidance. Try another minister.

Others seek help from marriage counselors. Marriage counselors come from a wide variety of backgrounds and hold many different philosophies, some practical and some outlandish. Basically, a marriage counselor gets people to talk. Hopefully, the couple will have a calm atmosphere with an impartial third party to referee while they exchange their grievances. This may be enough to get them back on the track. One drawback of dealing with a marriage counselor trained in psychology is that he may decide that one of the individuals is neurotic and not deal with the marriage itself.

RULE: SEEK DIVORCE WHEN
YOU CAN'T SURVIVE

This rule applies to both physical and mental survival. The physical survival is far more dramatic, but the mental survival is harder to deal with.

Physical survival is an obvious standard. Almost unbelievably, many women who have been physically threatened by their husbands are unwilling to leave the marriage. This subject is extensively covered in the chapter on battered women.

Mental survival is far more subtle. Individuals have different tolerances for unusual conduct. What one woman will find abhorrent, another will find amusing. The courts recognize these differences in personal standards. For instance, use of profane language could be grounds for divorce in one marriage, though it might not even be a subject for discussion for a less delicate wife.

Obviously, the point when you seek divorce is a matter of personal judgment. I recommend that you list the good points of your marriage and the bad points, weighing them against each other, so that the fact that your husband buys you nice presents does not outweigh the fact that he beats you. You must also consider what life would be like if you were not married to him. You may have to take on additional responsibilities which you would find impossible to handle. Some women, even today, cannot conceive of working. For them, life without their mate is incomprehensible.

RULE: YOU MUST CONSIDER
YOUR CHILDREN.

Often one parent will be appalled at the way the other parent is rearing the children. This attitude is sometimes realistic, and sometimes an excuse. In cases of outright cruelty, drug abuse, insanity, and other major issues, it is best to remove the children from the erring parent. However, all the arguments over proper discipline, the right school, or the children's friends may only be an attempt on the part of one of the parents to use the children as an excuse for a breakup. When considering your children's welfare, discount any minor differences you may have, since they probably are not relevant to your decision.

Divorce is not the only alternative you have if you wish to end your marriage. You may be able to choose annulment. Annulment is sought when there are grounds to declare the marriage invalid from the beginning. Legal separation is another alternative. It is used either as an in-

termediate step or when divorce is not desired due to religious principles.

RULE: ANNULMENT DECLARES THERE
WAS NEVER A MARRIAGE.

Annulment was once used very widely when divorces were less easy
to obtain. The concept of annulment grew out of the ecclesiastical
courts of the Church of Rome. Due to church doctrine, divorce was not
a possibility. But there was a biblical reference stating that it was a sin
for persons of the same family to be married. People seeking divorce
had to work very hard to prove that they were related.

Today, annulment is granted for a much broader category of flaws in
a marriage. The flaws relate to the state of the parties at the time they
were married. Certain types of fraud, underage partners, incestuous
marriages, and sometimes inability to have sex can all be grounds for
annulment.

Through annulment, marriages can be found to have been either void
or voidable. A voidable annulment means that the marriage could be
annulled if one or both of the parties wished it. A void marriage means
that the state declares the marriage annulled whether the parties want it
that way or not.

In any event, annulment is not used very often. In the 1950's, it ac-
counted for less than 3 per cent of marriage dissolutions. It is probably
less significant today, due to passage of no-fault divorce actions.

Annulments are usually based on fraud. One party will falsely represent to the other that he or she is in some particular condition or state
which affects the future of the marriage. Lies as to how good the
fellow's job is, whether or not he owns a house or has a fantastic
amount of money in the bank, are not grounds for annulment. It
doesn't sit well with courts for someone to plead that she wouldn't have
married the fellow if she hadn't thought he was rich. Lies which go to
the very heart of the marriage can be grounds for annulment. Agreements regarding children, prior marriages, church weddings, etc., are
examples. Any of these grounds may be waived if the woman continues
to live with the man after she discovers the lie.

Once the decision has been made to divorce, you and your spouse
have a great deal of thinking and arranging to do. You'll have to work
out a timetable by which the divorce will go forward, make property arrangements, and decide how to help the children through a trying time.
You both have to choose your own lawyers and work out separation
agreements, so that your arrangements will be realistic and meet the requirements of your state.

Parenthetically, there is a growing movement toward cheap divorces. In such cases, the parties represent themselves and do their own filing. It has the form of an uncontested divorce. New York, for example, is loaded with books telling you how to go about this. The cheap divorces are perfectly adequate for couples without children or much property. If custody rights or child support is part of the suit, seek professional help.

RULE: CHOOSE YOUR OWN LAWYER.

When selecting your lawyer, get recommendations from his or her clients. The clients know if the attorney has done a good job, whereas other professionals are likely to be more aware of his or her political abilities. It's also a good idea to make sure the lawyer has no connection with your husband, your husband's friends, or your husband's company.

You don't have to take the first recommendation you get. It's wisest to get the names of three lawyers and make appointments with them all. If you explain to them that you are interviewing attorneys to represent you, they probably won't charge you for a short conference. By all means limit your questions to his or her experience and a general discussion of divorce problems. You are not there to get free advice. Comparing these conferences, you'll be able to judge who you will get along with best. You might also keep in mind that many attorneys don't like divorce cases because the clients often require a lot of hand holding and the law of divorce is not very interesting. If you find the attorney less than enthusiastic, these factors may be part of the reason.

The separation agreements are written by the husband and wife through their lawyers and are generally worked out prior to the time the husband moves out of the home. The term "separation agreement" may be a misnomer since it provides for support while the divorce is in progress and may also be put before the court as the property agreement for the divorce. These agreements are private contracts and are only distantly controlled by case law or statute.

RULE: THE AGREEMENT MAY NOT
INDUCE DIVORCE.

Courts generally hold that separation agreements which tend to promote divorce or separation are invalid. Since the very nature of a separation agreement furthers divorce, the position is foolish. Aware of the difficult standard they have set, most courts will uphold separation agreements if the separation has already occurred or if the husband moves from the home immediately after completion of the agreement. Agreements made prior to marriage seeking to control property rights in the event of divorce are never honored, since these openly promote divorce. New Jersey does not allow separation agreements; North Carolina and Oklahoma are reluctant to honor them. All other states will accept some type of separation agreement.

RULE: THE AGREEMENT MUST BE FAIR.

A separation agreement is a contract. All contracts must contain an element called consideration. Consideration springs from the view that contracts should have a more or less even exchange. Contracts will be found invalid if this element of exchange is missing. Valid consideration for a separation agreement will be found in mutual promises, a release of one spouse of rights she may have in the property of the other, a promise of the wife to take care of the children, the wife's acceptance of the agreement in exchange for her claims of alimony, the promise to live separately, or the husband's obligation to support his wife. Consideration is an important element in a support agreement, since courts will use consideration to overcome the separation agreement if the court feels it is not fair to the wife.

It is possible that an agreement will meet the technical standards for consideration but the court will overturn the agreement as unfair. Although the cases are inconsistent on what will be judged unfair, unfairness itself is strong grounds for attack. The court is free to accept the agreement, modify it, or throw it out altogether. Homer Clark, an expert in this field, claims that it is virtually impossible for a husband to win if the consideration has been inadequate. Some states have modified this common-law principle by allowing questionable agreements when the wife has been given full disclosure of the husband's assets or independent advice about the agreement prior to the time it was signed. But even when there is full disclosure, the wife can still argue fraud or duress. The duress can be as simple as economic necessity. The court will also overturn an agreement if the judge suspects that something is undisclosed.

The law of consideration is heavily on the wife's side because of the public interest that she and the children be supported. Support is far more important than an arbitrary contractual idea called consideration.

RULE: BE CAREFUL WHAT YOU PROMISE.

Often a woman will sign a separation agreement in which she promises to release all claims of support in exchange for the agreement. Most jurisdictions hold this provision valid if the woman has received a reasonable settlement. New York, Illinois, and New Jersey do not allow such statements. Indiana, North Carolina, and West Virginia rarely honor them.

Another standard agreement is that the periodic payments to the wife will continue to her death or remarriage. This provision is readily accepted but runs into difficulty if the husband dies. In such a case you will have to sue the husband's estate to collect the amount owed to you. It is best to avoid this situation by covering the possibility in the agreement.

Many separation agreements now include clauses which impose various modifications upon the payment of support. The percentage of a husband's salary to be paid as alimony is one type. Another type makes the alimony dependent on the wife's income. Such provisions are usually honored by the court, since the purpose of them may be to avoid litigation when the circumstances of the parties change.

Sometimes the support agreement will require that the woman remain chaste until the divorce is final. Courts will usually honor this provision until the final decree. After that time, the ex-wife's chastity is her own business.

RULE: DON'T MOLEST HIM.

Most separation agreements contain a "non-molestation" clause. The parties agree not to molest or interfere with each other. The primary goal of the non-molestation clause is to prohibit a spouse from poisoning the minds of the children against the other spouse.

Sometimes the husband will try to avoid his support payments if his wife interferes with his life, such as making midnight phone calls, etc. The court will hold him to his support payments regardless of the wife's violation of the non-molestation clause. The courts perceive non-molestation and support as independent issues which do not rely upon one another. However, if he violates the non-molestation clause, his behavior does excuse the wife from her part of non-molestation.

Separation agreements can come off without a hitch as long as the spouses conduct themselves as ladies and gentlemen. Any other sort of conduct will probably not have financial penalties attached, but will make life more unpleasant than it need be.

RULE: RECONCILIATION CANCELS
THE AGREEMENT.

Although this rule is overly broad, it is a good rule to follow, since many states will void separation agreements which are followed by a reconciliation of the parties.

Reconciliation itself is not occasional intercourse between the spouses. Rather it must be a full resumption of the marital relationship, including sexual relations, living in the same house, and presenting yourselves as husband and wife. If the parties live together as often as circumstances permit, this fact may also be considered reconciliation. Unfortunately, the only safe course of conduct is to avoid events which might appear to be a reconciliation. The avoidance of friendly relations is not relevant to the separation agreement itself, but may affect the defenses to divorce which you will read about later in this chapter.

Under English law, divorce could not be obtained through the courts until 1857. Prior to that time, divorce was possible only through an act of Parliament. Consequently, it was available only to the rich and powerful. In 1857, English law changed. Divorce was then allowed only on the grounds of adultery. Ironically, husbands could divorce for adultery alone, whereas wives could obtain divorce only if the husband added a further insult to his adultery such as incest, bigamy, or cruelty. This attitude of sinful divorce spilled over into the United States. American law has now been modified from the tough English standard to the more modern position allowing divorces when the marriage has already dissolved from its own unworkableness. The first American divorce we found was *Jones* v. *Jones* in Tennessee (1804). There were probably some before that, but our law keeps published records only if there is an appeal. The grounds for divorce in the Jones case were adultery.

RULE: SUE FOR ADULTERY.

Adultery is certainly the most dramatic and interesting of all the grounds for divorce. It is a ground for divorce in every state, but very few persons sue on this ground because adultery is so embarrassing. In fact, only slightly more than 2 per cent of the cases cite adultery as grounds.

Adultery is normally defined as the "voluntary sexual intercourse of a married person with a person other than the offender's husband or wife" (West's Ann. Civ. Code—Cal., paragraph 93). One writer on the subject says that North Carolina, Kentucky, and Texas will grant the husband divorce on proof of a single act of adultery by his wife. However, the husband must actually be living with another woman before the wife can sue on those grounds. Homosexual contacts are probably adultery, although this is unclear.

Some acts of intercourse are not adulterous. If the wife is raped, no adultery has been committed. If the husband rapes another woman, adultery is found. When the party is insane at the time of intercourse, it is not adulterous. Intoxication is sometimes pled as a defense to adultery. However, intoxication will not excuse adultery, since the defendant became drunk of his or her own volition.

A very interesting development in the area of adultery has been suits based on the wife's use of artificial insemination in order to bear children. It is argued that since artificial insemination introduces genetic materials other than the husband's into the family, the wife is guilty of adultery. These strange cases seem to occur only when the husband's consent for artificial insemination has not been obtained. In all likelihood this issue doesn't belong in the area of adultery at all, and indeed fits into no existing area of the law. The best policy is to obtain your husband's consent before participating.

You may have seen movies in which a private detective takes pictures of a couple in bed. Although this makes a good movie scene, the courts want nothing to do with lurid photographs. They prefer circumstantial evidence. Most courts will find adultery if (1) the opportunity to commit adultery existed, and (2) the other party had a disposition or inclination to commit adultery. For example, a detective's report that the spouse frequently met persons of the opposite sex alone at night under intimate circumstances or that he visited an apartment or a hotel with a female would be proof of adultery. In a woman's case, if the husband can prove non-paternity of a child, adultery can be grounds for divorce. The same may be true if a spouse is infected with syphilis or gonorrhea.

In a majority of the states you do not have to prove that the adultery occurred "beyond a reasonable doubt." That's a criminal standard. All you have to prove is that there is a preponderance of the evidence on your side.

RULE: SUE FOR DESERTION.

Desertion normally requires all of the following four elements: (1) a voluntary separation of the spouses, (2) with intent of ending cohabitation, (3) without the approval of the other spouse, and (4) without justification. The requirement that the desertion be unjustified prevents battered women from being guilty of desertion. In fact, the most liberal view of justification of desertion states that departure from the home is justified when it is impossible to live there in safety, health, and self-respect. This interpretation is obviously broader than mere physical cruelty and can be used in many cases when the couple simply isn't getting along.

Desertion statutes vary from state to state. In some there must be an actual abandonment of the home, one year being the most common length of time required. Delaware will grant a divorce on the continual refusal of marital intercourse.

An interesting legal wrinkle in desertion is that periods of desertion which are interrupted by a reconciliation cannot be added together to meet the minimum time requirements of desertion, such as one year. If your husband offers a reconciliation, consult your attorney before you accept. By the way, a single amorous adventure between you and your deserting spouse does not qualify as a reconciliation, but be discreet.

Another odd element of desertion is that the intent to cease living together may happen long after the couple's actual physical separation. For example, the husband could join the Army and decide two years later to not live with his wife. The desertion would begin from the time he decides that he will not return. Hard to prove, but that's the way it is. Sometimes departures from the home are thoroughly justified, such as a temporary job in another city, joining the Army, being sent to prison, etc.

A colorful type of desertion divorce is the "Enoch Arden" divorce, named for Tennyson's poem of a sailor who returned after ten years at sea only to discover his beloved wife remarried. He unselfishly walked away, so as not to disturb the couple's happiness. The modern Enoch Arden divorce is much less romantic. In this case the deserted spouse can sue after some passage of time. The period which the spouse must wait can be as long as seven years but five years is adequate for most states. She cannot have heard from her spouse in this time and must have no idea of his whereabouts, or even if he is alive. The deserted spouse claims that the person has been gone five years without anyone knowing his whereabouts; that she believes the spouse to be dead; and that she has made a diligent search without uncovering any evidence that the spouse is still alive.

RULE: SUE FOR NON-SUPPORT.

Five states allow a woman to sue for divorce on the grounds that her husband is not supporting her. These states are Arkansas, Louisiana, Maine, Massachusetts, and Rhode Island. More states allow this suit under a broader term called gross neglect of duty. These states are Idaho, Kansas, Ohio, Oklahoma, South Dakota, Utah, Vermont, and Wisconsin. The difference between non-support and gross neglect of duty is that non-support must continue for a period of time, usually one year, whereas gross neglect of duty requires no passage of time. It does not exist in the other states, although grounds such as desertion may also cover non-support.

RULE: SUE FOR MENTAL OR PHYSICAL CRUELTY.

Cruelty is a strange and very broad ground for divorce. Prior to the passage of no-fault divorce, nearly 90 per cent of uncontested divorces were based on mental or physical cruelty.

Because cases of cruelty are usually uncontested, judges are placed in a legal box. If the wife charges cruelty, and the husband does not contest, the court has no right to interfere, and the judge must find cruelty and is not called upon to write a decision. Therefore attorneys have very little written reference as to what constitutes cruelty, and only practical experience, or rumor, as a practical guide.

The statutes merely refer to "mental cruelty," and have left it to the judges to decide what acts constitute cruelty. This standoff has allowed these grounds for divorce to expand without legislative action. All states grant mental cruelty as grounds for divorce, except North Carolina, Maryland, and South Carolina.

To give you an idea of how far this area has enlarged, the original English definition of cruelty in 1790 was that cruelty occurred only when there was bodily harm or a rational fear of bodily harm. Hurt feelings were not enough, nor were "mere austerity of temper, petulance of manners, rudeness of language, a want of civil attention and accommodation, even occasional sallies of passion, if they do not threaten bodily harm." This position has radically changed, so that cruelty is now the name often given to any marriage which has irredeemably fallen apart. If the grounds for cruelty are challenged, the court will decide the meaning of cruelty within the plaintiff's own education and background. Therefore, when defining cruelty, the daughter of a minister might be given better treatment than the daughter of a slattern.

There is a defense for cruelty. If the woman provokes her husband into acts of cruelty, she will not be granted a divorce unless his cruelty greatly outweighs her provocation. For example, if he hit her with a steam iron because she yelled at him, that would be cruelty. However, if he just yelled back at her, she could not get him on cruelty grounds.

Cruelty is not normally a single event, but a whole string of events which when put together illustrate how unworkable the marriage really is. Cruelty falls into particular types of cases. The clearest example is violence or threats of violence. Sexual abuses can be cruelty if the plaintiff's health is harmed. Attacks on self-respect or reputation are by far the most common, since this encompasses the psychic warfare of unhappy people. Neglect can also be called cruelty and will be used as such in states where non-support is not grounds for divorce. Improper relations with other persons whether heterosexual or homosexual are cruelty, and this ground is resorted to when adultery cannot be proved. More minor types of cruelty are baseless legal suits, drunkenness, and drug addiction. There is another classification called general marital unkindness, which can include practically anything, such as locking the spouse out of the house, verbal abuse, living with relatives, attempts at converting the spouse to a particular religion, and even political activity. The range of these cases is limitless. They include name calling, threats of harm to children, insistence that the wife continue working, bad language, and the country club syndrome in which the wife plays cards all day, drinks, and neglects her husband.

The only difficulty with the cruelty ground is that it is not very exact. Since some judges like to assign fault, they may get entangled in blaming, and confuse this with alimony and the division of property. This shouldn't be necessary since financial settlements and the grounds for divorce ideally should be handled separately, regardless of the fault.

RULE: SUE FOR INCOMPATIBILITY.

Incompatibility is a Scandinavian concept which sneaked into the United States through the Virgin Islands, which was once a Danish possession. Though incompatibility was once not an important ground for divorce, it has blossomed over the last ten years. Now thirty-three states allow for incompatibility, but may call it irretrievable breakdown or irreversible differences. This ground is *not* allowed in the District of Columbia and the following states: Arkansas, Delaware, Illinois, Louisiana, Maryland, Mississippi, New Jersey, New York, North Carolina, Ohio, Pennsylvania, South Carolina, South Dakota, Utah, Vermont, Virginia, and Wisconsin. If your state is listed among these, don't lose hope. Every state now has some form of no-fault divorce, which may accomplish exactly the same thing as the ground of incompatibility.

RULE: NO-FAULT GROUNDS ARE
ALWAYS PREFERRED.

Over the last ten years every state has passed a no-fault divorce statute. The essential idea of no-fault divorce is that the marriage has broken down to such a degree that it cannot be repaired. The state legislatures have recognized that the assignment of fault is really very useless in a divorce. Instead, they have substituted grounds under which no fault is assigned. This type of divorce is preferred whenever it is possible. No-fault divorce may be less expensive and faster, usually involves less emotional strain, and requires only limited evidence of the improprieties of your spouse. Even if one spouse has done something outrageous, no-fault is preferred by nearly all divorcées, since it is simpler for everybody. It avoids many of the procedural difficulties discussed later. The no-fault divorce may also preserve what love there is left in the family.

There are two basic approaches in no-fault divorce. The pure no-fault divorce is based on evidence showing that the marriage has broken down. Sometimes evidence will be admitted which might have been a fault ground before the no-fault statute was passed. Now this evidence is used only to show marital breakdown. This marital breakdown can also be called irreconcilable differences, irretrievable breakdown, irreversible differences, or incompatibility.

The Supreme Court in one decision defined incompatibility as "conflicts in personality and dispositions so deep as to be irreconcilable and to render it impossible for the parties to continue a normal marital relationship with each other." This definition sounds a lot like cruelty. Many courts actually include it within their own definition of cruelty.

This type of no-fault divorce is available in: Arizona, California, Colorado, the District of Columbia, Florida, Hawaii, Iowa, Kentucky, Michigan, Missouri, Montana, Nebraska, Nevada, Oregon, Virginia, Washington, and Wyoming. The judge merely hears the evidence. If he or she thinks the evidence shows a complete breakdown he or she declares a divorce. This decision does not modify alimony or child-support provisions. There is no other type of divorce available in a pure no-fault state.

The other type of no-fault divorce is a modification of a classic divorce statute. The states which have this type of divorce maintain the old-fashioned divorce action with faults, and have added the no-fault divorce to handle certain situations. New York is one example. Although it maintains a regular divorce statute, it has added a living-apart clause. In New York, if the spouses live apart for one year, they can apply for a no-fault divorce on the basis that their marriage has already dissolved. The following states and Puerto Rico have either living apart or some type of irreconcilable differences as a way to gain divorce without assigning fault: Alabama, Alaska, Arkansas, Connecticut, Delaware, Georgia, Idaho, Illinois, Indiana, Kansas, Louisiana, Maine, Maryland, Massachusetts, Minnesota, Mississippi, New Hampshire, New Jersey, New Mexico, New York, North Carolina, North Dakota, Ohio, Oklahoma, Pennsylvania, Rhode Island, South Carolina, South Dakota, Tennessee, Texas, Utah, Vermont, Virginia, West Virginia, and Wisconsin.

Don't let this short treatment of no-fault divorce minimize its importance in your mind. It is just not as complex as other kinds of divorce, and is by far the most important ground for divorce we have discussed.

RULE: SUE IF YOU ARE LIVING
SEPARATE AND APART.

This ground for divorce was the first step to no-fault divorce, since all that is required is that the persons live apart for a prescribed period of time, between one and ten years—one to five years being the most common requirement. The qualifications vary. Some states require legal separation; other states grant this divorce on the presentation of proof that the parties have lived apart for the time required. About half of the states now have this rule as a ground for divorce. It is different from desertion in that both parties agree to live apart. They simply indicate that at no time during their separation was a reconciliation likely. This rule is a wonderful development, since the court can readily recognize the marriage breakdown without assigning guilt.

RULE: SUE FOR DRUNKENNESS AND NARCOTICS USE.

Most state statutes allow for divorce when a spouse is truly an alcoholic—that is, he is unable to resist getting drunk whenever the opportunity arises. Although fewer states specifically mention narcotics addiction as grounds for divorce, it can probably be sued on under the drunkenness statute. The drug use must be truly an addiction, as opposed to the mere use of drugs.

RULE: SUE FOR VENEREAL DISEASE.

Venereal disease which you catch from your spouse is a specific ground for divorce in only two states: Delaware and Illinois. However, the plaintiff's contracting of venereal disease from her husband can be either proof of adultery or grounds for a possible cruelty judgment.

RULE: SUE FOR INSANITY.

Insanity is grounds for divorce in the majority of states. However, since the insane person is unlikely to be able to represent himself adequately, the courts have erected a series of protections. Depending on the state, the safeguards could be testimony that the insanity is incurable, that the person has been confined for a number of years, that the person has been adjudicated insane or, at the very least, considered insane on the testimony of a specified number of doctors. Some state statutes require that the divorcing party continue to support the insane person.

RULE: SUE THE CONVICTED FELON.

Practically every state allows the spouse of a convicted felon to sue for divorce on that ground alone. A few other states require that the crime be infamous. In other words, the crime must violate the marriage or involve moral turpitude. Occasionally a divorce can be granted simply on the basis that the fellow has to serve a specified time in jail. Two years' imprisonment is standard in these statutes.

RULE: SUE FOR FRAUD.

These states allow for a divorce on the basis of fraud: Connecticut, Georgia, Ohio, Oklahoma, Pennsylvania, and Washington. The plaintiff charges that there was some impediment to the marriage on the date it was performed. For example, the fellow had no intention of having children. All of this is discussed in the section on annulment.

Fraud is an odd ground for divorce, since the charge of fraud assumes that a basis for marriage never existed. Therefore, an annulment is the proper action. However, to prevent a perfectly honorable woman from being cut off from alimony, a selected number of cases have allowed divorce for fraud. If annulment had been chosen, alimony would not have been available.

RULE: SUE FOR NO SEX.

The following states, as well as Puerto Rico, allow the wife to seek a divorce on the basis of her husband's impotence: Alaska, Arkansas, Georgia, Illinois, Indiana, Maine, Maryland, Massachusetts, Mississippi, New Hampshire, North Carolina, Ohio, Oklahoma, Rhode Island, Tennessee, and Utah. There are three separate types of divorce actions having to do with the sexual relations of the partners. They are the grounds of impotence, physical defect preventing intercourse, and refusal of sex. By far the most prevalent statute is the one allowing divorce for impotence, the husband's inability to complete an act of intercourse. Far rarer is the physical defect preventing intercourse. This suit would be brought if a woman was incapable of having intercourse. However, many of these problems can now be remedied by surgery. Refusal to have sexual relations is clearly grounds for divorce in Delaware. In many other states this marital problem is lumped under either desertion or cruelty.

One woman refused to have her children inoculated because of her religious principles. The schools would not accept the children until they had inoculation certificates. The wife wanted to fight the issue in court, but the husband felt that his children's schooling was more important. One Saturday he marched them all to the pediatrician and had them inoculated without his wife's consent. She subsequently refused to have any physical contact with him. He divorced her for refusal of sex.

RULE: SUE FOR BIGAMY.

There is a whole group of statutory grounds for divorce which are
also grounds for annulment. These include prior undissolved marriages
(bigamy), a marriage against a person's will, incestuous marriage, and
pregnancy of the wife by another man at the time of her marriage. All
of these grounds are based either on fraud or on a marriage the state
would simply not allow. They are included in some divorce statutes so
that the wife may be eligible for alimony. Three states definitely allow
alimony when the husband has been bigamous (Florida, Maryland, and
Mississippi). A few more may allow it.

RULE: SUE WITHIN ONE YEAR
OF THE OFFENSE.

States vary by both statute and common law as to what time delay
will render the divorce grounds void. Peculiarly, most states apply the
statute of limitations only to the grounds of adultery. Adultery lapses as
grounds after one year in Hawaii and after ten years in Wisconsin. Two
or three years is the normal statute of limitations. The rule above sug-
gests that you sue within one year because this period covers all states
and most situations.

Even if no statute of limitations exists, the court may not allow a suit
if there has been too much delay since the grounds arose. The common
law holds men to much shorter delays than women. Women may have
to protect their source of income until they can acquire training to support themselves or the children are in school.

RULE: DIVORCE CAN BE
DEFENDED AGAINST.

The defenses for divorce come down to us from English law. Connivance is usually a defense in adultery cases. If the plaintiff originally
consents to the adultery of the mate, he cannot later change his mind
and revoke his consent. (This includes wife swapping.)

Collusion could be called conspiracy to commit divorce. All states
recognize collusion, either by statute or by common law. For example,
it may be that the husband and wife have arranged to stage a fake adultery scene so that the divorce can go through without a hitch. Later,
one of the spouses changes his or her mind and shouts collusion. Collusion is a defense which the judge himself may raise if he suspects the
couple is cooperating in obtaining evidence for the divorce. It is not

collusion for the parties to cooperate through their lawyers to have the divorce come off smoothly. It is best to avoid all discussions of the divorce which are not in your lawyer's presence in order to forestall a judge's arbitrary finding of collusion. Collusion has been largely abandoned with the introduction of no-fault divorce.

The third defense is called condonation. Condonation arises when one of the parties has committed an act and the other party forgives it. It differs from connivance, wherein the spouse consents before the act. In condonation, she forgives after the act. The marriage is resumed and later the party who forgave sues for divorce on the very grounds she forgave. In this case the party who originally committed the wrong can raise a defense of condonation and will probably win. However, superficial statements of forgiveness, such as "I forgive you, and get out of the house by Tuesday," will not be considered condonation. The forgiving spouse never allowed the normal marital relationship to be resumed.

Recrimination is the principle that if both parties have grounds for divorce, the divorce will not be granted. For example, when he's guilty of adultery and she's guilty of cruelty, the court may let the marriage stand. The wrongs have to be of comparable magnitude. One legal authority calls recrimination "outrageous." Through recrimination, insufferable marriages can be forced to limp along, with neither party being released from his or her agony.

Comparative rectitude is a principle which weighs against recrimination. Wisconsin follows this doctrine. Arkansas, Ohio, and Utah may. When both parties have been cruel, they decide which party has been more cruel and assign fault this way. The usefulness of this principle is a little obscure.

Provocation can also be used as a defense when both parties have been guilty. One party says, "Yes, I was cruel, but only because he was cruel to me." If the provoked person doesn't use cruelty which outweighs the cruelty of the one who started it, the divorce will probably be granted. If provocation can be shown, the fact that both parties are guilty will not bar the divorce.

RULE: COLLECT YOUR OWN EVIDENCE.

It may make you feel very uncomfortable to go around collecting evidence of your husband's misdeeds, but the court may require it, even for a no-fault divorce. What evidence you need is largely a matter of common sense. For example, when a beating has occurred, photographs, a doctor's report, and witnesses would all be evidence. Any one would be sufficient to show physical cruelty. If your marital warfare is more psychological, a diary might be called for. The descriptions above for the grounds of divorce will help you figure out what you need. Most of them require building your case over a period of time, except for physical cruelty. When you feel that you have a preponderance of evidence on your side, you and the lawyer will be able to move forward.

Divorce actions in the United States fall into the general category of equity, meaning justice or fairness. Equity is distinguished from law in that under the law precedent of cases must be followed. Equity is different in that the judge has latitude to find solutions for unusual problems without strictly following precedent.

In this country, equity has been rolled into the procedure of ordinary civil courts. In England, equity decisions are made only in courts of equity. In the United States, judges have been given the power to decide when they should follow the law and when they should follow equity. So a judge may decide part of a case based on a statute and the other part on equity, if that area is not covered by the statute. Divorce often falls into this category, since both the divorce statute of the state and the fairness to the parties must be considered.

Once you have gathered your evidence, the next step is the actual suit for divorce. By this time you will have acquired an attorney and may be ready to proceed. The actual legal steps to divorce must be followed in the order of the ten following rules.

RULE: STEP 1—FIND ALL THE
PARTIES TO THE DIVORCE.

A party to a divorce is any person who has an interest in the proceedings. Obviously, the husband and the wife are parties, but other persons can be involved. For example, if the wife is suing for property rights in her husband's business, his business partners may also be parties to the divorce. They will appear at the proceedings so that all elements of the divorce can be decided at one time. If they do not appear at the divorce, and the divorce settlement infringes on their business interests, they will have the right to bring suit later. Surprisingly, the children of the marriage cannot be parties to the divorce, although some states, including Iowa, are now appointing an attorney for the children in custody cases.

Some states and the District of Columbia require that a public officer also be made a party to the divorce. They are Delaware, Georgia, Hawaii, Indiana, Kentucky, Massachusetts, Michigan, Nebraska, Washington, West Virginia, Wisconsin, and Wyoming. This requirement is for an uncontested or undefended divorce, since the state has an interest in protecting families. This state officer may be appointed to check if a fault divorce is collusive or arranged between the parties.

If one of the principal parties, the husband and wife, dies before the divorce decree is final, the whole procedure is automatically called off. The divorce is simply canceled and the remaining party is a widow or widower in the eyes of the law.

RULE: STEP 2—SELECT THE PROPER COURT.

Several different courts in different states may have the right to hear the same divorce. For example, the husband may live in Illinois, the wife in Iowa. In this instance both states would have the right to hear the case. They would have "jurisdiction." Where the suit is actually brought is a different issue. The wife may fly to Nevada, meet its residency requirements, and sue for divorce in the state of Nevada. In this instance, Nevada would also have jurisdiction.

The other part of selecting the proper court is venue. Venue is the neighborhood, or essentially the place where the case is actually tried. In most cases the venue will be in the county in which the persons last lived together, or the plaintiff's or defendant's current county of residence. The parties may apply for a change of venue to make the site of the trial more convenient.

RULE: STEP 3—YOU MUST NOTIFY YOUR HUSBAND OF THE DIVORCE.

The requirement that you notify your spouse when you bring a divorce suit is called "service," which means that the defendant receives the proper type of notification. This service can be in the form of a subpoena or other formal document notifying him of the grounds for divorce and where and when the trial will occur.

There are two basic types of service, personal service and constructive service. Personal service calls for an actual delivery to the party involved. The courts of your state may allow the personal service to be made through the mail by registered letter. If the defendant cannot be found, constructive service is allowed. It is broken into two categories: publication and substituted service. Service by publication involves publishing a notice in the newspaper. Some jurisdictions also require that the newspaper be mailed to the last known address of the defendant. Substituted service is the delivery of the notice to a party other than the defendant. The other party could be a close relative of the defendant, his lawyer, or a close friend. The person who receives the substituted service should be someone who is very likely to be speaking with the defendant, even though they deny any communication.

If the only issue in the divorce is the termination of the marriage, constructive or substituted service is perfectly adequate. However, it can be used only when the plaintiff cannot discover her spouse's whereabouts after a diligent search. If property rights are involved, personal service must be performed on the man or his property. For example, the husband may be missing, but he may own property within the state where the suit is taking place. In such a case, the property itself can be served with a summons in the likelihood that though the man may have disappeared from his wife, he has not disappeared from his property.

Service of notice is a very important step. Always try to make personal service, since your spouse can nullify the divorce for your lack of diligence in giving notice. Then you'd have to go through the divorce again.

RULE: STEP 4—THE GROUNDS FOR DIVORCE CAN BE CHANGED.

When the defendant has had notice, he may disagree with either the grounds for divorce or the nature of the action itself. The wife may only be suing for separation. He may prefer divorce. The pleadings of both parties can be changed through amendments which are very simple to obtain.

The complaint for a divorce should contain certain basic elements, and the language doesn't have to be sophisticated. The basic points are: that there was a marriage of the parties, the basis of the court's jurisdiction, and the grounds which the plaintiff is asserting.

Interestingly enough, some of the grounds for divorce actually occur after the complaint is filed. These can also be used in the divorce action, if a supplementary complaint is added to the case.

RULE: STEP 5—COOL OFF BEFORE YOU DIVORCE.

Many states have imposed a cooling-off period between the time the complaint is brought and the time the trial actually occurs. The cooling-off period is to allow for a reconciliation before the bother of divorce, and is somewhat of an improvement over the older laws which required a waiting period after the trial and before the final decree could be issued. The cooling-off period is preferred, since the parties are more likely to make a reconciliation before they've gone to a trial. The length of the cooling-off period runs between twenty days and six months. Thirty to sixty days is most common. In most cases the period

begins when the complaint is filed and the trial will be scheduled sometime after the cooling-off period has run out. The cooling-off period
cannot be waived by either the parties or the court. Many cooling-off
statutes do not allow for any equitable relief such as custody and support of the children, temporary alimony and peace bonds. The only exception to this is North Carolina, which allows waiver of the cooling-off
period when it can be shown that the husband is removing his property
from the state.

RULE: STEP 6—YOU ARE ALLOWED TO ASK
YOUR SPOUSE FOR EVIDENCE.

In the law, when you ask the other party to supply you with certain
evidence, it is called discovery. In other words, you are discovering
(finding out) what the evidence is in the case. Obviously, you have to
have a pretty good idea what to ask for, because he may not want to
volunteer certain information, such as the value of his assets.

There are four basic types of evidence which discovery will help you
obtain. These are depositions, interrogatories, physical exams, and admissions.

A deposition, or oral deposition, is often used for pretrial discovery.
In a deposition, a statement is taken under oath from either a witness
or a party to the divorce. Each party must be notified of the deposition
so that each can be present and ask questions of the witness.

Interrogatories are written depositions. In the case of an interrogatory, one party serves the other party with a set of written questions
which he answers in written form and under oath. Interrogatories can
only be obtained from other parties in the trial and cannot be used with
witnesses. Interrogatories are very helpful since they are inexpensive to
perform and can establish facts known only to the other party in the divorce. For example, an interrogatory might be made on the extent of a
person's business holdings or reasons for his absence over an extended
period of time.

Physical examinations are usually used when there is some question
as to the paternity of a child. There is an interesting blood-grouping
test which can prove that a certain man is *not* the father of a certain
child, although it cannot prove that he is the father. Physical examinations are rarely called for in a divorce action, but they are available.

The fourth type of evidence is admissions. An admission is essentially an affirmation or denial of a particular charge having to do with
the divorce. For example, the husband could be charging cruelty on the
basis that his wife refused to cook him dinner, clean the house, or see
that other wifely duties were accomplished. She could make an admis-

sion that this was indeed the fact. At the trial she could enter a plea of circumstances which prevented her from fulfilling these duties, such as holding a job which required her to be away at dinnertime, physical incapacity to do the work, etc. Such admissions considerably shorten trial time, and hence can be a money-saving device.

RULE: STEP 7—OBTAIN AN INJUNCTION IF NECESSARY.

Injunctions are orders by the court that one party to the divorce stop doing a harmful act; they are also used to prevent a harmful act from occurring. Injunctions are also called restraining orders. Most injunctions brought during the course of a divorce have to do with maintaining the property within the state until the divorce settlement can be arranged. Injunctions will also be granted when one spouse is threatening the other with words, violence, or general harassment. Through an injunction, one of the spouses may be barred from the home during the suit. Injunctions can also be brought against third parties who are holding the husband's property, so that it may not be sold until the divorce is settled.

In order to have an injunction issued, you will have to submit affidavits stating the facts which call for the injunction. These statements must be specific. The injunction must be served either on the defendant or on the person in charge of his property. These injunctions last only as long as the divorce proceedings and then automatically terminate. If you feel that it's necessary to have a permanent injunction against your spouse, you must ask for it as one of the remedies you seek from the trial. A permanent injunction is especially important in the case of a battered woman, and it must not be overlooked.

RULE: STEP 8—PREPARE TO BE CONFUSED DURING THE TRIAL.

Divorce trials make people feel crummy. The procedure that is used at the trial is substantially the same that is used in any civil court. You may want merely to have your marriage dissolved. You and your husband may have worked out all of the details. Nevertheless, if you're stuck with a fault divorce, the law requires that both sides argue their case in what is called an adversary proceedings, meaning that both sides present their own case and examine the witnesses of the other party. There may be a lot of legal talk between the lawyers and the judge which you may not understand. Additionally, they're following very specific rules of conduct which have been centuries in the making. These rules of conduct are obscure and sometimes rather strange. You may not be able to tell exactly what your attorney is doing at any given moment. The lawyer may also have the responsibility of keeping up the sham that this is an adversary proceeding, when indeed all you are seeking is a court-ordered divorce and the court's approval of a property settlement, worked out months before. The judge may also have the responsibility of maintaining the divorce action as an adversary proceeding, so that you may find your attorney coaching you on how to answer particular questions that the judge may pose. The judge is the only person in most jurisdictions who can prevent a collusive divorce, a divorce in which the parties agree to divorce and then invent grounds for divorce. A judge has to ask those embarrassing questions for this reason.

The rules in divorce vary slightly from other civil actions. The courtroom can be closed to the public in order to prevent scandal and protect children. Also, one spouse may testify against the other.

Custody cases may involve the admission of a social worker's report suggesting who would be the better parent for the child. Such reports can be made at the request of the court and admitted as evidence. The court will then hear the testimony of the social worker who prepared the report and may hear the testimony of the people whom the social worker interviewed. Now some jurisdictions appoint an attorney to represent the children.

The introduction of no-fault divorce has somewhat modified the character of court proceedings. If you are seeking a divorce under one of the new no-fault statutes, evidence is presented to show that the marriage partners are irreconcilable. This evidence may include proof of adultery, cruelty, etc., but the adversary element is diminished. It comes very close to divorce by consent of the parties.

RULE: STEP 9—GET WITNESSES.

About two thirds of the states require that the testimony of the spouses be corroborated (verified) by witnesses not a party to the divorce. The corroboration is required to prevent collusive divorces. An outside party must have some level of proof that what the plaintiff or defendant admits is actually the case. For example, the plaintiff could be suing for the cruelty of verbal abuse. A neighbor could testify that he heard a lot of loud voices from the apartment next door. Although he could not testify that what was being said was verbal abuse, his testimony would corroborate the likelihood of verbal abuse. Corroboration can also be established by physical or circumstantial evidence such as pictures of bruises received during a fight or the fact that the plaintiff was admitted to the hospital directly after she says the fight occurred.

There are no constitutional limits on how evidence in divorce cases can be obtained. The plaintiff can use evidence obtained from illegal searches and seizures.

RULE: STEP 10—DON'T TALK TO YOUR SPOUSE
        IF YOU HAVE AN INTERLOCUTORY DECREE.

An interlocutory decree is a temporary decree entered at the end of a divorce procedure but puts off the final decree of divorce for a stated period. This decree can last from three months to a year, depending on the state. Some states call this a decree nisi (*nee*-see). The original purpose of the interlocutory decree was to discourage divorce and to encourage reconciliation, although this has not been the effect. If the parties reconcile during the period of the interlocutory decree, the divorce action is voided. If the reconciliation doesn't work out, they will have to sue for divorce all over again. Obviously, an interlocutory decree does more to prevent reconciliation than aid it.

Fortunately, the interlocutory decree is not widely used. It seems to be restricted to California, Kansas, Massachusetts, New York, Utah, and Wisconsin. During the period of the interlocutory decree, the spouses are still considered to be married. They may live apart, but are not required to.

RULE: INVESTIGATE BEFORE YOU REMARRY.

When the final decree is issued, it will dispose of many elements of the divorce, such as granting the divorce, property settlements and alimony, child custody, injunctions, and the wife's name change. Normally, the parties are free to remarry when they obtain a final decree. However, a few states have some very odd rules concerning remarriage, especially if the defendant has been found guilty of adultery. For example, Iowa requires that neither party remarry within a year unless it has been allowed under the divorce decree. Oklahoma flatly forbids any marriage within six months. Pennsylvania prohibits a defendant found guilty of adultery from marrying his paramour during the ex-spouse's lifetime. Texas requires either party in a divorce on the grounds of cruelty to stay single for one year. In Virginia the court may prohibit remarriage, pending appeal. Many of these laws are based on the assumption that the normal grounds for divorce are another woman or man. Surveys of divorced people disprove this concept. Most people divorce simply to escape an unhappy situation. Second marriages which may be happier should not be prohibited.

RULE: WHAT'S DONE CANNOT BE UNDONE.

On general legal principles, once a case has been tried and everyone has had an opportunity to present his side of the story, the court is disinterested in hearing about the case any further. The matter becomes "res judicata," meaning the thing is decided. Res judicata bars all further suit on the same grounds. This rule does not prevent a couple with a legal separation from suing for divorce, but it does prevent all further trying of the facts upon which the first case was presented. If the couple regret their divorce after the final decree, they can always marry again. Other issues in the divorce, such as alimony, child support, and child custody may be modified under further suits, but the divorce itself will not be modified.

Divorces can be attacked on the grounds that the plaintiff brought the suit in a state which had no jurisdiction. If the defendant was not or could not be notified, mistakes can also be remedied. The defendant can present himself later, along with his side of the story. However, if he doesn't move quickly, he will lose the right to present his evidence. Divorces in which one party was not represented are called default decrees. These default decrees can be set aside when the absent party becomes available.

The most important elements of the divorce negotiations involve money and children. These issues are also the area where a woman is most likely to err. When deciding alimony, child support, child visitation rights, and division of the family's property, each woman must be very clear in her thinking. Her children's futures are at stake, as well as her own. She must ask herself certain questions. Out of her husband's resources, as well as her own, she must plan for her children's security. If the woman is older, she must also consider how she is to support herself when she is no longer working. Women are inclined to make two mistakes. Often they will assume the best is going to happen; the other mistake is giving up, so that they don't have to deal with any number of specific problems.

RULE: DON'T COUNT ON ALIMONY.

The award of alimony in divorce is of questionable value. As more women work, the courts have become reluctant to award alimony. Alimony originated in England for a type of divorce that was really more in the nature of a legal separation. At that time, the husband retained his title to the property which his wife had brought into the marriage. She was unable to remarry and also unable to work for more than drudge wages. Alimony was granted to women who were not at fault in the divorce. The higher the degree of the husband's fault, the higher the alimony the wife would be paid. Since women now have the right to retain title to their property, to work for a decent salary, and remarry, the need for alimony is substantially diminished.

Alimony is a payment in recognition of a marital relationship. One spouse pays the other some amount which the court has ordered, and usually pays it on a monthly basis, although sometimes the payment will be made yearly. Alimony is quite different from child support in that child support can be awarded even if the parents were never married. The purpose of child support is just what it sounds like, money to take care of the child. Normally, the father pays child support, but there are rare exceptions. Alimony is also different from a property settlement in which the wife receives some portion of the husband's property upon the final decree of divorce. Property settlements are usually a one-time transaction, but alimony is likely to continue for many years. Each one of these types of awards can be decided independently and the court may award all three to the same woman.

Alimony is difficult to collect. Many men experience some degree of breakdown after a divorce. They have a high likelihood of changing jobs, moving to a different state, or even disappearing from sight. Additionally, alimony awards are often inadequate to support the wife. It is the rare man who makes enough income to even minimally support two households. Indeed, alimony awards often range between $100 and $150 a month. This amount works a severe hardship on the woman who is awarded the custody of preschool children, since she will probably be unable to meet the family expenses without working herself.

Temporary alimony can be awarded while the divorce suit is pending. This type of alimony is considered a substitute for the husband's common-law duty to support his wife. By the same token, husbands will not be granted temporary alimony in cases where the husband might be awarded alimony, since the wife has no duty to support her husband. Temporary alimony may be denied to the woman with a glaring marital error such as an adulterous relationship. However, support may be granted to the children during the period of the divorce, regardless of the wife's guilt. The guiltless wife must show a need for her support during the divorce, but the level of need is entirely within the discretion of the court. The court will be greatly influenced by the woman's age, her ability to earn money, her state of health, and her accustomed manner of living. If a woman is not paid her temporary alimony, her husband can be found in contempt of court. Temporary alimony will

cease upon the final divorce decree. The court may also award her attorney's fees.

RULE: TEMPORARY ALIMONY CAN BE ENFORCED.

The types of enforcement used for temporary alimony are the same
as those used for permanent alimony and child support. We will cover
them here so that they do not have to be discussed again.

The first type of enforcement for any one of these payments is a contempt proceeding. In a contempt proceeding, the husband who has not
paid the amount the court ordered him to pay is called before the court
to explain. If he can prove that he was unable to pay as required, the
court will excuse him. However, if he made enough money to make the
payment and then used the money for something else, he will be held in
contempt. The penalty for contempt can be avoided if he catches up
with his payments. If he's not able to raise the money, he may be jailed,
usually on nights or weekends, until he's caught up. Although the Constitution says a person may not be put in prison for debts, alimony and
child support are exceptions. These are not considered debts, but
rather are regarded as marital responsibilities.

The second type of enforcement is something called execution. This
does not mean that you can shoot him. Instead, you bring yourself before the court with the assertion that your husband has not made payments as required. He is allowed to show why this was not possible.
The court may find his defense inadequate and execute your claim
against his income. You then have a lien against his salary or property.
Not only may you recover against normal property, but your lien may
also be effective against property which is normally exempt from creditors, such as a trust or your husband's home.

If your husband has moved out of state, you may collect your money
either through the doctrine of comity (*kom*-i-ty) or through the Uniform Reciprocal Enforcement of Support Acts now available in all
states.

The doctrine of comity is the principle that one court should ordinarily respect the judgments of another court. Comity is used in divorce proceedings quite often, since it is a convenient way to enforce
the policy that husbands shall not evade judicially established obligations to support their children and ex-wife. The effect of comity is to
prevent a court in the state where your husband now resides from modifying your divorce agreement after the fact.

The Uniform Reciprocal Enforcement of Support Acts are most
helpful to you. Uniform Acts such as these are often passed by states to
avoid conflicts between the laws of different states. The Uniform Sup-

port Acts were passed since so many husbands were moving out of the state, thereby avoiding their obligations.

Your first step under the Support Acts is bringing an action in your state of residence. Your state's court makes a preliminary finding of the amount due to you. Your court then forwards the action to an appropriate court in your husband's state. There, an officer of the court calls him in to show cause why a judgment should not be entered against him. If he cannot show cause, the court will act to collect your money and then forward it to you. This proceeding can take many months.

One of the benefits of using the Uniform Support Acts is that you may not need an attorney to start the proceedings. Many states have officers of the court who can handle this for you for a small fee. Use of the Uniform Support Acts does not foreclose the possibility of you using any other method of collection. You may still bring suit to collect.

Alimony and child support should be collected promptly. If you know where your husband is and make no attempt to collect, you may find that you have waived your right to collect, at least so far as alimony is concerned. It is possible that child support cannot be collected retroactively unless you move rather quickly to enforce it. Child support is awarded to support the children. The fact that you manage to support them without your husband's cooperation can be used to void past payments which he failed to make. However, if you could not afford attorney's fees for collection, or could not find your ex-husband, you will lose nothing.

You may be relieved to know that if your husband does not pay alimony and child support according to the agreement, he is responsible for paying the attorney's fees which you incur in the collection. Sometimes the court will also order a husband to pay your attorney's fees if he tries to modify the alimony or child-support agreements after the divorce is final.

RULE: TO GET YOUR ALIMONY, BRING
YOUR HUSBAND TO COURT.

Marriages may be dissolved without one of the parties being present. For example, your husband could be missing and the court would grant you a divorce. The court will not grant you alimony unless your husband is there to present his evidence. For this reason the law says that divorces are "divisible"—that is, the divorce may be decided now, and the alimony and property settlement decided much later, when you are able to bring your husband before the court. Therefore, it is important that your divorce judgment state clearly that the alimony issue was not decided, since your husband was not present. Two states will not allow the alimony to be separated from the divorce suit itself. They are Maryland and Vermont.

If your husband brings a suit for divorce in another state, you need not appear in that action, but you may start an action for alimony and child support in your own state, if your husband can be brought within its jurisdiction. However, if your husband sues for divorce and you make a general appearance, you may not later bring an independent suit for alimony.

Interestingly, divorce may not end separate maintenance orders which had been decided before the divorce. Your husband is obliged to pay the separate maintenance until you are able to appear. For your existing separate maintenance decree to be terminated, you must be living in a state where your husband also has the right to bring suit.

RULE: ALIMONY IS BASED ON
YOUR LIFE STYLE.

Normally, the amount of alimony you will receive is worked out by the attorneys prior to the trial. The court will then modify this amount according to its discretion. The court will base its judgment on the husband's ability to pay, the wife's need, the relative fault of the parties, and other factors we'll discuss in a moment.

The husband's ability to pay is considered. He must have an adequate portion left to support himself at roughly the same standard of living that the alimony will afford the wife. This rule places a temporary upper limit on the amount of alimony, because the wife's needs are also considered. The alimony should afford her substantially the same standard of living to which she was accustomed prior to the divorce. The husband's income may not be great enough at the time of the divorce to allow for this, so many divorce agreements will state that the alimony can be modified later if the husband's income increases. Although the wife's own property and income may diminish the amount of alimony, the court will also consider that she may have to quit work to care for young children.

The fault of the parties to the divorce may also modify the alimony. This rule is made on the general theory that either the wife should be compensated for wrongs done to her or the husband should be punished. Some statutes do not allow a wife to recover alimony if she is at major fault in the divorce. For example, adultery or physical cruelty to the husband might be a major fault, whereas mental cruelty wouldn't be. In the case of no-fault divorce, in which the divorce is awarded to both parties, the wife may still receive alimony.

Frequently, individuals, including the court, will get carried away with alimony as it relates to assignment of fault. Alimony seeks to minimize the financial impact of divorce on a woman, and perhaps to allow her to take care of her children instead of working. To some degree an issue of equity will also be recognized, in that it is unfair to turn a woman of fifty years out of a twenty-five-year marriage with no source of income. Especially in the case of the older woman with an affluent husband, substantial alimony will be awarded as a salute to her faithful service in the home.

Common sense is also a factor in the amount of alimony awarded. The court will consider the age and health of the wife, how long she was married, her standard of living prior to the divorce, a career the woman might have given up when the children came along, the wife's contribution to her husband's business either in money or in service, and how much property the parties may have accumulated.

RULE: ALIMONY COMES IN A LOT OF DIFFERENT FORMS.

Alimony is normally due monthly. But the court can make any arrangements which will suit the husband's income. For example, a fellow with a seasonal occupation, such as a construction worker, receives most of his income during half of the year. The court might order that the alimony be paid during that period only, such as six payments due monthly from May through October. It is also possible that alimony will be paid in one lump sum following the divorce.

An alimony trust can also be used. The ex-husband puts money into a trust, which is then paid out to the wife periodically. The court may also order the husband to carry life insurance in the wife's name as part of the alimony agreement.

One of the problems with monthly alimony is that it does not become due and payable until the time has passed. Therefore, even though the husband may be two years behind in his alimony payments, his property may not be seized for more than the alimony already due. In other words, even though he has been recalcitrant about paying in the past, you will not be able to seize his property to protect yourself in the future even though it is unlikely that he will ever pay his alimony without your suing him.

RULE: HUSBANDS CAN GET ALIMONY TOO.

If a husband is unable to work, and his ex-wife is a woman of property, judges may award him alimony. This recent U. S. Supreme Court decision of *Orr* v. *Orr* found it unconstitutional to award alimony only to women—men had to be able to get it too. A majority of states already had laws allowing alimony for men. Now men in all states can have it, if the circumstances warrant alimony. Alimony awards to men have been traditionally granted only if the man is disabled or has been serving as a house husband. Courts are likely to continue these limitations.

RULE: ALIMONY MAY BE MODIFIED.

Many states have statutes specifically allowing courts to modify alimony. These states are Alaska, Arizona, Arkansas, California, Colorado, Connecticut, Florida, Hawaii, Illinois, Iowa, Kansas, Kentucky, Maine, Maryland, Massachusetts, Michigan, Minnesota, Missouri, Montana, Nebraska, Nevada, New Hampshire, New Jersey, New York, Oregon, Rhode Island, South Carolina, South Dakota, Tennessee, Utah, Virginia, Washington, West Virginia, Wisconsin, and Wyoming. It is a good idea to allow for modification of alimony, since the situations of parties do change. If alimony were fixed for all time, it could work a hardship on either the husband or the wife, or both. Consequently, most divorce decrees contain some provision for adjusting the alimony. If there is no statement in the divorce decree and the statute does not allow for modification, most courts will refuse to change the original arrangement. Even if you live in a state which permits modification, it's a good idea to provide for modification in the agreement. You might move to a state with no modification statute.

In order to modify alimony, either you or your ex-husband file a motion on the original divorce action. Personal service on your ex-husband is not required as long as he appeared when the original decree was granted. If you can't find your ex-husband or he is out of the state, you may serve your notice on his attorney if his attorney has not been officially discharged. The divorce is not tried all over again. You merely bring in evidence of occurrences since the last time the alimony was adjusted.

Alimony will be changed or terminated for various causes. The most common basis for terminating alimony is the wife's remarriage. In fact, most divorce decrees state that alimony will cease immediately upon the wife's remarriage. In some states it automatically ceases by statute. California, Colorado, and Illinois have laws to this effect. Failing either a statute or a specific clause in the divorce decree, most courts will terminate alimony so as to protect the woman's legal rights during her second marriage.

If the husband remarries, courts will also entertain a petition for modification. If he is able to support both families to the same degree, his alimony will not be reduced, but the court is unlikely to condemn the second wife to poverty while the first wife lives in relative comfort.

The wife's needs may also change. She may obtain increases in alimony due to poor health, inflation, additional expenses for the children, and similar financial problems. If you are increasing your alimony, you should also calculate your income taxes on the increase, since alimony received is fully taxable, as we shall discuss later. The wife's needs may also diminish and her alimony be reduced.

If the woman starts to make more money, or inherits property, the court may reduce the payments. Although some authorities feel that a woman should not be penalized because she's doing well in her job, the majority of courts hold that alimony is a financial bridge to help a woman adjust to single life. If she's doing well in her job, she has obviously made an adjustment. If her husband is strapped by the alimony payments, the court may terminate them.

Often an ex-husband's financial circumstances will change and a modification may be granted on this basis. For example, an airline pilot may develop a heart condition and be unable to continue his normal work. The courts would allow the alimony to be reduced. The opposite of this is the man who quits his job and refuses to seek further employment. His alimony judgment will remain constant. Sometimes a man will make substantially more income after his divorce. In such a case the alimony will be increased only to allow for the standard of living the woman had at the time of the divorce. She will not share in his subsequent prosperity.

Many suits are filed seeking the continuation of alimony after the husband's death. Some courts are willing to do this, since the woman has lost her right to a share in his estate. Many agreements provide that alimony is to cease at the husband's death and substitute a life insurance policy for the ex-wife's share of the estate. In the case where the alimony awarded is a specific sum to be paid over a period of time, the treatment is somewhat different. For example, if the decree states the woman is to receive $20,000, payable at the rate of $2,000 a year for ten years, the court will allow the woman to collect the balance of her lump-sum alimony from her ex-husband's estate. Collecting a normal periodic payment, such as $250 a month until remarriage, might tie up an estate well past any normal period of settlement. It's probably not a good idea to keep an estate open for twenty or thirty years just so periodic alimony can be paid. This would severely prejudice the rights of a second wife and children by a second marriage.

Sometimes husbands will ask that their alimony be modified because their ex-wife is misbehaving. The courts generally hold that what a woman does after her divorce is strictly her own business. However, her actions may indicate that she really doesn't need as much alimony as she was originally granted. For example, if she gambles or drinks heavily, she obviously has extra money floating around. If she's being supported by another man, her alimony may also be excessive. Courts will sometimes suspend alimony if one of the parties has not lived up to the divorce decree. For example, if a woman moves her children from the jurisdiction in violation of the custody order in the divorce, the court may suspend her alimony until she brings them back again. If the husband falls behind in his alimony, the court may allow him to bring suit on the basis that his circumstances have changed and he is no longer able to pay the amount. If he has attempted to pay part of the alimony every month, the court will consider this evidence that he is attempting to live up to the agreement.

Sometimes the parties will make an independent agreement after the divorce decree. They may agree to change the amount of alimony, the child custody, the use of property, visitation rights, etc. This agreement will not bind the court unless it is formally presented for its approval. The court will then modify the decree.

Sometimes the court will allow payments to be modified retroactively. If the husband shows that his circumstances have changed and he was not able to make recent payments due to that change, the court may refuse to enforce them. As a normal rule, however, if the alimony is due on the first of the month and is not modified by that date, the amount will be unchanged and his ex-wife can hold him to the original decree.

Obviously, modifying alimony is a time-consuming and perhaps costly procedure which should be avoided if possible. One way to avoid it is to write a divorce agreement with built-in changes due to inflation, changing needs of children, etc. It's quite possible for alimony to be modified ten or fifteen times depending on how stable the needs and incomes of the parties are. Court-ordered modifications may be unduly difficult, especially in a mobile society where both husband and wife may be transferred to a new location every few years. In fact, there is only the remotest likelihood that either will remain in the state where they got their divorce. Courts have carefully worked out what to do in such cases.

Generally, if you are seeking the modification, you have to bring suit in the state in which you now reside. The court of this state will then consult the law of the state where the divorce was granted to see whether or not the alimony can be changed. This rule can work a hardship on the fellow paying the alimony, since he may have to travel two thousand miles to appear at the hearing. It is little wonder husbands become less and less interested in keeping up alimony payments, since the whole thing is so unwieldy, inconvenient, and expensive.

RULE: MAKE SURE THE INSURANCE IS PAID.

Often the ex-husband will carry a substantial life insurance policy on himself for his ex-wife's benefit. The title to the policy should be in the wife's name so that proceeds from the policy will not become part of his estate. If the title is in the wife's name, no estate tax will be paid. You should work out a method of checking on whether the life insurance has been paid as required under the agreement. Husbands have been known to let these policies lapse. The same thing is true of annuity policies.

Also consider who will carry the health and hospitalization insurance on the children. Often the man will be able to include them on his policy at work. The agreement should specifically cover this particular issue. There should also be a clause in which the husband agrees to pay all medical expenses if he lets the health insurance lapse. You will probably have to provide for your own health and hospitalization insurance. This insurance can be quite costly. You may wish to add an amount to the alimony to allow for this.

RULE: DIVIDE THE PROPERTY AT THE DIVORCE.

Gaining title to property acquired during the marriage is the most secure financial arrangement a woman can make. The divorce decree may pass the property to her free and clear of all encumbrances. However, the husband must appear at the divorce in order for there to be an adjudication of these property rights. A woman may not seize property outside the jurisdiction of the divorce. Very often the woman will obtain the title to the family home while the husband will continue to pay the mortgage and taxes. Obviously, this is a great advantage to the family.

If the couple has been living in a community-property state, each is entitled to one half of the property acquired during the marriage. Inheritances received don't count. Neither does property brought into the marriage. The community-property states are Arizona, California, Idaho, Louisiana, Nevada, New Mexico, Texas, and Washington.

If the divorce decree does not indicate that the property rights were settled, or if jurisdiction could not be obtained over one of the parties, the divorce decree will not modify property rights. The wife may sue at a later time to have the property divided.

RULE: YOU LOSE A LOT THROUGH DIVORCE.

When you divorce, you may lose the benefit of a lot of economic security that your husband has been building up through his work. For example, you will probably forgo any normal rights you would have to his pension. Unless you have been married ten years, you won't have any right to the wife's share in your husband's Social Security. On top of that, your spouse may remarry and be granted a reduction on his alimony payments.

Your rights of inheritance will also be nullified. You lose your right to a widow's share in his estate. The widow's share is one third to one half of the husband's assets upon his death. Additionally, it is within the power of your husband to disinherit his and your children if they are under the age of 21.

After the divorce you could easily be left in the position of total dependence upon your husband's alimony and child-support payments. These payments can be difficult to collect and can be modified later, whereas your husband may retain many of his property rights, his pension rights, and his full Social Security. For these reasons you must plan for your future, since you can't really count on your ex-husband. Many women hope to avoid this insecurity by getting the largest property settlement available at the time of the divorce. They use the theory that it is better to take the property now than to hope that they will continue to receive a substantial alimony payment. What is certain is that the divorced woman must find herself a good job, so that she can begin to accumulate her own pension and Social Security. Another argument in favor of a large property settlement is that it avoids any difficulty when rights of inheritance are involved, and assures the children some security for their future.

Often the divorce settlement will use life insurance or annuity insurance to bridge the gap of pension rights and Social Security. Most courts will uphold the life insurance provision, since it protects the right to receive alimony. Annuity insurance is a bit more difficult, since it would provide the woman with a retirement benefit. Some courts have been unwilling to enforce a requirement that the husband purchase an annuity for the wife's benefit. If your divorce agreement is complex enough to include such provisions as an annuity policy, you must certainly have an attorney. He will be able to guide you through the prejudices of your local court.

RULE: BEWARE OF ODD PROVISIONS.

Occasionally, a husband will insist on including some unusual provision which restricts the wife's conduct. For example, the divorce agreement might include her promise not to go out with other men, that the children will be raised in a certain religion, not the wife's, that she will never work, and about as many other unusual things as there are wrinkles in the human mentality. These provisions may or may not be upheld, depending on the prejudices of the judge. Your potential problem with this sort of clause is that it may prompt further litigation. The saner the divorce agreement is to begin with, the better off both parties are.

In addition to alimony and property rights, child support is usually decided during the divorce. Sometimes a child-support order will be finalized prior to the divorce and will continue on through the divorce unchanged. A father's duty to support his child exists in all American jurisdictions. This duty is modified only when he becomes incapable of work. At that time the wife takes up the duty. Child support is independent of any fault of the wife. The courts will not allow a child to suffer because of inadequacies in the parents. Even in the rare case when a court denies a divorce, it may still order child-support payments. The courts will not allow any legal problem to interrupt the payment of child support. The parents may move, disappear, or do other things which would cancel alimony, but the child support continues. An additional interesting element to child support is that the child may sue for it himself through a guardian.

RULE: CHILD SUPPORT CEASES AT AGE 21.

As a general rule, the father can sue and have support canceled as each of his children reaches majority. The majority is age 21 if the child is in college. However, the child may leave high school at 18, get a job, or join the Army, and show that he is capable of taking care of himself. If a child marries, the father's duty to support that child is over. Courts will occasionally rule that the father's duty to support his child will continue indefinitely if the child is mentally or physically disabled.

The amount of support will be decided by the trial court. The support will depend primarily on the father's income and property. The children of wealthy men will receive much higher awards than the children of poor men. The child will not be limited to a minimum standard of living. The amount is likely to allow for education, recreation, and other advantages the child would have received if his parents had not divorced. But if the father would be bankrupted by the child-support payments, the court will rely on the mother's income as well. Since realistic child support is burdensome to the average man, the wife's income level is normally considered when awarding child support. The courts place the children's welfare above the legal rights of the parents.

The most vexing problem with child support is who will pay for the college education. Many fathers assert that they have no duty to supply the funds for this. The courts are pretty well split on whether the father is obliged. The modern view is that he is if the parents' backgrounds and educations indicate that their child would attend college.

RULE: CHILD-SUPPORT ORDERS
CAN BE MODIFIED.

Changes in the amount of child support will be granted, but only for the strongest reasons. The change in the father's fortunes must be permanent. The amount of the child support will not be reduced to allow for temporary setbacks or unanticipated variables. The court will also not reduce child-support installments which have already accrued.

Modifications of child support are generally brought up as a continuation of the original divorce action. Sometimes a court will grant one sum covering both alimony and child support. When the two have been lumped together, courts will not offhandedly reduce the payment. The father must show both a change in need on the part of the children and a change in his ability to pay. Many divorce decrees which lump child support with alimony will have very specific schedules showing when the alimony will decrease. These schedules will usually be linked to the time the child is expected to graduate from college. These schedules are probably a good idea, since they may prevent further litigation.

The reasons for child support modification vary widely, depending on the specific circumstances of the parties involved. A large increase in the wife's income may be grounds for a reduction if the husband has a difficult time making his small payment. If the father remarries and has more children, child support may be reduced, since many courts do not think it's fair to take food out of one child's mouth in favor of another. If a child develops income of his own, the courts will reduce the payment only to a level which is not burdensome for the father. If the mother remarries, the father's obligation to pay child support is normally not modified. However, if the second husband adopts the children, the natural father's obligation ceases. The court will consider the child's welfare above all other elements when modifying the court order. Child support often becomes a real issue if the woman remarries, moves out of the state, or denies her husband visiting rights. The father usually feels justified in ceasing to pay his child support. In such a case neither the mother nor the father is in the right. The court will consider what is the best thing for the child.

Although courts are reluctant to allow alimony to be collected against someone's estate after his death, many courts will tie up an estate in order to provide for the children. The law's point of view is that children should not become wards of the state if a parent has died leaving an estate which would provide for them. This law may present a difficulty since the father may have remarried and may have children by his second wife. In such an instance, the children of the second marriage may be deprived while the first set of children are protected. The best way you can avoid this difficulty is to require the father to carry life insurance payable to the children upon his death.

> RULE: THE FATHER MUST LIVE UP
> TO THE SPIRIT OF THE
> CHILD-SUPPORT DECREE.

The law requires that the father be in "substantial compliance" with the child-support order. Substantial compliance means that the father provides for the maintenance of the child without violating another provision of the divorce decree. He does not have the right to substitute his judgment for the judgment of his ex-wife, who has custody of the children. For example, one decree stated that the father would pay for private schooling. He could not refuse to pay for school and then substitute a pony or other toys even though the amount spent is the same. However, he could very well take the child shopping for a school wardrobe and diminish his child support by a reasonable amount.

If a father is to modify his child support, he should do it with the approval of his ex-wife, since she may be counting on the child support to buy the groceries for that month. After all, feeding and housing the child is the point of child support. Using support money outside the normal course of the agreement should be done with great caution, if the father is to protect himself from suit.

The issue which causes the most flare-ups after the divorce is the father's access to the company of his children. Child visitation is the name the law has given to Sunday football games, staying over, going off on vacation, all with Dad. Custody is somewhat different. The custodial parent is the one whose home is the permanent home of the child. Of course, the parent with the right to the body of the child will have more to say about the child's upbringing.

Although women typically gain custody of the children, some men are quite persistent during a custody controversy. One man I know lasted through several years of physical violence from his wife just because he wanted custody of their two children. He had pictures taken of every bruise and bump. She finally pushed him down the stairs, causing massive bruises and several sprains. He got custody of the children.

RULE: LET THE FATHER SEE THE CHILDREN AS MUCH AS HE WANTS.

Another part of the divorce agreement concerns the times and days the father will take over the care of the children. Any reasonable requests the father makes for visitation rights should be consented to by the mother. There are several practical reasons for this rule. If the father is in close contact with the children, the child-support payments are likely to arrive on time. The possibility of custody battles after the divorce is diminished. The children also retain the benefit of having a reliable male to talk to.

The father's child visitation should not interfere with the children's schooling. A normal agreement on child visitation is that the father has custody of the children on weekends and during holidays. Sometimes the holidays are assigned so that the mother has the children for Christmas and the father for spring vacation, and sometimes the holidays are alternated.

RULE: CUSTODY IS DECIDED IN THE CHILD'S BEST INTERESTS.

The definition of custody is difficult. Normally, custody means that the child has his official home with a certain person who is considered the child's guardian. The difficulty with defining custody is that one parent has a right to discipline, care for, supervise, and educate the child. This can be done without having the actual custody of the child. One legal authority calls custody "a slippery word." Custody is used in divorce proceedings to mean with whom the child lives as opposed to who has the duty to support the child. The result of most modern proceedings is that the father has the duty to support, and the right to visit, while the mother will actually take responsibility for the physical care and education of the child.

Custody is generally decided on the facts of each case, with the judges paying little or no attention to precedent formed in other custody cases.

Since the welfare of the child is the primary interest, the courts will consider many issues which it would be unconstitutional to consider in other cases. For example, the religion of the child and the person seeking custody may be considered. Religion of the parent will be an important factor only if that religion has some unusual aspect, however; religion may also be weighed if the child has been raised as a Catholic and the parent seeking custody is a Protestant or a Jew. Additionally, if the parent has any particular objections to medical care, she may be granted custody only if she consents to allow the child to have medical care.

RULE: CUSTODY IS SETTLED DURING DIVORCE.

All states have statutes authorizing the court to decide the custody of the children of the marriage being dissolved. Children by a prior marriage of one of the parties will not be considered. However, if a custody issue is to be decided, both parties must be notified, so that their evidence can be heard. If it appears that neither parent will be able to take care of the children, the court may ask a third person to join the suit so that custody may be awarded to that party. This guardian will normally be a grandparent or aunt or uncle of the children whose custody is being decided.

Custody orders may also be decided after the divorce if the matter wasn't decided during the divorce itself.

RULE: USE HABEUS CORPUS TO GET CUSTODY OF YOUR CHILD.

A writ of habeus corpus is one of the most interesting types of actions in common law. The term "habeus corpus" means "you have the body," and the writ orders the custodian to present the child at the suit. Habeus corpus is normally a criminal writ but it is used in custody cases when a person claims custody of a child who is not in his possession. A writ of habeus corpus allows the court to determine if it is in the child's best interests that custody continue for the person now holding the child.

In a writ of habeus corpus, proper notice must be given to all parties involved. The writ is enforceable by contempt and the trial court's decision may be appealed.

RULE: SUE FOR LEGAL CUSTODY.

It is not unusual that a person will actually have possession of a child without a legal right to custody. For example, the custody of the children might not have been decided at the divorce, or a woman may be abandoned and not have an unassailable legal right to the custody of her own children. A person in this position may not use habeas corpus, since that may be brought only against another person who has actual custody. To remedy this and to establish legal custody, the woman may make a petition in equity or may ask for a declaratory judgment that she is the legal custodian of her children. This sort of suit is normally a matter of form, but it may be necessary to simplify collecting monies due to the child and other practical issues. Also it's best to have a clear right to custody of your children.

There is another type of suit which is also a matter of form—the petition for guardianship. This suit allows for an adjudication of custody, and may be accomplished either by the parent's last will and testament or by a suit under statutes available in all states.

Custody disputes may also be settled under statutes for the protection of dependent and neglected children. "Dependent" in this case means a child who has been abandoned or orphaned. "Neglected" is used to define the instance when the child has been improperly cared for due to cruelty, mental incapacity, immorality, or depravity on the part of the child's custodian. These statutes can also be called upon when the custodian, either his parent or another person, refuses to provide the child with medical, surgical, or institutional care and so endangers the child's health. They can also be used when the child's custodian is endangering the child's morality.

The court has a wide latitude in deciding what would be the best remedy for a child so unfortunate as to be involved in this situation. The court may award custody to one parent or the other, ordering that the parents fulfill certain requirements. The child may also be removed from the parent's custody, placed in a foster home or an institution, or the court may even terminate any rights the parent may have and allow the child to be adopted.

RULE: THE COURT WILL WEIGH ALL ISSUES.

No clear-cut forecast is possible in child custody cases. The court considers many factors. Each of these factors is given a different weight depending upon the child's age, and may be one of the reasons why there are so many child custody suits. For example, the sex of the child will not be relevant until the child reaches a certain age. A fourteen-year-old boy could state that he wishes to live with his father. The court would honor his request. The court would not honor the same request from a younger child. The court would also weigh how strong the child's statement is and might test the child for maturity of judgment.

Interestingly, under the old common law the mother had absolutely no right to the custody of her children. Only a totally corrupt father was denied custody. The law today states that both parents have an equal right to the custody of children. The court then goes on to decide which parent would best serve the interests of the child.

Children under high school age are usually thought to require the care of a mother. The child of high school age is thought to require much contact with a parent of the same sex. Therefore, girls of high school age will usually stay with their mothers, whereas boys will often live with their fathers.

Occasionally the morals of the parties will be argued when deciding custody. A few courts deny custody to the adulterous wife, but as a general rule, the custody will remain with the mother if she is in other ways acceptable. Morality is normally used as an index of the parent's capacity for supervising and training the child.

Far more important than the issue of morality is the parent's desire and ability to care for the child. In this case, the parent's history of child care is given a very strong weight. The court will also consider the remarriage of a parent and the willingness of the new spouse to welcome the child. The courts give some weight to the physical conditions in which the child would live and more weight to the mental health of the parents. Occasionally, a parent will argue that he has far superior financial resources and therefore should be awarded custody. The result of this assertion is usually a higher child-support payment.

In the end, the court will decide this issue based on the sincerity with which the parent seeks custody. Normally, the custody of all brothers and sisters will be awarded to one parent, since the value of living with siblings is very great. Occasionally, courts will be asked to change custody based on the fact that the custodial parent is intending to leave the state. The court will consider only the child's best interests. Courts used to think the child's interests would be properly served by the child remaining in the state and under the supervision of the court, but a trend is developing to allow the custodial parent to take the child with her.

The most telling factors in a custody case are the agreements which the parents have made concerning the children. The court is in no way bound by these agreements, but it will routinely consent to them as long as the child's welfare is not hampered by the agreement.

RULE: JOINT CUSTODY IS RARE.

True joint custody is the practice of splitting judicial custody equally between the parents. The child spends six months with one parent and six months with the other. Courts generally object to joint custody since it is likely to interfere with the child's schooling and the continuity of his or her life. However, courts often agree to school months with one parent and vacation months with the other. If you and the children's father are dividing the custody of the child, the agreement should also state who's going to pay for the child's transportation between homes. If not provided for, these practical issues will lead to disagreements.

A new trend has been developing in New York. So far it has been used only with prosperous parents. If the parents have income which would allow them to maintain three separate residences, the court may order that the children reside permanently at the family home. It is the parents who move in and out of the home, either weekly or monthly, and take care of the children. When they are not staying at the family home, the parents go to their own apartments and lead their own social lives. If the parents can afford to do this, it may be the most secure arrangement for the children.

Joint custody is turning into a cause celebre, and it's getting a lot of publicity. Fathers are fomenting for sole custody or the joint custody described above. Some states have changed their laws to specifically authorize joint custody (Iowa, North Carolina, Arizona, and Wisconsin). Others are considering it (California, Connecticut, Michigan, and Pennsylvania). Some states, like New York, have laws stating that neither parent will be presumed to be the better parent, and that each case must be decided on the best interest of the child.

However, judicially imposed joint custody, and any of its modifications, is rarer than the publicity implies. The husband's attorney will often argue for sole or joint custody just to bargain down the wife's financial demands. Judges know this and consequently take husbands' pleas for custody with a grain of salt. Attorneys are culpable in this too. They are often so interested in "winning" for their client that they throw the human issues out the window. However, *nobody wins a divorce*.

If you'll observe divorcing people, you'll notice that if they're both fairly sane, they come to an equitable and workable agreement about the children. If one or both of them is crazy, anything can happen. This is why joint custody is such an ephemeral issue. If the couple is sane, joint custody is what actually happens, whether or not the court order says so. If one of them is a lunatic, they make a battle of it in court. For the most part, judges have orderly minds, and they don't want craziness in their courtrooms. So, if a couple offers joint custody as part of the divorce agreement, the judge is likely to approve it. If they fight it out in court, the judge will get testy.

Obviously, joint custody is not as much a problem of the law as it is a problem of human behavior. I watched one couple going through divorce and custody arrangements. It took them three years of living apart before they were both clear in their own minds as to what was best for everyone, including their daughter. After the pain of failure had left, they decided how to do things. He picks up the daughter from school and makes her dinner. Then he takes her to her mother. Weekends are negotiated individually, but it is assumed they will split these equally. The daughter seems fine.

RULE: CUSTODY MAY BE MODIFIED.

Custody can be modified or even reversed after the original decision. The modification then becomes part of the original decision, although you must ensure that everyone has notice of the suit and an opportunity to be heard. It can happen that the circumstances of the child's welfare will require a change in custody. For example, the mother may become ill, lose her job, or have another disaster befall her. One of the parents may die, in which case a change in custody would also be called for.

If someone was fraudulently induced into not giving evidence at the original trial, he may present his case at a later custody hearing. Additionally, if some basis for the custody decision in the original trial has changed, the parent may sue for a change of custody. If the parent remarries and is now able to provide a home, a change in custody may be allowed if the child would benefit by the move.

The child himself, upon reaching the age of 14, can also ask the court for a change in custody. At the age of 14, most states allow a child to choose his own guardian.

Quite frequently a parent will be able to show that the other parent is attempting to alienate the affections of the child. In this case courts feel that a change in custody is justified. Above all, the primary principle of change in child custody is not the reward or the punishment of the parents, but the welfare of the child alone.

Amidst other serious personal issues, the tax man comes to call. Practically every step in the divorce settlement influences the tax return of both you and your ex-husband.

RULE: PROPERTY SETTLEMENTS ARE TAXABLE.

When your husband gives you title to his property, he may also have to pay capital-gains tax on it. Capital gains as a tax is discussed in the chapter on taxes. However, the fact that your husband may have to pay substantial tax when he gives you title to the house will affect the amount of property he can afford to settle on you. For this reason you may find your husband reluctant to make a property settlement in spite of the fact that it really is the best method for many couples.

As you will read below, your husband doesn't have to pay taxes on the alimony he gives you, but he will have to pay taxes on property settlements. Therefore, many husbands argue for alimony instead of a property settlement. If a woman takes the alimony in lieu of property, she may then be in the unenviable position of having to sue to collect alimony, all because her husband didn't want to pay taxes. This tax law leads to an unfair result. The tax law on property settlements should be changed so a woman can more easily obtain the property which is rightly hers.

If the husband sets up a trust to pay alimony to his wife, he does not have a taxable gain. However, the trust agreement cannot allow the wife to have a general power of appointment or the right to invade the principal. In other words, the trust must actually be the property of the husband and only pay a specific amount to the wife. The bank which holds the trust will be able to help you specifically with any alimony trust you and your spouse might wish to set up.

RULE: ALIMONY IS TAXABLE.

Husbands deduct alimony from their tax return. Women must add the alimony to their other income and pay income taxes on the alimony they receive. This is the primary reason you should require that alimony and child support be independently designated amounts, and not one lump sum. If the alimony and child support are one lump sum, you will have to pay taxes on the whole thing, thereby decreasing the standard of living of your family. If alimony and child support are separated in your agreement, you need pay taxes only on the alimony. You pay taxes only on the alimony you actually receive, not the amount you should have received.

The IRS defines alimony as periodic payments of an indefinite amount of money or for an indefinite period of time. For example, if a woman is to receive $50,000 payable in amounts of $10,000 every year, this is not indefinite. The woman knows exactly how much she will receive and over what period. However, if a woman were to receive $10,000 a year until she remarries, this would be considered alimony, since she may remarry two years from now or never. An exception to this rule is that any payment received regularly over a period of more than ten years is periodic regardless of whether a specific amount is assigned to be received.

Another requirement for alimony is that the husband must be obligated to pay it under an agreement incident to divorce or separation. A man couldn't make a gift to his ex-wife and subtract it from his income as alimony. The IRS will not allow people to make up their own alimony or to independently designate support as alimony.

Another type of alimony agreement which will be non-taxable to the husband and taxable to the wife is the agreement calling for a designated percentage of the ex-husband's income over a designated period of time, usually five or seven years. This is alimony since the amount to be received is indefinite and depends on the husband's fortunes.

RULE: CHILD SUPPORT IS NOT TAXABLE.

Child support you receive is not taxable on your tax return. Your husband may not deduct it from his taxes. Many divorce agreements allow the husband to take the child's personal exemption on his tax return in exchange for his child support. This provision is fair as long as the child support represents more than one half the cost of maintaining the child on a yearly basis. However, if you end up picking up more than half the cost, you should notify your husband that you intend to claim the child's exemption, so that he does not claim the exemption too (and earn both of you an audit).

RULE: CHANGE YOUR WITHHOLDING STATUS.

When employers withhold income taxes, they use tables to show them how much is to be withheld each week. Married persons have much less withheld than single persons. If your divorce may become final during the year (before December 31), it is best to change from "married" to "single" long before your divorce becomes final. The withholding status need not be your legal marital status, but only the status which will ensure that the proper tax has been withheld at the end of the year.

Your actual filing status is determined by whatever your marital status is on December 31 of the year in question. If you're still officially married on December 31, you and your husband may file a joint tax return. You can also file as "married filing separately." However, if your divorce becomes final, you *must* file as single, even though your employer has only been withholding on the basis of your married status. You could end up owing a lot of taxes. If you have children living with you, you may file as a head of household if you meet the other qualifications. The IRS publishes a booklet called *Tax Information for Divorced and Separated Individuals,* Publication No. 504. You may find it helpful. Ask the IRS to send a you a copy.

In New York, there are several books on divorce available such as *New York Divorce for Under $100*. Books of this type are guides for do-it-yourself divorces. They are sure to be available in heavily populated states. The do-it-yourself divorce is perfectly legitimate. Any young working couple without children can avail themselves of this form of divorce.

The do-it-yourself divorce is not recommended if there is a child, much property, or if the wife is over 35. If there is a child, child custody and support must be decided and it's best to have help. You must weigh many issues. Property settlements, beyond dividing the goods in an apartment, also need a lawyer because titles to property will have to be changed and perhaps judgments entered. If the wife is over 35, she has to consider her retirement, life insurance, Social Security, etc. Practically all people prefer help with such complex issues. The woman over 35 is also likely to have contributed much to the couple's prosperity, so a property settlement is also in order.

Marriages do fail. The individuals grow in different directions, the romantic dreams about the other become disappointed, personality flaws tolerated during the courtship become abhorrent in the marriage, people adopt new habits, the list goes on and on.

You are disbanding a partnership which everyone hoped would succeed. It is a big loss.

Divorce is an emotional time, but you must make many clear decisions. Take your emotions to your friends, your minister, your family, but keep them out of discussions with your husband and your attorney. Statements of anger, grief, propitiation, will only drive your husband crazier, and inflate your attorney's fee. If you establish your goals and keep your mind on them, divorcing will run more smoothly. When you feel tears welling up, remember you are there to assure your future. The past is gone.

Chapter 4
UNTIL DEATH DO YOU PART

RULE: READ THIS CHAPTER LONG
BEFORE YOU NEED IT.

Death is handled in different ways by different cultures. Irish immigrants keen, Italians kiss the body, Anglo-Saxons buck up, Indians dance, some cultures have a party and everyone drinks, and in New Orleans they have a parade. Whatever her culture, the widow will be conducted through the early parts of her mourning by her friends and family. Then a week or so later, the loneliness will start to hit.

Mourning itself usually takes about a year. Although it gets lighter as time passes, many widows experience a seeming renewal of their loss on the first anniversary of their husband's death. But this anniversary seems to be the last gasp of mourning and after this time things tend to get much brighter.

Individuals have all different kinds of abilities. One widow may never have signed a check in her life; another may have been running a business. They will have greater or lesser skills in dealing with the business and legal aspects of their widowhood. But both of them will have to confront the emotional vacuum created by widowhood.

During the period of mourning, you can find a great deal of help in your community. Your best and most immediate adviser will probably be your minister, priest, or rabbi. Even if you are not a religious person, these counselors can provide more accurate emotional help than just about anyone else. They have a great deal of experience in dealing with death. You may find the calm atmosphere of a religious institution to be soothing and allow you time to think. For more practical help, your bank, the lawyer who wrote your husband's will, and perhaps an accountant will help you sort out the practical steps to clear away your husband's affairs. Your adult children can be helpful. There are also some women's groups which may be able to give you a combination of spiritual support and practical advice.

The old saw "Keep busy" is still the best advice around. The law will help you here. It demands that you attend to several things concerning your husband's estate: debts, the will, taxes, etc. You should also allow yourself enough time alone so that you can mourn, get angry, and contemplate what to do next.

RULE: TAKE CARE OF THE BODY.

It's best to make arrangements for the body long before there is any likelihood of death. At this time you and your husband can make very practical decisions about the amount of money you have available for your funerals. Many communities have memorial or funeral societies which have worked out inexpensive and dignified funeral arrangements.

The new widow is in a weakened position, and is likely to become the subject of much persuasion on the part of the funeral director. He may play on her grief and guilt in an attempt to sell more elaborate services than are really required. If the deceased belonged to a memorial society, the arrangements may have already been made by the deceased himself. The funeral director has little to do, except carry out his function.

Around half of the memorial societies are connected with churches, but they never require that memorial society members join the church. Memorial societies are also run by senior citizen's groups, unions, cooperatives, and even concerned individuals. One need not belong to the larger group to belong to the memorial society. The local society arranges to have a list of funeral directors with standard prices for particular varieties of services. These charges are specifically itemized and cover anything from immediate cremation ($200 to $500) to a traditional funeral with full services ($500 to $1,000). A survey of the funeral homes participating with New York memorial societies showed that a wide range of locations and ethnic and religious specializations are available. The memorial society will also help you with the legal requirements of your locality.

The memorial society member is asked to fill out forms which will someday aid the funeral director and surviving family members with the burial and arrangements for the estate. The particular form we saw also included donation of body parts to various organ banks. The costs were much lower than we had anticipated for the New York area. The memorial society itself charged a one-time ten-dollar fee for a lifetime membership. The family then pays for the funeral separately.

The memorial societies can save you a lot of money, even thousands of dollars. They can also provide local information. If you would like to find a memorial society in your area, you can write to: The Continental Association of Memorial Societies, Suite 1100, 1828 L Street, N.W., Washington, D.C. 20036. They send out about 20,000 information packets every year. They also regulate their member societies. Our experience with the individual societies and the national association was that they are knowledgeable, efficient, and fast.

Most states have health laws requiring embalmment, cremation, or alternatively, a quick burial. Embalming is done only once. One widow paid for two embalmings of her husband's body. The funeral director told her the law required it. If the corpse is to be shipped to a different area for burial, it must be embalmed as a health precaution. Most areas also require some sort of a casket. A pine box is just as adequate for this regulation as the most elaborate mahogany casket.

Cemeteries come in two general types. One type is owned by a church. The church members provide the care for the cemetery as part of the church activity. A church-owned cemetery is the least expensive kind because a charitable organization is providing the land and maintenance for its members' use. Such cemeteries are more likely to be found in small towns and rural areas where land is not scarce. The more common type is a cemetery which is conducted as a business. The businessman sells the plots along the same lines as a real estate developer might. These cemeteries are more elaborate and are likely to have a chapel and perhaps a mausoleum. They are far more expensive. Plots in these cemeteries are often sold on a contract basis while the husband and wife are still very young. They pay off the plots at a set yearly fee, perhaps one hundred dollars a year for twenty-five years. These cemeteries usually provide a feature called "perpetual care." The cemetery puts part of the purchase price into a trust which will pay for the maintenance of the cemetery and its individual plots.

If you have not made funeral arrangements prior to the death of your spouse, you will probably sign a contract with the funeral parlor to provide the services described in the contract. Like any other consumer transaction, this contract has minor pitfalls. For instance, you will be held to the price quoted in the contract. You have only a few days to dispose of the body, whether by burial or cremation. After the funeral director has performed his part of the bargain, you will have no recourse but to pay the bill. It's not news that funerals can be outrageously expensive. You may find that the casket and all the services could exceed your expectations by two or three times. The average funeral cost nationwide is $2,000, not including the plot. Much more than this is fluff.

When you go to make the funeral arrangements, it's best to take a hardheaded friend. If you take the family, they'll have the same emotional involvement that you do. The friend is more likely to tell you when he or she thinks the cost is way out of line. Many people prefer to send the hardheaded friend first, have him or her make the arrangements, and then come by to personally approve the contract.

When making funeral preparations it's best to keep in mind that you are caring only for the body of your spouse. He is no longer there.

RULE: GET MANY COPIES OF THE DEATH CERTIFICATE.

The death certificate can be issued by many different parties, depending on your locale. In Tacoma, Washington, death certificates are obtained in the County City Building. In New York City the funeral director arranges for the death certificate and turns it over to the relatives. In Chicago, the death certificate is obtained from the funeral director or from the Bureau of Vital Statistics (Public Health Department in many communities). County coroners may issue death certificates in the case of violent or accidental death. Either the attending physician or the funeral director can tell you how to obtain one in your area. Incidentally, the original death certificate always stays with the Public Health Department. You only get copies.

The death certificate gives you the right to make claims and to stand in your husband's shoes. You will need it for practically every situation you deal with, from straightening out names on bank accounts to claiming Social Security. Make sure the death certificate meets the basic regulations of your state. Notarize it, if required. You'll need many copies of this, so have six or eight photocopied at once, even for a simple estate. If your husband owned stock or bonds, you'll need more copies.

RULE: FIRST COLLECT THE INSURANCE.

The most readily available source of cash for most estates is the life insurance policies. The wife is very likely to know exactly where these are and how much they are worth. You should call the insurance agent almost immediately after the death. Although to act so quickly seems bloodthirsty, you may need the money to pay for the funeral and to have cash to support yourself and your children while the other assets are being straightened out. Collecting the insurance takes some period of time. The sooner you act, the sooner you'll be able to pick up the reins of your life.

RULE: FIND THE WILL.

If your husband wrote a will, you probably know of its whereabouts. Take out the will and read it to see if there are any unusual provisions in it regarding his burial or the appointment of the executor. If there is no will, your husband's property will be distributed according to the statutes of your state which provide for this occurrence.

You or a member of your family should start to take the steps to clear up the estate. If the amount of money which was left is small, the estate can be settled under the small estate laws without ever setting up a formal probate. The small estate laws normally apply to persons who die holding no real estate and have personal property up to $5,000 or $10,000 in value. In this case a voluntary administrator can step forward without court approval to handle distributing title to the right people. The voluntary administrator of the small estate is usually the spouse, but any competent adult relative may also serve. A county administrator may also step in. The title to cars will be passed to the surviving spouse upon presentation of the death certificate to the Secretary of State. If the title to the car is changed, the auto insurance must also be changed, since the insurance company is entitled to cancel the policy on the grounds that the insured is dead. Your banker can help you clear title to your accounts. The clerk of your local probate court can point you to the state law which covers the administration of small estates.

If the assets left include real property or more extensive holdings than the small estate, probate is probably necessary. Probate means nothing more than proving that the document presented is the last will of the person who signed it. Proving the last will is rarely an issue. The primary purpose of probate is to assure that the directions in the will will be carried out. The executor or administrator of the estate is given the documentation she needs to carry out her job. The court then supervises the executor's job.

Probate doesn't happen by itself. Someone has to start the process, and that person is usually the executor. The executor can hire a lawyer to help her with the task.

RULE: PRESENT THE WILL.

It is traditional to have a reading of the will. At this time the will is read to all concerned family members, and additional letters from the deceased may be read too. These letters are often explanations to one family member or another of why the deceased took some particular action in his will. It will be up to the executor to carry out the deceased's wishes, both to the exact direction and within the spirit which the will intends. Since the executor is acting on behalf of another, she has the responsibility to carry out her job precisely.

RULE: KNOW YOUR DUTIES.

Whether you're an administrator or an executor, you will use your powers to perform your responsibilities, which in legalese are called the executor's duties. The duties are very straightforward and will be discussed in the chapter on executors. Essentially, the executor's duties are to collect and conserve assets, pay death taxes, and then disburse the assets under either the will or the laws of intestate. The probate process will not be finished until all of these steps have been completed to the satisfaction of the court.

RULE: EXPECT DELAYS.

One recent widow complained that her most serious problem involved unexpected delays in settling her husband's estate. Everything took months longer than she had anticipated. Her state inheritance tax form took nine months to complete. It was so detailed that she couldn't make it out herself.

She discovered that in her state disability insurance and Social Security are linked together. She had to fill out endless forms to make her claim and even had to turn part of them over to her husband's physician. He in turn charged her for filling out the forms. She did not disagree with this, but thought it was a shame that the forms were so lengthy and complicated that she had to pay to have them done.

Her lawyer charged her more than he had originally estimated. The higher charge was due to the fact that he ended up doing the inheritance tax form, which she finally had to turn over to him. To add insult she also had to make a payment to maintain her husband's share of stock in a co-op plant, where he had been an employee for years. There was nothing wrong with this, but she certainly didn't expect to have to do it. The co-op plant did turn out to be a big source of help to her in other ways in terms of advice, business counsel, and other services.

For the first time this woman was handling finance problems and tax problems. These had been her husband's jobs for years. She had no experience of how to do all of the things that she was required to do. Her advice to you is: "And all women should take care of the money along with their husbands, so they know what's going on."

Part II
WORKING

Chapter 5
GETTING AND HOLDING A JOB

Women's work was once tightly restricted. The law limited the types of jobs we could hold, the hours we could work, and our working conditions. Starting with the Civil Rights Act of 1964, most if not all of the proscriptions upon female workers have been overturned.

This area of the law—only fifteen years old—is not as well developed as other areas because it takes a great deal of time for cases to find their way through the legal system. Cases can be appealed up through many levels of courts. Then judges and legal thinkers must sort out the ramifications of various decisions. Eventually, the most workable decisions are universally adopted, and the law emerges. The law of hiring discrimination is currently in the appeals and thinking stage.

Legislation can never be as precise and as thorough as lawmakers would desire. The Congress was aware that rules would have to be made which the Congress could not anticipate. An administrative agency called the Equal Employment Opportunity Commission (EEOC) was set up to make these rules. The EEOC was also empowered to help people enforce their equal employment rights.

This chapter and the next one concern themselves with the rights and remedies that help women get and keep better jobs.

The Civil Rights Act affects all levels of the hiring process and employment itself. Employment agencies, labor organizations, and employers are all covered by the act.

RULE: EMPLOYMENT AGENCIES CANNOT DISCRIMINATE.

An employment agency is any person who regularly procures employees for an employer. The person can be an individual and need not work for pay. Newspapers can also be employment agencies because of the "Help Wanted" ads they print, and as agents, they cannot provide any special classification of their own, such as "job opportunities—women."

RULE: LABOR ORGANIZATIONS CAN'T DISCRIMINATE.

In order to be subject to the Civil Rights Act, the labor organization must have fifteen members or a special protected status. The special protected status arises from the peculiar nature of labor organizations and their bargaining power. The National Labor Relations Board (NLRB) may investigate a union and certify the union as the exclusive representative for a particular job. A represented worker, whether a union member or not, has very limited rights to bargain with an employer without the approval of the labor union. For these reasons labor unions must adhere strictly to fair labor practices and cannot refuse membership to any person (whether a woman or a black or other minority-group members) without a very sound reason.

It had long been a practice for skilled crafts unions, such as plumbers and stagehands, to restrict new membership to the relatives of the current membership. This nepotistic practice is now outlawed, since the relatives of these formerly all-white unions will usually be white and the practice of racial discrimination would therefore continue.

The labor union must also serve all of its members without hostility or discrimination. Once a person has joined a union, the hiring hall cannot discriminate against her nor may hostility be used to make the person leave the union. The union can't represent any particular class unequally in their negotiations. For example, a union could not negotiate one pay scale for women and another pay scale for men. It is allowed, however, to negotiate different pay scales for different jobs. For example, the United Auto Workers might negotiate a higher pay scale for utility workers than it does for welders. Utility workers have more skills than welders, as a utility worker can weld as well as do many other jobs in an auto factory.

Unions control grievance machinery and cannot exclude a person from this for discriminatory reasons. Complaints about the showers in the women's locker room would have to be taken just as seriously as complaints about the men's showers. If the union refuses to process an individual employee's grievance, the employee is then free to go outside of the grievance machinery and sue both the union for a breach of its duty of fair representation and the employer for its discriminatory practice. The two suits can be joined together, even though the employer and the union have different responsibilities.

If a union member-employee is dissatisfied because of some discriminatory practice which the union has failed to handle, the employee cannot take independent strike actions of his or her own. The union member must continue to live within the rules of good union membership. Wildcat strikes and slowdowns are not allowed in spite of the discriminatory practice. The employee can be fired if he or she does this. The lesson of all this is that the union member should remain cool-headed and work within the system. Complaints about the union can be taken to the National Labor Relations Board. It has the duty of investigating unfair representation by the union of its membership.

Professional licensing boards are also covered by the Civil Rights Act. Bar associations, medical associations, dental boards, and countless other boards regulate the persons who enter these professions. They also grant licenses which allow the professional to operate within the state. Since they operate under the color of law (their decisions have legal effects), they are also covered, and may not discriminate on the basis of race, sex, etc.

RULE: EMPLOYERS MUST AFFECT COMMERCE.

Federal laws never apply to a business unless the business affects commerce, and almost all businesses do. The business found to affect commerce could be an individual, corporation, partnership, trust, labor union, or even the local city government. Practically any action taken by one of these groups, even putting a letter in the mail, affects commerce.

The employer must have fifteen employees for at least twenty weeks out of the year. Without this number of employees, the employer is not covered and may discriminate to some degree.

Religious organizations are somewhat an exception. They cannot discriminate against a person because of race or sex, but they may discriminate on the basis of their own religion. It may not benefit them to have persons of varying religious persuasions on their staff. At this point, it is not clear whether religions themselves are constitutionally exempt from any prohibition regarding discrimination. It's altogether probable that if religious doctrine requires that all priests be men, the Civil Rights Act will not interfere.

RULE: EMPLOYERS CANNOT DISCRIMINATE
BECAUSE OF RACE, RELIGION, SEX,
AGE, OR NATIONAL ORIGIN.

Employers have the right to discriminate between individuals, but they do not have the right to do so using race, sex, etc., as the reason. For example, the employer is not allowed to say that a woman cannot do a particular job until he has proved that every woman candidate for the job cannot fulfill the tasks necessary. Additionally, once the employer has given the test, and one woman has failed, he may not exclude all other women from being tested. Each individual has to have an opportunity to see if she can do the job.

Race and religion cannot be used as a basis for discrimination either, except under very particular circumstances. Race, sex, or national origin can be used as a basis for discrimination whenever that particular qualification is so much a part of the job as to be considered "inherent." The qualification could also be used because it is "necessary for authenticity." Examples of this qualification are female models being sent for jobs as female models. A man would hardly fit into the clothing designed for a woman. Only black male actors could be sent for roles requiring a black male actor. By the same token a French restaurant could restrict its waiters to those who speak French, thereby primarily limiting its waiters to Frenchmen. A rosary company could require that all of its salesmen be Catholic, since this requirement is inherently part of the job.

Although we won't discuss age discrimination very extensively, the age discrimination act almost exactly parallels everything we will be discussing. Under the age discrimination act, persons between the ages of 40 and 65 cannot be excluded from jobs strictly on the basis of their age. If a person in this age category is fired and is replaced by a younger person, the middle-aged person may have grounds for a suit. Any person who thinks she has a complaint on these grounds should first contact her union, if she has one, and then the Secretary of Labor. The Secretary of Labor can either talk to the employer to encourage the employee's reinstatement or sue the employer under the age discrimination act.

RULE: EMPLOYERS MAY NOT
DISCRIMINATE AGAINST
A PARTICULAR CLASS.

No particular category of individual can be set apart as undesirable. Whether it's an employment agency, a labor union, or an employer, any use of classifications is prohibited. There cannot be women's jobs, men's jobs, black jobs, or white jobs. Each individual must be examined to see if he or she has the capacity to do a particular job. This law even goes so far as to restrict any type of benefit on an arbitrary classification. For example, women cannot be forced to retire earlier or later than men. They may not receive smaller pension benefits, or be kept from working in an area which by some arbitrary standard might be considered dangerous to them.

RULE: PROTECTED CLASSES CANNOT BE DISCRIMINATED AGAINST.

A protected class is any group of individuals which has been discriminated against in the past. The civil rights acts which were passed after the Civil War required that all citizens shall have the same rights as those enjoyed by white citizens. This act has grown to protect all "persons," which literally means everybody. Anything which would be normal for a white male must now be normal for everyone. Any group which has not always received the treatment and fairness that a white male would receive is aided by the 1964 Civil Rights Act. These classes can be women, any racial minority, any religious minority, or foreign-born persons. Age is also covered. No part of the employee's duties or work-related social functions may be separate, except by practical necessity, such as separate locker rooms for men and women, but not for blacks and whites.

RULE: WORK RULES MAY NOT BE BASED ON CLASS MEMBERSHIP.

Any work rule which is based on an arbitrary classification is outlawed. For example, women cannot be excluded from being telephone linemen on the basis that the job is dangerous. It is no more dangerous for a woman than it is for a man. The same thing applies to excluding women from night shifts or overtime. Travel rules for employees are also covered and women cannot have a different set than men do. Employee discipline must also be equal.

Chivalrous ideas which have become the law are also overturned. For example, state law often required that women get rest periods, a particular length of lunch hour, or so many trips to the toilet during the workday. State regulations also often required that a woman be paid time and a half for extra work, but didn't have the same regulation for men. In order to remedy this situation women have not lost their protections, but the court has required that these protections be applied to men as well. As a general principle, you can assume that if the employee benefits from an existing law, the law will be broadened to cover everyone. If some classes of employees suffer because of a particular rule, the rule will be outlawed.

RULE: SEX-PLUS IS DISCRIMINATORY.

The sex-plus regulations are defined as adding an additional qualification to sex which might have the effect of restricting hiring. For example, some corporations used to restrict their employees to any men, married or not, but would employ only unmarried women. This practice was common during the Depression. It existed until recently in the airline industry. Stewardesses were required to be unmarried. If they married, they lost their job. Sex-plus has been outlawed along with any other type of classification which discriminates between the sexes. Women with preschool children must be held to exactly the same standards in hiring as men with preschool children. Grooming standards must apply to both sexes, though of course the standards used will be different for men and women. If the grooming standard could rationally apply to both sexes, it must be applied. For example, the use of contact lenses, well-cut hair, and weight limitations can be applied to either sex. Beards and eye makeup cannot. Grooming standards also cannot vary between races.

Whenever you see your employer hold women to different standards than men, it is probably a sex-plus violation.

RULE: THEY CAN'T FIRE YOU BECAUSE YOU'RE PREGNANT.

Pregnancy is considered to be "neutral" classification. Even though pregnancy happens only to women, it's neutral in that it is natural for that particular class of workers. For a while, employers argued that discrimination based on pregnancy was not discrimination against women. They were merely discriminating against pregnancy to protect the mother and her unborn child. The court thought this reasoning was a little foolish and ruled that since discrimination based on pregnancy could only discriminate against women, it had to be considered sexual discrimination. Any loss of job rights due to the pregnancy, like denying sick leave or getting fired, would be discriminatory and is outlawed. Seniority will not be lost while the woman is on a pregnancy leave.

Since pregnancy is not disabling to many women, the court has found that it can be excluded from state disability programs. The disability programs are based on physical conditions, and the programs may choose what conditions it will cover. The court found that it was within the disability program's rights to exclude pregnant women on the grounds that to do so was necessary to protect the program's financial stability. This rule leaves a woman in a fairly tenable position. She may be granted sick leave in order to have a child. Many unions and employers allow a woman to accumulate her sick leave over several years' time. She may receive salary for as much time as she has in the sick-leave bank. If her health is good, and she has a sedentary job, she may be able to work up until the time she delivers, even though she is uncomfortable. Additionally, her hospitalization insurance at work may cover her medical bills. Most physicians agree that a woman can return to work very quickly after her child is born. All that she cannot do is collect benefits for disability. And after all, having a baby is not really a disability.

RULE: THE JOB REQUIREMENTS MUST FIT THE JOB.

In an attempt to define what would be considered proper job qualifications, the Congress invented a term called "bona fide occupational qualifications." Because this is such a mouthful, it's been shortened to BFOQ. (Each letter is pronounced.) BFOQ applies only to hiring. BFOQ means that the qualifications needed to get the job must be related to actually doing the job. BFOQ has opened up a Pandora's box of discriminatory techniques. There were a staggering array of these.

All distinctions arising from romantic notions of womanhood must now actually be tested against the job itself. Women cannot be denied jobs just because they contain traditionally male elements, like lifting, climbing, or even driving a bus. Stereotyped assumptions are also forbidden. Assumptions that a woman will leave a job more quickly than a man are legally considered to be as silly as they actually are. Keeping women out of traditionally male jobs like corporate sales work is also proscribed. If an employer wants to use any of these assumptions, he will have to prove that the assumption is correct.

Proving any of these assumptions for sex-based job qualifications has turned out to be difficult, if not impossible. Although the original decision about bona fide occupational qualifications stated that statistics could be used to show that the BFOQ is correct, an employer has rarely succeeded in doing so. What has actually become the law for BFOQ's is an opinion written by Justice Thurgood Marshall. Mr. Justice Marshall stated that using statistics to prove the assumption would still discriminate against individuals who could do the job in question. He concluded that the act required a showing that the job qualification was inherent to the job (male actors for male acting roles). According to Mr. Justice Marshall, a statistical showing that women with preschool children were unreliable was inadequate. One would have to show that one particular woman was not reliable. The EEOC has used Mr. Justice Marshall's opinion consistently and refuses to recognize statistics when BFOQ's are being used. Only proof that the individual would be unable to perform will satisfy the EEOC.

Sometimes a particular gender is needed to fulfill a certain job. Sometimes male hospital patients will insist on having a male nurse instead of a female nurse. Male prisoners may object to female guards supervising their showers. This individual prerogative on the consumer's part is not challenged, but by the same token women as well as men must be given the opportunity for non-sensitive jobs within the institution. A woman could possibly be a tower guard in a prison, or work in the prison library or the warden's office. She might even supervise in the exercise yard, and she would have to be allowed to apply for all these jobs. These types of exceptions are called "necessary qualifications."

RULE: NECESSARY QUALIFICATIONS ARISE
FROM THE ESSENCE OF THE JOB.

When deciding if a BFOQ is satisfactory, the EEOC and courts weigh the qualification against how essentially it relates to the gender, religion, or national origin of the potential employee. The stewardess cases are an example of this. There is nothing in the essence of the stewardess job which is the exclusive territory of either sex. Therefore, men must be able to have the job too. That's why we now have flight attendants instead of stewardesses.

RULE: PENSION BENEFITS HAVE
TO BE THE SAME.

Employers also tried discriminating against classes on the basis of economic necessity. Women live longer than men and are likely to get pension benefits for a longer period of time than men. However, the court found that all employees had to get the same size pension benefits. Therefore, employers have to make bigger contributions on women's behalf so that women will end up with the same size pension benefit as men. Women employees may actually be more expensive than men employees, though not by much.

Health insurance is also affected. Employers often have excluded

pregnancy benefits from omnibus health plans. They say that the cost of
pregnancy coverage is simply too high. However, since only women
employees get pregnant, it is discrimination against a class. Pregnancy
must also be covered by insurance. You'll notice that employers'
health, hospitalization, and disability insurance has different rules applied to them than state-run disability insurance.

RULE: REASONABLE ACCOMMODATION TO
RELIGION IS REQUIRED.

When an employee has very specific religious practices which require
that he or she be gone at a particular time of the week, the employer
must contrast the period of time during which the employee is required
to be absent against the actual necessities of the job. For example, if
two persons could do the same job, and one was Jewish, requiring Saturdays off, and the other was Christian, requiring Sundays off, they
could mutually accommodate each other. The Jewish woman could
agree to be available on Sundays; the Christian woman could agree to
be available on Saturdays. The job would be covered. However, if both
were of the same religion and required the same day off, the employer
would have the right to fire one of them and hire somebody new if the
job was so necessary to the operation of the plant that actual harm
would result if the job wasn't done.

Perhaps a retail merchant needs every employee available on Saturday, the big shopping day of the week. If a potential employee says to
him that she cannot work on Saturday, it is within his ability to reject
the application since he really does need everybody on Saturday.

Workers' safety is regulated by both state statute and federal statute.
Many states have inspectors for factories and other work places. The
federal agency is called the Occupational Safety and Health Administration or OSHA. OSHA researches workers' safety, makes regulations
on workers' safety, and inspects plants to make sure that employers
adhere to the rules. It is also within OSHA's ability to enforce its own
regulations. The OSHA regulations are incredibly complicated, though
they have recently been simplified. One of the rules thrown out in the
simplification was the exact height from the floor that a fire extinguisher
must be hung. This example gives you an idea of how specific OSHA
regulations are. Your union may work a great deal with OSHA.

The federal law sets minimum wages. The person must be paid a
minimum amount per hour. This amount is going up with inflation. The
minimum wage laws may not apply to you if you receive salary benefits

besides money. For example, household workers who also receive room and board are only partially covered. Waitresses also have a lower minimum wage, since a large part of their pay comes from tips.

Employers are absolutely liable to their employees for injuries which occur on an employer's premises. Workmen won this right through the Workmen's Compensation Act now in effect in all states. There is no question of negligence on the part of the employee or the employer. The only questions to be settled are whether the injury occurred on the employer's premises and if so, what amount of compensation should be paid. The statutes fix the amount of compensation in most cases. Under the normal workmen's compensation statutes, one can only recover compensation under the Workmen's Compensation Act. However, farm laborers, domestic servants, railwaymen, business owners, and employees of small businesses may not be covered by the statutes. These persons may still sue under the old common-law provisions.

The common law requires that an employer do the following things.
1. Provide a safe place to work.
2. Provide safe tools and equipment.
3. Warn of dangers.
4. Provide enough other employees to do the job properly.
5. Make safety rules for the employees.

The worker is also expected to take some responsibility for his own safety. The standard in this case is "reasonable care." Reasonable care still allows room for recovery on accidents, but reckless conduct will bar a person from recovering.

Two types of legal relationships exist between employee and employer. The first and more simple is the master-servant relationship. In this relationship the employee is subject to the control of the master to the extent of the employee's physical conduct. If the master exercises substantial control over the details of the work, the employee will be considered a servant. In this relationship the employer is always responsible for the employee's actions. Most factory jobs fall into the master-servant category.

The other type of relationship is the principal-agent relationship. In this particular relationship the employee acts on behalf of the principal, and by the consent of both of them. The employer has some control over the agent's actions, but not total control. A private secretary might be considered the agent of her boss. A typing-pool secretary would be a servant, not an agent. In the principal-agent relationship, the principal is responsible for the activities of the agent only to the degree that the principal has authorized the agent to act in a particular fashion. If the agent's conduct seems reasonable for her job, the principal is normally held responsible for the agent's actions and promises. For example, the vice-president of a company is normally empowered to spend the company's funds. A salesman normally does not have this power. A court would hold the company responsible for the vice-president's offer to buy goods. The company would not be responsible for precisely the same offer made by its salesman.

Another employer-employee relationship called "independent contractor" exists to be used when the "employee" has an extensive technical skill. For example, a plumber will often be hired as an independent contractor to install plumbing. In the independent contractor relationship the senior contractor controls only the *result* of the plumber's work. He has nothing to say about how the plumber does it. If someone is hired as an independent contractor, the employer has no liability for the employee's actions. Therefore, independent contractors usually carry their own liability insurance.

Many of us who have professional or semiprofessional occupations may be asked to sign employment contracts, especially if one has worked for a company for five years or more in a white-collar job. These employment contracts can be scary, since they seem to restrict us from holding any job whatsoever if we leave the company. If a person is making a great deal of money under a contract, the contract must be taken very seriously by the employee if she wishes to leave the company. If one is making less money in a semi-professional position, such as sales supervision or personnel, the clauses in the contract wherein you promise not to compete are less important. For example, when Fred Silverman left ABC to become the president of NBC, he had to wait out the end of his ABC contract before he could take up his new job. However, if a person had a job of lesser importance, such as product development, the person could probably go to another company in a similar field without fear of a lawsuit. However, if an employee in product development went to the company's main competitor, the employee could expect that the contract would be enforced.

Employment contracts also frequently contain a clause giving the company full rights to the patents and copyrights of the employee's work. These are usually not enforced unless the work has been done on the employer's premises. However, problems can arise, especially if the item the employee invented in her own basement turns out to be very valuable. The inventors that I know (mostly in the computer field) never become full-time employees in order to avoid this. They work out independent contractor arrangements instead.

Payroll withholding mystifies most people. Though this topic is covered in other chapters, there are a few things you may want to know right here. Employers are required by law to withhold income taxes and Social Security from your paycheck, unless you are an independent contractor. Withholding is never exactly accurate. As a normal rule, too much federal income tax is withheld. Almost everyone can count on some amount of refund, unless her marital status causes withholding to be off. (It almost always does for married persons when both work.) If your Social Security is overwithheld, you can recover it from your employer if you work for only one person all year long. You might also suggest to the payroll department that their computer needs fixing. If you are overwithheld on Social Security because you worked for two people during the year, you get your money back through your tax return.

A few states allow an employee who has not been paid to charge the employer with the crime of theft of services. This is a type of larceny. Under the common law, however, if you are not paid, there is nothing criminally wrong with it. If you've ever been on the receiving end of the employer absconding with the books on payday, you'd disagree with this. This theft of services law should probably be more broadly accepted, especially when the business owner also runs away with the company bank account, even though it is officially his own.

Now you know that the employer has to give you the same chance at the job as anyone else. The tests that he gives you for the job must be pointed toward the actual doing of the job, and not some theoretical qualification he might have. Once you get the job, it's up to you to do well, so that you can worry about the next chapter on equal pay and promotions.

Chapter 6
EQUAL PAY AND PROMOTIONS

The right to get a good job wouldn't do us much good unless we were paid equally for it. Women have also been discriminated against when it came time for promotions. Legislation has done a great deal to help us in this area as well.

Because of the long history of discrimination against particular classes in the society, regulations have had to be formed to help women and minorities make up for lost time. Discrimination tends to perpetuate itself unless strong action is taken. The effect of these regulations had been to allow white male workers to keep the jobs that they have already attained, and to give the protected-class employees the first shot at the next job that comes up. A white male factory foreman need not step down from his job because it should have gone to a black woman. The black woman's salary is increased to the level she should have had, and she waits for the next job opening.

RULE: RED CIRCLES ARE REQUIRED.

"Red circles" is a labor-law slang term used for the carry-over of higher salary and plant seniority to a new job. A red circle protects the employee's salary and seniority. For example, a woman could have been working in a beer plant and have accumulated a good salary and substantial seniority. She knows that if she transfers to the same company's ale plant across the street, she will have a chance for better advancement. But perhaps women were never allowed to work in the ale plant before. The employer cannot keep experienced women workers, or other protected classes, out of the ale plant by refusing to transfer seniority and salary. Instead, the woman's salary and seniority are "red-circled" and carried over to the new job.

RULE: TESTING MUST BE FAIR.

When an employer gives a test to see if hiring or advancement is appropriate, the test may not operate in a discriminatory fashion. For this reason requirements for a high school degree, passing IQ tests, or even tests of superfluous skills have been outlawed, since these can serve to disqualify a protected class. The employer has the burden of showing that there is a "manifest relationship" between the test and the job. A high school diploma may not be necessary at all for one to be a competent mechanic or a hairdresser. IQ tests may eliminate many minority applicants. The tests must meet particular standards in order to be considered appropriate. If the impact of the rule is such that it results in discrimination, the test will be thrown out whether the employer instituted it in good faith or not. Once a discriminatory impact is shown, it's up to the employer to prove that he has an actual "business necessity" for having the test. For example, if an employee would be frequently required to lift forty-pound boxes onto a table three feet off the ground, a weight-lifting test would be valid. However, the employer could not ask a prospective employee to lift an eighty-pound box to a four-foot-high table. If the test is more or less superfluous to the particular job at hand, the test will also be illegal. If once a day someone has to lift the forty-pound box, but not necessarily the person holding the job, the test cannot be included as a matter of business necessity. If the employer rejects an employee on the basis of business necessity, he must do so objectively, based on a particular person's ability to do a particular job. In other words, he must have actually given the employee an appropriate test.

RULE: ADVERSE IMPACT MEANS DISCRIMINATION.

If a policy of the employer has the effect of perpetuating discrimination, the policy must be changed. If the employee sees that some policy will keep her out of the good jobs, she may have grounds for a suit. The employee has to show that some rule which is neutral on its face will have a negative impact upon herself and other members of her class. An example of this type of neutral policy is the prevalent first-hired/last-fired idea. Some employers lay off in the order that their employees were hired. If the employer has been discriminatory in the past, most of his work force may be white males. If he maintains first-hired/last-fired, women and minorities will be continually cut out of chances for promotion and seniority, since they will be laid off more often.

There is an exception to neutral rules. If a policy is absolutely necessary for safety or efficiency, it may be valid. But it's up to the employer to prove this.

In 1963 the U. S. Congress passed the Equal Pay Act. The purpose of the act was to remedy pay discrimination based on sex. It did not go into racial differences, merely differences in gender. Women then, as now, were making much less than their male counterparts. The bill has not been as quickly effective as one might have hoped. However, many women have been able to make inroads because of it.

RULE: ALL PERSONS GET
EQUAL PAY.

The Equal Pay Act covers more businesses than the Civil Rights Act we have been discussing. Any enterprise engaged in commerce must pay men and women equally for the same job. Some businesses are specifically exempted, such as small retail stores, farms, and amusement parks.

RULE: IT'S UP TO YOU
TO PROVE IT.

It's the plaintiff's responsibility to show that the employer is paying more to a male employee for the same work. In this case the most difficult part of the proof is showing that the work is equal. The work must be performed in the same "establishment." Establishment probably means the same city, since employees in different cities can be paid differently. The exact meaning of establishment is yet to be clarified.

Equal work is not defined as "identical," but it does mean "substantially the same." When the jobs are substantially equal, equal pay must be given. Job titles are not convincing evidence that the job is different. For example, a man might be called an office manager, and a woman might be called an executive secretary. They might perform exactly the same functions. If the executive secretary replaces the office manager, and at a lower salary, she probably has grounds for an equal pay suit.

It's hard to make a specific statement on what will be considered equal work, but some general guidelines have been established.

RULE: THE JOBS MUST REQUIRE EQUAL EFFORT.

The effort can be either mental or physical. Men and women in the same jobs need not perform precisely the same physical efforts. If the man supplies slightly more physical effort and the woman slightly more mental effort, these two things will offset one another when making the equal-effort decision. The court will first examine the primary duties of the jobs. If the man's job and the woman's job have very similar primary duties, the effort will be equal. Sometimes there are secondary duties which may influence the court's opinion. For example, if a male employee must spend a great deal of time doing this secondary duty, such as loading boxes onto a truck, the jobs will not be considered equal. If a woman is assigned extra duties that are different from but require as much time as the man's extra duties, the jobs are still equal.

RULE: SKILL MUST BE EQUAL.

Skill is more difficult to judge than equality of effort, since it actually relates to the performance of the job. It will also include extra qualities such as education, training, experience, and general abilities. Pay differences can be justified by an employer if one worker is more skillful than the other. The employer is allowed to pay differently only if he can apply an objective test to show the degree of skill. If a person has a type of skill which is not used on the job, this fact will not justify a higher wage.

RULE: RESPONSIBILITY MUST BE EQUAL.

A readily apparent difference in the responsibility required of a jobholder may also justify a pay differential. An example would be a shop with a number of typewriter repairmen. One repairman has supervisory duties, but actually spends most of his time repairing typewriters. He would be entitled to a higher salary than the others since he has extra responsibilities. Sometimes the degree of responsibility can be very subtle. The employer may be able to justify paying the male assistant office manager more money than he pays the female assistant office manager, since the male assistant office manager has the responsibility for dispersing petty cash. However, if both of them have responsibilities of a similar nature though not the same—she might do the payroll, he might run petty cash—equal pay will be justified.

RULE: SIMILAR WORKING CONDITIONS
ARE REQUIRED.

The conditions need not be exactly the same, but they should be close. Sometimes an employee will make more money for putting up with more inconvenience. For example, a bookkeeper might be paid more for going to a construction site which could be muddy, cold, and even a little dangerous. Certainly a person who is tolerating all of this is entitled to more money. Physical circumstances are considered if one is seeking equal pay, but the working conditions really do have to be substantially different before a pay differential is allowed.

Which shift you are working may also justify differences in pay. It's common practice in factories and other twenty-four-hour operations, like hospitals, to pay more money to the swing and night shifts than to the day shift. This pay differential is perfectly acceptable as long as women are not foreclosed from working on the higher-paying shifts.

The best overall view of differences in pay is that pay differences will usually be found illegal unless the employer can come up with a good explanation.

If an employee thinks she has been wronged under either the Civil Rights Act or the Equal Pay Act, her remedy is very specific. Under the Equal Pay Act, the employee has three different routes through the justice system. No method has to wait on any lengthy administrative action of the executive branch, such as EEOC or NLRB, although either one of these organizations may help.

Under the Equal Pay Act, you may file suit directly against the employer. Or the Secretary of Labor may file an injunctive suit on your behalf if the Department of Labor discovers that your pay is wrong, or you write them asking for their help. The third method is a special suit brought by the Secretary of Labor, specifically on your behalf. This method is new, has been used once, and allowed the Secretary of Labor to gain damages, not just back pay, on behalf of the employee.

I was once witness to one of these back-pay suits, which proved to be very successful. The New York Telephone Company was forced to give back pay to a large number of female employees who had been discriminated against. One woman that I knew, a repair supervisor, got over $20,000 in lump sum to make up for pay discrimination in the past.

If the employee sues for herself, she may claim back wages and get liquidated damages in the amount equal to what she has been underpaid in the past. The court can deny liquidated damages. If the suit is successful, the employee can also be awarded attorney's fees and court costs. She must file her suit within two years of the damage, but since most of us get paid every week or so, the damage happens every week. One should not wait on a suit like this, however, because three years' back wages is the maximum recovery. The sooner you get the situation corrected, the more money you have. It is also unlawful to discharge an employee who brings an equal pay suit.

If you think you have been discriminated against unfairly in matters of hiring or promotion, you use a different process. You must file within 180 days of the time the discriminatory act occurred.

Many persons encounter the difficulty of not knowing which agency to contact to have their claim processed. Many states have their own fair employment agencies. If your state has its own fair employment agency, federal law requires that the state agency have the first opportunity with your case. If the state doesn't move on your complaint, you then can take your case to the Equal Employment Opportunity Commission (EEOC), which is the federal agency dealing with the same thing. The filing and administrative procedures are very complicated. In order to avoid the complications of this government procedure, it is recommended that you file your charges with the state agency and the EEOC at the same time. If the state doesn't act within 60 days, the EEOC may pick up your charge and carry it forward.

For you to make a proper charge, you must put it in writing, sign it, and swear to it (have it notarized). You must state your name and address, the name and address of the person who discriminated against you, and the nature of the charge. This letter need not be formal, or written in legal language. I suggest, however, that you take care in writing it, so that it will be as clear as possible. The letter goes to a government agency, and if you do not state your case well, your letter may not get action.

You cannot bring a civil suit for hiring or promotion discrimination for 180 days after you have filed your complaint with the EEOC. Theoretically, they take this 180 days to investigate your claim and to see if the statutes have been violated. They also try to persuade the employer to rectify the situation. The employer has 30 days in which to do this. The EEOC has exclusive jurisdiction over your case for the full 180 days, although it's nearly impossible for the EEOC to take any action within the six-month time period. EEOC employees are overworked and may have to select only the most needy cases. If after six months the agency has not taken action, you can ask it for a letter of authorization for your own private suit. It is require by law to issue this letter. However, you can wait for an indefinite period of time to file your own suit. You need not request the letter after precisely 180 days.

These regulations allow us to go into the job market on an equal footing with any other group of people, but the battle isn't won yet. Many women are still underpaid, or tied in jobs where they will never have more pay than they have now unless they do something about it.

Your rights are only as effective as you make them. We have the legal ability to firmly establish ourselves in the job market, but if these laws are not used constructively by women at large, they will have no effect on the lives of the rest of us. We can't leave this responsibility to the few firebrands among us. We owe it to our daughters to make headway in job discrimination, so that they will never have to suffer through the tough times that many of us did with our own jobs.

Part III
HOUSING

Chapter 7
LANDLORD AND TENANT

Apartment living can be a joy. The tenant is released from many maintenance tasks and may have more leisure time. It also has its drawbacks. If the landlord doesn't uphold his maintenance responsibilities, the tenant may be in for a long and arduous war of wits. What the landlord must do depends on local city ordinances. These ordinances are structured on the building code and the health code of each city. Fire codes also influence the landlord's responsibilities. There is no one rule that would cover so many individual towns, but there are broad rules which will tell you how to start out if your landlord is not living up to his or her responsibility. New York is used as the sample state in this chapter since landlord-tenant law in New York is rather advanced. The law of your state may be less liberal. The landlord is the person who rents out the property. He or she usually owns it, but not always. Often real estate owners have a management firm take over running the building. The tenant is the person who takes over possession of the property, usually in exchange for rent, but occasionally in exchange for services.

Under the common law the landlord has no duty to repair the premises. The tenant might or might not be required to repair, depending on the lease. The tenant does have the obligation to prevent the property from wasting. In other words, the tenant has to keep the property watertight and windtight, so that the elements will not destroy the subject of the lease. These are the minimum obligations of both parties. If there are absolutely no laws or building codes in your city regarding residential housing, the above paragraph will be true for you. However, this is very rare.

When you read a lease, it is likely to contain a lot of language that you don't understand. The law has its very own language. Landlords prefer to use this technical language because it may have the effect of overwhelming the tenant and discouraging her from taking action. To prevent this, New York has passed a plain-language act which requires many documents, including leases, to be written in non-technical, everyday language. Your lease may include many synonyms, like the demised premises (apartment), arrearages (back rent), covenant (promise), and so on, which are incomprehensible to the average lessee (tenant). The landlord is likely to do nothing to help you understand what the lease actually says. If you really want to know, get out your dictionary. You could also consult an attorney. However, this is usually done only when commercial property is leased, as for a store, restaurant, etc. This problem seems irresolvable except for the following rule.

RULE: THE LEASE IS NOT THE LAW.

Even though the lease is a private agreement and will govern your use of the property to some degree, the lease cannot take rights away from you which you are granted by the building codes of your city. For example, if the building code disallows residential occupancy of any apartment without adequate heat, the landlord cannot take away this right by excluding his responsibility for heat in the lease. Although few landlords are this outrageous, they do try to modify their responsibilities. For example, the landlord may argue that he has no duty to repair your broken window. He points out that it says so in the lease. The city health code states that broken windows must be repaired promptly. The landlord must repair the window, since the city health code is a law superior to the lease. The same thing is true of wiring violations, dangerous hallways, and even dangers in the apartment itself due to falling plaster or peeling paint, leading us straight into the most important tool that a tenant has.

RULE: THE APARTMENT HAS TO BE HABITABLE.

Although this is not the law throughout the country, an increasing number of courts are finding that the landlord makes an implied warranty of habitability when he leases out an apartment. The warranty of habitability started out in cases where huge numbers of housing code violations were found. The landmark case was decided in 1970—very recent as legal concepts go. In this case over 1,500 building code violations were found in an apartment complex in Washington, D.C. The court decided that under modern concentrated urban conditions, it could no longer be feasible for landlords to be free of the responsibility of repair. Since the tenants' rent did not change, the landlord had the obligation to keep the property in the same condition it was in when the tenant took up occupancy.

The warranty of habitability started out as an attack against slum landlords. But the law knows no social boundaries, and many middle-class persons have been successful in charging their landlords with the selfsame warranty of habitability. One New York case allowed tenants in a luxurious building to deduct the cost of renting air conditioners when the air conditioning supplied by the landlord broke down and failed to work throughout the summer. You can see that the warranty of habitability is not restricted to slum housing.

The New York legislature has passed a law stating that there is an implied warranty of habitability which lease terms cannot modify. The services warranted are likely to expand greatly and already include such divergent areas as garbage pickup, water leakage, roaches, rodents, broken windows, defective door locks, and plumbing. One warranty of habitability case was successful when cat urine fumes from a neighboring apartment in the building penetrated a bedroom and made it unusable. Another case involved a young woman whose stove remained unfixed for 17 days. She figured that eating out cost her $10 a day more than eating at home. She won a judgment of $170, $10 for each day her stove remained unrepaired. For the benefit of New Yorkers, the warranty of habitability is contained in Section 235-b of the New York State Real Property Law.

The enforcement process for the warranty of habitability is very straightforward. You notify the landlord by registered letter that your apartment has developed a problem. Explain the nature of the problem and why you consider it dangerous. Also call the landlord, but don't anticipate that you will get any immediate action from the phone call. The registered letter is proof to him that you intend to handle the situation. Keep a copy of the letter you have sent to him along with the postal registration. Chances are the minute he receives the registered letter, he will jump into action, because he knows that you're starting to build a case.

If he receives the registered letter and does not take action, have the problem repaired on your own. You will probably recover if you deduct the cost of repair from your rent. You may try deducting the cost of repair from your next rent check. You may also withhold your rent and wait for the landlord to sue you. In New York State one can also take the repair bill to small claims court. In the small claims court, one needs no attorney and the court costs are very small—under five dollars. The tenant presents proof that the landlord was notified, that the landlord took no action, and shows evidence of the cost of having the difficulty repaired.

The small claims court is very informal and all the plaintiffs have pretty much the same level of expertise as you do. However, the judge is a real pro and will help you sort out things. If you win, the judge will give you a judgment against your landlord. If the landlord refuses to pay, you can deduct the judgment from your rent. The small claims court approach is favored above withholding all or part of the rent. If you go to small claims court and win, you'll get a judgment against the landlord, and the law will protect you if you subtract the judgment from your rent.

You should take steps to repair when there is a dangerous condition in your apartment which the landlord has been unwilling to rectify. How quickly you act to repair depends on how dangerous the problem is. However, there is no legal standard here. It's a matter of common sense. The basic meaning of dangerous is a threat to the health or safety of the tenants. A leaking gas stove presents an immediate threat in that persons could become sick or the apartment could blow up. You needn't wait more than a day to call in your own repairman for something this serious. Broken windows could be very serious if there are infants or elderly people in the apartment. It could also be very serious if the window is on a fire escape. The broken window might invite casual burglars. In such a case you could repair and deduct within two or three days. One case in this area involved wet plaster in the ceiling of a closet. In spite of the tenant's warnings, the landlord ignored the problem until a pipe upstairs burst, flooding both the apartment upstairs and the apartment with the wet closet. The landlord had to pay for the damage to the contents of both apartments.

If a warranty exists, the landlord is held absolutely liable for any damages which are incurred. Strict liability is not subject to any modification through the lease. If the plaster falls, smashing a cloisonné lamp and a Hepplewhite table, the landlord is responsible for the whole cost of the lamp and the whole cost of the table. He is also totally responsible for personal injuries which might occur.

At this time the warranty of habitability is absolutely the law in New York, Massachusetts, and Ohio. More states are joining this view every year. New Jersey has a form of the warranty of habitability and most populous states are likely to honor this in the near future.

There's often a chasm between the law and the real world. The actual application of the law may be a lot tougher than the success stories described above. Before undertaking legal action on your lease, investigate the different courts in your city; sit in and see how the law is applied. Try to settle the matter without withholding rent. If you don't pay your rent, you're in for a fight. Prepare yourself for the emotional strain.

The perfect method is to write the landlord a lot of letters about the problem if it's not immediately dangerous. Then have it repaired yourself, remembering that the repair must be necessary to maintain the apartment up to the condition required by local housing codes. If possible, get before-and-after photos of the repair. Then get a judgment against the landlord in small claims court. If you've continued to pay your rent, you can now deduct the judgment with no fear of eviction.

RULE: YOU CAN EVICT YOURSELF.

A concept called constructive eviction started out as a way to end a lease when the landlord got outrageous. The courts found that if the landlord removed the door or windows, the tenant could move out without paying rent. Constructive eviction has grown somewhat to include cancellation of the lease when the landlord has not provided heat and hot water. Cancellation is really no solution at all, since the tenant has to pack up her possessions and family and move them off to some other location. The only advantage is that the tenant will not be stuck with the rent for the rest of the lease period. The constructive eviction becomes a defense against the landlord's claim that the rent is owed. If the warranty of habitability is not yet the law in your state, and your landlord isn't providing major services, you can argue that constructive eviction ended your lease.

If services in your building get truly bad, and you cannot recover through the warranty of habitability and you cannot move out, you and other tenants may wish to consider a rent strike. Although most state laws prohibit a rent strike, it still may be an alternative, even though you have to break the law. She who holds the money holds the power.

New York has a law which enables tenants to get together and have the court appoint an administrator to receive their rent. The administrator then runs the building out of the funds he has received. Even if your state does not have a statute allowing a rent strike, there is very little a landlord can do if more than a third of his tenants have gotten together and started to pay their rent into an escrow account. Financial conditions alone can bring the landlord to his knees. The tenants may also use their rent money to repair the premises. The repairs must be carefully supervised and the tenant should watch the costs to keep them within reasonable bounds. If you're going to do this, it's best to hire your own lawyer right from the start, so that you end up with a repaired apartment in your possession. If you violate the law too outrageously, you may find the sheriff has moved you out while you were at the grocery store.

Sometimes you will find that you have to break a lease. It could be a job transfer sending you to another city or your financial condition could change for the better.

RULE: FIND A NEW TENANT.

If you want to leave your apartment just because it's gotten too small or too expensive, the landlord is within his rights to hold you to the balance of the lease term. He can keep on collecting his money and, in most parts of the country, not even attempt to find a new tenant. Additionally, many leases do not allow a tenant to sublet the apartment to someone else or to assign the lease.

Subletting is turning over the apartment to someone else for part of the period remaining. In this case the tenant becomes the landlord for the sublessee. Assignment of the lease is turning over the entire remaining period of the lease to someone else who will pay the rent directly to the landlord. Most of the transactions that people call sublets are actually assignments. Under either term, you remain ultimately responsible for payment of the rent.

Since the landlord can collect the rent from you for the rest of the lease, the only way to protect yourself is to offer to find a new tenant. This offer must be in writing and should be sent by registered letter. This puts the landlord on notice that he had better cooperate with you in finding a new tenant. If you have made the offer to find a new tenant, the courts are loath to enforce the remainder of the lease, especially for a lengthy period. One New York case only allowed the recovery of three months' rent after a major New York City landlord had kept the couple's apartment unrented for seventeen months after they had moved out.

Because our population is so mobile, many leases include a transfer clause. The transfer clause automatically cancels the lease should the tenant be transferred to another location. Sometimes the landlord asks for proof and sometimes he doesn't. The transfer clause has been known to be used to cancel leases in situations other than transfers. The landlord usually doesn't know that the transfer was not real.

RULE: REPAIRS DO NOT REDUCE YOUR RENT.

Although it seems unfair, you are not allowed to reduce your rent because the landlord has not repaired. The requirement that the landlord repair is only one part of your lease agreement. If he fails to repair, it does not modify the amount of money you are supposed to pay. There are three different circumstances under which a landlord has a duty to repair, and three corresponding ways in which the tenant recovers the cost of the repair.

The first circumstance under which the landlord has a duty to repair arises from a clause in the lease. If the landlord fails to uphold his duty, the tenant can go ahead and repair. The cost of the repair is offset against the rent, instead of reducing the rent on a month-by-month basis. For example, you live in a rented home. The landlord has agreed to repair the heat and hot water systems and fails to do so in spite of your efforts. The hot water hasn't worked properly for several weeks. You go ahead and have the hot water heater replaced. The bill comes to $400. Your monthly rental is $325. Instead of your rent check, you present the landlord with a copy of the bill, which wipes out the first month's rent. In the second month, you reduce your rent from $325 down to $250 to pay you back for the $75 that the first month's rent did not cover. More major replacements, like a furnace, should be undertaken with great caution.

The second circumstance is the repair and deduct statute. These statutes require a residential landlord to keep his premises in livable condition. If he doesn't, the tenant can pay out up to one month's rent to effect repairs. The tenant probably cannot recover expenses in excess of one month's rent. This statute is helpful to middle-class persons, but is not much aid to persons living in substandard housing.

The third circumstance arises from the implied warranty of habitability. Under this warranty the landlord promises that the dwelling currently does and will continue to meet the standards of the local housing code. If the property is found to violate such a warranty, the tenant's rent is reduced by the court. The tenant starts the warranty of habitability proceedings by not paying her rent. She then goes to court when the landlord starts eviction proceedings and raises the defense that she need not pay the rent because her housing is in violation of the local building code. She must also present proof. Photographs of bad conditions either in the public areas of the building or in the tenant's apartment will be helpful. If at all possible, she should also have a city building inspector come in to find violations in her apartment or in public areas of the building. Unfortunately, it's not always easy to get an inspector to inspect. Health inspectors can also be asked to look at the premises. In New York City it is much easier to get a health inspector than a building inspector. In fact, health inspectors frequently come the same day you call them.

While the case is being heard, the court may require that the rent be paid into the court. This way the court is assured that you have the money to pay. At the end of the case, the court may reduce your rent to reimburse you for the loss of value of your apartment, based on the housing code violations.

Rent devaluation is difficult for a judge to decide upon. He wants to reduce the rent an accurate amount. He has no desire to punish the landlord. Punishment isn't part of this particular law. If your request for a lower rent is well thought out, well presented, and not exaggerated, the court may honor your request to the penny. You may also take the warranty of habitability action to a small claims court as we discussed before.

Many states are disallowing attempts by the landlord to evict tenants when they try to assert their rights under these various circumstances. The techniques that they use for eviction can be an outright eviction order or ridiculous jumps in rent. Either way the landlord may get a quieter tenant. Just get your case in early and have it well documented in writing. This will forestall the landlord's attempts at retaliatory eviction.

RULE: YOUR LEASE TELLS YOU WHEN
YOUR RENT IS DUE.

The lease describes the date on which your rent is due. It's usually the first of the month, but not always. Sometimes leases have a grace period. The lease will tell you just how long that period is. If you're late, the lease may impose some fee for lateness. The whole amount of the rent is due and not just part of it. In fact, some landlords will reject a part payment of rent. They just don't like to keep records of part payments. The tenants also get confused about how much has actually been paid. If your landlord is a human being (not all of them are), and you're in a jam, he may accept a part payment if you've been a reliable tenant. If you have already created a lot of problems for him, he may not accept part payment. If you pay in part, he can still bring eviction proceedings based on the balance due.

In the case of eviction proceedings, which we will be discussing more fully in a moment, the landlord may try to reject any attempts to pay less than the whole amount. If he accepts part payments, he may have to amend the eviction papers. If the amount you're paying is insignificant to your total bill, it may cost him more to amend than the rent you are offering. If you offer a significant amount and the landlord refuses it, go straight to the post office and send the check by registered letter. If, for example, you owed $600 and you tried to pay $300 of it, and the landlord rejected it, you'd send it to the landlord by registered mail. This would show both the landlord and the court that you were serious about catching up. In many jurisdictions the landlord might have to start eviction procedures all over again. This may help you delay eviction until you can catch up.

RULE: FIND OUT IF THE LANDLORD WANTS
HIS MONEY OR HIS APARTMENT.

Evictions happen for two basic reasons: either the landlord wants back rent or he wants possession of the apartment so he can lease it to someone else. If all he wants is back rent, you have a good chance of keeping the apartment by paying your rent. However, he may want possession, if you made yourself a nuisance by requesting a lot of changes, or even requesting that the landlord live up to his responsibilities under a warranty of habitability. You may be a bad tenant, allowing damage to occur, making too much noise, not taking care of your animals, or throwing wild parties. You may also be carrying on a business which the landlord considers undesirable for his property. The landlord may also want the apartment for some purpose of his own. He might want to give it to his children, he may live next door and want the extra space for himself, or he may be able to rent it out at a much higher price.

Most eviction actions have two steps. In New York the first step is a three-day notice. The three-day notice tells you the amount of rent which the landlord considers outstanding. In New York you have three days to pay up before the eviction procedure actually starts. However, the notice calls to your attention that the landlord is about to take steps to collect. The next step is a notice of petition, sometimes called a dispossess.

The notice of petition is the actual beginning of a legal action. If you do not pay up on your first notice, you will be taken to court and will have to pay court costs, probably around twenty dollars. If you have a dispossess, you may have the option of paying your rent to the clerk of the court in your jurisdiction.

The clerks of the court have a very practical knowledge of the way the law works in your community. If you get a notice, ask the clerk for his advice. If you want to go to court and fight, instead of just paying up, you'd better get a lawyer. When you go to court, you will probably make a counterclaim against the landlord demonstrating that he owes you money. You argue that the money is owed to you due to his breach of the warranty of habitability. You tell the judge that you didn't pay your rent since the landlord failed in his duty to maintain the property. If you lose, you cannot be evicted until the judge issues an order of eviction. In most jurisdictions, the judge puts this off for a period of time, three days to a week. Up to the time the warrant of eviction is issued, you can still pay off the rent plus the court costs and stay in the apartment. If the landlord won't take your money, you can pay it to the clerk of the court. However, if you don't pay it before the warrant of eviction is ordered, you'd better find someplace else to live. There is no way to keep the apartment.

Evictions can also be ordered for reasons other than non-payment of rent. If your lease has expired, you have no right to be in the apartment. It is well within the landlord's privileges to take the apartment back. However, he must work through the entire eviction proceedings before he can make you move. You'll get a dispossess order and have to go to court. Chances are you won't win, unless there is some unusual quirk in your local law. In New York these quirks are called rent control and rent stabilization. Tenants under these particular leases have the right to remain in the apartment indefinitely with certain limits on the next rent increase. You may also be a month-to-month tenant. The month-to-month tenant has the right to stay on until the landlord gives her thirty days' notice to vacate the apartment. He can evict you if you don't move out after he gave you notice. You may also substantially violate your lease: repeated late payment of rent (like nine or ten times in one year), damage to your apartment, refusing the landlord entry to your apartment, carrying on an illegal activity, creating a nuisance, or a continual disturbance to other tenants' quiet enjoyment of their own apartments. If you've conducted yourself badly, it's best to mend your ways upon the first notice that you're creating a problem. Most normal people get along fine. The only group I know of that's been evicted for a nuisance was a prostitution ring. It wasn't the prostitutes that the neighbors minded so much as the pimp's pals hanging out in the lobby.

You may also be evicted for physical changes you make to the apartment. Anything you attach to walls or that you replace is not likely to be grounds for eviction. However, if you remove any walls or tear up the flooring, you may be committing waste, and the landlord could evict you.

From a practical viewpoint, it is best to keep in mind that the landlord can't have things fixed unless you tell him they're broken. If a landlord is sincere about maintaining his property, he'll be happy to hear from you. There are landlords who are shocked when you don't report a dripping faucet. Others don't care if the plaster is falling down. For this less responsible sort of landlord, the best policy is to put all your complaints in writing. You'll probably end up taking him to court and you'll need proof.

Chapter 8
LIVING TOGETHER

If you are planning to enter a living-together arrangement, it is best that you do it with your eyes wide open. There are basically three reasons why people choose to live together: economic necessity, passion, and trial marriage. Depending on the reason why people decide to live together, the negotiations for the living arrangement will vary.

Economic necessity may prompt a very clean relationship which may be free of emotional involvement, regardless of the sex of your living partner. In this situation the living partners are roommates.

RULE: YOUR NAME ON THE LEASE
MAKES YOU RESPONSIBLE.

If your name is on the lease, the landlord can sue you if the rent is not paid. Additionally, many landlords are unwilling to have more than one person be responsible for the lease. Therefore, it often happens that one person will own the lease and the others will become sublessees of the person whose name is on the lease. The person who owns the lease is responsible for the whole rent. She also may be responsible for all of the electricity bill and all of the telephone bill, since many utilities are unwilling to extend service to anyone except the leaseholder. Obviously, the leaseholder won't have as much freedom and flexibility as the other persons who live with her. She may occasionally get stuck with an extra portion of the rent.

The best way to protect yourself if you are a leaseholder is to write up a contract with each of your roommates. The contract should have the following elements: (1) an agreement to divide the rent equally, regardless of the number of roommates, (2) an agreement to pay an equal share of rent, regardless of periods absent from the apartment, (3) a requirement of one month's notice before leaving, (4) a deposit of one full month's rent, and (5) an arrangement for an estimated deposit of one full month's share of the telephone and electricity costs. Of course, the agreement should also state the parties' names and addresses. If you have such an agreement, you will be able to take the roommate who departs prematurely into small claims court. No roommate should be allowed to move in without having already paid her share of the first month's rent and the deposits.

RULE: DON'T BUY FURNISHINGS TOGETHER.

Occasionally people fall into the trap of sharing big purchases. Neither may be able to pay the whole cost of a large item, like a color TV, air conditioner, or couch. So the living partners pool their money. Then the household breaks up for one of a multitude of reasons. But you can't split a couch or TV set. Moreover, it's difficult to determine a fair price for selling or buying the other half, since the goods are now used goods.

It is always best to buy household furnishings independently, so that you own the couch, he or she owns the TV set, etc. This way, if you have to split up the household, the ownership of goods is clear-cut.

RULE: SOME ROOMMATES STEAL.

It's not unheard of for one roommate to steal from another. The theft can be money, but more often it's goods. The roommate may admit an accomplice to the apartment in order to steal the television set, or practically anything else which could be resold. However, the roommate might not be guilty of theft under the criminal-law statutes. The roommate had the right to be in the apartment, and may even own part of the television set. Roommates are seldom prosecuted for theft in spite of the criminal nature of this activity.

Many insurance companies are reluctant to insure the goods of a shared apartment. The statistics on losses simply aren't good. If your roommate relationship is not romantic, it's best to leave Grandma's diamond ring with your parents.

RULE: YOU CAN RECOVER FOR DAMAGES
TO YOUR PROPERTY.

Even though the criminal law may not help you, if your roommate has operated on your property with wild abandon, there may be a way to recover through the civil courts or the small claims court in your jurisdiction. One type of action you could bring is an action for negligence. Under negligence, the other person has to have conducted herself in such a way as to fail to protect your property against loss, damage, or theft. For example, she may have left the front door wide open allowing someone to come in and grab your stereo. In such a case you might be able to recover the cost of the stereo by suing in small claims court for negligence.

The action of conversion is also available. To qualify as conversion, your roommate (or any other person) must exercise a control over goods which is inconsistent with your rights in the goods. The roommate's possession must be wrongful, but need not be consciously so. The roommate must change the physical location of the goods and then dispose of them in an unauthorized manner. The roommate may either sell the goods or keep them for herself. You must make a demand to have your goods back, and if your demand is refused, you then have the basis for conversion.

The remedy you get for a conversion is a "forced sale" of the goods to the erring roommate. She has to pay you for what she took. If she destroys the goods, she also has to pay for them.

If your roommate temporarily takes something of yours, and then returns it, you may also recover, but the taking has to be rather serious. For example, you could have loaned her your car for a short shopping trip. She decides to visit her boy friend in Alaska and to use your car to get there. This would also be conversion. If you go away on a vacation and return to find that your roommate has substantially changed your living arrangements, it may also be unlawful conversion, although your goods would have to be harmed or misused in the process.

Remember that your roommate need not intend to misuse your goods or be negligent for you to assert conversion. The most important issue is what she actually forgot to do or how she actually used your goods.

If you go to court and get a judgment against your roommate, you can recover against either her goods or perhaps her salary. If you win your case, you get a judgment. A judgment creates a lien. The sheriff or marshal can help you collect your lien. Liens can be renewed every year, often for seven to ten years. Sooner or later you will be able to collect the money she owes you.

Roommating can be a wonderful thing, if you're young in the big city, you travel a lot, or you have a need to have someone around. Don't let this material put you off on getting a roommate, but do adhere to the agreement stated in the first rule. This will save you a lot of heartache and possible financial embarrassment.

The generation of the sixties changed many things. The institution of marriage was modified along with practically every other social pattern. As the iconoclastic young people of the sixties matured and acquired property, the law has had to change to allow for what they were actually doing. And one of the things they were doing was living together.

The law is slow, but ever flexible. Common-law marriage is nonexistent in most states, so some highly inventive attorneys began to help their unmarried clients through the law of contracts.

A contract is nothing but an agreement. These agreements can be in writing and are called express contracts. A contract can also be taken from the conduct of the parties. This is an implied contract. Marriage itself is a contract, but the conditions of the contract are controlled by law and not by the special agreements of the parties involved. Unmarried partners are not subject to the marriage contract, and are therefore free to make their own agreements.

The most famous of these contract cases is the Marvin decision in California. This renowned case involved the actor Lee Marvin and his longtime companion, Michelle Triola Marvin. They lived together for seven years and then split. The Supreme Court of California, on appeal, found that there could be a valid contractual relationship for services between Mr. Marvin and Ms. Marvin. However, when the case went back to the trial court for a decision on the facts, the trial court *did not* award damages for breach of contract. Ms. Marvin did receive some money for her "readjustment," much like a property settlement after a divorce. I suspect the court awarded this under the law of equity. The primary principle in equity is a just result. This California decision sets a precedent that unmarried couples in other states may be able to use. However, some questions remain unanswered. Only time and experience with these cases will give us an adequate prediction of the amounts that can be recovered or how long the couple must be together before recovery is possible. About a thousand contract cases are now pending in California. The outcome of these cases should supply us with some answers.

Informal marriages have long been accepted among poor people. In the South there was a longtime practice of the so-called shoe-box divorce. If a poor (usually black) couple married, the clerk would put their marriage license in a shoe box instead of registering it as required. If the couple later wanted a divorce, they went to see the clerk. The clerk retrieved their marriage license from the shoe box and handed it back to them. They tore up the license and became divorced.

With the growing incidence of divorce, many persons thought the only alternative to divorce was not to marry in the first place. However, the worst difficulties surrounding divorce have been rectified by the almost universal adoption of the no-fault divorce, which you read about in the chapter on divorce. In spite of the ease with which divorce is now possible, many persons continue to form semi-marital relationships. Some of these partnerships are based on passion, and some on trial marriage.

Passion alone tends to muddy up the relationship. In my observation, living arrangements based on passion have little chance of success. The partners' view of fairness and responsibility may become completely submerged in the emotions of the relationship.

Trial marriage may work out better, although it is by far the most complicated of the relationships. The living situation may have every factor of the roommate relationship, with passion, and added to the bargain, plans for the future. At the base of a trial marriage is each partner's intentions for a responsible relationship. And yet the partners have few or no guidelines by which to conduct themselves.

Many trial-marriage partners are afraid that if they try to submit their relationship to contract negotiations, their relationship will fall apart before their eyes. This may be true. A person who is unwilling to directly confront the responsibility of marriage may be just as unwilling to confront contractual responsibilities arising from the relationship. This all boils down to whether or not the parties forming the relationship are willing to accept the responsibility. If they are, the relationship is likely to be successful, whether or not a marriage ceremony is actually performed. If they aren't willing to be responsible, they've both picked the wrong partner.

If you want to do this right, there are certain steps you can take. First we'll talk about what living together isn't. Then we'll talk about how to make it into something, maybe even turning it into a marriage which has a better chance of lasting.

RULE: LIVING TOGETHER IS NOT MARRIAGE.

Thirty-six states out of the fifty have outlawed common-law marriage. Common-law marriage is the idea that persons become married after they have lived together for some period of time. Fourteen states and the District of Columbia currently recognize a common-law marriage. These states are: Alabama, Colorado, Florida, Georgia, Idaho, Iowa, Kansas, Montana, Ohio, Oklahoma, Pennsylvania, Rhode Island, South Carolina, and Texas. Because so many people move, common-law marriage should never be counted on as a way to be sure that you're married. One could move out of a common-law marriage state, or one could move from a state which bans common-law marriage to a state which allows it, only to find that one is married, whether one wanted to be or not. A catch-22 exists in common-law marriage. The state allows the relationship, but may penalize it under the misdemeanor of cohabitation, which you'll read about later. The states which recognize common-law marriage but also have cohabitation misdemeanors are Idaho, Kansas, and South Carolina. Establishing your common-law marriage could cost you thirty days in jail.

RULE: SEVEN YEARS DOES NOT
MAKE YOU MARRIED.

Contrary to myth, seven years together does not tie the marriage knot. There is no specific time period after which the marriage becomes valid. If you want to prove the marriage, you will have to either sue or be sued.

Common-law marriage requires that the couple conduct themselves as though there is a marital relationship. They must live as husband and wife and tell people that they are husband and wife. They must have the intent to be married. The intent will be surmised from their conduct. If the relationship actually works as a marriage, that's exactly the way the common-law marriage state will treat it, whether the couple is together for one year or fourteen. But until these issues are decided in a court, no marriage exists in the eyes of the law.

The hardest part of common-law marriage is finding evidence that the marriage existed. Proving the marriage is the responsibility of the person seeking to enforce the marriage. The issue of proof usually arises in an attempt to get some property right as a result of the relationship. Claims for the widow's share of Social Security, Workmen's Compensation, inheritance rights, and alimony are examples of the rights sought in common-law marriage suits. The court and jury are more likely to find a common-law marriage if the widow is seeking some government benefit like Social Security. If she's suing for alimony, or a share of property under a will, the marriage will be harder to prove. The ability to recover through common-law marriage may be liberalized by the Marvin contract case.

Common-law marriage is still marriage as far as the IRS is concerned. If you both work, you'll have to pay the higher tax, just like all married working couples, if you live in a common-law marriage state.

RULE: LIVING TOGETHER MAY BE ILLEGAL.

Some states have laws prohibiting persons of the opposite sex from living in the same house without a marriage license. This living arrangement is called cohabitation. These states are: Alabama, Alaska,

Arizona, Florida, Idaho, Illinois, Kansas, Kentucky, Massachusetts, Michigan, Mississippi, Nebraska, New Mexico, North Carolina, South Carolina, Virginia, West Virginia, Wisconsin, and Wyoming. The penalty can be a warning, a fine from $50 (West Virginia) to $1,000 (Kansas), or even jail. Kansas can jail you for thirty days and Arizona can put you away for up to three years.

Some states also have laws prohibiting a man and a woman of different races from living together. These are called miscegenation statutes. Georgia, Mississippi, and Tennessee have such statutes. Chances are that these statutes are not constitutional, since a similar Virginia statute was found unconstitutional. These states simply haven't prosecuted on the statutes since the Virginia decision came down.

If this isn't enough, some states have a crime called fornication, a sexual act between unmarried persons of the opposite sex. The penalty for this crime can be two months to one year in jail. The fines can run from $10 in Rhode Island to $500 in Florida. The states which prohibit fornication are: Florida, Georgia, Hawaii, Idaho, Illinois, Massachusetts, Mississippi, North Carolina, Rhode Island, South Carolina, Utah, Virginia, West Virginia, and Wisconsin; the District of Columbia also has laws against fornication. In some of these states, the couple must be living together in an open and notorious fashion. We found one 1977 New Jersey case which stated that fornication statutes are unconstitutional if the defendants are consulting adults. This decision affects only New Jersey, since it was decided by the New Jersey Supreme Court. A Florida case in the same year found Florida's fornication statute to be too broad. This case is a little muddy, since the person charged was a felon out on probation and the case dealt more with probation than fornication.

These laws are rarely enforced. You can also expect this area of the law to change more than other areas. When these laws are enforced, it is normally against persons whose conduct is abnormal for the community which surrounds them. This was especially true in the hippie era when communes were stomped on by local regulation. Many communities passed ordinances prohibiting more than a certain number of unrelated adults from living together. One such ordinance I know of restricts more than five unrelated adults in one home. The more isolated the home, the fewer problems the unrelated adults should have. These hippie ordinances are rare in big cities. A type of reverse isolation occurs there too. Everyone is so close physically that people seem to pay less attention to what other people are doing.

Living together can also modify other marital relationships already formed. For example, if one of the parties is married, even though separated, the living-together arrangement would be proof of adultery to that person's spouse.

When the couple decide to form their partnership, they face the self-same issue which disrupts many marriages. The issue of money. Who makes the money, who spends money on what items, and what belongs to whom are still issues whether one is living together or married. Elizabeth was living with Frank, a prosperous businessman. Frank bought a house in the suburbs and Elizabeth quit her job so she could spend her time on the house renovation. She scraped paint, hung wallpaper, supervised the installation of the new kitchen. After a year and a half the house was done, but so was the relationship. Frank had put all the money into the house, and Elizabeth had done all the work. The house belonged to Frank. Elizabeth had no legal right to any part of the house.

This case was decided before the Marvin decision, so it might turn out differently today. However, just because there is a new law in California, you should not assume that your state will adopt this legal policy. In order to get a remedy you or Elizabeth would have to get your state to adopt the Marvin precedent. You might have to take your case to the highest court of your state. It might or might not adopt the policy. The lawsuit would be very expensive and you might not get anything in the end.

Your protection is to make a written contract with the person with whom you will live. The purpose of this contract is to sort out your financial relationship before emotional items get in the way. While you're still thinking clearly, get your agreement talked out and written down.

RULE: PUT EVERYTHING IN WRITING.

A writing, even though informal in nature, can become a contract. The writing should cover who is responsible for each different type of expenditure and whether it is to be shared.

RULE: DIVIDE EXPENSES ACCORDING
TO YOUR CAPACITY TO PAY.

A normal roommate arrangement is a strict split of rent, food, gas, electric, and telephone. However, when the relationship is a trial marriage, the couple will very often modify this even split. One partner may be making much more than the other, so the couple may want to work out proportions according to income. The party who makes more money might pay the whole rent. The reason for this variation is that the party who makes more money may not wish to sacrifice her own standard of living to one that the partner could equally afford. Sometimes, if one party is unusually prosperous he or she will take over the whole cost of running the household. The other party, usually the woman, will be responsible only for her own clothes and perhaps for household beautification. She may even be responsible for saving her whole salary for a house down payment. One couple I know used this last method. They are now married.

RULE: DECIDE WHAT YOUR EXCHANGE WILL BE.

If both parties continue to work, there is little difficulty in determining what services they perform for one another. If the couple are apartment dwellers, they will probably both pitch in on the household duties. If the couple live in a house, they may split up their responsibilities differently.

If one of the parties doesn't work, the contract becomes more complex. If the woman has given up her job to keep house for the man, a contractual relationship will arise for services which she renders. These services are usually called those of companion and adviser. Even when a contract is written, sex as a service is never mentioned. It is illegal to make a contract, other than a marriage contract, which involves sexual favors. (Sex is called meretricious services.)

It is appropriate to mention in the contract the services which you will exchange. The description can be anything as basic as companion and housekeeper, or it could be more specific, such as acting as administrative assistant or editor for your partner. These agreements for services depend solely on the means and talents of the individuals. This area is so new that there are hardly any guidelines for the preparation of these contracts. The two of you will simply have to work out the most practical solution for you.

RULE: HOUSEHOLD GOODS BELONG TO THE WOMAN.

Tradition stated that household goods such as pots and pans, sheets, bedclothing, etc., belonged to the woman. Traditionally either her family supplied these items for the couple as part of the dowry or the girl supplied it for herself from a hope chest. These basic implements of householding are called paraphernalia. Since the woman supplied them, they're hers. In modern life, often both parties have maintained their own households before combining as one household. In this case the rules change.

RULE: IT BELONGS TO WHO BUYS IT.

Goods which are purchased belong to the person whose name is on the bill of sale, unless there are extenuating circumstances. We'll discuss the extenuating circumstances in a moment, but you should operate on the premise that any item belongs to the person whose name is on the sales slip. This is what the law will find unless you can prove otherwise.

It is possible that the other person was able to buy a particular item because you picked up some cost of running the house. For example, he might say, "I can buy a television set if you'll pay for the food this month." You go ahead and pay for the food and he buys the TV. If the cost of the food and the cost of the television were roughly the same amount of money, you now own one half of the television set, since the money you spent buying food allowed him to save the money to buy the television.

Proving such a complex transaction is another story. You will have to keep month-by-month accounts of who purchased what. For example, in one month the accounts may show that you both paid half the rent, you paid for food and the phone bill, and he bought a television set. Since the rent, food, and telephone were mutually consumed, you own half the TV. Many couples rankle at keeping such detailed records. Their attitude is understandable, since the primary purpose of these records is aid in dissolving the relationship should it break up. Each time you have to do the accounting, you are reminded that the relationship need not continue. Love is delicate enough without having the continuing difficulty of financial negotiation.

RULE: NEVER ASSUME A PROPERTY RIGHT.

Traditionally, unmarried couples had absolutely no right in the property of one another. The Marvin decision may have modified this, but it's likely to take ten years or more before this decision becomes a reality in the lives of more ordinary people. For now, it is best to assume that you will acquire no property rights unless you keep specific records of your contributions of dollars.

RULE: YOUR NAME ON THE TITLE WILL
GIVE YOU PROPERTY RIGHTS.

When a married couple buys a house, often both names will go on the title as "tenants by the entirety." Tenants by the entirety is the particular form which says each owns an undivided one half of the property, and if one owner dies, the other owner gets the whole thing. This type of title is only given to married couples. An unmarried couple can get many of the same advantages by owning a house or car in joint tenancy. Tenancy in common has other advantages. Consult the real estate chapter for more information.

If you and your partner want to buy a house or car, lenders have to treat you like any other couple, married or not. The federal Equal Credit Protection Act requires that unmarried mortgage applicants receive the same consideration as married applicants.

RULE: YOU HAVE NO RESPONSIBILITY FOR HIS DEBTS.

In a marriage, it is possible to hold a wife responsible for her husband's debt, if her name is also on the loan, as creditors frequently require. Unmarried couples do not have this difficulty, unless one co-signs a loan for the other. In this case the creditor can collect against the other party, not as a result of the relationship, but because the party acted as a co-signer on the note. It's not a good idea to co-sign for each other. Any relationship which breaks up because of your refusal to co-sign would have broken up anyway. The co-signing issue would only be an excuse.

RULE: YOU PAY YOUR OWN INCOME TAX.

The area of federal income tax for persons living together is potentially tricky. If you are living in a state that either does not allow common-law marriage, or has a law against fornication or cohabitation, you cannot be forced to file as married. If, however, you live in a common-law marriage state, the IRS has the potential of taking you and your spouse to court to have you declared as married. Since the idea of the IRS making you marry is so ridiculous, they are yet to try it. However, the possibility remains.

Whether or not you are married is important, since marrying can cost you tax money if both of you work.

This tax injustice toward married couples need not go on forever. As the tax structure stands now, working couples are penalized for taking on the responsibility of marriage. Because of inflation, both may have to work to maintain their standard of living. Therefore, the only practical reason to marry is to protect the good name of your children.

New York State has an alternative method of computing income taxes for a married couple. Under this system the tax is the same as though they were single and both working. The only additional advantage they have is the right to pass back and forth deductions and exemptions so that they pay the lowest possible combined tax. This method of computation could be a ready solution to the federal tax problem for working married couples.

One common question for the unmarried couple and their income taxes is the filing status of those involved. If there are no children, and one party does not work, the other party can file as single claiming the exemption of the person whom he or she supports. That other person cannot have more than $750 in income from any source. The exemption cannot be claimed in states in which it is illegal for persons of the opposite sex to live together. Even though it's legal, the IRS does not like it when someone claims the exemption of an able-bodied adult, so you may be audited.

When there are children born to the relationship, the tax situation is somewhat modified. One of the parties can claim the head of household status and take the exemption of the child. The other party must file as single. The party who claims the head of household status should be the person who makes more money than the other, since the head of household status saves more in higher income brackets. I would never recommend that a working couple marry to save on taxes. The fact is, it's likely to cost them money.

The issue of children born to an unmarried couple is discussed in the chapter on children. You should be aware that under the current law children born under these circumstances have very limited rights of inheritance. It is also more difficult for the children to claim benefits under Social Security if one of the parents dies. It is not recommended that children be born without their parents first being married.

It is questionable whether divorced people with custody of their children should ever undertake a living-together arrangement. The other parent will discover the living-together arrangement, and may use it as the basis of a child custody suit. For the custodial parents, the choice is pretty much marriage or nothing. It is also questionable whether alimony should be paid to a woman in a living-together arrangement.

If you are considering undertaking a living-together arrangement, analyze your motives carefully. A lot of people choose this arrangement because they have found marriage to be too heavy a responsibility. If the living-together arrangement is to work, however, the partners need an even higher responsibility level than they need for marriage. Living together is fun, but it's no way out of responsibility.

Chapter 9
REAL ESTATE

This chapter is about buying and selling your house. Unlike other chapters which are written with the expectation that you will be handling a matter yourself, this chapter is written to act as a bridge of information between you and your attorney. There are people who successfully form their own corporations. Others handle their own divorces. However, real estate should never be bought or sold without the services of an attorney. By all means shop for the lowest attorney fees, but never cut out this very necessary ally in a real estate transaction.

RULE: GET AN ATTORNEY.

The approach of this chapter will be why you need an attorney, with some explanation of the steps involved in selling your house or buying another one. You will also need a real estate agent, but this person can only find you a buyer or seller. An attorney will make sure that ownership is correctly changed to fulfill all the legal requirements.

RULE: LAND IS UNIQUE.

Land and houses are called real property. Real property always means land and things permanently affixed to it, like houses, wells, and power lines. No two pieces of land are exactly alike. Even if the land is right across the street and has the same dimensions, it will still be different. The sun will strike a different side of the house at a different time of day. One parcel may have adequate water; the other may not. One may have a beautiful tree; the other may be barren. One may be in the city; and the other may be just outside the city limits. The tax could be different.

Then when a home is placed on the land, the land becomes even more special. No two homes are ever alike, regardless of the similarity of floor plan. Your neighbor gets water in the basement and you don't. Your tree becomes diseased; his doesn't. Roses grow in your yard, and not in his. The law long ago recognized that every piece of land is unique unto itself and cannot be substituted for. The law regarding a sale of land is far different from the law regarding the sale of personal property.

RULE: FIRST YOU DRAW UP THE
CONTRACT OF SALE.

The contract of sale is the first step in selling a piece of property. It is not a deed, but is a promise to sell. It must be in writing, although oral contracts are occasionally enforced if there has been a partial performance on someone's part. This agreement is sometimes called an earnest-money agreement.

Earnest money is like purchasing an option to buy the property—the seller cannot sell it to anybody else. If for some reason the deal doesn't go through due to the inability of one of the parties to perform, the earnest money will be returned. If, for example, the seller cannot deliver the title, the escrow agent who is holding the earnest money will return it to the buyer. (An escrow agent is a third party, usually a bank or an attorney for the seller, disinterested in the contract, who holds either funds or a document until the contract is performed.) If the buyer cannot perform, the money will also be returned. For example, the buyer could have a heart attack, be unable to find a mortgage, or suffer other disasters.

In the contract of sale the seller promises to deliver a marketable title for a certain price. The price is decided upon before the contract of sale is entered into. Up to this point the buyer, the seller, and often a real estate agent can handle the negotiations on their own. The marketable title is an issue which requires a lawyer. The following paragraphs illustrate why you'll need an attorney to manage this stage.

Titles are unmarketable if the seller lacks any part of the title which he has said he owns, or the title has any outstanding obligations on it, such as a mortgage, or there is a reasonable doubt that either of these two situations exist. The seller has the time between the contract of sale and the actual closing to go through the steps to "perfect the title."

The seller usually promises to deliver a title which is called an undivided fee simple absolute. This term means that the seller owns a clear title to all of the property without anyone else having any interest in it. If the seller has promised to have such a title and does not, the buyer can withdraw from the contract. Some of the encumbrances to a fee simple might be a joint tenancy with his wife, an interest in the land which lasts only for the seller's lifetime, or some unusual title obligation, such as a condition that liquor would never be sold on the land or no more than a one-family dwelling be built upon it. The property can be sold with such title differences, but the title reservations must be made part of the contract of sale. At this point arrangements for passing the title can get very complicated.

The title must also be free of a wide category of title faults which are called encumbrances. An encumbrance is a right or interest to the property held by someone other than the seller. An encumbrance does not negate the seller's interest, but only modifies it. Power lines, public roads, and leases are examples of encumbrances. The most common encumbrance is a mortgage outstanding on the property.

The seller must also deliver a title which is free from doubt. If the seller has any chance of making the title good before the closing, the buyer is required to wait, and the buyer cannot avoid the contract of sale. The waiting period is called giving the seller an opportunity to "cure the title." The buyer will have the choice of whether or not to waive defects in the marketable title. The buyer might waive leases outstanding, public roads across the land, or mortgages outstanding upon the property. This last waiver is what people are talking about when they say they have taken over the mortgage. The contract of sale will include these waivers. The contract of sale may also state that the buyer is buying what is called an insurable title, a title that a title insurance company is willing to write insurance on. However, the buyer should never agree to taking insurable title but should insist on marketable title. Though the buyer might not lose any money with an insurable title, she may lose the house itself, or alternatively she may end up with a house she can't sell.

RULE: GET HOME INSURANCE BEFORE YOU
SIGN THE CONTRACT OF SALE.

Most states require that the risks of loss due to fire, wind damage, and perhaps even injuries to persons, fall on the buyer when the contract of sale has been signed. Even though the property may not have been delivered into the possession of the buyer, the rule still stands. Some states, like New York, say that the seller is responsible for damage. As an overall operating policy, it would be best to talk to your insurance man before signing the contract of sale.

Between the time the contract of sale is signed and the actual closing, the seller and his agents are busy making arrangements to deliver a marketable title. On the date of closing, everybody who has an interest gathers so that all encumbrances to the property can be cleared up at the same time. If you are buying a house, you may go to the closing to find three or even more attorneys facing you. However, the seller may not be there. One attorney is yours, one is the seller's, one is probably employed by the bank which held the seller's mortgage, and there may be others. The title insurance company may send one, the bank writing your mortgage may send one, and persons owning easements on the land may send their own. If the couple selling the house had joint ownership and were divorced, they may both send attorneys. You will sit there with your checkbook and different attorneys will order you to write out checks for different amounts of money. You won't have any idea what's going on. They are all there to watch each other, not to watch you. You are totally incidental to the sale of property and are only there to write checks. You don't even sign the deed in most cases. You leave with a very empty bank account and nothing else. Your lawyer or the title insurance company representative takes the deed to record it. You may not even be entitled to possession of the house at this point. You may get the keys to the house at another time.

To add one more body, the real estate agent or his representative will be there to collect the commission from the seller, or the seller's attorney.

At the time of the closing, you and your husband will get title to the property. One of your attorney's tasks is to help you get the most advantageous type of ownership.

RULE: PICK THE TYPE OF OWNERSHIP
WHICH SAVES TAXES.

When deciding whether you and your husband will hold joint title to your house, you will consider two estate-planning issues. The most obvious issue is how to protect your property if one of you dies. The other issue asks who will make the mortgage payments, and it has become more important as more women have started to work outside the home. Although both of these questions have practical ramifications for your everyday life, they may also modify how much is eventually paid in estate taxes.

Many couples automatically put everything, from the house to the savings accounts, into joint ownership. If you and your husband have wills, this act is a duplication of effort since the passage of title would be taken care of through the will. If you and your husband don't have wills, title to your house must be in joint ownership. If you don't have joint ownership and he dies without a will, you could discover that the laws of your state have forced a joint ownership in the house. You, your minor children, and your mother-in-law may all own a share.

Another aspect of estate planning is keeping a lid on the estate taxes. If you and your husband own everything in joint tenancy, and he dies, you could end up paying higher estate taxes, depending on the size of the estate. An estate worth less than $250,000 would not incur extra estate taxes because of joint ownership. (You shouldn't dismiss this limit as being too high to include your own family. See the chapter on wills.)

Joint ownership of property in no way excludes that property from estate taxation. When someone dies owning property jointly, the whole value of the property will be taxed if the person who died is the person who paid for the property. Joint ownership on the legal title may not save a penny if your husband paid for the property. This principle is true for houses, savings accounts, or any other type of property. The IRS will exclude half of jointly held property from estate taxes only if the other joint owner actually paid for her half of the property. This actual payment is called a "contribution." In order to exempt part of the property, the surviving spouse must be able to prove how much she actually contributed to the purchase of the property.

There are instances when the husband is the only wage earner but the wife is the major contributor to the purchase of the house. One young couple bought a house for $36,000, and the wife contributed the $11,000 down payment. Her husband paid the mortgage payments because she quit work to have children. Four years later they sold the house for $93,000. He had only paid about $3,000 in principal on the mortgage. The balance of the mortgage payments had been interest. When the house was sold, they actually put $14,000 of capital into it, but they made a $57,000 profit. She owned 11/14 of the $57,000, or $44,460 (her $11,000 down payment divided by their joint contribution). He owned the balance of $12,540. When they bought a new house for $125,000, she was still the major contributor, since she put all her proceeds into the initial payment for the new house.

As more wives work away from the home, more women are actually able to make the contribution that the IRS requires for the exclusion from estate taxes. The woman may be able to make the mortgage payment out of her own salary. As in the example above, she may have used her savings to make the down payment. Records should be kept of the sources of the money which paid for the house, since it may save your family estate taxes many years from now.

From a traditional point of view, the husband usually pays for the house and its upkeep. The wife's income is more likely to be used for luxuries like vacations or a second car. It may be smarter for the wife to use her income to pay the mortgage, since this might save estate taxes. The payments all come out of the communal family pocketbook anyhow.

RULE: GET THE RIGHT TITLE ON THE DEED.

Title defines who has the right to possession of the property. The title can be sole (one person owns everything) or joint (two or more persons share possession). You and your husband can pick any one of the forms of title discussed here if you live in a common-law state. If you live in a community-property state, or have ever lived in one, the rules are somewhat different. Community-property titles are discussed at the end of this rule.

The name on the title has nothing to do with who pays for the property or who lives there. However, if your name is on the title you have the right to live there. You will be held legally responsible for the mortgage. You may also have to give your consent if the property is used as security for a loan or mortgage.

As you learned in the previous rule, an owner who contributes all of the purchase price will have the house included in his or her estate at death. If the husband is the only contributor to the house purchase, and he has a will, he may hold sole title to the house without creating legal or tax problems. Sole ownership is very common in affluent families, since no practical advantage would be gained by joint ownership. If you are a single woman who buys a home, you can also hold sole title to the property. However, even single people will sometimes hold title jointly with their children or a sibling. The house may be the single person's major asset. They may put it in joint ownership to avoid probating their estate.

Joint ownership of the house by the husband and wife is far more common than sole ownership. There are three common types of joint ownership. Each type has a slightly different legal significance.

Joint tenancy is the most common joint ownership. Both owners have an undivided one-half interest in the entire property. If one of them dies, the other owner automatically owns the entire property. No will can modify the passage of the ownership. Passing of the title upon death is called the right of survivorship. Any persons can be joint tenants. No particular relationship, such as husband and wife, is required. If one of the joint tenants sells his share of the estate, the joint tenancy comes to an end (is severed) and a tenancy in common rises in place of the joint tenancy.

Tenancy by the entirety is a type of joint ownership restricted to husband and wife. Not all states have this type of ownership. Tenancy by the entirety is exactly like joint tenancy except that neither spouse can sell his or her share without permission of the other. In most states, the husband and wife are entitled to share rents and have joint control of property management.

Joint tenancy and tenancy by the entirety must both fulfill certain title requirements. The ownership of both owners must be created at the same time. They must both get their ownership from the same person. They must have equal interests in the land and be equally entitled to possession. Therefore, it is theoretically impossible for a husband to give his wife a share of their house in joint tenancy if he already owns it. (Under the common law, they can arrange joint tenancy by transferring the house to a third person, who can then transfer title back to them as joint tenants or tenants by the entirety. Some states have statutes which make a direct transfer possible.)

Tenants in common each own a share of the property which cannot be partitioned off. The owners need not be husband and wife, and may own unequal shares, depending on how much each contributed to the purchase. The tenant in common's ownership survives his or her death, and the property share can be willed to a person other than the co-owner. Joint tenancies or tenancies by the entirety which fail for some legal technicality will be treated as tenancies in common.

If your common-law state makes tenancy by the entirety available, you and your husband will probably prefer this ownership, since your interests in the property are protected. Joint tenancy is the next-best method. Tenancy in common is usually reserved for ownership of business property, or when spouses want to preserve ownership proportional to their individual contributions.

If you live in a community-property state, you have much less choice about the form of ownership. (The community-property states are: Arizona, California, Idaho, Louisiana, Nevada, New Mexico, Texas, and Washington.) If you or your husband buy property while you are living in one of these states, you will probably take a type of ownership which is much like tenancy by the entirety. Even if you later move to a common-law state, the ownership must stay in the form it had when you acquired it. Each community-property state has slightly different rules, and due to the modern mobility, they affect many more persons than one might expect. If you are buying a house, your attorney will see that your form of ownership satisfies the local statute.

RULE: A DEED TRANSFERS TITLE.

There are three basic kinds of deeds. The quitclaim deed usually contains the language "I release all my interest in the property to you."

The seller in this case makes no promises that he or she ever owned any part of the property. This type of deed is used to settle outstanding claims which might make the property unmarketable. The quitclaim deed is said to "quiet title," or clear up the title so it can be sold. The quitclaim deed is not very desirable, since the seller promises nothing about the title itself. A quitclaim deed would be used to sell the Brooklyn Bridge.

The grant deed is somewhat more trustworthy. The seller in a grant deed promises that he or she has owned the property, and that he or she has not previously sold or encumbered any part of it. The grant deed is preferable to the quitclaim.

A quitclaim or grant deed is fine, if it is backed up by title insurance. Buyers get the most effective protection of their house title, or any real estate title, through the purchase of title insurance. Title insurance companies promise to pay damages if the title to the property turns out to be incomplete. In the Midwest, title insurance companies tend to be the ultimate authority on the ownership of property. These midwestern companies have been keeping records since the property was first homesteaded. In order to insure property the company will do a title search to see if there are any flaws in the title. Title insurance is very desirable and should be purchased under all circumstances. If title insurance is not available, you can protect yourself by requesting a warranty deed.

The warranty deed is by far the most secure type of deed to have, but it's not as good as a quitclaim deed with title insurance. In a warranty deed, the seller promises that six things are true of his title and the deed he is giving you. The first promise is that the seller has possession of the property. The second promise is the covenant of good right to convey which says that the buyer can recover from the seller if the seller was in wrongful possession of the property. The third promise by the seller is that he will pay off all liens outstanding against the property, such as taxes, mortgages, or leases. The fourth promise is that the seller and his agents shall give the buyer the right to quietly enjoy the property. In other words, the seller will stay out of the buyer's hair. The fifth promise or covenant is a warranty covenant, in which seller promises to defend the buyer against lawful claims of third parties. In other words, the seller will compensate the buyer if the buyer is disturbed. The last is the covenant of further assurances. The seller promises to turn over to the buyer any further rights to the property which the seller may acquire after the deed has been delivered. The warranty deed is just that, the seller promising to protect the buyer against damages due to flaws in the title.

Even if a warranty deed is offered, you should still get title insurance. The seller may be far away if and when you need the protection of the warranty. He could also be dead. The title insurance company is very likely to still be around.

RULE: DEEDS ARE VERY SIMPLE.

Very little is actually required to turn over the title. The seller (grantor) has to sign it, but a seal is no longer required. The buyer has never had to sign a deed. No money has to change hands at all, although deeds which are bought from the stationery stores usually include some rhetoric to the effect that "consideration" has been paid. Most states do not even require that the seller's signature be witnessed. A few do. The title to the property passes when the deed is delivered to the buyer (or grantee, if the property is a gift).

RULE: DELIVERY IS MORE THAN HANDING OVER THE DEED.

Deeds become effective when they are delivered to the buyer. The seller may sign them months before and leave the deed with his attorney, instructing the attorney to turn over the deed when the money is paid. Delivery requires that the seller intend that the deed be delivered and have the effect of passing title to the buyer. If there is more than a thirty-day gap between the date of signing the deed and the date of delivery, the title company may require proof that the seller is still alive.

The issue of delivery is rarely a problem when property is actually bought or sold. However, if property is a gift to another person, delivery of the deed becomes all-important. For example, you might want to give one of your daughters your vacation house and your other daughter the family home. You could make a quitclaim deed and then say, "Here are the deeds, kids. You can have this property when I die." The deeds are not effective because you did not make the delivery of the deeds with the intention that the deeds pass the titles. If you would like to accomplish the same effect, you can do it through the use of an escrow agent. If you deliver the deeds to an escrow agent, instructing him to hand over the deeds upon your death, you have made a proper delivery. The escrow agent must be a true escrow agent, and you cannot call back the deeds. Your attorney or bank could act as the escrow agent. However, make sure that your children witness the act of handing over the deeds. The attorney should sign a receipt. I have seen cases where attorneys embezzled property held in escrow.

One of the most interesting developments in home buying has been the enlargement of warranties to new homes. At one time the principle of caveat emptor (let the buyer beware) persisted in all of real estate. In 1965 a mass-production builder was held strictly liable for burns a child received due to a defective hot water system in a new home. The court refused to recognize any difference between mass-produced automobiles and mass-produced homes.

RULE: ALL BUILDERS WARRANT FITNESS
FOR HABITABILITY.

If the home is new, the builder is considered far more expert at detecting defects than the purchaser ever could be. For this reason it is the total responsibility of the builder to put the house in safe and habitable condition. To avoid this, some builders have included clauses in the purchase agreement disclaiming any liability for flaws. The courts are developing a way to handle this by tying the warranty of habitability to the local building code. If the house meets the requirements of the building code, it also meets the warranty of habitability.

So far the courts have been unwilling to extend the warranty to old houses. The old house is more likely to have minor defects. However, the seller probably has the responsibility to disclose any defect which renders the property unsafe or unhabitable. For example, if the house needs a new hot water heater, you'd better tell the buyer, or expect to be sued. The same thing would be true if you sold a property with an unsafe staircase. If you warn of the unsafe staircase prior to the sale, the buyer assumes the risk. Your sales price will be somewhat lower to allow for the repair of the stairs.

Most of the law of real property has been excluded from this chapter since a lay person would not benefit from an explanation of these laws. Most of the words used in real property law are highly technical (for example, reverter, fee tail, seisen, tacking, shifting or springing uses, etc.). The attorney's primary job in a real estate transaction is to prevent the situations described by these unfamiliar words.

The family home is usually the largest single investment the family has. Although homes are rarely lost because of difficulties with the title, an owner may not be able to sell her house easily if she has been careless when she bought it. These problems can crop up years after the purchase and long after everyone's memory has faded. As in so many other areas of life, prevention is the best policy. Hiring an attorney for the purchase and getting title insurance are your best preventions. If you do these things when you buy your house, you will be sure you can sell it easily.

Chapter 10
MORTGAGES

After you have found the house to buy, and you sign the agreement to buy it, your next step is to get a mortgage. You will need to have the mortgage arranged before the house becomes yours. If you are one of the few people who can afford to pay cash outright, you will skip this step.

Mortgages aren't always easy to obtain. The first reason for the difficulty is an economic one. Most mortgages last twenty to thirty years. Because inflation has been such a prevalent factor in our recent economic life, mortgages are the first type of loan to disappear when the total amount of money available to be loaned diminishes. Commercial bankers would prefer to loan out dollars which will return to them before the value of the loan is wiped out by inflation. Some banks have no choice about the sorts of loans which they can make. For example, in New York State, savings banks are restricted to making loans on real property, unless the loan is secured by passbook savings. This type of law is not unusual. Therefore, in tight-money periods, a savings bank may be the only source of mortgage money. However, when commercial banks aren't lending mortgages, everyone goes to savings banks and the amount of money available at the savings bank is quickly used up.

Mortgages are standard agreements. Even if you shop for the best deal, you will find little difference between the interest rate one bank will charge as opposed to another. However, you may find differences in the amount of money they charge for drawing your mortgage. This difference can be quite substantial. One shopping trip in New York City turned up a difference of $1,000 in these costs. The highest would have charged $1,300 for credit checks, appraisals, insurance, bank fees, etc. The lowest charged $335. In this case the buyer had to assume the appraisal fee (about $75). The mortgage interest rates at the highest bank and at the lowest bank were the same.

It has long been the practice to carry the largest mortgage possible. The reason for this was that real estate did not appreciate at the same rate as investments in other areas, such as the stock market. It was felt that money held in savings or stock was a better investment than cash put into a house. However, in light of the inflationary spiral in real estate and anticipated interest rates on mortgages of 10 per cent per year, you should investigate paying as much cash as possible, and carrying a smaller mortgage, if you are just now buying a house. Keep in mind that this book is being written in 1979. You will have to examine the real estate market and the mortgage market at the time you're making your purchase to decide what the best policy for you would be, assuming, of course, that you do have the cash to put into a house.

There are three different kinds of mortgages. They are: the so-called "purchase money mortgage," the building loan mortgage, and the collateral or security mortgage.

The purchase money mortgage is the most common type. In the strictest legal sense, a purchase money mortgage is an agreement between the seller and the buyer. The seller may have the power to resell the property if the buyer falls behind on his payments. Depending on the state, title may stay with the seller until the buyer pays off the whole mortgage. Mortgages between the seller and buyer also do not have a maximum legal rate of interest.

In its most common usage, a purchase money mortgage refers to the mortgage a buyer gets from a bank. An agreement is made to buy property and the buyer goes out and finds someone willing to loan him the money to pay off the balance. The money changes hands at the closing of the deal.

The building loan mortgage is sought by someone who already owns land and wishes either to build a house or to add to an already existing house. This type of mortgage is different in that amounts of money are paid to the borrower periodically as the building progresses.

The security-collateral mortgage is loaned when money is needed for something other than the house itself but the real estate serves as security for the loan. The money might be borrowed to send the kids to college or to start a business.

Second mortgages can be modifications of either a building loan or a security mortgage. The second mortgage is a mortgage in addition to one which is already outstanding on the property. If a lender feels that the value of the property can support a second mortgage, he may make the deal. (The law restricts savings banks from lending on second mortgages, except in rare instances. You'll probably have to seek a second mortgage from a commercial bank.)

Sometimes mortgages can be refinanced, instead of taking on a second mortgage. The first mortgage is paid off and a whole new mortgage starts up. However, in light of the substantial increase in interest rates, it is probably best to maintain the old mortgage at what is hopefully a lower interest rate and add on a second mortgage at the higher interest rate. If you entirely refinance the old mortgage, you will be paying on both amounts at the higher rate.

The decision of taking on a second mortgage requires a lot of thought and figuring. Your income may have increased substantially since you first bought your house. Carrying a second mortgage to make improvements to your house might not strain your pocketbook a bit. On the other hand, it may be the proverbial straw which breaks the camel's back. Conservative investment lore advises against a second mortgage. The rate of inflation may make this obsolete, if you have a job in which your salary is likely to increase at least in step with the inflation rate.

Generally bankers don't like second mortgages unless they're home improvement loans. The law says that the first mortgagee has the first right to recover if something happens to you or the property. The second mortgagee will not receive any funds until the first mortgagee has been entirely paid. Of course, the problem only arises if the property must be foreclosed upon. As long as you continue to make your mortgage payments each month on each mortgage, both mortgage lenders will be happy.

RULE: YOU RETAIN TITLE.

One of the qualities of a modern mortgage is that the person who borrows the money retains title to the property. The person who borrows (the mortgagor) also retains the actual possession of the property. The mortgage allows the person who loaned to have a lien on the property for as long as the mortgage is outstanding. The different states use one of three basic theories of mortgage which split up the rights of title and possession differently. These theories have more to do with the default on the mortgage than its being paid off. These theories will hopefully not affect you.

You can sell the property, but you will have to notify the bank that you will be paying off the mortgage. They may wish to be present at the closing so they can collect their money. Indeed, you won't be able to sell the property with a clear title until the mortgage is paid off, since it is an outstanding lien and you cannot deliver a clear title until it has been paid off. (The buyer could also agree to take over the mortgage. The seller should be cautious about allowing the buyer to take over the mortgage. If the buyer defaults on the mortgage, and the house doesn't bring enough at sale to pay off the mortgage, the bank may be able to collect the balance due from the seller. Ask the bank about your state law.)

RULE: YOU HAVE TO PROTECT THE PROPERTY.

It is your responsibility as the mortgagor to keep the property in sound condition, and not make any unusual additions to it. If you plan any additions, it is best to clear them with the bank first. You may think that gutting the inside of your four-bedroom house to turn it into one large studio with a kitchen and one bathroom would serve your purposes very well. The bank may take substantial objection to this, since your house may be much harder to sell after you have made the changes. You may have destroyed the value of the home as far as the bank is concerned, and the mortgage probably contains a clause allowing them to foreclose.

The bank is very unlikely to inhibit you if you want to put in a new kitchen or add on a recreation room. As a matter of fact, they'll probably jump for joy, but it's always best to notify them, so they can check things out if they'd like to.

RULE: YOU HAVE TO PAY YOUR TAXES.

The bank is very interested in protecting your rights to the property. The mortgage will contain some type of provision allowing them to foreclose if you fall behind on your tax payments. Many banks collect the taxes right along with your mortgage payments. Then they pay the taxes for you. The only problem with this arrangement is that they collect from you monthly for your taxes and build up an escrow account. At the end of the year they pay off your tax bill. They may or may not pay you interest on your tax money which is in escrow. If they're putting the interest in their own pocket, your interest rate on the mortgage is actually higher than the interest rate which is stated. The escrow account may be one of the things which you can negotiate about when you are shopping for a mortgage.

RULE: YOU HAVE TO CARRY INSURANCE.

In all likelihood the mortgage will state that it is your responsibility to keep the property fully insured. If you don't, the bank may also foreclose.

RULE: LOOK FOR A FLOATING
INTEREST RATE.

A type of interest has been available for the last several years which puts a ceiling on the percentage of interest charged but diminishes the interest rate charged if the bank lowers its interest rate. This way you will never have to pay more than the interest you have agreed to, but the interest will go down if the mortgage interest rates go down. This beneficial clause saves you additional work if the mortgage rates decrease after you get your mortgage. For example, at the time of this writing mortgage rates are about 10 per cent per year. This rate is exceptionally high and can be expected to decrease. In order to prevent refinancing when the rates go down, the bank will be willing to incorporate a floating interest provision. This provision saves you work too, since you may not have to find another bank to refinance the mortgage.

RULE: GET A SATISFACTION
OF MORTGAGE.

Even though it seems that you will never finish paying off the mortgage, the day will come when your last payment has been made. The mortgage itself is canceled and the mortgagee issues you a document called a satisfaction of mortgage. This document *must* be filed with the county clerk to show that your property is free and clear. Although you have always had the title, your title is now unencumbered.

Paying off the mortgage is usually the subject of great celebration. My mother had a hole drilled in the newel post, rolled up the mortgage, stuck it in the newel post, and attached an antique ornament to the top of the post. In Mississippi River homes, such an ornament was indicative that the mortgage had been paid off and the ornament was necessary to cover up the hole in the newel post which now held the mortgage.

Although most mortgages end this happily, some do not. The mortgagee hasn't been getting his payments and is forced to foreclose. He may do this in two different ways. The most common way is to take the mortgagor to court and seek a judicial sale of the home. The second way is used in a minority of states which allow mortgagees to write foreclosure clauses into the mortgage itself. They then foreclose under a clause in the mortgage called a power of sale.

RULE: JUDICIAL SALE IS VERY SLOW.

The actual mechanics of the judicial sale vary widely from state to state. The statutes in this area normally provide for notice, hearing, the judge's decision that there has been a default, a public notice of sale, possibly an appraisal, the sale itself, and then the delays begin. The judge has to confirm the sale, which he may or may not do. The statutes in some states allow the person whose property was sold to redeem the property. This period of redemption may last for months or years. The judge may also enter a deficiency judgment if the sale has not brought enough money to cover the mortgagee's loss.

The ability to redeem the property is the most important issue to the consumer. Depending on the state in which the consumer lives, she may be able to redeem her home under a principle called equitable redemption. In this case the homeowner can stop the foreclosure by paying off the entire amount of the debt due plus foreclosure costs. Even if the foreclosure has gone along so far that the sale of the property has occurred, about half of the states will allow her a further opportunity to redeem the property. Under these statutes the period of redemption may be extended beyond the actual foreclosure from several months to several years depending on the state. In such an instance the mortgagor must come up with the whole sale price, as opposed to only the amount of debt which was outstanding when the foreclosure action was brought.

As mentioned before, the court may or may not actually confirm the sale under the foreclosure. The person who buys the house at a judicial sale is not entitled to enforce the sale. Some states require that an appraisal of the property be obtained prior to the sale. The sale price must meet at least a certain percentage of the appraisal. If the price is so inadequate as to shock the conscience, the judge will not confirm. Adequacy of the price is often considered in these cases, although no clear-cut outcome could be predicted, and is one reason why mortgage sales are so unattractive to buyers. The sale may not be confirmed, and the whole effort would be a waste of time, and there is a substantial risk that a large amount of money will be lost.

The power of sale clause in some mortgages may allow foreclosure without judicial process (under deeds of trust). Sales under these clauses are restricted in some states and used commonly in only eighteen states. In these states, statutes require many steps in order for the power of sale to be effective. The steps include a public sale, a very detailed public notice, etc. Courts don't like power of sale, and will overturn the sale on the smallest failure to comply with the requirements. Because of this, buyers are far less willing to participate in a mortgage sale. The fewer buyers bidding, the lower the price may be, and the more likely the sale is to be overturned for an inadequate price. This downward spiral makes the power of sale close to useless.

Although it is unlikely that your mortgage will ever be foreclosed upon, you may now understand better why mortgage lenders check out prospective clients so carefully. Even though the house absolutely secures the debt outstanding, the mortgagee will have to work very hard to get his money back.

Real estate and mortgage transactions are in no way immune from the credit requirements which will be discussed later in the chapter on credit. That chapter also has information you will find helpful in the particular area of consumer credit as it applies to mortgages. However, mortgages do have their own special rules.

RULE: REAL ESTATE FINANCE CHARGES ARE COMPLICATED.

The area of finance charges and mortgages is more complex than a normal consumer credit finance charge. The mortgagee may charge the following forms of interest: points, a time price differential, transaction charges, activity charges, carrying charges, appraisal fees, loan fees, discounts, and any number of other charges which the imagination could conceive. These charges must be included in the finance charge, since they all modify the amount of interest. However, the total finance charge which you will pay over the twenty-five- or thirty-year mortgage need not be disclosed as a total amount. For your own illumination you may want to figure the amount out. The finance charge will easily double the amount you pay for your house. These days the amount is usually far more than double the actual mortgage debt. The one finance charge clause you must insist upon is a no-penalty clause if you pay the mortgage off early.

RULE: YOU HAVE THREE DAYS TO CALL OFF THE MORTGAGE.

The truth-in-lending provisions discussed more extensively in the chapter on credit also apply to real estate. Consumers have three business days to call off a mortgage contract, or any other contract which would create a lender's right in your property. The lender has to tell you that you have a right to call it off. The three days begin when you have received all disclosures regarding the credit transaction. If the creditor never tells you, you have three years after the agreement is signed to call it off. Rescission of a real estate mortgage is a fairly complicated proceeding. If you've already received your mortgage money, it's best to hire an attorney to handle this. If you have not received the money, chances are you can cancel the agreement by mail without any difficulty. In fact, most mortgagees wait about seven days before delivering any money to the consumer. They have to do this in order to protect themselves. (Many banks have been exempted from this rule. Other mortgage lenders have not been.)

RULE: INTERSTATE LAND SALES REQUIRE
PROPERTY REPORTS.

Because of a great deal of fraud and misuse in the area of interstate land sales, there is now a federal law governing the sale of unimproved land. The promoter of these land sales must live up to certain standards, and file certain reports, including the prospectus you receive, with the Department of Housing and Urban Development (Office of Interstate Land Sales Registration). Consumers also have a private right to sue for fraud or misrepresentation.

The consumer also has the right to rescind these purchases. The property report must be furnished to the consumer, and the consumer has forty-eight hours to rescind any agreement made after the report is furnished. If no property report is furnished before the sale, the seller cannot hold the consumer to the bargain.

RULE: THE HOUSE BUYER MUST HAVE
CERTAIN INFORMATION.

If the consumer is buying a one- to four-family residential dwelling, the mortgage lender is required to make sure that the buyer has received certain information from the seller. These rules only count if the house is more than a year old. The information required is the seller's name and address, the date the seller acquired the house, and if the house was owned less than two years without being used as a residence, the seller must disclose his purchase price and the cost of any improvements.

The mortgage lender is also required to make two separate disclosures of all of the charges to be paid by either the buyer or the seller.

This information must be made on a uniform disclosure settlement statement, which is an HUD form, and must be furnished to all of the parties at least twelve days prior to the actual closing.

This chapter is overly detailed, but may give you some idea of what all those pieces of paper are which are given to you in the complicated procedure of buying or selling a house.

Practically everybody buys his house with a mortgage. There is nothing frightening about it, but it is a new experience for many women. For years many bankers made it a practice to deny mortgages to single or divorced women. They can no longer do this unless the woman's income is inadequate to pay for the mortgage. This change occurred because of the Equal Credit Opportunity Act.

In times when the economy is more or less normal, obtaining a mortgage is not very difficult, and not even confusing. You just go around to the banks and ask a lot of questions. You may have to visit them several times before you feel you have enough information to make a decision. Then you just contact the bank which is making the best deal. It's rather like shopping for the best buy on a TV set, except the obligation you make is about two hundred times as big.

Part IV
MONEY

Chapter 11
TAXES

Taxation began in prehistory. The Babylonians made an art of it; the Romans, a science. During the medieval period, taxation, like everything else, fell into disorder. But the Renaissance reinstituted it with a Machiavellian hand.

In America taxation has become such an elaborate game that even experts get baffled. The federal income tax regulations of this country exceed 40,000 pages, not including judicial opinions or other extra-statute matters. There are no doubt simpler ways to pay for the operation of the federal government. But for the time being it's up to us to deal with this mess.

In this chapter we will talk about the elements of taxation that confuse the uninitiated. We will start with United States federal income taxes and federal estate taxes. Once you understand the basic principles, you'll find it easier to acquire the more specific information which applies to you.

RULE: THEY CAN TAX YOU ANYWHERE
IN THE WORLD.

If you are a United States citizen, you must pay taxes whether you live in Pocatello, Idaho, or Hong Kong. If you move abroad, your tax situation becomes even more complex. If you live abroad, you will generally have to file a United States tax return, a tax return of your country of residence, and an extensive foreign tax credit form to prove to the United States government that you've already paid taxes on your income to a foreign country. If you live abroad, the local American consulate can help you with your United States taxes. Persons who live abroad file their tax returns on June 15 instead of April 15.

RULE: ALIENS PAY TAXES TOO.

If you are not a United States citizen, and you intend to stay in this country for a prolonged period of time, you may have to pay taxes on all of your income from anywhere in the world. The type of visa you use to enter the country is an indication of your intention. However, we all change our minds. You could enter on a tourist visa, be offered a job, and decide to stay. If you decide to stay, you will have to pay United States taxes on all of your income from all over the world. If you only come to make occasional business transactions with no intention to stay, your tax is a flat 30% of your profit. Foreigners earning wages in the United States are subject to a type of regular income tax, but they are not entitled to a standard deduction. Tax treaties which the United States has with the taxpayer's country of origin may also affect taxes paid.

Some foreign visitors to this country have to file a tax return before leaving the country. If they owe tax, it must be paid before they can obtain a permit to leave the United States. A branch of the IRS, the Alien Tax Service, helps foreign citizens with the peculiarities of tax returns for non-residents. Any foreign-born person who has been in this country for less than the entire tax year (January 1 to December 31) should contact the Alien Tax Service. Call your closest IRS district office and ask for the phone number of Alien Tax Service.

RULE: INCOME IS ALL THE MONEY YOU RECEIVE.

In theory, all money you receive is taxable. However, laws exempt some particular types of income from tax. Exempt income includes: gifts, bequests from a will, welfare payments, veteran's benefits, Social Security benefits, loans, disability benefits, interest from municipal bonds, insurance benefits, money from certain kinds of lawsuits, the principal of a loan repaid to you, child support, scholarships, and a few other minor items.

RULE: SOME SPECIAL PERSONAL EXPENSES ARE NOT TAXABLE.

These certain types of personal expenses are called adjustments to income. An adjustment is quite different from ordinary deductions and exemptions. Adjustments to income are subtracted from your income before ordinary deductions and exemptions are subtracted. An adjustment will benefit you even if you can't itemize deductions.

Adjustments to income are: moving expenses, employee business expenses, individual retirement accounts, alimony paid, and interest penalties on the premature withdrawal of long-term savings accounts.

So the first step in figuring a tax return is to accumulate all of your income. The next step is to subtract the adjustments, if you have any. The result is called the adjusted gross income. The adjusted gross income is your real income, according to the IRS.

RULE: CERTAIN PERSONAL EXPENSES ARE
DEDUCTIBLE FROM YOUR INCOME.

These personal expenses are called itemized deductions. Many taxpayers call itemized deductions "the long form." Itemized deductions include medical expenses, taxes, contributions, etc. The adjustment to income is "non-taxable," and has an advantage over an itemized deduction, which is merely "deductible." An expense which is not taxable has no taxes paid on it whatsoever. An expense which is deductible will end up being partially taxed.

The reason for this distinction is subtle, but important for a taxpayer. The reason is—the standard deduction. The federal government allows everyone a standard deduction, and the amount depends on his or her marital status. In 1978, the standard deduction was $3,200 for a married couple. Taxpayers don't have to spend any money at all to get this standard deduction. However, the taxpayer who claims itemized deductions must accumulate more itemized expenses than the standard deduction in order to gain a tax advantage. The married taxpayer must spend at least $3,200 to get any break at all.

The person who chooses the standard deduction hasn't actually spent the money. The one who uses the itemized deduction has. So the one with the standard deduction is actually in better financial shape, even though the taxpayer who spent his money has lower taxes. Additionally, the person who spent the money gets a tax deduction on his expenditures only after they have exceeded the standard deduction. In effect, all the money he spent to reach the standard deduction is taxed anyway, since it represents no tax savings.

Alimony is a good example of the difference between a deductible expense and a non-taxable adjustment to income. In fact, alimony used to be an itemized deduction. In 1977 it was changed to an adjustment to income because it was so unfair as a deduction. For example, Henry Carlisle pays $1,800 a year in alimony, $500 in union dues, and $300 in state income taxes. His itemized deductions before 1977 were

$2,600. Now that alimony is an adjustment to income, Henry subtracts $1,800 in alimony plus a standard deduction of $2,200 before his income is taxed. Under the new method, his deductions total $4,000. After 1977, he has a net gain of $1,400 in deductions. At any income level, Henry saves a great deal of tax.

You may find yourself being confused by terminology. This is not unusual, since taxes make very little sense in the logics of law, accounting, or semantics. Not only that, but the IRS occasionally changes the meanings on us. However, adjustments are different from deductions. And deductions are different from our next topic, exemptions.

> RULE: THE NUMBER OF PERSONS IN YOUR
> FAMILY AFFECTS YOUR TAXES.

The tax reduction you get for the number of persons in a family is called your exemptions. There is no clear way to explain this. Exemptions are based on the fact that there is an actual person there. The current $750 value assigned to an exemption seems to have little to do with how much it costs to support, let alone feed, an individual for a year. At one time it may have been linked to some practical issue, but this has disappeared into tax history. Now, like the standard deduction, exemptions are merely an amount that is subtracted before the tax is arrived at. Each $750 exemption will actually save a taxpayer between $75 and $300, depending on the tax bracket, so obviously the tax exemption is merely a token salute to the cost of support.

Exemptions are granted because a person was alive during the year. So a child born in December is just as valuable an exemption as a person living all year. A person who dies during the year gets the same exemption as one who lived all year long.

To confuse the issue, additional exemptions are allowed which don't directly relate to the fact that a mere person is there. Additional exemptions are granted if a person is blind or has reached age 65.

> RULE: THE AMOUNT OF TAX YOU PAY
> IS COMPUTED ON YOUR INCOME
> AFTER ALL DEDUCTIONS AND
> EXEMPTIONS ARE SUBTRACTED.

Many people have no idea of the percentage of taxes they actually pay. There are two tax rates which you should be aware of in your own tax return. The most important of these will never be found on a tax return. It is called the effective tax rate. That is your final tax as a percentage of your income (tax÷income=effective tax rate). Most of you will find that your effective tax rate is about 10%. If Social Security is included, the effective tax is about 16%. The effective tax rate for well-to-do individuals is frequently 40% or 50%.

The other tax rate which is important is your tax bracket. Remember that nobody pays any income taxes on standard deduction plus exemptions. Everybody pays 14% on the next $500, 15% on the $500 after that, and so on, until you start to pay 50 cents of every dollar as federal tax. A single individual will pay 50 cents of every dollar he earns above $36,000. Married individuals pay 50 cents of every earned dollar above $52,000 of their joint income. That 50 cents is what's referred to as a tax bracket. If a person in the 50% tax bracket has income she didn't earn, like interest on savings accounts or capital gains, the tax rate on the unearned income will be higher than 50%. A tax bracket can be anywhere from 14% to 70% depending on the amount and the type of income.

The tax bracket tells you how much of your itemized deductions are returned to you by lower taxes. For example, if you're in a 39% tax bracket, 39 cents of every dollar of your deductions will be returned to you through lower taxes. Sometimes your deductions will lower you from one tax bracket to another. For example, if you and your husband have combined earnings of $55,000 and you have $12,000 in itemized deductions, your tax bracket is reduced from 50% to 45%. Your $12,000 in deductions can save nearly $6,000 in taxes.

If another couple making $55,000 had spent the $12,000 as adjustments to income, like employee business expenses, they would save more money. Their adjusted income would be $43,000 ($55,000—$12,000). In addition, they could claim a $3,200 standard deduction, lowering them to a 42% tax bracket. In the process, they would save an additional $1,400 in taxes.

RULE: TAX SHELTERS ARE
AVAILABLE TO EVERYONE.

One of the earliest Supreme Court decisions on the income tax ruled that it was no crime to avoid income taxes. Tax shelters were originally set up to help risky businesses raise money by allowing tax advantages to the investors. For example, investments in movies and real estate development used to have substantial tax advantages. The Tax Reform Act of 1975 abolished many of these shelters. More tax money is now collected from prosperous citizens, but risk businesses have a harder time raising money. However, not all tax shelters are risky or expensive.

The basic quality of a tax shelter is that income from this year is invested tax-free or at reduced tax rates. In a future year the return from the investment may be either partially or entirely taxable. The most common example of a tax shelter is home ownership. In the case of home ownership the price of the house itself is not sheltered. However, the interest and the real estate taxes are partially sheltered because they are itemized deductions. The appreciation on the value of your home is entirely sheltered because your profit on the sale can be carried forward indefinitely until you purchase a less expensive home than the one you sold. Home ownership is the most widely used tax shelter and is readily available to the majority of American families.

A newer but also broadly used tax shelter is the retirement plan known as an Individual Retirement Arrangement or Keogh Plan. The principle of this shelter is that income is placed into such a plan tax-free. When the principal and interest are withdrawn, income tax is paid on both. Since this income will be drawn after retirement, theoretically the taxes will be much lower, depending on your current income and the number of years you have to go until you retire. However, this shelter may cost the exceptional wage earner higher taxes. If you are self-employed, earning $60,000 a year at age 30, and you put $7,500 of it into one of these plans every year for the next forty years until you retire at age 70, your contribution plus the interest will be well in excess of one million dollars. The law now says that all the money from the account must be taken within a ten-year period. This withdrawal requirement would give you an income of over $100,000 a year. The future taxes on $100,000 would be higher than today's taxes on $7,500. However, over the next forty years, or even over the next ten, practically anything could happen to our income tax structure. Obviously, someone who will retire ten or twenty years from now can invest in one of these shelters with far more assurance of what she can expect to receive as income and what she will pay in taxes.

The Tax Reform Act of 1975 has left us with very little in the form of "fancy" tax shelters. What is left is cattle raising and oil exploration. They're both expensive and risky. The only way to make a profit on these shelters is to have a lot of money to invest and to spread it over a number of different investments.

RULE: THE INCOME TAX PRIVACY ACT
PROTECTS THE GOVERNMENT'S PRIVACY.

Prior to the Privacy Act of 1974, an individual's income tax return could mysteriously find its way into the hands of credit investigators and other individuals who had absolutely no right to it. The Privacy Act abolished this practice but gave the right to the IRS to distribute your tax returns to any government agency. They did this anyway before the Privacy Act, but now they have the legal right to do it. Some people don't consider that very private.

The Privacy Act has a real disadvantage to the taxpayer. In New York, anyway, the IRS now refuses to discuss practically anything over the telephone, even when you call to inquire about your refund.

There are some areas of taxes which most people have heard of and everyone finds confusing. My financially sophisticated mother called me one day for an explanation of capital gains. Other knowledgeable people have astounding gaps in their understanding of taxes. This book will only talk about the things most tax books never tell you. If you'd like more extensive information, just about any tax book on the market can fill in the details.

RULE: THE MIDDLE CLASS HAS MOST OF THE MONEY.

Occasionally a politician will contend that taxation should be used to further social reform or to redistribute income. A politician who makes such a statement probably hasn't checked his facts, because if he wants to redistribute income, he's going to have to take it away from the middle class, which comprises the vast majority of the population. At least 85% of U.S. taxpayers consider themselves to be middle class. The middle class bears the great burden of taxation in this country. Of the total taxes collected, 67% comes from personal income taxes and Social Security taxes. Only 13% comes from corporate income taxes; 11% is attributed to government borrowing; and the balance is derived from minor federal taxes like the excise tax.

Occasionally, a cry will be heard to "soak the rich." Unfortunately for the rest of us, there aren't many of them around. If the U.S. government confiscated all personal fortunes of one million dollars or more, the proceeds might be enough to pay for one year of the operation of the federal government. Since rich people really don't hold much total wealth, the taxing bodies have to take it from the group who really does have money—the middle class.

RULE: INCOME TAX LAW IS COMPLICATED.

As mentioned earlier, we have a graduated income tax system, meaning the more money we make, the higher a percentage of taxes we pay. The graduated income tax system is the primary contributor to the complexity of the tax law.

The theory of the graduated income tax system is that it will tend to equalize income. The actual effect of it is quite different. First of all, the graduated income tax system doesn't really change the standard of living of the more well-to-do, but it does leave them less money to save and invest. The well-to-do may also cut out unnecessary items, such as household help, thereby costing the frustrated worker a job. The same effect of less money to save affects the middle class also. As the wage earner makes more money, he or she is taxed more heavily. She then has the choice of saving and living at her old standard, or living slightly better and saving the same amount. She is therefore unlikely to ever be able to save enough to move herself from middle class up to well-to-do. The effect of the graduated income tax on the savings of the middle class is its most serious aspect.

Because the graduated income tax takes a greater percentage of large amounts of money, multitudes of exceptions have had to be created to equalize unfairness. For example, a woman's husband had a mental breakdown and lost his job. She was fired from her job of twenty years, but found another. They had two children. He needed a housekeeper to watch him while she was at work. The children had to be placed in day care. She made $12,000 in that year, but got a $20,000 lump-sum pension plan payment from her former employer. The husband also got a pension plan distribution of $20,000. Her taxes were nearly $12,000. She was not allowed to deduct the day care because she had income of $52,000. She also couldn't take off the housekeeper who cared for her husband, since the housekeeper wasn't a medical person. She had to pay graduated income taxes on the pension benefits from their employers. After the taxes were paid she had spent practically all of the money, much of it for day care and the housekeeper. This situation is obviously unfair, and tax laws were passed later to modify both the lump-sum distribution problem and the day care problem. However, both of these laws became necessary because of the graduated income tax system. Herein lies the nuisance of graduated tax—it isn't basically fair, which gives rise to countless exceptions and manipulations by taxpayers. It also creates a lot of work for attorneys.

The next part of this chapter discusses some complications arising out of the graduated income tax.

RULE: CAPITAL GAINS TAX APPLIES TO
INVESTMENTS WHICH ARE SOLD.

Investments such as a home or stock or antique cars are likely to appreciate in value over the period of time you own them. Until you sell them, the appreciation or depreciation in value cannot be actually determined.

An individual may hold property for many years before she sells it. It would not be fair to tax the entire profit, because a substantial depreciation in the value of the dollar has occurred since the time the property was purchased. Additionally, investments such as a home or stock are likely to represent an individual's main avenue of savings for the future. Many people will only sell their stock or business once in a lifetime. It seems fair that they should be able to keep a large portion of their life's work. It would be unlikely that an individual would place her hard-earned savings in any major investment if it seemed likely that taxes would confiscate the fruits of her efforts.

RULE: CAPITAL GAINS TAX HALF OF YOUR PROFIT.

Just to confuse the issue, there are two types of capital gains—long-term and short-term. As of 1978, short-term capital gains apply to investments you have held for less than one year from the date of purchase. Long-term capital gains apply to property you have owned for more than one year. In short-term capital gains the entire profit is added to the rest of your income for the year and you pay regular graduated income tax on the entire profit. For example, if you make $30,000 in salary and have a short-term capital gain of $20,000, your income is $50,000. Depending on your marital status and other variables, the tax on your $20,000 profit would be around $10,000. However, if it's a long-term capital gain, only 40% of your profit is added to your other income to determine your income tax. If you make the same $30,000 in salary with a long-term capital gain of $20,000, the 40% ($8,000) is added to your salary, giving you an income of $38,000. Then the tax on the $20,000 profit could be as low as $3,750, since only part of the gain is taxed.

Although capital gains is a fairly decent tax on long-term investments, it is not accurately responsive to a particular situation which often arises. Indeed, this is one of the saddest events in tax practice. For example, Susanna Clemens retired from Sears after forty years with the company. On retirement, Sears handed her a profit-sharing retirement plan in the form of Sears stock. Susanna had been a secretary and thought that her $500,000 profit sharing was just wonderful. The Sears stock had appreciated substantially over the forty years and her actual investment had been very small. Susanna sold the stock expecting to live very grandly on bank interest. What she did not anticipate was that her income taxes on the sale of the stock were over $155,000. Even worse is the case of the private businesswoman. She may have started her business on a shoestring, worked hard her whole life to build the business into something, only to find her security for her retirement disappear into taxes.

There is a new tax law which could now help the lady who retired from Sears. It is called Special 10-Year Averaging, and is different from the regular income averaging, mentioned later. Ten-Year Averaging applies only to total distributions of employee pension and profit-sharing programs. If you receive your whole profit sharing, either when you leave your company or retire, make sure this special tax method is used.

Special 10-Year Averaging is not applicable to someone who sells her farm, business, home, or stock.

RULE: THE IRS CAN'T TAKE MORE
THAN 50% OF YOUR SALARY.

With inflation pushing salaries up and the tax rates remaining the same, you may find that you soon reach the 50% tax bracket, which is $36,000 for a single taxpayer and $52,000 for a married couple filing jointly. These days a hard-working truck driver can make $36,000 a year. An excellent gas station owner-operator can make over $50,000. You can see that high taxes can affect blue-collar occupations just as easily as they affect the president of a corporation. To modify this, Congress passed the maximum income tax. This tax holds the income tax on salaries, wages, and pensions to 50% of the amount earned above the $36,000 for a single person or $52,000 for married couples.

RULE: INCOME AVERAGING CAN
SAVE YOU MONEY.

Income averaging is one of the least understood tax breaks. Most people are under the impression that their income is actually averaged out over a period of years. This is not true. What really happens is that the top tax brackets of the last four years are averaged. The tax on this year's income is limited to the next tax bracket above the average of the last four years.

The IRS doesn't tell you that if you wish to income-average you must have filed tax returns for the four previous years. Even though you may not have had a penny of income to report, it's mandatory that a return has been filed. This way you can income-average when you return to work. If you haven't filed tax returns for the four previous years, and you anticipate an increase in salary of $3,000 or more, it would be a good idea to file the years you missed.

RULE: IF THE IRS OWES YOU MONEY,
        YOU DON'T HAVE TO FILE
        BEFORE APRIL 15.

The penalty on late filing becomes active only if you owe the IRS money. You must file your tax return on the due date (usually April 15) or pay a penalty of 5% per month. The penalty is waived if you have a refund coming. The only hitch in this is that if you don't file a tax return within three years of the date it should have been filed, the IRS is under no obligation to refund you your money.

In 1977, the IRS processed 133,700,000 tax returns. They do a pretty good job as long as everybody follows their rules. When an individual starts doing things with his tax return which a computer can't handle, it causes the IRS problems. Any non-standard thing you might do, like forgetting to sign your return or sending your return to the wrong office, will cause your refund to be delayed.

Many people suspect that the IRS has particular standards which cause a return to be selected for auditing. Any person making more than $50,000 per year has a greater chance of being audited, as do people who claim high business expenses, unusual charitable contributions, or larger total itemized deductions than a statistical average. Many returns are examined by the IRS to decide whether the individual should be called in for an actual audit. Actually, only a very small percentage of returns (1.75% in 1977) are selected for any audit at all.

Some returns get a face-to-face audit. Many other returns receive a treatment called a letter audit. The IRS sends the taxpayer a letter requesting further information, or perhaps some proof that the tax return is true. It is common for the IRS to check on the dependents a taxpayer claimed by writing the taxpayer a letter requesting copies of birth certificates or school records. If the dependent can be proved, it's usually the end of the communication with the IRS. If the taxpayer can't prove the dependent, or fails to answer the letter, she may either be called in for an audit or find a treasury agent on her front step.

RULE: YOU HAVE NOTHING TO
        FEAR FROM AN AUDIT.

Being audited by the IRS is a traumatic event in most people's lives. In fact, they will do almost anything to avoid an audit—anything from not taking legitimate deductions to refusing to show up. If you can prove a deduction, by all means take it. If you don't take it, you will get less of a refund than you are entitled to. The only thing you have to do to protect yourself is to keep your proof of the deductions. If you have added some deductions to your return for which you do not have proof, you may have to pay the extra tax. However, you were the one who didn't keep the receipts.

To be totally safe, hang on to proof of your deductions for seven years. To be moderately safe, keep them for three years.

The fellow who audits you at the IRS is likely to be a recent college grad in accounting. He may have taken this job to get the training he needs for some very lucrative position in a private accounting firm. Or she may be a professional who feels she is rendering a service to the people of the United States. In either case these auditors audit every working day of the year. They know you're nervous but they really just want to get your audit finished. If you come prepared, are businesslike, and present yourself as a person willing to answer any questions, the outcome won't hurt too much. For example, at the end of one year I accidentally sent off tax-deductible expenses in the wrong envelopes. The hospital insurance company got the check made out to the doctor and the doctor got the check made out to Blue Cross. I finished my tax return on January 10 and sent it in before the error was discovered. Since the checks did not clear in the year of the tax return, I wasn't entitled to either tax deduction for the year. Because my medical deductions were overstated by $60, I owed additional tax of $24, and I still had the opportunity to take those expenses the following year.

RULE: NEVER LOSE A TAX RETURN.

If you lose your returns, the damage caused is not irreparable, since the IRS can provide you with copies of the tax returns. However, it takes six to nine months to get the copies. That's at least six months when you might have had an income-averaging refund sitting in your bank account.

RULE: THERE'S NO SUCH THING AS
A PERFECT TAX RETURN.

Tax returns have so many variables that you or the most experienced tax preparer can hope only for a tax return which is more or less correct. A well-trained treasury agent can find some fault with almost any tax return that was ever written. The IRS is well aware of this and does not hold taxpayers to a standard of perfection.

Tax fraud is quite a different subject. You cannot be jailed for mistakes or differences of opinion, but you can be jailed for fraud. Fraud is rarely charged unless the taxpayer omitted substantial income from the tax return. There are only about 8,000 tax fraud investigations every year. Only about 1,500 taxpayers are prosecuted, since many either pay off or aren't guilty in the first place.

The second most significant type of tax is property tax. Property tax is an older form of taxation than income tax. This tax arose out of feudal tributes once paid to kings and princes. Prior to escalation in the size of government, property taxes were the main source of public revenue. Today property taxes are primarily used to build and maintain city streets, maintain sewers, run schools, and pay the local police and firemen. Many states collect part of the property tax from the city or county and use this tax to help run the state government. In addition, many communities are now met with the difficulty of having part of their school taxes siphoned off by the state government for the use of poorer school districts.

Property taxes are paid on any sort of real estate, whether it be a farm, home, or factory. The amount of tax will be different depending on the nature of the land use. For example, a factory may utilize the sewage system of a county in a far different way than a home would. Therefore, the sewer tax collected from the factory may be out of proportion to a home sitting on the same amount of land. Property taxes on the whole are quite logical and sensible in contrast with income taxes. Many communities even break up the taxes so that a property owner will pay school tax, sewer tax, and a blanket tax which will cover roads, police, etc. It's comforting to be able to see where your money goes.

RULE: THE TAX BASE IS THE TAXABLE
VALUE OF YOUR PROPERTY.

Local authorities maintain records that are usually called property rolls. The property roll assigns a value to each piece of real estate in use within the tax authority's jurisdiction. This tax authority can be a city, township, county, sewer district, school district, or state. The taxable value of the property is unlikely to be equal to the cost of the building and land, or the last sale price of the house.

The tax authority may use a number of different methods to arrive at the taxable value. Any of the methods are all right as long as the tax authority uses the same method for all property of the same classification. For example, the taxable value of all new homes may be carried at 75% of the actual cost of land plus construction. The same community may value all office buildings at 95% of construction and all factories at 100% of construction cost. Occasionally factories will be valued at only 30% or 40% of the cost as a tax incentive to attract industry. Older homes are sometimes revalued. For example, a house that was built in 1920 for $6,000 might bring a sale price of $70,000 today. Of course, it would be unfair to owners of newer homes to pay higher taxes than owners of older homes, since both receive much the same services.

There is a move afoot to carry all property at 100% value. Each time a house is sold, the sale price will be entered on the tax rolls at the taxable value. New York is doing this as well as several other states. In the long run, this practice will probably raise taxes in rural communities, since the state will apply the same tax to equivalent values all over the state.

One of the uses of a building permit is that the taxing authority will be notified that improvements are being made to your home. If you add a new room or any other major improvement, you will find that your taxes increase. Normally, all or part of the cost of improvements will be added to your tax base.

> RULE: THE TAX RATE IS APPLIED
> TO THE TAX BASE TO DETERMINE
> PROPERTY TAX.

The tax rate is the actual dollars and cents you will pay per $1,000 value of your home or other property. For example, if you have a tax value (tax base) of $50,000 and the tax rate is .045 ($4.50 per $1,000), your real estate taxes would be $2,250 ($50,000 × .045 = $2,250).

If you are trying to modify any type of property tax in your community, you must consider both the tax base and the tax rate in your negotiations. It would do you little good to lower the tax rate only to find the tax base increased.

> RULE: YOU HAVE NO RIGHT TO DETERMINE
> DISTRIBUTION UNLESS THERE IS
> A REFERENDUM.

The constitutions of most lesser taxing authorities require that the people consent if that tax authority is going to issue bonds to pay for a project. Bonds are normally brought up for a referendum—the consent of the property owners who will be responsible for the debt. Referendums on school bonds and other types of municipal bonds can bring out the best and most exciting times a community has. Fifteen years ago the good citizens of Park Ridge, Illinois, twice defeated a bond issue to build a new high school. They felt that $18 million cost was excessive. They preferred that their school tax money be spent on instruction rather than repaying the cost of an elaborate building. Twice the architects went back and modified the design. The final product was a beautiful school costing $6.9 million. Because of the community's interest in how the money was spent, this school, Maine South, is now considered to be one of the best high schools in the country.

RULE: REAL ESTATE ASSESSMENTS CAN BE CHANGED.

In talking to your neighbors you may find that you're paying substantially more tax than they are. In such a case most tax authorities have a hearing board which considers your arguments regarding the overvaluation of your home. If you can show that your home is valued higher than other houses in the same area, they are likely to adjust the value. You may wish to hire an attorney to handle this matter for you. You may be able to argue the case well by yourself, but a local attorney may be privy to information about the community which you would find difficult to obtain.

RULE: SENIOR CITIZENS MAY BE ELIGIBLE FOR A REAL ESTATE TAX REDUCTION.

Many communities allow senior citizens to modify their taxes on reaching age 65. Somers, New York, reduces senior citizens' taxes by 50%. Other communities cancel the school tax portion. If you are 65 or over, the tax assessor's office at your local town hall will be able to assist you.

RULE: IF YOU DON'T PAY YOUR TAXES THEY TAKE AWAY YOUR PROPERTY.

If a property owner gets behind in his taxes for more than two or three years, the tax authority will put the owner on notice, giving him a specified time period (usually ninety days) to pay the back taxes. If the property owner cannot meet this demand, the tax authority will foreclose. The property will then be sold at auction, where it will probably not get the best price. The property owner will receive the proceeds of the sale after the back taxes are paid up. (See the chapter on debts and bankruptcy.)

Property taxes can be levied on the value of personal property you own. Personal property taxes are now fairly rare. Before the advent of state income taxes, personal property taxes were widely used by state governments. This type of tax has fallen into disuse since the income tax is a much more efficient type of tax collection.

RULE: PERSONAL PROPERTY TAXES
ARE LEVIED ON THE VALUE OF THE
PROPERTY YOU OWN.

Many people are confused by what personal property is. If it's attached to land, it's real estate or real property. If it's in any way portable, it's personal property. Florida, which does not have an income tax, levies a personal property tax against holdings of each resident as the property is valued on December 31 of every year. Florida limits its tax to stocks, bonds, and savings accounts. Other states may levy taxes on cars, home furnishings, jewelry, or any personal property of value. For example, in Florida, the taxpayer tells the state the dollar value of his stocks, bonds, and savings accounts on December 31, and multiplies this value by .001. The Florida tax is sensible, because the taxpayer can easily determine the value of his property. When personal property taxes are based on home furnishings, jewelry, etc., the possible decline in value makes the tax far more difficult to determine.

Personal property taxes are hard to collect. First of all, the taxpayer has to declare the value of his holdings. The state is unable to check his declaration without investigation. In the case of furniture and jewelry, the state may have to send an appraiser to determine the tax base for the personal property taxes. The cost of appraisal would probably exceed the amount of tax collected. Additionally, it's very easy for a taxpayer to hide his assets by holding them in another state.

If you live in one of the few states which still levy a personal property tax, you may challenge the valuation. You can have your own appraiser look at your property to see how accurate the state appraiser's estimate was. For example, the state appraiser may have wrongly decided that your Chippendale highboy was an American original. You know it to be a high-quality nineteenth-century copy. The American antique might be worth $25,000. The nineteenth-century copy would be worth only $1,000 to somebody who really wanted it. Normally, just a letter to the tax authority with your appraisal attached would handle the matter. The tax authority may also have a hearing board, but you probably won't have to go into that stage.

If dying isn't insult enough, the federal and state governments tax the dead person's assets through estate and inheritance taxes. Estate taxes are different from inheritance taxes. Estate taxes are levied by the federal government and by most states on the value of the holdings of the person on the date of his death. Inheritance taxes are paid by the heirs on the value of the property they receive. The states which levy taxes on the estate do not also tax the heir's inheritance. Sometimes a state will confuse the issue by calling its estate tax an inheritance tax.

RULE: EXECUTORS PAY ESTATE TAXES.

When someone dies, the property he leaves behind is called the estate. The estate becomes a legal entity of its own, just like a corporation is a legal entity. The executor is the person who is responsible for the estate. She has particular duties and privileges which are covered in the chapter on executors. One of the executor's responsibilities is to pay estate and inheritance taxes. The executor is held personally responsible for the payment of these taxes and the tax due can be collected from her personal assets if she fails to pay the taxes.

RULE: ESTATE TAXES ARE BASED
ON A PERCENTAGE OF THE
VALUE OF THE ESTATE.

The Tax Reform Act of 1975 rewrote the federal estate tax law. The most outstanding feature of the new federal law allows the spouse to inherit tax-free one half of the estate or $250,000, whichever is greater. The rest of the estate is taxed at escalating percentages based on the value of the estate. Then the estate tax has a tax credit subtracted from it. This tax credit partially takes the place of the old gift tax.

As an example of how taxes are computed, let's look at Raymond Jones and his family. Mr. Jones died in 1979, leaving an estate of $400,000. Of this, $250,000 passed to his wife tax-free. Tax was then computed on the $150,000 remaining, resulting in a tax of $38,800. A credit was subtracted against the tax due. The credit for 1979 is $38,000, leaving a tax due of only $800.

If Mr. Jones leaves the $150,000 in trust to his children, and leaves the $250,000 to his wife, Mrs. Jones will probably leave her $250,000 to her children. If this plan is followed, the estate taxes on her death will be $23,800. The combined taxes on the estates of Mr. and Mrs. Jones is $24,600.

Sometimes the husband will leave his whole estate to his wife. This distribution is fine if the estate is smaller than $250,000, but in larger estates, it can be very costly. If Mr. Jones had left everything to his wife, the taxes when Mrs. Jones died would be $74,800 for a total between them of $75,600. Leaving the whole estate to Mrs. Jones cost over $50,000.

The huge tax savings represented by leaving title of part of the estate to the children on the husband's death and part on the wife's death can be arranged through a pour-over will and trust combination. This estate-planning combination is discussed in the chapter on trusts.

You may think that $400,000 is an extraordinarily large estate. In my experience, it has not been remarkable for a family to accumulate this much in the course of a lifetime. The value of the home, life insurance, profit sharing, and savings can easily accumulate to this very substantial figure. If you do a financial statement of your assets and liabilities, you may be pleasantly surprised, even at a fairly young age.

RULE: GIFT TAXES ARE PART OF ESTATE TAXES.

Under the reformed estate tax laws, you may still give up to $3,000 a year to a person, and not have any tax consequences. You and your husband can each make a $3,000 gift, for a total of $6,000 a year. If you give more than this, you start to use up the estate tax credit discussed in the rule above. However, if you give more than $25,000 in a year's time, you will have to file a gift tax return.

RULE: INHERITANCE TAXES ARE LEVIED BY STATES.

Heirs pay inheritance tax. If you inherit $25,000 and go to the lawyer's office to pick it up, you may find the state tax man there too. The attorney may hand the tax man a check for your share of the taxes and give you a check for the balance. Or the executor may just send you your share and your $25,000 has magically become a smaller amount, say $22,500. Inheritance taxes are fairly rare, since states find it easier to follow the form of the federal estate tax.

Certainly taxes are the least-loved area of the law. Tax rebellion is foolhardy and yet nothing affects the quality of our daily life more than the substantial tax burden the American people carry. To the taxpayer, it often seems that the good guys can't win. In fact, taxpayers often win, but such suits are so expensive that usually only the rich can afford them. Political foment and your vote are the best ways to control your taxes.

Chapter 12
INSURANCE

Nearly six thousand years ago, a Babylonian merchant borrowed money to buy his stock in trade. He made a deal with the moneylender. If the ship carrying the goods were lost, the principal of the loan would be canceled. The moneylender agreed, but he raised the interest. This was the first insurance. It was called bottomry. The Hindus and Greeks used this too. The Romans added burial societies, an early type of life insurance. Marine (ship) insurance was perfected in the fifteenth century. The English developed fire insurance after the Great Fire of London in 1666. The famous Lloyd's of London was actually a coffeehouse which was popular with insurance men and bankers after the fire. The name Lloyd's became synonymous with underwriting—the practice insurers use to limit their losses by placing their risk contracts in a bigger group, a pool, so they can average their losses against each other. Pooling allows insurers greater predictability on the claims they must pay out.

Insurance has become more businesslike than coffeehouse meetings, but the basic principle remains the same. When you buy insurance, you are guaranteeing everybody in your insurance pool against the cost of a risk. The risk can be a lot of different things: the loss of life, loss by fire, car accidents, burglary, errors in your profession, or the mailman falling through your front steps. This list is infinite. If you want to insure against something, you can probably find an organization willing to assume your risk in exchange for a payment. According to Webster's Dictionary, risk is the chance of loss, damage, or injury. When the risk is an odd one, writing insurance is akin to gambling. If the risk is very normal, such as loss of life, insurance is a strict contractual agreement with almost no gambling aspect.

An insurance contract is an agreement between yourself and the insurance company that their own pool will take over your risk. The insurance company is really nothing but a clearinghouse between yourself and other people who want to pool their risks. Insurance companies can be operated for a profit, such as Aetna Life, or can be not-for-profit, such as Blue Cross, or they can be mutual associations, such as the Prudential Insurance Co. or Equitable Life Assurance. The price of insurance may be somewhat influenced by profit motives, but there is no guarantee that the not-for-profit or mutual company will have lower prices.

The cost of insurance is determined by how many persons out of a group are likely to suffer a particular type of loss within the year. If one house out of a thousand will burn down, the company can use this figure to determine how much your insurance will cost. One house out of a thousand translated into mathematics is one tenth of 1 per cent. If the value of your house and its contents is $60,000, it will cost the insurance company $60 to assume the risk ($60,000 $\times$ .001 = $60). Operating expenses will be added to the cost of risk to determine the price of your premium.

The cost of life insurance is determined in a similar fashion. Statistics are gathered as to how many people of a particular age will die every year. These statistics are put together to form the life-expectancy tables. The insurance companies use your age and these tables to decide how much it will cost them to assume the loss caused by your death. As you grow older, more and more people of your age group are likely to die, and therefore the cost of life insurance increases as one grows older. One of the most interesting elements of life-expectancy tables is that the older you get, the longer you are likely to live. For example, a man at age 62 may have a life expectancy of only four years. If the same man lives to age 66, he may have a life expectancy of an additional six years. If he reaches age 72, he may then have an additional life expectancy of five years. You can see from this that life expectancy does not mean that you will die at that time, only that of all persons of your category, more than half of them are likely to die before the life expectancy runs out. (Life expectancies are getting longer and depend on many factors, such as a person's occupation. The above figures are probably not true for you.)

The law of insurance is not very complex. Insurance is a private contract between the person buying the insurance, called the insured, and the person selling the insurance, called the insurer. Since these are professionally written contracts, there are very few lawsuits about what an insurance contract means. The parties can agree to any terms reasonable under the circumstances.

Many states have boards which regulate insurance companies that sell policies within their state. However, the primary function of these insurance regulators is to promote the financial stability of the companies, thereby protecting the interests of the insured persons.

RULE: INSURE THE BIG RISKS.

When deciding whether or not to get insurance, a person should weigh the dollar value of the loss in relationship to the cost of insuring against that loss.

Most people's homes represent a major portion of their personal assets. If the house burned to the ground, they would lose most of their money. Therefore, almost everyone insures his house against fire. On the other hand, the contents of the house may not be very valuable and the cost of carrying burglary insurance may outweigh the value of the contents which would be lost if they were to be burglarized.

By the same token, if the wage earner of a young family dies, the loss is very great. An older person without the responsibility for the care of children may have no need to insure against the loss of life, just as a young person with no family would need only enough life insurance to take care of burial.

Liability insurance has the purpose of paying for legal judgments against you as the result of an accident. For example, if a mailman fell on your icy steps, injuring his back, he might be unable to work for an extended period of time and he might sue you to recover on the damages to him. The damage award might be very high and cost you all of your assets. Since liability insurance is really very inexpensive, almost everyone carries it to protect himself from an unlikely risk which could be very costly. Liability insurance is written for homeowners, car owners, businesses, and just about anyone else subject to liability.

RULE: YOU MUST HAVE AN
INSURABLE INTEREST.

The only basic requirement for any kind of insurance is that you must have an interest in the person or property you are insuring. You must suffer a loss if the person dies or the property is destroyed. You need not own the property or be married to the person.

Courts have found insurable interests in someone's life based on family relationships or business relationships. Everyone has an insurable interest in his or her own life. Husbands and wives have insurable interests in each other, as do minor children in their parents, and vice versa. Beyond this level of family relationship, it could not be stated with absolute certainty that an insurable interest would be found without some particular extenuating circumstance.

Business relationships give rise to many insurance contracts. The creditor has an insurable interest in his debtor's life. A mortgage holder has an insurable interest in the property of the mortgage as well as in the life of the property owner. Business partners have an insurable interest in the lives of each of their partners, as does the corporation which carries life insurance on its key executives. If the party seeking the insurance would lose money because of the death of the insured, or if the insured property were destroyed, an insurable interest will be found. More subtle losses can also be insured. Losses due to an unfulfilled contract, because of the assumption of legal liability, or from the loss of property, whether or not it belongs to the insured, are all insurable. "Insurable interest" is rarely used to deny recovery if the insurance has been sought for a sensible purpose.

RULE: THE INSURANCE CONTRACT
TELLS YOU EVERYTHING.

Because insurance is a private agreement, you and the insurance company can decide what will be in the contract. In fact, many large businesses will negotiate extensively as to the terms of the contract. As consumers, we rarely negotiate, but just sign the contract as presented. The terms of the contract have been worked out through years of experience and are most often entirely fair.

Before you sign the contract, you should scan it to see if it states the amount of coverage you requested. If you read more deeply into the contract, you may be left with the impression that you are insured for almost nothing. When a legal contract is written, main clauses will be modified by other clauses which state when the insurance company will not pay on the insurance. You should concentrate on what the main clauses of the contract state. The insurance agent may be able to help you with the contract, but of course his explanation in no way modifies the written contract. You can also refer to this book's chapter on contracts, but I assure you that your insurance company's attorneys will have written a valid contract.

There is a move afoot in all states to require that all contracts be in plain language if a consumer is to sign them. This is to prevent consumer misunderstandings of the contract. The plain-language bill is being sponsored by the insurance companies themselves. By 1985, it is likely that all insurance contracts will be written in plain language.

The best indicator of a good insurance company is the practical experience of your friends and co-workers. If you have some experience in dealing with a particular insurance agent, and have found him trustworthy, you may also rely on his opinion. Or you may write to the insurance regulatory agency of your state government for a report on the insurance companies you are considering. It is also recommended that you find out the rating of the insurance companies from *Best's Reports*. Their rating system runs from A+ down to C, with A+ as the highest rating. This rating is a combination of various elements which indicate the financial stability of the companies you are considering. The more stable the insurance company, the more likely you are able to collect on your loss.

Life insurance is used to protect a family against the premature death of one of its members. If the member is a wage earner, the loss will be greater than if the member is a child. The amount of life insurance contracted for will depend on the amount of loss the family will suffer if the person dies and on the family's budget for insurance. For example, a person may determine that if he or she died before the children reached age 21, the family would need living expenses plus the cost of the children's college educations. This may require $150,000 in income over a period of years. This income can be drawn from a number of different sources. Social Security is the most basic of these. Practically every wage earner is covered, often very substantially. One should refer to the chapter on Social Security for more information in this area. In addition to Social Security most people have life insurance at their work. They also have personal assets and probably some type of insurance to cover the mortgage payments on their house. The amount of insurance which must then be purchased is substantially reduced when all other assets are considered. The insured may discover that he needs to carry only $40,000 or $50,000 in individual life insurance in order to meet his goals.

The family's budget for life insurance must also be considered. It is possible that the ideal amount of life insurance simply couldn't be afforded. In such a case many different sources could be investigated for the best combination of coverage and price. For example, many credit unions offer no-cost life insurance along with their savings accounts. The life insurance coverage may be as high as double the amount of the money on account. This is a fine way to double or triple one's assets in case of premature death. Many fraternal organizations offer low-cost life insurance to their members, as do unions and professional organizations.

Life insurance comes in three different types: term, whole life, and endowment insurance.

RULE: TERM INSURANCE IS WRITTEN FOR A SPECIFIC PERIOD.

Term insurance is usually the least expensive type of insurance coverage. Everyone who owns a home should have term insurance to cover the amount of mortgage principal outstanding. Term insurance is written for a specified period in exchange for the payment of a premium. For example, one might purchase $10,000 in term insurance for a five-year period. The insured would have the option of paying for the whole thing at the beginning, paying for it annually, or even every month.

As long as the insured person is paid up, the policy will pay his beneficiaries the specified amount if he dies within the term. For example, if someone has $10,000 of term insurance for a five-year term, he must die within the five-year period in order to collect the insurance.

Term insurance comes in two varieties: level term and decreasing term. Under level-term insurance both the proceeds and the premium are a stable amount for the entire period of the contract. Decreasing-term insurance proceeds and premiums may get smaller and smaller as the period continues. Decreasing term is often used to cover a home mortgage, because the amount of the mortgage steadily decreases as time passes. It is also used as college education insurance for the children. As each of them finishes his education, less and less insurance is needed.

RULE: STRAIGHT LIFE INSURANCE IS PURCHASED FOR A WHOLE LIFETIME.

Term insurance becomes increasingly more expensive as a person gets older. Straight life insurance ordinarily maintains the same premium price as long as the person keeps the insurance. In addition to this, straight life insurance has a built-in savings account. As more premiums are paid, the savings account grows, and along with it, the ability to borrow money on the policy increases. The insured person can take loans from the insurance company at a low rate of interest, usually specified in the contract. Straight life insurance is also called whole life or ordinary life. If premiums are to be paid over a specific period, such as thirty years or until age 65, the insurance is called limited-payment life insurance.

If someone has straight life insurance, she is insured for the face value of the policy whether she's been paying for it one month or thirty years. If she wishes to cancel the life insurance, her savings account in the insurance will be returned to her. This type of insurance has the additional advantage of paying for itself after a certain period elapses. If enough savings have accrued, you can assign the interest to pay for the premiums.

RULE: ENDOWMENT INSURANCE COMBINES LIFE
INSURANCE AND PENSION PLAN.

Endowment insurance is primarily a pension plan which adds life insurance as an extra advantage. The primary purpose of the endowment plan is to provide regular income upon retirement and should not be purchased for the insurance factor alone, since the cost is so high. Under an endowment policy, life insurance is provided for a certain number of years, usually to age 65. After age 65 the person has a choice of taking the whole amount in the savings portion or taking monthly payments over a period of years. If you're interested in the pension aspect, the IRA and Keogh plans with a savings bank are currently a better investment. Keogh and IRA plans are discussed in the chapter on taxes.

These are the basic types of life insurance policies and all policies will fit into one of these categories. Insurance is a very broad field, and each company's policies will vary slightly. These policies may combine one or more aspects of any of these basic types. Regardless of the type, all life insurance policies have certain basic contract provisions. These provisions are standard, and many are regulated by state insurance boards.

RULE: GIVE THE POLICY AWAY.

All life insurance can be transferred (assigned) to another person, unless there is a policy provision which forbids it. There are two types of assignment available: absolute assignment and collateral assignment. In absolute assignment, all interests the insured owns can be given away. Collateral assignment is more limited, since the only type of assignment available may be the ability to take out a loan on the insurance. The only type of assignment which is desirable is absolute assignment.

According to the Internal Revenue Code, LIFE INSURANCE CAN PASS TOTALLY FREE OF ESTATE TAXES if all the requirements are satisfied. The insured must give away all "incidents of ownership" more than three years before his or her death. The only part which will be taxable is the premiums paid in the three years preceding death. Under most circumstances this amount will be insignificant in relationship to the proceeds of the life insurance.

The incidents of ownership which you must give away forever to satisfy the IRS are: (1) the right to change the beneficiary, (2) the right to surrender the policy for cash, (3) the right to borrow money on the policy, (4) the right to collect dividends, (5) the right to designate the type of settlement option. If you do not have the right to absolute assignment, you will not be able to satisfy these requirements. All of these rights must be given away permanently (irrevocably) to your primary beneficiary, usually the spouse.

These incidents of ownership may be given away at any time, as long as it is more than three years prior to the insured's death. However, if you kept the policy long enough before making the gift so that the savings feature builds to more than $3,000, the gift will modify your estate taxes. It is best to give away the policy in its early years for the estate tax reason.

You may not currently have enough assets to worry about estate taxes, but you don't know how much you'll be worth twenty years from now. So be sure you're entitled to make an absolute assignment, so you can use it if you need to.

This donation of the rights to the insurance policy should be done on at least one of the family's policies. Most people have some sort of life insurance with their employer which will become part of the decedent's estate anyway. In addition to estate tax advantages, giving away your rights in the policy will also help your family in the months after your death, since the insurance will not become part of your probate estate.

RULE: YOU HAVE 31 DAYS
TO PAY YOUR BILL.

Practically all insurance policies allow a "grace period," the amount of time that you can be late with your payment without the policy lapsing. In most policies, the grace period is thirty-one days, but you'll want to check the policy to be sure this is true for you.

RULE: INSURANCE CAN BE REINSTATED.

Most policies allow the insured to start up the policy again, even if he hasn't paid the premium for a rather long time. The reinstatement clause in the policy will tell you how long you have to start the policy back up again. Reinstatement clauses allow for periods as long as three years after you have let the policy lapse. All you have to do is pay up the back payments and the policy goes back into effect as though you never missed a single payment. Reinstating a lapsed policy should always be considered first if you are seeking additional coverage. It may be cheaper to pay up the back payments due than to start out all over again. There may be hidden charges for starting a new policy, but usually none for reinstating an old one. In addition, you'll have to pay a higher premium on a new policy, because you're older.

RULE: INSURANCE COMPANIES CAN DELAY PAYMENT.

State regulatory agencies require insurance companies to include a clause in the contract allowing them to delay payment for some period, usually six months. This delay clause is to protect the financial stability of the insurance company in times of national economic distress, when the insurance company's investments may have diminished value. This delay clause is very rarely used by an insurance company.

RULE: THE INSURANCE COMPANY MAY NOT CONTEST THE CLAIM.

Most policies provide that the insurance company cannot cancel the insurance due to errors, misstatements, or even fraud if the policy has been in effect a stated period of time, usually two years. This clause allows the beneficiaries an absolute right to collect if the policy has been in effect for the required length of time.

RULE: SUICIDE MIGHT NOT CANCEL THE INSURANCE.

Many policies have a suicide clause which automatically cancels the insurance if the insured commits suicide within two years of the date of issue. The premiums paid are returned to the beneficiary appointed in the policy. If the insured person commits suicide more than two years after the issue of the policy, the insurance company has to pay the entire benefit.

RULE: YOU CAN BORROW MONEY ON YOUR POLICY.

All straight life policies can be used as collateral on a loan. The loan limit will be the paid-up value of the insurance. When the money is borrowed from the insurance company, it is really an advance on the life insurance itself. This advance does not have to be repaid and will be deducted from the death benefit before the beneficiary collects it. The interest rate on these loans is generally stated in the contract. These loan provisions should be investigated as part of the advantages available under a straight life policy. It's not unusual for a policy loan to cover part of a house down payment or the kids' college educations.

Another type of loan which may be available is an automatic premium loan which pays the premiums if the insured person is unable to pay. Though this automatic premium loan provision is not ordinarily included, it will be added at no extra cost if you request it. This provision is desirable, since it may carry your life insurance intact through periods of illness or unemployment.

RULE: THE POLICY TELLS YOU HOW
TO APPOINT THE BENEFICIARIES.

All beneficiaries must be appointed by the official process which the insurance company outlines in the policy. Beneficiaries are appointed when the policy is first purchased. The beneficiary is the person who will receive the proceeds if the insured dies while the policy is in effect. The primary beneficiary is usually the spouse. Secondary beneficiaries are appointed in case the primary beneficiary is not alive when the insured person dies. Secondary beneficiaries are usually the couple's children. Secondary beneficiaries are also called contingent beneficiaries.

Beneficiaries may usually be changed. Most policy owners appoint revocable (changeable) beneficiaries. The policy owner may also appoint an irrevocable (unchangeable) beneficiary. There is an estate tax advantage with the irrevocable beneficiary, but his or her signature will be required if the insured wants a loan on the policy. If the insured wishes to change a revocable beneficiary, he may do so at any time without the beneficiary's consent. An irrevocable beneficiary cannot be changed.

The insurance contract states specifically how changes will be made. Ordinarily policies require that the insured send in an official change-of-beneficiary form along with the contract itself. The beneficiary is then changed on the face of the policy.

If the beneficiary refuses to give up the policy so the insured can make the change, there are cases which hold that the change-of-beneficiary form is adequate. The insured must have made every attempt short of burglary to fulfill the contract requirements for changing beneficiaries. It's best to adhere to the insurance company's procedure so that the insurance proceeds are not held up while the insurance company gets a court order directing who is to receive the proceeds.

By the same token, the insured cannot change an insurance

beneficiary in his will. Insurance is a contract, independent of the will, and can only be modified by an amendment to the contract itself.

When a beneficiary is appointed, it is customary to add a descriptive term to the beneficiary's name, such as "creditor," "wife," "fiancé." This description shows the insurable interest. In life insurance the insurable interest arises under the relationship that exists at the time the policy was issued. Even though that relationship may cease, due to divorce or an end of a business relationship, the policy will remain in effect as long as the premiums are paid. Your insurance agent may also recommend that your beneficiaries be appointed with the reservation that they survive you for thirty days or more. This rule is to prevent the life insurance proceeds from flowing through two estates and being taxed twice, and is called a simultaneous death provision. It will protect your family in case you and your spouse are killed in the same accident.

Life insurance contracts may also contain an aviation clause which suspends payment of the policy if the insured is killed in an airplane accident. Most of the policies containing such provisions are quite old, and this provision is rarely included in more modern contracts. If insurers see war on the horizon, they will start to include war clauses in the insurance contracts of young men. War clauses suspend payment if the insured is killed in a war.

RULE: THE INSURANCE COMPANY CANNOT KEEP YOUR SAVINGS.

State statutes require that your savings be returned to you if you decide to cancel a straight life insurance contract. These elements about to be discussed are not applicable to term insurance. If you elect to cancel, the insurance company must give you back the savings feature if you have been paying premiums for some period, usually three years. Some policies will return your money after the first or second year. If you take all of your cash back, the policy will be canceled.

If you don't need your cash, you have other alternatives. The contract may allow you the option of choosing a reduced amount of paid-up life insurance in exchange for your cash value. For example, you may have been paying premiums for five years on $40,000 of life insurance when you choose to end the policy. You can leave the money in, and depending on your age, the policy will continue, but for a lesser amount of insurance. The amount of insurance coverage will be determined by your age and the amount you paid in prior to conversion of the policy.

You may also have the option of choosing paid-up term insurance for the face value of the policy. For example, your $10,000 face value policy may provide you with six and a half years of paid-up term insurance of $10,000. If you're finding the premiums a heavy financial burden, you may wish to choose this particular option. Under the paid-up term insurance option you maintain the same coverage for some period of time without the responsibility of the premium.

RULE: INVESTIGATE YOUR CHOICES
FOR THE DIVIDENDS.

Some insurance policies grant policy holders a type of interest which the insurance companies call "dividends." You will want to investigate which options you have according to the contract.

Cash dividends are the most common type. The policy holder receives a check for cash dividends. If you are insured by a mutual insurance company, the amount is not taxable, since it isn't really income. Mutual insurance dividends are a return of part of your premiums. If you receive what amounts to savings account interest, it is taxable. If the insurance company sends you an IRS Form 1099, it indicates that your dividends are taxable.

You may also take the option of leaving your dividends with the insurance company to accumulate the interest. This amount is not income-taxable while it is being accumulated, but will be taxable if you receive the proceeds later, such as in an endowment policy.

You may also choose for your dividends to buy you more insurance. The dividends may be accumulated to provide small paid-up amounts in addition to your ordinary policy. The amounts can also add a temporary term insurance to the policy.

You will want to investigate your policies to see which of these options might be available to you. You may also find that your accumulated dividends might bring you more interest in another kind of institution, such as a savings bank.

RULE: YOU DECIDE HOW THE BENEFICIARY
GETS THE MONEY.

The most common type of insurance settlement is a lump-sum payment. With a lump-sum payment the insurance company simply pays the beneficiary the face value of the policy plus accumulated amounts. However, there are other settlement options available.

The interest settlement option agrees to pay a specific interest on the face value of the policy if the beneficiary leaves the lump sum with the insurance company. The policy may guarantee a 2.5 or 3 per cent interest rate on the insurance proceeds and will pay an additional amount if the company is making a good return on their investments. The additional amount may be another 2.5 per cent. Most savings banks are now paying 7.5 to 8 per cent interest, so this particular option is not currently desirable.

You can also elect that a certain amount be paid per month to the beneficiary until the funds are exhausted (a fixed-amount option). Each payment is partly principal and partly interest. Additionally, it may be taxable as income to the beneficiary. Fixed-amount options should be critically investigated before choosing this method. The fixed-period option is very much the same, except that the insurance company guarantees to pay over a specified period of time.

There are also a great number of choices which guarantee some amount of income for the life of the beneficiary. The choices here are practically infinite. The beneficiary will receive a monthly payment based on his or her life expectancy. The longer the life expectancy, the smaller the payment will be.

It is recommended that a policy owner *not* exercise any of these options. Many things can change between the time of the option and the time of death. The beneficiary is free to exercise any one of these options if the insured has allowed for it.

RULE: THE BENEFICIARY COLLECTS
THE PROCEEDS.

In the normal course of events, it is usually the beneficiary who actually collects the life insurance. Often the insured will give the written policy to the beneficiary, or the beneficiary is the spouse and he or she will know the whereabouts of the policy. The insurance agent or a representative of the insurance company will help the beneficiary fill out the required forms. The forms, the policy, and a certified copy of the death certificate are sent to the insurance company. After the company has approved payment, the insurance company will issue a check to the beneficiary. If the beneficiary is a minor, the company will issue the check to the guardian of the minor beneficiary. The insurance company may pay off very quickly, perhaps even two weeks after death, although a month is not uncommon.

Insurance companies usually request that the policy be sent in with the claim form, but there is no legal requirement that you do so. The insurance companies collect the policies in order to prevent duplicate claims on the same policy. (Duplicate claims are usually mere errors.

The executor of a deceased woman's estate finds a policy on her long-deceased husband's life. The executor is duty-bound to try to collect.)

Property insurance is quite different from life insurance. Life insurance is written on the life of a person and requires no responsibility on the part of the insured to do anything in particular. Property insurance is a personal contract between the insurer and the property owner, who promises to take normal precautions to guard his own property. In life insurance the insurable interest need only exist at the time the insurance is purchased. In property insurance the insurable interest must exist at the time the damage occurs. There are two basic kinds of property insurance. The most obvious sort is property insurance (fire, theft, etc.), which reimburses the property owner for all or part of his cost. The other type is liability insurance, which pays for injuries received to others as a result of problems which occur on or are caused by the insured's property.

Property insurance comes in five basic types, ranging from insurance which pays for only limited kinds of damage to insurance which pays for any type of damage which might be inflicted. The all-risk type of coverage will have certain types of damages excepted from coverage, such as earthquakes in California or tidal waves in Miami. Special insurance riders can be added to cover damage due to these "acts of God."

Homeowner's policies generally pay a replacement value for real estate damages. For example, if your house is destroyed, the insurance company will pay you its cost multiplied by the increased cost of house construction since the house was built. The personal furnishings are insured at their depreciated value—that is, their value after they have been used. Unless you buy special personal property riders, the amount of personal property insurance included in a homeowner's policy is only one half the value of the real estate. For example, if you have an $80,000 insurance policy on your home, your personal possessions will be automatically insured at $40,000 or their depreciated value, whichever is less. It's very important to insure your home for its current construction cost plus a little extra for appreciation over the next few years. If you don't do this, the replacement cost provision may not apply.

RULE: CARRY HEAVY LIABILITY INSURANCE.

All homeowner's or renter's policies contain some type of liability coverage. It may be a small amount, such as $25,000. This liability insurance covers you both for attorney's fees to defend against personal injury actions and for the judgments which the court might bring against you. Unfortunately, personal injury judgments in excess of a million dollars are no longer uncommon. If the judgment exceeds your liability insurance, the injured party can collect the judgment against your personal assets and your salary, perhaps for the rest of your life. For these reasons it is imperative to carry extraordinary amounts of liability insurance. Fortunately liability insurance is probably the best buy on the insurance market. This liability insurance rule applies most especially to automobile insurance.

RULE: BE READY TO PROVE YOUR LOSS.

It is relatively simple to prove the damage to a house which has been destroyed by fire, but it is far more difficult to prove damage to your household goods. It may take you months to remember all of the things that burned up in the fire. The best way to protect against this is to take a complete inventory of your household goods. This inventory should include all of the items in your household, how much you paid for them, and the year in which they were purchased. This inventory can be updated periodically to include new items you acquire. The inventory should be done on a room-to-room basis, so that all kitchen items are together, all living-room items, all bedroom items, etc. Your insurance agent will probably have inventory forms for you to use. Keep the inventory in a safe-deposit box, and never in your house. If you have a fire, the inventory may go up in smoke as well. The inventory has the additional value of showing you how much your household goods should be insured for. You may be quite surprised at how much you have accumulated over your life.

RULE: CARRY SPECIAL POLICIES
FOR VALUABLE ITEMS.

Valuable items like silver, jewelry, furs, coin collections, paintings, etc., will have a small limited coverage under your policy. If you feel you wish to insure against the loss of these items by either theft or fire, have the items appraised and carry a special rider to cover them. The amount paid will be the amount of the appraised value, as opposed to the depreciated value for most personal items. This type of insurance is rather expensive, and you may want to consider putting these things in a safe-deposit vault in lieu of paying the high premiums. I know a woman who is the proud possessor of a fortune in diamond jewelry. She has had facsimiles made of her favorite pieces. The real stuff is in the vault and the facsimiles are in her jewelry box. Nobody seems to know the difference.

RULE: YOU MUST KEEP YOUR HOUSE SAFE.

The insurance company is entitled to suspend or reduce your coverage if you leave the house unattended beyond a certain period, usually thirty days. Losses due to vandalism and accidental water damage will not be recoverable unless you make a special arrangement with your insurance broker. He can cover you while you go to Florida for the winter, but it will require a special effort.

If you store hazardous materials, your coverage will also be suspended. For example, an extraordinary amount of gasoline or paint in your basement will substantially increase the hazards of fire. The insurance company did not agree to the risk of special hazards, and so hazards must be specially insured for. The insurance company will send out an inspector to see what precautions you have taken to protect your family and your property from the risk of fire.

RULE: PROPERTY INSURANCE HAS
NO GRACE PERIOD.

If you do not pay your premium on time, your property insurance expires. If you suffer loss after the date of expiration, the insurance company is not obligated to pay you anything.

RULE: INSURE YOUR HOUSE BEFORE
YOU CLOSE THE DEAL.

When you buy a home, be sure that you have fire and vandalism insurance which starts immediately with the closing of the sale. If the house is destroyed between the time you signed the papers and the time you move in, you may have no recourse unless you've insured prior to the closing on the house.

Auto insurance is another type of property insurance, but is usually separate from the homeowner's policy due to the special risks involved. The normal insurance policy covers all persons who drive the automobiles which the family owns. If a member of the family has an accident in a car the family doesn't own, he will also be covered, except when he is driving a car which is a public conveyance, such as a taxi or limousine, or when the car has been rented. It is mandatory to carry separate collision and liability insurance if you rent a car. You buy this at the time you rent the car.

RULE: CONSIDER DROPPING COLLISION INSURANCE.

Collision, the damage to the automobile in an accident, is the most expensive part of most people's auto insurance. If the car is older, it is possible that its value has diminished to such a point that the collision insurance is more expensive than the car itself. If your car is three to five years old, you can consider dropping collision without much financial harm to yourself. However, in no instance should you reduce your liability insurance.

RULE: REPORT YOUR LOSS IMMEDIATELY.

If you suffer damage to property, regardless of the cause, you should report the occurrence as quickly as possible to the fire department, police, and most especially your insurance agent. Many insurance companies maintain a twenty-four-hour claims service. Your loss should be reported immediately, so that your insurance company can inspect the premises. Indeed, your insurance may have a clause requiring notification within a specified period of the discovery of the loss. Notification within a week will always be adequate. Only a phone call will be required.

When you've reported the loss, the insurance company swings into motion. If you've been in an auto accident, they contact the insurance company of the person who hit you. Between the two of them, they decide who will pay what. In all likelihood your only further function will be taking your car to the required number of garages to get estimates of the cost of repair.

There is much agitation to pass "no-fault" auto insurance—a way of making sure the accident victim is compensated. Blame is not assigned according to who did what bad thing; rather, the emphasis is on compensating the victim. At this time only Puerto Rico and Massachusetts have adopted these measures. It is generally argued that no-fault insurance would be very expensive. A few more states require liability insurance (Massachusetts, New York, and North Carolina). More states have a fund to pay unsatisfied auto liability judgments (New Jersey, North Dakota, South Carolina, and Virginia). All other states lie in between, requiring insurance after the first accident or posting a bond after the first accident. Alaska is the exception. It has no auto liability legislation, but with such a small population in such a big area, it may not be necessary.

RULE: PROPERTY INSURANCE CANNOT
BE GIVEN AWAY.

Life insurance can be given away to any person the insured appoints. Property insurance, whether it be fire, theft, or auto, is in effect only while the person owns the insured property. The insured cannot sell the insurance along with the property. One should be careful that the insured person and the registered owner of the property are one and the same. A recent case denied recovery when the insurance was held by one member of the family and the title of the car by another member.

Like every other form of insurance, nothing is more important than health insurance when you need it. Most people are covered at their work. However, if you must buy private health insurance, it can be outrageously expensive.

One way to handle the expense of health insurance is a concept called self-insurance. You decide how much risk you are willing to take. For example, you may decide you can afford to lose $2,000 in hospital expenses before the insurance starts to pick up the tab. (This figure is arrived at since health insurance for a 35-year-old single woman will cost around $600 a year. Three years at $600 is $1,800. The insured takes a risk that hospitalization will not happen over the next three years.) If you don't get sick, the $2,000 will remain in your own pocket or your savings account. If you lose the wager with yourself and end up in the hospital, you have to pay out the money you saved by not carrying full hospitalization insurance. A major medical policy can be purchased to pick up most of the cost above $2,000. This type of insurance is much less expensive, running about $80 a year.

RULE: INSURANCE COMPANIES PAY
REASONABLE COST.

The biggest of the health insurance companies are the Blue Cross–Blue Shield Associations. The Blue Cross Associations have a different organization for every state. They keep records of average charges for each type of service rendered. Their reimbursement will depend on the average charge. They won't pay ridiculously high bills for the medical service rendered. Blue Cross itself is a hospital plan which normally provides seventy days of semi-private hospital care plus other specified hospital services. Other insurance plans vary from this slightly. Blue Shield pays for surgery and some doctor's services. An al-

ternative to Blue Shield coverage is the relatively new Health Maintenance Organization (HMO). The insured person and his family contracts with the HMO for medical services exclusive of the hospital
costs. The HMO then provides physicians to handle every kind of family illness, generally regardless of its type. For example, the HMO will
provide pediatric care, obstetric care, normal health checkups, emergency treatment, and even common surgery such as appendectomies,
broken legs, and run-of-the-mill health emergencies. The HMO is a
very good investment for a family. A healthy single person may find the
price rather high.

RULE: DIVORCED WOMEN CARRY THEIR OWN HEALTH INSURANCE.

Group medical insurance normally covers a worker's family and his
dependents. The definition of dependent varies from one insurance plan
to the other, but will always include the worker, the spouse, and their
unmarried dependent children below a particular age, usually age 19 to
23. The definition may also include dependent parents and handicapped children of any age, but this is less ordinary.

If there is a divorce, a non-working spouse can end up with no insurance, since the divorce cancels the relationship covered by the insurance. The children will continue to be insured, since the divorce didn't
change the fact that they are the worker's children. However, a worker
may need to pay a small additional sum to insure the children. If he
ceases to do this, their insurance will drop. The ex-wife will have to
find her own insurance or go to work for an employer who will provide
it for her.

RULE: EXERCISE YOUR RENEWAL PROVISION.

If you are leaving your work, you may find it slightly less expensive
to pick up an individual health insurance contract through your former
employer's insurance. If you've had no experience with buying individual health insurance, the cost may astound you. You will want to consider whether or not the policies you are examining contain the following elements.

The renewal provisions give you the right to continue your health
coverage from one period to another. This right to continue is important should you develop a chronic health condition which may require
a great deal of care. If you cannot automatically renew the policy, the
insurer may find you unattractive and cancel.

Many health care policies refuse to pay for health problems due to accidents or sickness which occurred prior to the beginning of the policy. Group health plans such as one gets at work usually do not include such a clause. Private health plans normally cannot deny coverage on a pre-existent health condition if the policy has been in effect for two or three years. However, the health plan can avoid covering this if it specifically excludes that illness or injury from your coverage.

Much like life insurance, health insurance may continue despite misstatements if the policy has been in effect for a two- or three-year period. In other words, the insurance company has to catch you before the period expires or they are your insurer for good. You are also allowed a grace period—the amount of time you can be late with your payment. The grace period can be fifteen to thirty days, depending on the policy of the company. You are also required to make your claim on the company in a timely fashion, usually within three months, but this ninety-day limit will be extended if you could not reasonably make the claim within the ninety-day period.

It's often said that this is an age of insurance. We can buy insurance for practically anything, whether it be errors in our profession, such as malpractice insurance, or accidents we have, such as falling through an empty manhole. Indeed, insurance is so pervasive that the government conducts a large number of insurance functions. The most widespread of these plans is Social Security.

I've heard people say, "You can never have too much insurance." This statement is especially true for liability insurance, since the cost is insignificant in comparison to the protection. However, straight life insurance is not the most profitable investment which is available. Insurance is only one type of savings to help you plan for the future. You also need ordinary savings and perhaps some investments.

An insurance agent can be an important asset to your family. He may actually do more to help you than any other type of consultant, such as a lawyer or an accountant. To find the very best one, consult three or more, lay out your financial situation and what you want, and listen to what they have to say. The guy who comes up with the most coverage for the least amount of money will probably be the best for you. I once had an auto accident in a remote place. My insurance agent contacted my family, gave them a report on my health, and arranged everything. He performed an important service at a difficult time. If you can find a similar person who is genuinely interested in the welfare of his or her clients, you may have found a friend who will last a lifetime.

Chapter 13
INVESTMENT LAW

This chapter is about the law of money, keeping money safe, and investing it. Fortunately, investment law is rarely a problem. Banks and stockbrokerage firms tend to be highly responsible and conservative, and surprisingly few individuals lose money through the error of investment or banking firms.

At least part of the reason for this stability has to do with the quality of money itself.

RULE: MONEY IS ONLY AN IDEA.

Money is not based on any concrete principle. In the United States, our money is no longer exchangeable for gold or silver. It probably wouldn't make any difference if it were, since gold and silver themselves have no particular value, except a traditional acceptance as valuable metals. Gold and silver can be manufactured into a product, or they can be exchanged for other goods. So money is nothing more than a means of exchange. If our society accepted cowry shells as an item for exchange, cowry shells would be money.

If we are to exchange goods freely, we must be able to exchange goods for a stable and portable item. If you wanted to buy a chicken and had to barter your goods for it, you might have a difficult time finding someone with a chicken who wants something you are willing to give in exchange for the chicken. The process of buying a chicken is greatly simplified if you and the chicken owner can trust the idea of money enough to use it as your means of exchange.

RULE: FINANCIAL INSTITUTIONS
ARE BASED ON TRUST.

Because money has no intrinsic value except that which people are willing to assign it, banks and stockbrokers intuitively know that their clients must trust the institution which keeps their money. Therefore bankers, and to a lesser degree stockbrokers, tend to conduct themselves by conservative standards, so as not to insult anyone's idea of trustworthiness.

To help the money industries stay trustworthy, they and the federal government have formed many supervisory and regulatory commissions. These commissions guide and discipline the money institutions. The end product of these commissions is greater public confidence in the money firms.

In the banking industry, the primary regulator is the Federal Reserve Bank (the Fed). The Fed requires that a certain percentage of the bank's deposits be held in reserve—in other words, not loaned out. The percentage of required reserve will change, depending on the Fed's current economic policy. The Fed also sets interest rates. Along with other federal and state agencies, the Fed inspects banks, regulates banking practice, and publicly criticizes individual banks when they refuse to comply with the regulations. Since the banking industry is based on trust, criticism by a banking regulator can destroy the bank's ability to do business.

The stockbrokers are self-regulating, which means that they have set up their own watchdogs. Above these industry watchdogs sits the Federal Trade Commission (FTC), which acts as a further check on the brokerage industry. Brokerage customer problems rarely go as far as the FTC.

Because of good regulation, banks rarely abuse their position. They do, however, make errors. As a general rule, the bank is responsible for its errors.

RULE: THE BANK IS RESPONSIBLE FOR
DAMAGE TO YOUR CREDIT.

If a bank deposits your money in somebody else's account, and then bounces your checks, it has committed an error. Of course, the bank has to give you credit for the money you deposited. The bank must also write letters to the persons to whom you wrote the bounced checks. The bank has damaged your credit reputation by wrongfully bouncing your checks and is responsible for rectifying the damage by sending letters of apology to the recipients of the bounced checks. If it doesn't write these letters of apology, you can sue for breach of contract and slander of credit.

RULE: YOU ARE ONLY ENTITLED TO
THE MONEY YOU DEPOSIT.

If the bank makes an error in your favor, and deposits someone else's money in your account, you'd better leave the money there. If you spend the money, you could be charged with theft. In a recent case, a New York bank accidentally deposited $1,100,000 in a man's account. He drew out the money and left for Finland. When he was caught, he had only $700,000 left. He was brought back to the United States and charged with theft. This case is unusual since so much money changed hands. In an ordinary case, the whole procedure would be handled informally with a phone call.

RULE: BANK ACCOUNTS ARE INSURED.

The Federal Deposit Insurance Corporation (FDIC) insures bank deposits up to $40,000 for one individual in one bank. If the individual keeps more than $40,000 in a bank, he or she can transfer the excess over $40,000 to another bank and get insurance there.

In the rare case of bank failure, the FDIC has the choice of paying off the depositor or selling the bank. The depositor might have to wait a week or two while this decision is being made. In the end, the depositor will get every dime of deposits under $40,000.

RULE: THE BANK IS RESPONSIBLE
FOR EMBEZZLEMENT.

Sometimes a dishonest bank employee will embezzle money from customers. The employee is most likely to embezzle from inactive savings accounts. The bank is totally responsible for paying you what you deposited, and it must make good the interest and principal in your account.

When you open an account, the bank makes a promise to pay all amounts you deposit. The promise can be unconditional (a checking account) or conditional (a long-term savings account).

RULE: THE BANK IS RESPONSIBLE
FOR FORGERIES.

The bank cannot pay any checks on your account except the ones you write. If someone forges your name or alters one of your checks, the bank is responsible for detecting the crime. If the bank does not detect the crime before it pays out the money, the bank has to put enough money into your account to make up for the error.

The bank which paid the forged check then becomes a "holder in due course," meaning it must absorb the risk of honoring a forged check. It will be up to the bank to get the money back. For example, a California bank presented a forged check to your New York bank and the New York bank paid it. When you inform your New York bank that the check has been forged, the New York bank, in its role as a holder in due course, can ask the California bank for its money back. It's ultimately up to the California bank to press charges against the forger.

RULE: BALANCE YOUR CHECKBOOK.

If the bank doesn't know it has made an error, it won't be able to do anything about it. You can't tell the bank about errors if you don't balance your checkbook.

Most bank bookkeeping is computerized. The computer can make many errors if it is fed incorrect information or the computer program isn't adequate. Sometimes bank errors can be astounding. One woman had her personal check bounced because a check she had deposited hadn't cleared yet. The bank charged $5.00 for a check returned due to uncollected funds, but the computer charged her sixteen times for this one check, bringing the total charge to $80. The bank fixed it up, but it took time. If she hadn't inspected the monthly bank statement, she wouldn't have discovered the error.

Banking has been operating in its current form for over five hundred years. The industry has had much experience and has used this experience to work out ways to handle problems. Most of the problems are handled informally. The consumer rarely needs to do more than phone or visit to have a problem rectified.

Stockbrokerage is a newer business than banking, but it is well organized and surprisingly honest. At least twenty-five million shares of corporate stock are traded daily, and there are far fewer errors and disputes than one would expect.

RULE: STOCKBROKERAGES ARE SELF-REGULATING.

The stockbrokerage regulators are oriented toward protecting the consumer. Stock prices are subject to many factors. One way the industry avoids depression in stock prices is by cleaning its own house of dishonest operators.

The New York Stock Exchange, the American Stock Exchange, and the over-the-counter traders each regulates its own market. They gather evidence of wrongdoing and have arbitration boards which settle disputes between brokers and customers. If the broker makes too many errors or is guilty of dishonesty, the broker will lose his seat on the exchange. He won't be able to trade stock.

If a customer feels she has been wronged, the broker is likely to make the damage good without any arbitration. Too much arbitration is a symptom of a sloppy broker, and the industry will discipline him. Examples of customer complaints are: the broker not selling when ordered, not buying when ordered, misuse of customer funds, paying too slowly, and bad investment advice. The consumer is generally protected from these errors by a very sophisticated set of safeguards.

RULE: THE BROKER MUST GIVE YOU
APPROPRIATE INVESTMENT ADVICE.

The brokerage industry insists that brokers use good judgment when advising clients. The broker has the responsibility to examine whether his or her suggestions are suitable for the client's overall welfare. Any suggestions the broker makes must fulfill the suitability requirement. For example, a broker cannot advise an unsophisticated person to place a large part of her money into a particular risky growth stock. Advising the same stock to a more sophisticated investor might be suitable.

Of course, investors can order a broker to buy a stock or bond, even if it is risky. The suitability requirement implies that the broker has a duty to warn when the client initiates an unsuitable purchase order, but the broker would not have responsibility.

RULE: NEVER GIVE A BROKER DISCRETION.

Discretion in this instance means that the client gives the broker the power to buy and sell stock, bonds, or commodities on the broker's judgment alone. The client may not even know that her holdings have been sold. This practice is very dangerous and should be followed only on rare occasions.

Stockbrokers make their commission when you buy and sell stock. It is therefore to their advantage for you to trade stock more often. There have been instances when this profit motive has been behind the transfer of substantial assets from the client to the broker. One woman was trading in commodities (grain, sugar, etc.) and doing very well. She was doing so well that she decided to go off to Europe for two months. She gave her broker total discretion over her account. When she got back she discovered that her $75,000 in assets had disappeared through bad investments. In the two months she was gone, the broker had traded her account often enough to earn $28,000 in commissions. Of course, the broker had disappeared. This tale represents the extreme. Discretion can be used well by a broker, but it is never recommended to give a broker total discretion.

Sometimes a client will have to give a broker limited discretion. If the client will be out of the country, she may wish to provide the broker with specific guidelines for trading. She may order ahead of time that stock be sold if it appreciates or depreciates in value. She might also give the broker the power to reinvest the funds, but she would be more likely to order that he hold the proceeds of the sale. Banks may also be able to arrange for sales in your absence if your stock is held by their safekeeping department.

RULE: TALK TO THE BROKER FIRST.

If you think you have been wronged in the sale or purchase of securities, talk to the broker first. He may admit error and pay you out of his own pocket. If he gives you an explanation which seems too complicated, you'll want to talk to the firm which employs him. If they disagree with their broker, they may give you your money back. If you still don't have satisfaction, you can talk to the stock exchange itself (for example, the New York Stock Exchange). If this fails, consult the Federal Trade Commission.

You will need some type of documentation to prove your claim. However, most customer buy and sell orders are issued over the telephone, leaving no written proof. Some investors will issue the order over the phone and then jot out a covering note to the broker, reiterating their conversation. They keep a copy of the note as proof of the order to buy or sell.

Incidentally the broker will rarely buy or sell a stock at the exact price he quoted you. Prices on the stock exchanges change in small amounts from moment to moment. Prices normally vary by at least twenty-five cents from hour to hour, even if the stock isn't active that day.

RULE: BROKERAGE FEES CAN BE NEGOTIATED.

Broker's fees used to be set at a certain percentage of the price, and the more shares purchased, the smaller the price would be. Set fees have been eliminated, but the private individual still pays the highest rates. If she trades in even lots of 100 shares, she pays lower fees than if she trades odd lots.

Some small brokerage houses have become discount brokers. Their fees are lower than those of the major brokerage houses, and they give limited investment advice. The offices tend to be less plush. If all you want to do is buy or sell, you may like this type of broker. Sometimes banks will sell stock for you. The trust departments of major banks often have ways to trade stock at no cost to the customer. The bank may be unwilling to sell your stock unless you are a large depositor.

RULE: KEEP SECURITIES SAFE.

If securities are stolen, someone may be able to forge them and sell them, just as one could do with a check. If you take the proper steps, you can avoid harm to yourself.

If you own securities, like stocks or bonds, each will have a certificate number printed on it. You should keep a record of these numbers along with the name of the company and the number of shares represented by each certificate. The number of shares will be printed or typed on the certificate. It is also helpful to have a record of the names on the certificate. Sometimes a couple will hold some shares individually and some shares jointly. If you want to sell some shares, you might need to know who owns them without taking a trip to the safe-deposit vault.

Certificates should be kept in a safe place. A common thief will probably not be interested in certificates, but you will want to protect the certificates from fire. A fireproof safe in your home and a safe-deposit box are the best storage places. Very few home strongboxes are totally safe in a fire. Another fireproof storage place is your freezer.

If a certificate is stolen you should immediately notify the company. The shareholder's service office will take steps to protect your ownership. If a certificate is lost or stolen, a new certificate can be issued, but it will greatly aid the shareholder's office if you can give them certificate numbers.

Securities can be safely moved in a number of ways. The safest is for you to deliver them personally. One woman puts them in the bottom of her shopping bag, underneath the groceries. You can also hire a bonded messenger to make the delivery. If anything happens to your securities, the messenger's insurance company will pay you back. Messengers are not as costly as you might think.

If you have to send securities through the mail, it's best to send them registered, return receipt requested. This way you will know the transfer agent got them. If the security is a stock or bond, it will have an area on the back beginning with "I appoint . . ." If you fill this in with the transfer agent's or stockbroker's name and address, no one else will be able to transfer the securities (like endorsing a check: "For deposit only . . ."). Alternatively you can send a stock power in a separate first-class envelope. When the transfer agent receives the stock power, she can transfer the stock. You can probably get a stock-power form from your banker or stockbroker.

The only type of security which is sent in a different way is a bearer bond. The person who has the physical possession of a bearer bond can sell it. The bearer bond doesn't have an owner's name on it, and it's just as negotiable as a dollar bill. If you have to deliver a bearer bond, you might want to carry it in your pantyhose or girdle. Since the face value is often as high as $10,000, no precaution is silly. If you mail the bearer bond, you send it by registered mail, but you must also buy insurance. If a bank sends a bearer bond to you, it will also insure the envelope and pay for the insurance itself. A stockbroker may charge you for the insurance.

Investment and money law are surprisingly free of trouble. Chances are you will never encounter a problem, but if you do, this area responds to customer complaints more readily than any other area. You can use an attorney to do your negotiating for you, but it's probably totally unnecessary. In this area of the law, you can certainly "do it yourself."

Chapter 14
WILL OR NO WILL

Your control over your property stops with your heartbeat, unless you have a will. Many persons use a will as a way of providing for their families after their death. Some people even get mischievous and include statements in their wills as parting shots to friends, a sure way of getting in the last word. You can see that a will does not have to be a somber document. Much of it has to do with your own style, and the style of your attorney.

Your will tells your family and the court how to divide your property after your death. The types of provisions it makes depend solely on your desires. You can do almost anything you want, with a few exceptions you'll read about later in this chapter.

There are many misconceptions about wills. Some people think you will die sooner if you have a will. The statistics do not bear this out. Fifty per cent of the people who die every year do not have wills. They still die. Some people are confused by the pledge a person makes in his will that "this is my last will and testament." This phrase means only that it is the most recent will the person has written. It can be changed at any time. Many people think they do not need a will because they own such a small amount of property. However, many people underestimate the value of their holdings. And even if the person has very small holdings, a great deal of family conflict can be avoided if a will is written.

An unfortunate number of us have witnessed the chaos which occurs following the death of a family member. Too often the family descends on the household of the dead person and raids the contents. This situation happens in part because there is no will describing how household goods should be divided. Recently a friend's 80-year-old grandfather died. Within six hours one of the more aggressive family members had backed a truck up to the man's front door and taken everything of value. The whereabouts of the man's small amount of jewelry, family records, and memorabilia are unknown. The television set also disappeared.

RULE: HANDWRITTEN WILLS ARE SELDOM VALID.

Handwritten wills are sometimes called holographic, a fancy word for handwritten. Holographic wills are reserved for emergency situations.

The state laws surrounding will writing are very specific and only rarely does a lay person satisfy all of the requirements for a valid homemade will. Letters and other simple documents have been found to be valid wills, but this is by far the exception. Most states do allow soldiers and seamen to make a holographic will, but this will is valid for only one year after their discharge from service. Holographic wills by soldiers and naval personnel are allowed because of the impossibility of making a valid will on the battlefield.

An even rarer type of will is an oral will. The dying man says, "Leave my farm to John." This will may be honored if the man was dying due to an accident, had only moments to live, John was his only child, the dying man had no wife, and he had made no other wills. Obviously, oral wills are not very reliable. If the dying man had said, "Give my gold pocket watch to John," the request would have been honored because of the relatively small value of the pocket watch compared to a farm.

RULE: HAVE AN ATTORNEY WRITE YOUR WILL.

If you want to be sure that your will is honored, it's best to have it drafted by a professional, so that all the peculiarities of local law are followed. These peculiarities include the number of witnesses required, your intention that this is your last will, strange issues such as the order in which things will be paid, and an infinite number of items depending on the complexity of a person's affairs.

Many people are curious about the books which contain standardized will forms which the person fills out. These may be adequate if the person's finances are simple. However, these are not recommended if the person owns more than a house and savings accounts.

If an attorney is writing a will, he can make allowances for current events as well as events into the future. He can analyze the holdings and may suggest ways to plan the estate for substantial tax savings. He can also tell you how much your estate taxes will be so that the family will have a firm idea of what assets will be available after the estate has been settled.

We are now entering the part of this chapter where technical language becomes inescapable. Attorneys have spent hundreds of years developing precise terms for each element of a will and its settlement. The person who orders that the will be drafted is called the testator. The testator must declare that he understands this document to be the most recent and possibly final distribution of his property. This statement is called a statement of intention, and is usually the first element in the will. The next element is normally an order to pay debts acquired while alive and the funeral expenses. Then the testator usually makes specific bequests (gifts under the will). These specific bequests can be either personal property or real estate. Typical bequests would be: "I give my car to my grandson, Tom," or "I leave my house to my wife, Tessie," or "My diamond ring goes to my friend, Susan Zuckermann."

These gifts seem simple on their face. However, the testator may not own a car at the time of her death, or she might own two diamond rings. For this reason property in specific bequests must be specifically described. For example, the diamond ring could be described as: "My 2.7 carat diamond in the platinum setting which has been inscribed inside with the initial 'M.'" The house could be described as: "My principal residence on the date of my death." An address would not be used in this case since the house at a certain address might be sold and another one might be purchased between the time of writing the will and the subject's death. If the address were specific, the spouse may end up not owning any house. Also, specific bequests should describe the person to whom the bequest is to be given. "My wife, Tessie," is clear, as would be "my grandson, Tom," unless there is more than one grandson named Tom. The description of the friend, Susan Zuckermann, would be fairly clear, but the person who settles the estate would have to be certain that the ring was given to the right Susan Zuckermann, and not to another Susan Zuckermann whom the dead person didn't know.

RULE: TO DISINHERIT, MENTION THE PERSON.

Occasionally a parent will wish to cut a child out of his will. The reason is not necessarily antagonistic. A person may have two daughters, one who is married to a wealthy man and the other who is divorced with children. If the parent's estate is small, all of the assets may go to the divorced daughter. This situation also applies to a beneficiary who is mentally or physically incapable of self-care or who has unusual financial responsibilities, such as the care of a retarded grandchild of the testator.

Since most state statutes allow a child to contest a will if he is not named in it, the safer course is to mention the child and perhaps give him a token gift. For example, the testator can state: "I fully remember my son, Jack, but for my own reasons, which I deem to be adequate, I leave him the sum of $10.00." You'll notice that this sentence includes the information that the testator remembers the existence of his child. If the child was not mentioned, the will could be contested on the basis that the testator made an error.

When a child is being disinherited because of the need of some other member of the family, the description of the disinheritance tends to be softer. "I remember my beloved daughter, Janet, but make no provision for her in my will, since her grandmother has already left her a small sum of money and she is well cared for by her husband."

RULE: TRUSTS CAN BE SET UP IN WILLS.

Trusts can be set up by an independent agreement called inter vivos trusts or they can be set up in a will. You will read a great deal more about this two chapters hence. Trusts under a will are normally the next step after specific bequests.

RULE: THE BALANCE OF THE ESTATE IS
USUALLY LEFT TO THE SPOUSE.

The federal estate tax structure exempts the first $250,000 of the estate from taxation when one spouse survives the other. For this reason most testators leave the bulk of their estate to the spouse, since this method of distribution can constitute a substantial estate tax savings, depending on the size of the estate. (See the chapter on taxes.)

The legal term for this balance is "the rest, residue, and remainder." These particular words are used because of the peculiarities of property law. This phrase includes the rest of all holdings of any nature which have not been specifically left to someone in the bequests portion of the will. Since large specific bequests are rare, the "rest, residue, and remainder" is usually the major part of the estate. The remaining portion may be willed outright so that the spouse gets possession of the property and the right to sell it. The remaining portion may also be put into a trust for the benefit of the spouse. (See the chapter on trusts.) Occasionally, the remaining portion of the estate will be divided between the spouse and children.

RULE: THE WILL MUST BE WITNESSED.

The law of every state requires that other persons be present when the will is signed so that they can later testify as to the testator's state of mind when the will was signed. The witnesses sign an attestation clause by which they swear that they were present at the signature and that the testator declared himself to be signing his will. The witnesses' names and addresses are taken so that they can be contacted if their testimony is needed. The witnessing of the will helps to prevent fraud. The witness does not know what is in the will, but she can swear that there was no indication that the testator signed it under duress. The witness can also say that the testator appeared to be in a normal frame of mind. The witness cannot give testimony that the signing she witnessed was that of the last will. She might not know if another will was drafted later. The witness states only that a particular will was signed and that the testator was aware that the document was the testator's will.

If you are planning to write a will, the first step is to list your assets and your liabilities. This is called a statement of net worth. Additionally, you will want to consider your family and how you can best effect their happiness and security. You may also have special business problems to handle through your will. Your attorney will need all this information to help you come up with the best solution. Many people find this process interesting and even heartening, especially if they've done it before. It can be a measure of the progress the family has made.

RULE: DETERMINE YOUR ASSETS.

The assets in your estate include all money and property you currently hold, as well as property that would come to your heirs if you died, such as insurance. The assets should be listed at their purchase price or current value if you can count on that value holding up. You should include your contribution to pension plans, retirement plans, the current value of your life insurance, savings accounts, checking account, and a low estimate for personal property, such as your household goods or stamp collections.

In addition to these assets, there are others which you must take into account but which will not be included in your estate. The primary of these is Social Security. A young widow with children receives substantial monthly Social Security benefits. Workmen's Compensation may also be sizable. Sometimes the proceeds of life insurance will not be included in the estate because the spouse actually owned the policy. You may also have hidden assets which might not normally occur to you, such as good friends who can find jobs for your children, a business associate who might give your spouse a partnership, or the reputation you have earned in your community. This good will is not to be discounted, since it may provide a way for your family to earn their own way after you are gone.

Your liabilities are the amounts of money you owe. A liability, most properly, is the amount required to pay off the bill if you did it tomorrow. It does not include interest you will have to pay in the future if the debt goes to its full term.

Net worth is assets minus liabilities. This is the amount of money your family is worth today. To your net worth you should add monies which would be paid to your family if you die.

ASSETS		LIABILITIES	
Home (purchase price)	$57,000	Mortgage	$36,000
Savings		Charge cards	
⚹462	3,260	Sears	1,376
⚹35784	4,271	Visa	623
Stock		Macy's	3,267
100 sh Standard (Ind.)	5,370	Car loan	2,762
100 sh G.M.	7,261	Personal loan	6,275
40 sh H&R Block	621		
Bonds			
City of Chicago	5,000		
Pension plan	6,275		
Checking account	626		
Paid-up life insurance	2,721		
Loan to Tom Harrison	1,000		
Personal property			
House furnishings	8,000		
Stamp collection	1,500		
	$102,905		$50,303

Assets	$102,905	
Liabilities	50,303	
Net worth	$ 52,602	$52,602

PAYABLE ON DEATH

Term insurance (S.B.L.I.)	$100,000
Pension plan life insurance	75,000
Life insurance on mortgage	36,000
Paid-up life (30,000—paid-up 2,721)	27,279
	$238,279 $238,279

RECAP

Net assets	$ 52,602
Death benefits	238,279

TOTAL WORTH FOR WILL	$290,881

With a statement like this, you and your attorney can determine the estate taxes—in this case, probably zero. Then you will know how much you will have left over to provide for the family. In this case, if there are young children, the surviving spouse is likely to get the whole amount outright. When you do your planning, you may find that you need to carry more life insurance, or less than you thought you needed. When making this decision, you can also include the amount of Social Security your wife is entitled to. (See the chapter on insurance.)

RULE: PLAN FOR YOUR FAMILY AS THEY
ACTUALLY ARE.

It's possible that each of your children needs a different type of provision, since individuals are so different. One family had the following plan. A widower with three children divided his assets equally among his three kids. His older boy, who was a responsible and well-educated man, got his $100,000 outright. His daughter was married to a nice fellow to whom the testator had loaned money to start his own business. The $40,000 loan had not been repaid and was subtracted from the girl's $100,000 share, leaving her assets of $60,000 in her own name. The younger boy's life had been filled with problems, and although he was beginning to straighten out, his father felt that the $100,000 should be placed in trust and the assets be paid to the younger boy's children after the boy's death. The younger boy received the interest on the trust but could invade the principal only to pay medical bills.

RULE: CARRY INSURANCE TO
PAY YOUR DEBTS.

Younger people are inclined to have more debts in relationship to their net worth than older people. Not as much of the mortgage is paid off and they may not be as far ahead on a savings program as they would like to be. It's not uncommon for a young widow to be unable to maintain the mortgage payments on her home. Fortunately, term insurance for young people is relatively inexpensive. Term insurance can be carried to cover the amount of principal needed to pay up the mortgage if the husband dies. Many credit card companies carry a type of life insurance which pays off the debt in the event of the debtor's death. You may have noticed in the statement of assets above that this couple was carrying life insurance to cover the principal of the mortgage. It can be carried in decreasing amounts as the mortgage debt is reduced.

RULE: PLAN FOR SPECIAL BUSINESS PROBLEMS.

The family-owned business can present a very serious estate-planning problem. Since continuance of the business is probably the family's best security, arrangements will have to be made to run the business during the settlement of the will. If the business is neglected, its value will severely diminish, even if it is sold later. Additionally, if the wife is experienced enough to run the business after her husband's death, the business is likely to do better than it would in the hands of a manager or trustee hired to take over.

If the business is a partnership, the partner may object to the wife's coming in on equal footing. The partner may want his own children to continue the business, and may even liquidate assets of the business for his own use. The preferred method for a partnership is to arrange for the partnership to buy out the widow. The partnership agreement itself should carry this provision. Partnerships often carry insurance for this particular purpose.

In addition to the practical problems of continuing the business, estate taxes may make it impossible to continue the business as it has been conducted. This situation has been especially true of family farms, restaurants, and other medium-sized businesses. The value of the business is sufficiently high to pay substantial estate taxes and yet too small to afford an $80,000 to $100,000 estate tax bill. Of course, inflation has had a great deal to do with the high values of these businesses, especially in farming. In addition, the new estate tax law requires that capital gains be paid on property if it is sold by the estate for any purpose, even to pay the estate tax bill. Since the capital gains tax currently runs as high as 28 per cent of the profit and the estate tax is similarly high, the family can be left with around half of the estate's assets if they are forced to sell their business. This situation is another argument in favor of carrying adequate life insurance, since in this case it would be imperative to have life insurance proceeds in order to pay estate taxes. You'll find a discussion of estate taxes in the chapter on taxes.

RULE: DON'T MAKE LARGE BEQUESTS.

Specific bequests such as "I give $10,000 to my aunt, Sarah Jordan," are paid first. The widow normally takes the balance after all specific bequests are paid. If the value of the estate increases between the time the will was written and the time the husband dies, all will go well. Unfortunately, it's not unusual for an estate to decrease in value, forcing the widow to take less money than she needs, or expected to have. If the value of the estate has decreased, the widow may have to contest the will in order to protect herself. Will contests are costly and time-consuming.

For these reasons states have statutes outlining the order of abatement (reduction) of bequests. The first group to have their inheritance lessened are the residuary devisees. These are the people who take shares after all other money has been distributed. The next group are the general bequests, such as "I give $10,000 to my Aunt Sarah . . ." The last group to be abated are the specific devisees: "I give my gold watch to my Uncle Frank." This abatement is something which every testator should consider. He should decide how much money he wishes the most important person to have and order his own abatement in the will, so that the favored person gets the amount of money intended. A testator can change the statutory order of abatement through his will, and need not follow the state statute if it doesn't suit his purposes.

RULE: DO NOT MAKE WILLS BY CONTRACT.

Although it is fading out, there was a tendency for many years in this country for a husband and wife to make mutual wills. They would promise to leave their money to each other and the last to die would leave all assets to their children or perhaps some other family member. Although the wills themselves were not a contract, the mutual will formed a contract between the spouses which implied they would not change their wills. Since women statistically will live ten to fifteen years longer than their husbands, the woman's assets were tied up well past her husband's death. Such wills often included a clause that the woman would not remarry.

These wills cause a lot of litigation, tie up the estate for years and years, and restrict a woman's ability to make her own will, free and clear of her husband's influence. Wills by contract are *not* recommended.

A will by contract can be used to borrow money. A person can make a contract to leave his property to a nephew in exchange for a $20,000 loan, or the nephew's taking care of the person's property, etc. The only real objection to this sort of will by contract is that it creates confusion. The person who loans the money, does the work, etc., should have very thorough documentation of the will, the contract, and his fulfillment of his side of the contract, so that the executor can turn over the property with the least amount of investigation.

RULE: A WILL CAN BE CHANGED BY CODICIL.

Codicil is the word the law gives to an official document which modifies a will. A codicil is used when minor changes need to be made in the will. The testator can sign a codicil at any time. Codicils save money in attorney's fees, since they rarely run more than a few paragraphs. The codicil is witnessed, just like a will, and is incorporated into the will at the time of the testator's death. Codicils can be used to modify the mutual or contractual wills discussed above.

Codicils can be used to change any particular part of a will, such as changing the person to whom the gold pocket watch is bequeathed, changing the individual or individuals who will receive the balance of the estate, or may substitute property in a bequest when the original property described has been sold.

Writing the codicil is simple and can be achieved by a short letter or a telephone call to the attorney. The attorney then writes the codicil for your signature.

RULE: PLAN FOR WILL CONTESTS.

Will contests occur under two circumstances: when the surviving spouse can get more money under the local intestacy statute or when children have been left out. In rare instances, wills will be contested when a wealthy person leaves a large part of his estate for some seemingly frivolous enterprise, such as the care of a pet.

The majority of the states have statutes requiring that a widow or widower get a share of the estate. The share is one third or one half of the estate, depending on the state. This is a substitute for the original widow's share, called dower. Dower had many legal complexities attached to it and the modern statutes were passed to simplify the dower concept.

The rest of the states grant widows a share through community-property statutes. Under these statutes, the wife is entitled to an undivided one half of the property accumulated during the marriage, unless the will provides for more. The balance would go to the heirs. The husband can give his wife as much in his will as he desires to, but the wife can overturn the will if she is not given at least as much as the community-property statute will allow.

Community property only affects property accumulated while the marriage was in existence. It does not apply to money either spouse brought into the marriage. Nor does it apply to money inherited during the marriage. Because of this, the woman in a widow's-share state may often get a bigger statutory settlement than a widow with community-property rights.

Eight states currently have the community-property system. About one third of the population of the United States lives in these states. The states are: Arizona, California, Idaho, Louisiana, Nevada, New Mexico, Texas, and Washington. All other states have the more typical widow's share described above.

Widows are generally given a certain amount of choice as to what they will take for their share. The widow frequently keeps the family home, furnishings, and the more secure investments.

There are two ways of dividing estates among descendants. One method is called per capita—that is, by the head. Under the per capita method all grandchildren receive the same amount of money. For example, there may be $100,000 allocated to the testator's five grandchildren. They would receive $20,000 apiece. The other method is called per stirpes—that is, by the root. Let's suppose the testator has three children. At the time of his death, the testator had five grandchildren, three by one son and one by each other child. If a per stirpes distribution were made, the $100,000 would be divided among the three children and then each grandchild would get his share through the parent. The grandchildren in the three-child family would get $11,111 apiece; each of the only-child grandchildren would get $33,333 apiece. Since this result is unfair, many states statutes require that all persons in the same relationship, such as "grandchildren," share equally.

Per stirpes distribution is used most commonly when a single person has died without leaving a will. In this instance each of her brothers and sisters and their descendants will share in the estate.

Will contests can be avoided if the will is written along the guidelines of the state statutes. If one group of your descendants or your husband is to be disinherited, you may speak with your attorney. He or she can help you set up ways to avoid the contest. One of the best ways to do this is to fund a trust for the benefit of that class of heirs which you will disinherit. A further description of this area is included in the trusts chapter.

RULE: NO WILL—NO VOICE.

If you don't leave a will, your state will determine how your assets are to be distributed. A person who dies without a will is said to be intestate. Every state has statutes determining the distribution of assets in this case. These statutes can vary widely. If the spouse and children survive the property owner, the spouse will take one third to one half of the assets; the balance of the estate will be equally divided among the children. If a widow dies leaving children, the estate may be split equally between her children. If a single person dies, one half of the estate may go the parents and the remainder split among brothers and sisters. This representative statue may vary slightly from state to state.

Although this distribution is fair, it doesn't really take into account the family's individual needs. For example, many persons would prefer that the spouse take the entire amount of the estate, especially if the children are young. The federal estate tax has recently been reformed. If the estate is small, estate taxes may raid the estate if the widow doesn't get all the money. (State intestacy laws are slowly changing to provide for the change in federal estate taxes.) A single person may have well-fixed parents and siblings who need every penny they can get. The usual laws of intestacy would deprive a sister of money she needed now, while granting the affluent parents unnecessary funds.

For many years a number of small farmers in the South have not made wills. The property passes per stirpes to succeeding generations, which become harder and harder to find. Eventually there are so many owners to the property that it cannot be sold, since the likelihood of getting 80 to 100 signatures on the deed is remote. This situation has continued for over a hundred years, but its relevance to the person dying intestate today should not be lost. Titles to practically everything can become confused in intestate estates, so that actual ownership may be years in the unwinding.

A will is not a complicated procedure. Many attorneys charge moderate fees for will preparation, usually $75 to $150, with higher fees for more complex estates. A simple will may cost only $50. Should you die prematurely, the value of a will to your family will be far beyond these

amounts. You may even find your attorney willing to arrange installment payments. Attorneys think wills are very important.

Perhaps the reason half of the population dies without leaving a will
is influenced by the human unwillingness to confront death. For most
people, a will is a one-time undertaking. To save your family money,
time, and confusion after your death, it is well worth confronting for
that short period.

Chapter 15
EXECUTORS

Many a man appoints his wife to be the executor of his estate. The executor is the person who has the responsibility to carry out the provisions of a will. Many women like doing the job of executor because it gives them the chance to settle the last details of what was a lovely marriage. Having done this, they are in a position to go on with their own lives, perhaps even stronger than they were before.

The executor is usually appointed in the will. Executors are often the spouse or an adult child of the deceased or a professional executor such as an attorney. An administrator has all the same duties, except that the word "administrator" is used when the deceased did not make a will (died intestate). Administrators are usually adult relatives, but others may also serve. Creditors of the deceased are sometimes appointed as administrators. In this chapter we will use the word "executor" to describe the duties of both the executor and the administrator.

The first duty of the executor is to present herself and the will to the probate court. The probate procedure proves that the document presented is the last will of the person who signed it, although this one point is rarely an issue. The primary purpose of probate is to assure that the directions of the will are carried out. The court then oversees the executor's acts.

Most populous states have a separate probate court (also called surrogate or orphan's court, or a court of ordinary). Less populous states may handle the probate in a trial court of general jurisdiction. The inexperienced executor's best friend in these courts is the court clerk. He or she usually knows the ropes and is a good source of practical advice.

After the executor opens the probate, the court issues a document to her called "letters of administration" (also called letters testamentary). This document gives the executor the official right to represent the estate. These letters of administration are important since no one will deal with the executor without them. You will probably need many photocopies of this document, since it will have to be sent every time you request a title change in the decedent's property.

An estate is not settled automatically. Somebody has to start the process and that somebody is usually the executor.

RULE: KNOW YOUR POWERS AS EXECUTOR.

All states have laws which give the executor the ability to take certain acts on the part of the estate. All executors are required to furnish a bond to insure the estate against the executor's faults in upholding her responsibilities. This bond is not a substantial amount of money, and can be purchased from a surety company. This bond cannot be waived if there is no will. If there is a will, the person signing the will can waive the bond. Exempting the executor from bond should not be done as a matter of course, since the point of the bond is insuring that the beneficiaries get their assets. The bond should be waived only if the person writing the will has experience with and trusts the abilities of the executor.

The will may give you other powers in addition to those which the state allows you. The normal executor may only have the right to transfer the property. The will may give the right to the executor to sell property and transfer the cash to the beneficiaries. Many wills also allow the executor to mortgage or otherwise transfer property. Most states give the executor the right to pay the deceased's debts, but the will document may give the executor the additional ability to negotiate debts. The executor may also be allowed to assign values to the property without having the property appraised. This power can save the estate money. All of these powers outlined above allow the executor to operate without turning to the court for an official ruling each time a situation arises which is not defined in the state's listing of executor powers. In the absence of these provisions in the will, you as the executor will have to obtain the court's approval each time you do something unusual. For example, you may have negotiated with a creditor so that he is willing to accept less money in payment of a debt than the face value of the credit agreement. If you do not have the power to negotiate debts, you would have to first obtain the court's approval for the compromise. If you are an administrator, you are limited to the powers that the state gives you. An executor has all the powers the state gives plus whatever extra powers the will may grant.

RULE: KNOW YOUR DUTIES.

Whether you're an administrator or an executor, you will use your powers to perform your responsibilities, which in legalese are called the executor's duties. The duties are very straightforward and will be discussed in more detail in the rules below. Essentially, the executor's duties are to collect and preserve assets, pay debts and death taxes, and then disburse the assets either under the will or under the laws of intestate. The probate process will not be finished until all of these steps have been completed to the satisfaction of the court.

RULE: COLLECT THE ASSETS.

The first task of the executor is to find all of the property of the deceased. This property may be in the form of bank accounts, stock certificates, employee benefits, Social Security and Workmen's Compensation Benefits, real estate, insurance, or any of the other myriads of property interests modern man can own. The existence of this property can be detected through the deceased's tax returns and other records he has kept around the house. The executor's duty is to find as many of these assets as she reasonably can. Her search must be prudent, but she is not expected to find assets which the deceased might have hidden away without a clue. All of the assets in which the deceased owned any interest at all must be collected. The fact that the home was owned in some type of joint tenancy does not remove it from the probate estate, even though the title passed with his death.

The executor or administrator is charged with making an inventory of the estate. Any form is adequate, as long as you are orderly and careful. The normal inventory divides the assets into categories. All savings accounts are listed together along with the current value of each account. Stock is listed together with the company name and how many shares are owned. The value on the date of death is also listed. Personal property can be lumped together if no item is of outstanding value. For example, the personal property inventory might read: "clothing and accessories—$500, 1976 Chevrolet Impala, two-door—$1,800, stamp collection—$1,200." This way the court can readily see the thoroughness and accuracy of the executor's work.

The executor is charged with obtaining appraisals of assets. The will sometimes allows the executor to determine his own appraisal without seeking the help of a professional. The executor can appraise stock by looking in the newspaper stock quotations for the date of the deceased's death. Automobiles can be appraised using the Blue Book value. A friendly real estate broker can give you an approximate value on the house. Personal items such as clothing or furniture are more difficult to appraise, but any realistic estimate is usually accepted. With personal items such as clothing or furniture, the depreciated value on the date of death is the value used for the inventory. The inventory is typed up neatly and presented to the court for its records.

RULE: FIND THE DEBTS.

Most people die owing some money. It's the responsibility of the executor to find the creditors and pay them before distributing the assets to the beneficiaries. No outlandish search is required but it's best to check with all persons the decedent regularly dealt with. As a normal rule, the creditors will make sure they collect their money.

Most states do not allow an estate to be distributed prior to a particular date, say six months from the opening of probate. This period allows the creditors time to present their claims. If a creditor has not presented his claim prior to the time the period has expired, he will be barred from collecting the money owed him.

The executor is always empowered to pay the debts. Some wills give the executor the additional power to negotiate the amount of payment. The executor is required to pay everything due and to present lists of the debts and payments to the probate court.

RULE: PAY THE TAXES.

You may be wondering why all the fuss over probate. There are two basic reasons. The first is an orderly way to pass title on property. Passing title is especially important for real estate. However, the title of the property, if it's held in joint tenancy or some other type of joint ownership, can take care of this. The most essential function of probate is paying the taxes. If someone dies leaving a surviving spouse, the estate must be substantial before taxes will be paid to the federal government. However, many states are not as kind to widows as the federal government. They will insist that the state death taxes be paid prior to the widow's getting clear title. If someone dies without leaving a surviving spouse, the estate need not be very large before the federal government as well as the state government demands its share. Consult the chapter on taxes for more information.

Paying the taxes is the last step before the estate is distributed. You will have to show the receipt for the taxes paid and a release from the taxing body before you can distribute assets. This step also takes time while the tax authority looks over the tax return and the records of the estate. You'll probably want to hire an accountant to complete the estate return for you.

RULE: DISTRIBUTE THE ASSETS.

The final step of settling the estate is paying everyone his share. This must be done in accordance with the will if there is one, or under intestate statutes if there is no will. The distribution is not always as straightforward as we would like it to be.

In most estates the wife of the deceased takes clear title to the house and the most secure investments. The children equally divide the remaining assets. However, problems arise when assets cannot be split. For example, the deceased may have owned a business which one of the children wishes to run by himself. There may be a corporate bond with a large face value. The children may be unwilling for many reasons to hold the bond in joint ownership. Also, the decedent may have left a letter with particular instructions as to how he wishes to have his property distributed. Although this letter is not law, executors generally adhere to these instructions as closely as possible. For these reasons many executors sell assets which cannot be split and pay cash to the family. This prevents later disagreements among the heirs.

Changing title on stocks and bonds is a fairly simple administrative function, but it does require some paper work. It's best to write a letter of inquiry to the corporation which issued the stock or bond, or the governmental agency which issued the bond. They will forward your letter to the stock transfer agent, usually a bank, which will actually change the title. The bank will send you a list of instructions so you can fulfill the requirements of your state.

If you and your husband held stock or bonds in joint tenancy, and you as the survivor wish to have the certificates placed in your own name, you merely send the original stock certificate, a copy of the death certificate, and a letter of instructions to the stock transfer agent. You sign the back of the stock certificate. In the section which says, "I hereby appoint," you fill in the transfer agent's name. By filling in the agent's name, you can ensure that the certificate cannot be cashed by anyone else should it be lost or stolen. This appointment to the agent has the same effect as endorsing a check with "for deposit only."

If you are acting as executor for an estate, and you are arranging to have the title transferred to the heirs, the procedure is different. In this case you send in a copy of your letters of administration, a copy of an affidavit of domicile (where the deceased lived), the original stock certificate with your signature, and a letter of instructions. Depending on the state, you may also have to send a tax waiver. The transfer agent will tell you this when you inquire. You can mail the papers as described in the above paragraph. Alternatively, you can sign a stock power to be sent in an envelope separate from the certificate. The transfer agent holds your papers until the stock power arrives. See the chapter on investments for information on how you mail more unusual types of securities.

When all the titles have been changed, the assets can be distributed. After you have worked out your distribution schedule, the court will probably have to approve it prior to the actual distribution. Whether or not court approval is required depends on your powers in the will. If court approval is required, you present a schedule stating who will get the particular assets. When the court approves it, you can proceed. The beneficiaries must sign receipts for assets they receive. This is to protect you from accusations of wrongdoing. After the assets have been distributed, you appear once again, show your receipts for the assets, the court verifies them, and the probate is closed. Your job is over.

As you can see from this description, the job of an executor is really not very hard. There is a lot of detail involved. You'll have to keep very good books and probably write a lot of letters. At first the amount of work seems enormous, but as you chip away at it, it becomes simpler and simpler.

Chapter 16
TRUSTS

A trust can do many things that the creator would have done herself had she lived. The primary purpose of a trust is to care for those left behind. The trust does this by preserving the property of the creator and paying regular income to the beneficiaries.

Trusts are not the exclusive reserve of stodgy rich old folks. Indeed, most trusts are set up by middle- or upper-middle-class people in their forties. These families probably have teen-aged children to send to college and graduate school. Their main source of security is likely to be life insurance, and not substantial personal assets.

Most trusts have a small amount of money in them, like $1.00. The papers are signed, but no substantial money may go into the trust at that time. Usually, the money will go into the trust when the creator of the trust dies. The money will come from any assets or insurance available at the time of the creator's death. The creator can arrange for the assets to flow into the trust in two ways: through her will or by designating the trust as the beneficiary of her insurance policies.

The person who sets up the trust is called the creator or the donor. The institution or individual who holds the property is called the trustee. The most common type of trustee is a bank or a trust company, which is usually a subsidiary of a bank. The persons who will get the income and principal are called beneficiaries. The creator of the trust herself may be a beneficiary, but the most common beneficiaries are the spouse and the children of the creator. The money in the trust is called the corpus, or the body of the trust, and can include both principal and accumulated interest. Income is the money a trust earns, and income normally comes from interest on bonds and savings, and from dividends on common stock.

RULE: TRUSTS PROTECT THE CORPUS.

The job of the trustee is to protect the corpus of the trust, and beneficiaries normally have no right to the corpus. When the trust ends, the beneficiaries receive the corpus of the trust to hold as their own property. As long as the trust lasts, beneficiaries only have the right to income.

Trusts end upon the happening of some event. This event might be the beneficiary reaching a particular age, getting married, or more commonly, the death of the primary beneficiary. As you will read below, trusts are often funded for the benefit of the wife. Upon her death, the trusts will normally be distributed to her children, if they have reached maturity.

Sometimes part of the corpus will be used to insure the beneficiary of a certain standard of living. For example, the trust agreement might order the trustee to pay $20,000 a year to the primary beneficiary (usually the widow). But if the trust income is only $18,000, each year some part of the corpus will have to be paid to pay the $20,000 as the agreement requires.

RULE: TRUSTS SAVE ON TAXES.

The primary advantage of a trust is to hold a portion of the person's property free of estate taxes and to diminish income taxes. The principal (corpus) can skip from one generation to the next with the lowest amount of estate taxes paid, while still protecting the income of the surviving spouse. Trusts do this by splitting the estate into two parts. Since estate taxes get higher as the estate gets bigger, the trust can save substantial tax money by allowing one half to be taxed when one spouse dies. The other half is taxed when the other spouse dies and the money goes to the children or other heirs. The total tax on the two halves is much lower than the tax on the whole amount in one lump.

The most ordinary sort of trust arrangement is structured in the following way. The creator arranges for the trusts while he is alive. He signs the papers, but only a token amount is put into the trust. There is one trust for the spouse and a trust for each of the children. When the creator dies, the will instructs that his assets at death be "poured over" into the trusts, usually one half into the wife's trust and equal shares of the remaining one half into the trusts for the children.

The wife has the right to income from all of the trusts as long as she lives. She designates in her will who is entitled to what share of the trust which is in her name. Under the estate tax laws, her trust remains tax-free until her death. The children's trusts pay estate taxes at the time of the creator's death. Although their mother has had the use of the income from their trusts, no estate tax is paid on the children's trusts when the mother dies. Using this method, the mother has the maximum income and the children receive the biggest amount of money because of the taxes saved.

For example, Allen Carpenter has the trust arrangement discussed above. He dies with an estate valued at $600,000. His wife's trust is funded with $300,000. She receives income for life and has the right to appoint who will inherit her trust. There are no estate taxes paid on her $300,000 because that's her widow's share under the federal estate tax. The balance of the $600,000 is divided among the children's trusts, but this amount is diminished by the estate taxes they pay at the time of the creator's death (about $50,000, depending on a lot of issues discussed in the chapter on taxes). If there are two children and two trusts, they would divide what is left of the $300,000 after the estate taxes have been paid ($250,000). The money would go into their trusts in equal shares with their mother having the right to the income for her life, but no right to appoint who is to receive the children's trusts upon her death. When the mother dies, she will probably leave her own trust to her children in equal shares. The children will then have the right to the income from their own trusts plus their share of the mother's trust after estate taxes have been paid on her $300,000 (another $50,000 in tax). This arrangement is a fair exchange, since the mother has gotten the maximum use of income and the children have gotten the greatest amount of principal. The $300,000 taxed on two separate occasions accumulates a total tax of about $100,000 in estate taxes. If the entire $600,000 went to the widow, the tax would be $50,000 when she inherited it and $150,000 when she left it to the children. So the trust method would save about $100,000 in taxes.

RULE: TRUSTS PRESERVE PROPERTY.

Aside from the estate tax advantages which have the effect of preserving property, a trust can also be used to hold property free of the influence of the beneficiaries. This provision is made when the creator feels, whether rightly or wrongly, that the spouse and offspring need protection from bad investments. Most trust companies have very conservative investment policies and are required to prove that the investments they make on behalf of the trust are prudent and in the best interest of the beneficiaries. Additionally, the trust agreement can be written in such a way that the beneficiary is protected from his own bad judgment. This trust is the so-called "spendthrift" trust, to be discussed below.

RULE: TRUSTS PROTECT THE INNOCENT.

The creator may have a young child or a retarded child. A trust is probably the most adequate way to insure the care of a minor or an incompetent. The trustee can oversee the child's education and can be given the discretion to make certain judgments on behalf of the beneficiary.

The more common type of protection offered by a trust is the spendthrift trust, wherein the creator seeks to protect the income and corpus of the trust from the creditors of the beneficiaries. The beneficiaries will lose their interest in the spendthrift trust if they attempt to sell their interest in the trust to another person. The spendthrift clause is not acceptable in all jurisdictions. Where it is acceptable, the judges may restrict the beneficiaries' right to sell their share of the income but will not restrict their right to sell the corpus.

You may be amazed that people sell their interest in a trust. Selling trusts is now a minor industry, but it once flourished in both England and the United States. The beneficiary wanted his money now and was willing to sell his interest in order to have cash in hand. This area is called future interests (an interest in property one may actually own at some time in the future), and is rather like taking your tax return to a loan company and giving the loan company the right to receive your refund. You get part of your money immediately and the company makes a profit.

RULE: TRUSTS ARE SECRET.

Some people are unwilling to have others know the exact value of the estate. They may set up a trust specifically to avoid this. They can either fund the trust before their death or arrange through their will that all assets at their death "pour over" into the trust. In neither case are the assets ever a matter of public record. Additionally, some families own business interests which might be considered sensitive. If the owner of these interests creates a trust, the business holdings may remain secret forever.

Trusts come in many shapes and sizes, and within certain limitations the creator of the trust is free to do almost anything. Besides their flexibility, trusts can also isolate creditors from assets, provide business advantages, and act as a way to preserve personal assets while the creator goes off temporarily to do a different job.

There are at least ten different types of trusts. They are: revocable, irrevocable, testamentary, private express, charitable, business, blind, Totten, Claflin, and trusts under the Uniform Gifts to Minors Act.

Revocable trusts can be changed. The creator of the trust and the trust company may agree that the creator can change only certain parts of the trust, such as who is to receive the corpus when she dies, or the entire trust agreement altogether, so that the trust is canceled and the corpus returned to the creator. Most private express trusts and blind trusts are revocable. The revocable trust is an additional attribute of a more specific type of trust, so that a trust would be spoken of as a revocable blind trust or a revocable private express trust.

An irrevocable trust cannot be changed. Although the creator may have the income for life, he has already determined who will be the beneficiary. Irrevocable trusts are also a subsidiary quality of another type of trust. For example, a trust may be an irrevocable business trust or an irrevocable private express trust.

A testamentary trust is set up through a will. It will probably be irrevocable, but the purpose of it may be either to benefit heirs or to create a charitable trust.

A private express trust is set up during the creator's life, and funded or not, according to the creator's wishes. If it is not funded, and litigation arises, the court may find that a private express trust which was not funded during the creator's life was in fact a testamentary trust. The testamentary trust is the most common type.

A charitable trust is set up for the benefit of a charity or some class of individuals who are not relatives. For example, the Ford Foundation is a charitable trust for the benefit of many organizations and artistic endeavors. Often scholarship funds are charitable trusts as well. The trust may read: "To pay income each year to the daughter of a farmer for her use in the study of medicine."

A business can also be the corpus of a trust. A businessman may put part of his business or a building he owns into a trust for the benefit of his children. For example, one father had a garment business and on the side sold odd lots of scrap fabric to fabric stores. This business netted him about $4,000 a year. He put the scrap fabric business into an irrevocable trust and continued to operate the business. He no longer had to pay income tax on this profit. The trust could then accumulate the money for his children and pay compound interest on it besides. The purpose of this trust was to pay for his children's college education. As it turned out, there was money left over and each child got the surplus as he or she reached 25 years of age.

Blind trusts are used by politicians to hold their assets while they are in public office and to prevent conflict-of-interest problems. Blind trusts are usually revocable, so that the politician gets his assets back when he is no longer in office.

A Totten trust is really a type of joint ownership. The creator of the trust keeps the trust in his own name, in trust for the beneficiary, such as "One in trust for Two." Two gets the title when One dies. The Uniform Gifts to Minors Act has adopted the form of the Totten trust, but generally allows the minor to take the title at age 21, instead of at the death of the creator of the trust.

A Claflin trust is also often used when making gifts to minors. Under the Claflin trust the gift is made along with directions to pay specific amounts at specific ages. Most commonly, this would read: "Susie is to receive $10,000 at age 25, $10,000 at age 30, and the balance of the trust at age 35." The beneficiary has no right to the principal before reaching the required ages.

There are many other kinds of trusts, but most of them refer to the way the trust is conducted or the purpose of the trust. These types of trusts outlined above are the basic garden variety trusts.

RULE: SATISFY THE REQUIREMENTS OF A TRUST.

Trusts must be written. An oral trust will almost never be honored. The trust must state who created the trust, what person or institution will act as the trustee, who the beneficiaries will be, and what payments the beneficiaries are to receive from the trust. It must also state what property will be used as the corpus of the trust. The corpus need not be put into the trust at that time but must be in existence at the time the trust is signed. For example, if the trust corpus will consist of the creator's assets at the time of her death, the designation of those assets is sufficient to create a trust. It is not important that the creator know what the assets will actually be. That specific knowledge may be thirty or forty years in the future.

There is little or no litigation about the basic validity of a particular trust if it has been professionally written. Practically all litigation having to do with satisfying the requirements of a trust arise out of family transactions or the efforts of the debtor to hide his assets from a creditor.

RULE: YOU CAN SET UP A TRUST
FUND WHILE ALIVE.

Trusts that you set up during your life are called inter vivos trusts. The creator of such a trust may simply set up a trust, sign the papers, and not fund it until she dies. If she cares to, she may donate property to it. The inter vivos trust may be either revocable or irrevocable. The revocable form is far more popular. In either case, the creator sets up the trust, and need not fund it until she dies. Her will directs that the assets of her estate be "poured over" into the trust. The trust is revocable because she may later change her will so that the trust is never funded.

The irrevocable inter vivos trust is far less common. The creator of the trust must designate the beneficiaries at the time the trust is signed. The trust is funded and the creator retains only the right to receive the income. Occasionally very wealthy persons will use the irrevocable inter vivos trust for income tax purposes.

Depending on the practice of your state, you may save some probate costs by fully funding an inter vivos trust while you are alive. There can also be some other obscure capital gains savings. The probate savings will not be substantial, however, and you should fully investigate your tax savings before you do this. You may find the several thousand saved is not worth the loss of control of your assets.

RULE: WILLS CAN ESTABLISH TRUSTS.

Trusts can be established through a will, but then one is generally not dealing with large estates. For example, a will could state: "$10,000 to my daughter, Jennie, to be held in trust for her until she reaches age 25 or marries, whichever comes first." A trust of this type will generally be held in a savings bank with a close relative of Jennie's as trustee. This trust is frequently used when the beneficiary is a minor. This type of trust is very similar to the trust established under the Uniform Gifts to Minors Act, where a parent holds assets in trust for her child, and is much like a Totten trust, where a person changes the title of an asset from her own name, "Sarah Jones," to a trust account, "Sarah Jones, in trust for Erica Jones." The Totten trust is used to avoid probate, since the title to the trust passes automatically, and the beneficiary of the trust takes the whole thing when the creator dies.

Major trusts established in a will used to be quite common, but have less popularity now for the practical reason that a trust document can be very lengthy. Besides the extra cost of writing a long will, trust companies in some states prefer that the creator of the trust use the company's own trust agreements, rather than one written by the creator's own attorney. Additionally, most creators prefer to have an agreement with a trust company before setting up the trust. Trust companies have been known to reject a trust as being too small. A special trust arrangement may be needed, through either a smaller bank or perhaps a relative.

The will can then refer to the trust document and make the trust part of the will through a process called incorporation by reference. The only requirement is that the trust must be set up prior to the time the will is signed. The will can be changed many times after the trust is set up and the same trust can be incorporated into each will. This type of arrangement is called a pour-over will, because the will pours assets into the trust.

An additional point in the favor of setting up a trust independent of the will is that a trust is much harder to contest than a will. It's not uncommon for disappointed beneficiaries to overcome the provisions of a will. A will requires that the testator have testamentary capacity (the mental ability required to draw a will), a difficult standard to prove at any time, but most especially difficult if the decedent was elderly or eccentric. A trust requires that the creator be competent, a lesser level of ability than testamentary capacity and a standard much less open to criticism of the creator's behavior.

Whether or not you choose to set up a trust has little to do with how great your assets might be. When deciding about trusts, your primary interest is the welfare of your beneficiaries. If you decide that your beneficiaries would be best served by a trust, you can then find the proper institution or person to administer the trust.

RULE: PROVIDE A TRUST FOR MINOR CHILDREN.

If at the time you draw your will your children are still under age, you can easily set up a trust for them through the will. The provision would read: "To my son, James Hancock, I give the sum of $10,000 to be held in trust for him until age 25. The income is to be distributed only for the payment of medical bills. I appoint as trustee my husband, Patrick Hancock. If he is not willing to serve, I appoint my sister, Madeline Schmidt." In all likelihood, this bequest would be put into a savings bank and the interest accumulated until the boy reaches 25.

When your children grow older, you need not change the will, even though they have already attained the age at which the trust would end. They would merely take possession of the whole bequest as an ordinary beneficiary under the will.

More affluent persons, or those carrying large amounts of insurance, will probably set up trusts for minor children to provide for their college educations and living expenses after the creator's death, but before the child is able to make his own way in the world. Of course, trusts would also be constituted for the benefit of a mentally or physically incapacitated child, regardless of the child's age. The parents of such a child find great security in the knowledge that the child has the trustee as a protector after the parents' death.

RULE: FIND THE RIGHT TRUSTEE.

If your assets and insurance are quite substantial, the appropriate trustee is most likely to be a trust company. Trust companies offer a wide range of services to the beneficiaries, although their primary purpose is to collect income and pay that income to the beneficiary. They may also pay bills for the beneficiary, supervise the beneficiary's schooling, purchase a home, or provide any other comforts of life that the creator of the trust commands. In exchange for this service, the trust company is paid a percentage of the income from the trust. Trust companies will not accept every trust offered to them. Some trust companies require that the total assets exceed certain amounts. Small banks may require $50,000. Medium-sized banks may require $100,000 to $200,000. Large banks in large cities may have higher requirements.

Private trustees may be a better choice for a person of modest assets. In this case the best trustee may be either a spouse or a trusted relative with business ability. The private trustee could also be a professional. Relatives are preferred, since they generally have a thorough knowledge of the creator's desires and the needs of the children who are the beneficiaries. The private trustee is not to be confused with a guardian of minor children. A guardian must report to the court each time an expenditure is made on the children's behalf. The trustee need not have expenditures approved as long as the trust agreement has given him the power to make the expenditure. The private trustee can choose a number of different ways to invest the money in his care. Although it is possible for him to invest in stocks, bonds, etc., the private trustee normally chooses a savings account.

You can also set up a trust yourself and appoint yourself as trustee. This procedure is done frequently for the benefit of minor children. You can hold stock, savings, bonds, or any other sort of property for the benefit of the children. The title of ownership would read: "Bernadine Munson in trust for Scott Munson." The child is then entitled to the corpus of the trust upon the death of the creator.

Income taxes must be paid on the income from the trust, whether it is drawn out of the account or not. However, a child beneficiary will probably pay lower income taxes than the parent would. The parent trustee has the option of paying the income taxes on his own tax return, but is not required to do so. The bank or corporation will be able to assist you in changing the title.

The Tax Reform Act modified the gift tax. The creator of the trust may no longer pay a gift tax if the trust is set up during his or her life.

The assets of the trust are now included in the creator's estate for estate tax purposes. The estate tax is then figured on the assets at death plus the assets of all trusts funded while the creator was alive. The estate tax credit takes the place of the gift tax. (See the chapter on taxes.)

Being the beneficiary of a trust sounds like one plateau just short of heaven. The idea of free money rolling in is about as good a definition of being rich as most of us could conceive. However, being a beneficiary is not without its problems.

RULE: BENEFICIARIES PAY INCOME TAX.

The beneficiary of a trust is not exempt from the income tax on the income he receives from that trust. At the end of the year, the trustee sends the beneficiary a listing of the different types of income she received. This income could include interest, dividends, rents, royalties, capital gains, and other types of income. The beneficiary is required to include this income along with other income earned during the year. Income taxes must be paid on the total of all sources of income. Since no withholding tax is collected on trust income, the beneficiary must also pay quarterly estimated income tax, so that the whole tax bill is paid up each quarter.

RULE: IT'S HARD TO GET AT THE PRINCIPAL.

Although the beneficiary may have a good business opportunity or may wish to buy a house, the trustee is restrained from cooperating with every whim, or even a very good idea the beneficiary may have. If the trustee has been instructed to pay income only, he must do that. If he does anything more, the beneficiary can turn around and sue him later on the grounds that the trustee violated the trust agreement. The beneficiary could then recover from the trustee's personal assets.

Many trusts make allowance for this particular situation by giving the trustee certain discretionary powers over distribution of the corpus of the trust. The powers the trustee has are described in the trust agreement. If you, as the beneficiary, wish to acquire some or all of the corpus for your personal use, you will have to do it under the specifications of the trust agreement, or by overturning the trust—a very difficult task.

RULE: TRUSTS CAN BE REFORMED.

Reform in this instance means modifying the trust to fit the intention of the creator. Sometimes a trust agreement will be unclear on particular points. Many of the beneficiaries may have died, leaving the intention of the creator unfulfilled. In such an instance the remaining beneficiaries may petition the court to have the trust reformed within certain reasonable limits, although this is a rare and costly process and may or may not succeed.

RULE: YOU CAN PUSH AROUND THE TRUSTEE.

Trustees have specific responsibilities to protect the corpus of the trust and to uphold their responsibilities to all beneficiaries. Trustees tend to be very conservative about this, since their liability for an error in judgment can be very great. If there are many beneficiaries to a trust, the trustee is likely to be very conservative in his conduct. If there are only one or two beneficiaries, the beneficiary and the trustee may be able to modify the agreement slightly to aid the beneficiary. For example, if there were many beneficiaries, the trustee would be unlikely to loan any of them even a small amount of money to start up his own business. However, if there was only one beneficiary, the trustee may possibly be willing to make a loan to the beneficiary based on the trust corpus.

Trusts are a good thing. They give the parent a secure knowledge that her children are provided for. The child knows that there is money for her, even though it may be far in the future. Any good bank and competent attorney can set up a trust in a matter of days. The cost of starting and maintaining a trust is moderate in comparison to the advantages gained.

There may be some residual resentment lingering about trusts, since this has so long been the tool of the rich. However, in spite of recent economic problems, many of us have become quite wealthy. The tool of the trust is now available for many middle-class families and should be used. Indeed, it is one of the best ways to make sure everyone gets taken care of at the lowest possible cost.

Part V
YOUR PERSON

Chapter 17
CIVIL RIGHTS

Civil rights form the basis on which all other American law rests. Our civil rights keep us from chaos and despotism. Whenever they are infringed upon, take a stand, build a barricade, and fire your warning shots. Your life is in danger.

A strong statement. However, within the memories of most of us is a disaster based on the denial of civil (human) rights. During World War II, 18 million civilians died, due to some denial of their rights. The Jews of Europe were the most clear-cut example of this injustice. They were cordoned off from the rest of society, their children denied schooling, their property confiscated, their bodies experimented upon, and their lives taken at whim. Our own revolution was not severe, but our forefathers had learned how people can be subjugated if all rights belong to the state. The warlords who forced the signing of the Magna Carta knew it, as did Pericles and Plato.

You might think that nothing could happen here, but it already has. Witness: the Japanese-American incarcerations during World War II; the McCarthy hearings, where, believe it or not, even Santa Claus was suspect because of his red suit; union organizers being beaten by company gangs and denied the right to speak publicly; LSD experiments on uninformed subjects; the chaos in Little Rock; Watergate; and the battle over the ERA. Only through the strict guarding of our civil rights have we survived thus far.

Our civil rights are in writing. They are found primarily in the Bill of Rights, the first ten amendments to the Constitution. Some of the other amendments are also important as civil rights documents, since these amendments give many different kinds of people the right to vote. The

Constitution itself was adopted in 1789. Individual human rights were not enumerated at that time, since they could not be agreed on. Two years later an agreement was worked out as to which rights should become the guideposts of our society. When ten of the thirteen colonies voted to accept the Bill of Rights, it became law. By the way, "Bill of Rights" was also the name of a less radical English document of 1688. It recognized freedom of speech in the English Parliament, but not anywhere else.

There is no record of Connecticut, Georgia, or Massachusetts having ratified (accepted) the Bill of Rights. They are governed by it though, since two thirds of the other states accepted it.

The Constitution is called the mother of laws, since no law passed can conflict with it. There are two essential issues in constitutional law. The first of these is the topic discussed in political science classes. That is, what powers do the different governmental units have? The other issue is the one which we hear the most about—when do private liberties take precedence over governmental powers? This basic issue is civil rights.

The powers the different governmental units have is primarily a sorting-out process. This process has been going on for over two hundred years, and is likely to continue as long as time passes. For example, only the federal government can control trade between the states. This trade is called "interstate commerce." A hundred years ago a state could make laws concerning the required axle width for a commercial farm wagon. Chances were that farm wagons would rarely go out of the state. Today, any truck is likely to travel out of the state because of remarkably improved transportation systems. Therefore, as the country has grown, the right of a state to legislate in the areas of commerce and transportation has consistently shrunk. Although allocation of governmental powers is very important to the way our country is conducted, it does not radically affect the life of an average citizen.

However, private rights affect our lives every single day. It is sometimes a near thing when a court has to decide which is more important, the private right of the citizen or the governmental power. For example, when a government employee swears to uphold the Official Secrets Act, it becomes a crime for him to leak government documents, even if they are evidence of wrongdoing. Is it more important that national security be protected or that the people know of wrongdoing? Some of the violations of the Official Secrets Act have included information leading to the discovery of the Army experiments with LSD, the Pentagon Papers, and the CIA assassination of Allende of Chile.

Private rights are basically divided into two parts: personal freedoms and the due process of law. Personal freedoms include freedom of speech, religion, assembly, and the right to keep and bear arms. Personal freedoms cannot be restricted. Due process of the law is the body of superior principles which govern what laws can be made or how laws can be enforced. For example, due process does not allow the government to make a law which would take away personal privacy. When a person is arrested, due process requires that the arresting officers follow a certain procedure. The part of due process which governs the rules of arrest, trial, and incarceration is called procedural due process. When due process is applied to lawmaking, it is called substantive due process. "Substantive" means existing independently. Substantive due process is used in modern times to enlarge the coverage of the Constitution. This expansion is justified by a public policy argument—if the framers of the Bill of Rights could have anticipated long-range microphones, they certainly would have prohibited the government from using them. (In fact, our constitutional fathers probably would have. Our revolution was started by a widespread conspiracy against the state. This conspiracy would not have been possible without the free exchange of ideas.)

The issue of constitutionality is rarely entertained anywhere but in appellate courts. Trial courts, police, and government agencies must conduct themselves under the constitutional rules set up by appellate courts. When somebody has been found guilty, he has the right to appeal various elements of his trial. One of these elements can be the constitutionality of something which led to his conviction. The appellate court then decides if the right was denied. This appellate court can be either a federal appellate court or a state appellate court. If the prosecutor of the case disagrees with the finding, or if the convicted party disagrees with the appellate finding, they can then appeal to the next court level, which might be the U. S. Supreme Court or a state Supreme Court. The last court where the case is heard will make the final decision concerning the case. For example, the case may reach only the first appellate level, be decided, and will end there. That decision will become law for that particular jurisdiction. If the case goes all the way to the U. S. Supreme Court, the decision of the Supreme Court will become law for all federal cases, and depending on the kind of decision, perhaps all state cases where that particular constitutional issue is involved.

The recent death penalty decision shows how this works. A convicted murderer on death row in Georgia appealed on the basis that the death penalty was cruel and unusual punishment and a violation of the due process clause in the Constitution. He did not appeal his conviction; he merely appealed the death penalty which the judge and jury, in their discretion, had assigned him because of the conviction. The Supreme

Court found that this particular Georgia capital punishment statute was cruel and unusual punishment and in violation of the due process clause. The majority of the Supreme Court offered no explanation beyond this, thereby outlawing all death penalties. (For more on the death penalty, see the chapter entitled The Criminal.)

The concept of private rights was new when the United States adopted it. To understand why private rights are so precious, we'll look at some history of the most liberal country of the Old World—England. Up until 1476 English society had been monolithic. The king had an unfettered power over life and death. The Church controlled thought. Thought was strictly religious in nature. Under the doctrine of the Catholic Church at that time, to err was a sin. It was the moral obligation of every man to keep his fellow from hell, by discouraging error.

And then the first book was printed. This event exploded on English society with an impact similar to the one our society felt with the splitting of the atom. Suddenly knowledge was available to the people. Ideas could be spread more quickly. The upper classes started to read for the first time. Bright children of the middle class were educated outside of monasteries. Thoughts, criticism, and the Reformation seemed to hit all at once. The society had remained essentially unchanged since the Romans left England. Now, change, political foment, and communication became the watchwords of the day.

Within a generation, Luther in Germany and John Knox in England had reformed religious thinking. Because religious thinking had formed the basis of political structure, the Reformation caused tidal waves of effect far beyond the shores of religion, and the political structure itself began to crumble in the fresh wind of informed thinking.

The king feared for his throne and began to take measures to suppress the change sweeping the land. He instituted the Star Chamber, the English version of the Spanish Inquisition. The Star Chamber's purpose was to protect the king and the government from criticism and political change. The Star Chamber was willing to go to any end to accomplish its goal. Charges of treason became commonplace, and the Star Chamber brought charges, tortured confessions from the accused, and tried the cases. They also charged people with the hanging offense of sedition (criticizing the government). In less than fifty years, the Star Chamber managed to suppress political thinking and publication of political literature.

The Star Chamber was disbanded in 1641, but the crime of sedition remained in the most liberal country of the Old World—England.

John Twyn was found guilty of treason in 1664 for printing a book

whose theme was that the king was accountable to the people, and that
the people had the right to take matters into their own hands and revolt
if the king did not live up to his responsibilities. For publishing this
thought, John Twyn was hanged, drawn, and quartered.

About one hundred years later, John Twyn's philosophy became the
war cry of our own revolution. When the signers of the Declaration of
Independence swore to uphold independence with their lives, fortunes,
and sacred honor, they took the oath seriously. If John Twyn had
suffered such agonies for publishing a book, imagine what would have
happened if we lost the revolution.

RULE: YOU CAN SAY WHAT YOU THINK.

The First Amendment to the Constitution says: "the Congress shall
make no law . . . abridging the freedom of speech." At the time this
amendment became law, it was considered to be radical in the extreme.
No country on earth gave its people the right to criticize the conduct of
their government. Although this amendment began as a prohibition on
the U. S. Congress from making laws modifying the right to free
speech, it has become an absolute right of Americans to say what they
think regarding the conduct of their government.

There have been various attempts, usually in time of war, to restrict
various parts of the freedom to speak out concerning the government's
conduct. Among these, the most prominent was the Espionage Act of
1917. This act restricted persons from willfully causing insubor-
dination, disloyalty, mutiny, or refusal to serve in the armed forces. In
one case, Eugene Debs, a socialist, was indicted. In another, Abrams, a
communist, was charged. Although their convictions stood, Oliver
Wendell Holmes wrote a brilliant opinion which differed with the majority. Mr. Holmes's dissent has become the philosophical point of view of
free speech in the United States.

But when men have realized that time has upset many fighting faiths,
they may come to believe even more than they believe the very founda-
tions of their own conduct that the ultimate good desired is better reached
by free trade in ideas—that the best test of truth is the power of the
thought to get itself accepted in the competition of the market, and that
truth is the only ground upon which their wishes safely can be carried
out. That at any rate is the theory of our Constitution. It is an experiment,
as all life is an experiment. Every year if not every day we have to wager
our salvation upon some prophecy based upon imperfect knowledge.

Mr. Justice Holmes, dissenting opinion
Abrams v. *the United States,* 250 U.S. 616 (1919)

RULE: THE RIGHT TO SPEAK HAS LIMITS.

Freedom of speech is restricted to criticism of governmental action. Freedom of speech does not allow a person to injure another's reputation, to lie, to incite to riot, or to interfere with the orderly course of justice.

Injury to another person's reputation by speaking is called slander. Slander may be a lie or an opinion intended to maliciously harm another's reputation. It is not protected by freedom of speech since slander is merely one person harming another. It's not a constitutional issue. Lying is also not protected by the First Amendment. For example, perjury (lying in a court of law) is not a First Amendment privilege. Lying to obtain money, called fraud, is also not protected.

Interfering with the orderly course of justice is also not allowed under freedom of speech. The person who interferes may be denying the right of another to a fair trial. Practically every community has ordinances prohibiting the picketing of a courthouse. Imagine the chaos of a full-blown demonstration complete with bullhorns and chanting while a trial is being conducted inside. By the same token, freedom of speech is strictly suppressed within the courtroom itself. Once again, freedom of speech will become subservient to the accused's right to a fair trial.

RULE: YOU HAVE THE RIGHT TO HOLD A MEETING.

Being able to speak would not do you much good unless you had a place to do it and could meet with other persons of a similar mind. This rule is called the right of assembly. You may speak in the town council, on a street corner, and any other place where you think your opinion should be heard. However, when you say it is a matter of local regulation. Neither the town council nor the Congress of the United States need listen to an unlimited amount of public opinion and will set limits on the amount of opinion they listen to.

The right to hold a meeting can be modified when people may be injured. The laws controlling meetings are usually called inciting to riot or clear and present danger statutes. In order to protect people from physical harm, freedom of speech can be temporarily held in abeyance until the threat of clear and present danger has passed. The meeting can take place at another time, hopefully under safer circumstances.

Whenever local authorities consider who is to speak as opposed to what they will say, the courts have found that freedom of speech has been denied. Local and state authorities may require that you get a license to hold your meeting. This licensing is legal as long as everyone needs a license and not just certain groups. The license may not be denied on some broad basis, such as the meeting would cause "consternation and alarm," as this is too broad to be enforced. However, the local authorities do have the right to maintain order, to be present at your meeting along with the police, or to make other provisions to provide for the community's safety.

RULE: THE PRESS CAN SAY WHAT
IT THINKS TOO.

Freedom of the press is another type of freedom of speech. It wouldn't do much good to speak unless you could also publish what you say and disseminate your thinking to a wider audience.

When questions of fact are involved the press must print the truth— what actually happened, or a reasonable report of what happened. It's hard to get a straight story, but the reporter must have made an effort to verify his information. The famous journalistic precepts of who, what, where, and when are guidelines for a reporter to follow. Why can also be included but it is a matter of opinion. Opinion is also protected under the First Amendment, but there are certain limitations on it. Libel (damage to a person's reputation) is not protected under the First Amendment. When a reporter runs across something which could be injurious to someone's reputation if he reported the story, he has a higher degree of duty to check his facts before the story is published.

The press is also protected by a Supreme Court decision stating that persons in the public eye are more open to criticism than a private person. The public person has a lesser right of privacy than a private person. For example, reports that a movie star has been seen in the company of a female who is not his wife might not be grounds for libel. However, if the same statement were made about a fellow who ran a local hardware store, it might be libelous. The reporter would be required to check with the hardware store owner, whereas he might not have to check with the movie star.

RULE: FREEDOM OF THE PRESS
PROTECTS OBSCENITY.

The issue of obscenity is also protected by freedom of the press. You are probably aware of the difficulties of the obscenity issue. First of all, obscenity is largely a matter of opinion. What one person finds obscene another person may consider artistic. For example, the movie *Midnight*

Cowboy had an "X" rating. Many persons considered this movie a work of art. Some people consider violent murder scenes obscene and find nothing wrong with watching lovemaking on the screen. Other persons think anything is obscene if it contains the word "sex." In the light of so much variation between individuals, the Supreme Court has more or less fallen into confusion with the rest of us. It has held that an item will be judged obscene based on the general standard of a particular community. This ruling has merely opened the floodgates of lawsuits, so that any pressure group may represent themselves as the community. This law is not very effective. Nor does it really make any sense.

Freedom of the press had the original purpose of keeping Americans safe from the sedition laws which had plagued England. You'll remember that the thrust of these sedition laws was forbidding independent political thought and criticism of the government. Since obscenity has nothing to do with sedition and even less to do with politics, any Supreme Court decision on obscenity which mixes the two elements must essentially be in error.

The other side of the obscenity argument is how to allow persons of differing opinions the freedom to act within their own codes of honor. Certainly there is no question that literature like Henry Miller's *Tropic of Cancer* should be available to those who do not find it offensive. On the other hand, the girlie magazines with their prominently displayed bosoms on the front cover would tend to interfere with one's experience at the local newsstand or drugstore. Perhaps the resolution lies within a respect for each individual's rights. Many communities have taken to shielding the covers of these magazines so that the beckoning postures cannot be seen by a casual viewer. This action seems entirely fair, as effort will be required in order to discover the contents of these magazines. Then individual choice begins to take its place over the assault on our eyeballs.

RULE: THE PRESS MAY NOT INTERFERE WITH A FAIR TRIAL.

Just as freedom of speech must be limited when somebody's right to a fair trial is involved, so the press must limit what it says if a fair trial might be sacrificed. The court may order that coverage of a trial be limited to certain types of reporting so that the defendant's case will not be prejudiced. For example, photographs will not be allowed in the courtroom, nor will the attorneys be allowed to make statements concerning the trial or its evidence. Attorneys are permitted to make general statements such as "The defendant is holding up well," and that's about all they can say.

Recently, television cameras have been allowed in some courts. However, at this time, television coverage of a trial is purely experimental. The courts have outlined very specific rules about the television equipment. The cameras are small and stationary, the microphones are unobtrusive, and the attorneys are instructed to pay absolutely no attention to the fact that they are there. Normally, the defendant must give his permission to have his trial taped. The tapes are for private or educational use only and may not be used on news broadcasts.

The press has recently had a Supreme Court decision imposed upon it which may affect its ability to protect sources of information. The state's right to gather evidence and witnesses in criminal prosecutions has been found to be more important than the reporter's right to protect confidentiality of information. The reporters argue that their sources of information are private. People might not talk to reporters if the police were allowed to search news offices, even if the police have a proper search warrant. The police contend that the reporter is obstructing justice by refusing to tell the police where he got his facts. According to a recent decision, police can search newspaper offices as long as they have a proper search warrant.

Under modern legal interpretation, a reporter can be subpoenaed and required to give testimony concerning the sources of his information. If in the end he refuses to reveal his sources, he can be found in contempt of court and remain in jail for as long as the trial in which he refused to testify lasts.

RULE: PRAY AS YOU CHOOSE.

As a man's right to speak his mind is protected, so is his right to know his own spirit in the way he may choose. Freedom of religion is guaranteed under the First Amendment. Most countries have an official religion. England has the Church of England, Italy the Roman Catholic Church, and so on. These state churches are remnants of the days when the king held power by the approval of the Church. In exchange for this support, the king made the Church the official religious body of the country and protected the Church against those who would differ. It was a monopoly on religion. The framers of the Bill of Rights had historical knowledge of two very bloody battles based on religious differences in England, the reign of Bloody Mary and the Puritan Revolution when Oliver Cromwell and his cohorts deposed Charles I. America had been peopled by groups of religious dissenters. Puritans, Quakers, Catholics, Huguenots, Protestants from Catholic countries, Catholics from Protestant countries, and Jewish refugees from the

Spanish Inquisition. The framers thought the only way to handle so much diversity was to call a permanent and everlasting truce between the government and religion.

The position they took was that no law should be made restricting freedom of religion. The courts implemented this with the fallacious position that religion and government stand side by side but never touch, when in fact the two do keep bumping into each other. For example, the IRS may tax an institution if it is not a church. They therefore have to decide what a church is and to do so they must decide what a religion is. By deciding what is a religion, and what is not, they have interfered with the freedom of religion.

Many new religions have grown up in America. For example, Mormonism started in western New York State. Though the tenets of this religion may sound exotic to the uninitiated, there is no doubt that it is a religion and is beneficial to many of its members. There may not be a way to solve the problem of separation of church and state, due to a fundamental opposition between spiritual values, which are hard to put into words, and governmental values, which are anything but mystical.

Ideas can exist side by side without difficulty, but when taxation sneaks into the picture, things start to change. The law says churches can't be taxed, either on income or on property. This right creates problems for the IRS or the local taxing body which must decide what is a legitimate church and what is not. Often, they cannot decide. The line has yet to be clearly drawn.

There are no significant cases regarding the freedom of religion. The cases have only gone as far as whether a Christian Scientist may be compelled to be vaccinated, whether a religious pacifist could be forced to serve in the military, or whether an athiest's children could be forced to pray. These cases concern themselves with the individual exercise of religion. They do not test the relationship of religion and the government.

RULE: YOU CANNOT BE FORCED TO VIOLATE
YOUR OWN RELIGIOUS DOCTRINE.

Some religions do not allow their members to kill. Conscientious objectors to military service must be allowed an alternative form of service to their country, since killing would violate their religious code. However, if the doctrine of their church is not well established and clear or if the alternative service is objected to, the fellow will either have to fulfill his military obligation or go to jail.

By the same token, some religions will not allow a person to swear an oath. Many trial courts require that witnesses swear that their testimony will be true. If a person cannot swear, he is allowed to affirm his testimony without resorting to God as his witness.

Persons who choose to send their children to parochial schools argue that they are taxpayers too and that their children are entitled to aid. Persons whose children attend public schools say that their tax money should not be used to further a particular religion. Unfortunately, this issue plays on both the fairness and the prejudices of a society. The elements of the issue are difficult to separate. Now the situation is further confused by the issue of school busing. Religious schools in many areas have attracted new students due to the threat of the children being bused out of the community.

RULE: CHILDREN IN RELIGIOUS SCHOOLS CAN BE AIDED.

As long as it is the child who is being helped as opposed to the religion, the courts will find tax money allocations to be constitutional. As of this date, state aid for school buses, textbooks, and health programs for parochial schools has been accepted by the courts. Communities may even allow religious instruction in public school buildings. However, if the money is used to promote the religion rather than to help the child, the aid will be declared unconstitutional. The law is yet to be clearly drawn in this area.

RULE: YOUR CHILD CAN BE RELEASED
FROM SCHOOL FOR RELIGIOUS INSTRUCTION.

The courts have decided that children can be let out of regular classes to study religion. The religious classes may take place either in public school buildings or in church facilities. The children may also receive public school credit for their religious classes. However, children may not be forced by the school to take the religious instruction.

In recent years there is a growing concern that churches are often using their nonprofit status to shelter profit-making enterprises such as active farmland and large office buildings. These tax shelters put an extra burden on the rest of the community since the church might not be paying its share of city costs.
Reversing this trend may require a constitutional amendment.

The civil rights we've just discussed are called the four freedoms of the Bill of Rights. They are speech, assembly, press, and religion. Two other articles of the Bill of Rights involve arms and the militia. The

Constitution gives us the right to keep and bear arms because "a well-regulated militia is necessary to the security of a free state." The Constitution also tells us that soldiers cannot be quartered in private homes in peacetime without the consent of the owner. In time of war, there must be laws passed describing under what circumstances a soldier shall be quartered in a private home.

The other section of the Bill of Rights is due process. Due process requires that all people receive the same procedure and treatment under the law. These requirements are well defined. Due process essentially limits the actions of the police and the conduct of the court in criminal cases. We are discussing criminal, not civil cases, which have slightly different rules.

RULE: YOU HAVE THE RIGHT TO COUNSEL.

If you are charged with a crime, even a petty offense such as a parking ticket, you have the right to counsel. Although this right was once restricted to a felony trial alone, it has been widely expanded to include petty offenses, proceedings before and after the trial, habeas corpus, and filing fees. Since the ability to afford counsel has nothing to do with guilt or innocence, methods have been set up to help indigent persons find legal representation. The local bar association or the public defender's office will step forward to help those in need of criminal defense. For civil matters, the local legal-aid society may provide assistance. Occasionally attorneys will take on civil cases without a fee, as a favor, but this situation is rather rare.

RULE: YOU MAY REQUEST A TRIAL BY JURY.

The U. S. Constitution ensures you of a trial by jury for all federal cases involving more than $20. In 1789, when the Bill of Rights was passed, $20 was considerably more money than it is today, but the requirement still exists. Under the due process clause in the Fourteenth Amendment, the right to trial by jury is applied to the states as well.

Jury trials are available only to persons who plead innocent. Juries decide the facts in the case. If you plead guilty, you are saying the facts you are charged with are true, so therefore a jury trial is unnecessary.

Judges normally decide the penalty. In some states, the jury recommends the penalty. Some states require that a crime bear a certain minimum sentence. In the instance of the death penalty, the Supreme Court has ruled that the jury's determination of guilt and their decision to impose the death penalty must come in separate deliberations.

RULE: YOU OR YOUR PROPERTY MAY NOT BE
SEARCHED OR SEIZED WITHOUT CAUSE.

One of the most delicate areas of constitutional law is that of search and seizure. It is in the best interests of the police to be able to go anywhere, searching out evidence and seizing what they find. It is in the best interests of the people, especially the guilty, to strictly limit the police's ability to do this. Therefore, the Constitution requires a warrant issued by a court, with probable cause, taken under oath. The warrant must specifically describe the place to be searched and the persons or things the police or other authority may seize.

A normal warrant will be issued by a court when a district attorney or police officer comes before the court and makes a statement under oath to the effect that he has circumstantial evidence of illegal activity being conducted at a certain place. His evidence may include information from an informant and observation of the property. He would make a charge, such as possession of stolen goods. The court would order the warrant for a specific address, such as 137 South Cumberland, Park Ridge, Illinois. This warrant will entitle the police to search the house, garage, garden, and any other buildings on the property. The warrant would also include the information that the officer was looking for stolen goods. The persons at that address have the right to examine the warrant before they allow the police to enter. But if the warrant states the address correctly, they have no right to deny the police entrance. If after searching the property, the police find no evidence of stolen goods, but do find heroin and evidence of drug dealing, they may retain the heroin since the warrant was legally issued. Heroin itself is evidence of a crime.

There are many other kinds of documents which cannot be seized since they are not obvious evidence of a crime. For example, if the police raided the house looking for stolen goods and they found no obvious evidence of stolen goods, like boxes stacked up, or seventeen TV sets, they would have no right to seize goods from the household just on the off chance that the goods are stolen.

An even finer issue involves documents being seized that might possibly be evidence of wrongdoing. For example, if the Treasury Department is looking for evidence of a business's tax fraud, it may wish to seize every document of the business. However, this action is unreasonable, and the owner of the business could fight the seizure in court and get his papers back.

Warrants are not necessary if the police have a reasonable cause for the search and seizure itself. For example, if the police have seen someone rob a store and they follow him, they may gain entry to any place the robber goes. The more difficult case occurs when a police officer stops someone for a speeding ticket. Something in the person's behavior is peculiar and the officer feels that he may be in the midst of some illegal activity, such as the possession of drugs or stolen goods. Many states have passed statutes defining what is a reasonable search under the circumstances.

Male police officers cannot conduct a search of a woman's body. Female police officers can. Searches of the body will start with a total disrobing, usually in the presence of a female officer. Depending on the regulations of the police department, the matron will search the mouth, the rectum, and the vagina. At this time, body cavity searches are done on *all* women arrested in Chicago, even for traffic violations.

There is probable cause for arrest when a person similar to yourself in appearance and clothing has committed a crime in the neighborhood. For example, if you are walking down the street in a red raincoat and a green scarf, you may find yourself surrounded, arrested, and whisked off to the station house. This arrest would be legal if a woman in a red raincoat and a green scarf has just robbed a local bank.

Probable cause and a police officer's instincts can travel over into chance and even psychic sense. Chicago had a series of hideous Friday-night rapes. The young man was described as having medium-brown hair and wearing an Army fatigue jacket. The officer who finally arrested the man merely decided to follow every young fellow in a fatigue jacket. The third one ran and the officer caught him. It was the Friday-night rapist.

The requirements of illegal search and seizure can be waived by the citizen and is a good policy as long as the citizen has a choice. For example, the police knock on your door and say something like "Police. There's been a shot reported in the building." Let them in. They're trying to help someone and if you don't allow them entrance to your apartment, one officer will have to stay in front of your door while the other goes off to search. By refusing the police entrance, you won't be helping the person in trouble, and may endanger the policeman who is off looking by himself. Just open the door slowly, let them look around, and offer the use of your telephone if they need it. Good citizens have to stick together.

RULE: THEY CAN'T KEEP YOU WITHOUT
CHARGING YOU.

The Constitution also guarantees that a person shall "be informed of the nature and cause of the accusation." Today this means that you must be informed of the crime you are being charged with or you must be released. The procedures of each individual state vary slightly as to how long you can be held without being charged. New York requires twelve hours as a maximum, though as a matter of procedure, everyone is charged immediately, so that no slip-ups occur. Other states allow a person to be held as long as twenty-four hours. If you have not been informally charged, your attorney or a friend can ask for a writ of habeas corpus, meaning, literally, you have the body. Habeas corpus demands that "the body" be presented. When your friend asks for a writ of habeas corpus, the state must show that they have a good case for your retention. The judge will order that you be either charged or released.

RULE: YOU MAY KNOW YOUR ACCUSER.

In a federal case, the formal charge is brought by a grand jury. Ideally, the grand jury screens the charge to see if the charge appears valid. Twenty-three people, civilians like yourself, hear the evidence presented by the federal prosecutor. Witnesses are heard and examined by the federal prosecutor. The defendant is allowed to have an attorney accompany him into the grand jury room. Transcripts of the grand jury proceedings are not available to the accused. All states also have grand jury systems, but there is no constitutional requirement that a criminal held by a state be indicted by grand jury.

In most states the district attorney or state prosecutor will bring the formal charge. Generally, the federal prosecutor or state attorney will be the person accusing you. At the point you are being formally indicted, you need not know who the witnesses are or what the evidence is against you. This information must be supplied to you prior to your trial. You do need to know the exact crime you are accused of.

RULE: YOU CANNOT BE FORCED
TO CONFESS.

The Fifth Amendment protects all Americans against self-incrimination. If a person is to be proved guilty, it must be done on evidence gotten from other sources. You have the right to confess, if you wish to, but no brutal or coercive methods may be used to extract this confession.

Of course, no police agent may beat an individual, nor may he deprive him of minimal needs such as food, sleep, or communication with the outside. Confessions which have been coerced are not admissible as evidence. A coerced confession may color the case so much that the police may be forced to release the prisoner.

By the same token spouses cannot be forced to testify against one another. In the eyes of the law, husband and wife are almost the same person. Consequently, it would violate self-incrimination if the spouse were forced to testify. The spouse may choose to testify, but may not be forced to do so.

RULE: STAY OUT OF GRAND JURIES.

The exception to the right against self-incrimination is testimony of witnesses before a grand jury. The person who is being charged need not testify, but witnesses guilty of the same crime can be granted immunity from prosecution (use immunity). If the federal prosecutor acquires use immunity for a witness, the witness must testify even if in doing so he incriminates himself in other crimes. He can then be charged with the other crimes. The federal prosecutor need not confine his questioning to the matter at hand. The witness may not even know who is being charged or what questions may be asked of him. The federal prosecutor can go on hunting expeditions and need not follow any particular rules of conduct. No judge is present, or any other authority to modify the prosecutor's conduct. Any question the witness answers besides name, address, telephone number, and age, will open up literally any portion of that witness's life to investigation. The witness must answer. If he does not answer, he can be charged with contempt and jailed for as long as 180 days. Perjury can also be charged if a witness lies before a grand jury. If you're called to be a witness before a grand jury, you can get an attorney and have the subpoena overcome before you appear. Once you appear, there's not much to do, except talk.

The reason for the rule recommending that you stay out of grand juries is modified if you have witnessed an ordinary crime like murder. Your testimony may be needed to charge the criminal.

Unfortunately, grand juries have been badly used in recent times. Especially during the late 1960s, the grand jury was used for fishing expeditions to gather evidence against those in the peace movement. The most famous case involved Benjamin Spock, the pediatrician. He was eventually charged with conspiracy—talking to other people about how to end the Vietnam War. The law makes it possible for politicians to use grand juries as a weapon against their political adversaries. When it is misused, the grand jury becomes reminiscent of the English Star Chamber.

RULE: YOU CAN FIND OUT WHAT THE GOVERNMENT IS SAYING ABOUT YOU.

Testimony given in a grand jury, whether it is true or not, may find its way into government files. The government may also gather information on you and your family if you: have been in the news, been charged with a crime, been active in a social reform group, lived next door to anyone with a file, done business with a politically active person, run for office, have a name similar to that of any person doing any of the above. And, believe it or not, you may have also been watched because an FBI agent had to fill his quota of political subversives but couldn't find a real one to list.

In 1966, Congress passed the Freedom of Information Act (FOIA). FOIA tore off the veil of government secrecy. Citizens now have an absolute right to see their personal files. But more important, the people have the right to ask for any government documents. FOIA has turned up some exceptional information. When one citizen asked the CIA for their 1962-to-1976 files on mind-control experiments (subjugation of the individual through pain, drugs, and hypnosis), the CIA's reply stated that they had 130 file drawers of documents for the period between 1962 and 1976. The CIA had previously stated that all mind-control experiments had stopped in 1961. Obviously FOIA is as important to the public at large as it is to individuals.

The Freedom of Information Act does not require that the citizen show any special need to see particular files. The burden of proof is on the agency to show cause why the files should not be released. The form for making a request is simple. You merely state that you are making a request under FOIA, and then give a general description of the subject matter of the documents you would like to see. If an agency turns you down, you have the right to appeal.

Sometimes a person will fear reprisals if she should make an FOIA request. There may be some truth in this, but generally, government workers are more afraid of you than you are of them. The most experienced group in the use of FOIA has published a pamphlet describing the procedure of FOIA. It has made several thousand FOIA requests and most of them have been successful. (For a free copy of *How to Use the Freedom of Information Act,* write: Church of Scientology Information Service, 5930 Franklin Avenue, Hollywood, California 90028.)

RULE: EVERYBODY MUST BE TREATED THE SAME.

The same Fourteenth Amendment which contains the due process clause also contains the equal protection clause. It is through the equal protection clause that many modern civil rights cases have been decided. School desegregation and school busing are outgrowths of the equal protection clause.

The equal protection clause has an exception as well. All persons must receive equal treatment except those who have an outstanding history of discriminatory treatment. These people are entitled to an especially good standard of treatment. Blacks, women, and disabled persons may have special laws passed to give them advantages over other segments of the population. However, the Supreme Court has recently made a modest retreat from this principle. The Bakke decision from California concerned a white male who felt he had been unjustly denied entrance to medical school by the university's preference for minority students. The court held that there was no showing that the school had ever been guilty of discrimination in the past. According to the decision, the school did indeed discriminate against Mr. Bakke, but the court approved an affirmative action program (favoring of minority students) as long as that program didn't interfere with regular admissions of all qualified persons. This area is obviously a muddle with no true beginning, middle, or end. Nobody really has a clear idea of what to do about it, either. Only time, and more cases, will tell.

The equal protection clause is especially effective when the state or federal government attempts to set up a so-called suspect classification, a group of persons that will be watched more closely or held to a higher standard of conduct than other persons. Equal protection means that aliens or Presbyterians or green-eyed females cannot be held to a different standard of conduct than other people. For example, if an alien commits a crime, he may be deported, but this law applies to all aliens. The only reason why a United States citizen would not be deported is that there is no place to send him. By the same token, a Greek alien could not be deported for a more minor crime than that committed by an English alien who was not deported. The importance of the right which is modified will affect how much restriction is allowed. The more important the right, the less restriction is allowed. Every person, alien or citizen, has the right to travel, freedom of speech, due process, etc. However, no right is being violated when the federal government requires all aliens to register their location once a year.

Procedural due process, which we have just discussed, controls how people are tried and convicted. There is another type of due process, substantive (independent) due process, which tests the law itself, to see if it is fair. After all, the legislature could make laws which limit your rights.

Substantive due process is now called the peripheral rights theory. Under this theory, the court acknowledges that persons have rights that the legislatures may not control. Among these undescribed rights is the right of privacy. The peripheral rights theory arose out of a 1968 appeal of a case brought under a criminal statute in Connecticut which prohibited married couples from using contraceptive devices. The court said that zones of privacy were implied in the Bill of Rights. Contraception was one of these zones of privacy.

This Connecticut case started a whole string of cases in the area of contraception and birth control which have revolutionized women's rights. Surprisingly, the court relied on the little-used Ninth Amendment, which states that the Bill of Rights "shall not be construed to deny or disparage [certain rights] retained by the people."

RULE: YOU HAVE THE RIGHT TO AN ABORTION.

Two abortion cases were decided by the Supreme Court in 1973. The first of the cases is called *Roe* v. *Wade*. This case found that due process requires that a woman's personal liberties include the decision whether or not she will terminate her pregnancy. The second case was called *Doe* v. *Bolton*. In this case the court found that only a *compelling* interest in maintaining life and medical standards could justify government regulation or prohibition of abortion. Since life cannot be maintained outside the mother's womb during the first three months of pregnancy, state legislatures or state courts are not allowed to interfere. In the second trimester, the second three months of pregnancy, abortions could be prohibited if the mother's life was not in danger. Third-trimester abortions are generally dangerous to the mother; also the child might survive. This judicial stand is a bit confusing, since it seems to rest on the ability of the child to live outside the womb. As one expert has pointed out, if the inability of the child to live if aborted during the first three months is the reason for allowing a first-trimester abortion, then why would the state suddenly develop an interest in the fetus during the second three months? It is currently possible to keep a fetus alive outside the womb during the second trimester. There is no reason to assume that medical science will not also be able to maintain the life of an embryo even in the first three months. This stand may be an intermediate step, an effort to reconcile a woman's freedom with the interest of unborn children.

The backlash on these abortion decisions has been highly verbal, even violent. Various states have adopted laws requiring husband's consent, criminal penalties against doctors who destroy the fetus which could have survived outside the womb, and prohibition of abortions in public hospitals as well as the refusal to use public funds to pay for the abortion. These measures have been more or less effective. The law requiring parental consent for a minor who seeks an abortion has been overcome by the courts allowing a minor to seek a court-ordered abortion. Physicians have avoided laws affecting them by insisting upon the husband's consent in writing.

There is a rather famous case in Massachusetts in which a doctor was indicted under the homicide laws of that state. The prosecutor charged that the doctor had let a child die which could have survived a different type of abortion than the one the doctor used. The court ruled that if a physician fails to protect "a live-born infant," he will be subject to prosecution. However, any statutes which require extraordinary medical procedures to maintain the life of a fetus during any stage of pregnancy are unconstitutional. There was some social significance in this case as well, since the doctor was black, practicing in heavily Roman Catholic Massachusetts. Once again, the ability of the infant to live outside the womb (viability) came up. Viability may continue to haunt this area.

After the Roe and Doe decisions, many state legislatures passed bills prohibiting public health insurance from covering so-called non-therapeutic abortions, that is, abortion where the mother's life is not in danger. The court allowed the states to do this on the grounds that although the state may not interfere with a constitutional right, it is not obliged to encourage the exercise thereof. The same was found true of non-therapeutic abortions in public hospitals. If a woman is poor, or too young, the absence of public funds and facilities can present a difficulty, since at least $100 will be needed to pay for the abortion. Middle-class women are likely to be able to acquire the funds, but for others, $100 can be an unobtainable amount of money.

Abortion clinics are occasionally operated as rackets. The clinic offers free pregnancy tests in the hope that the abortion will be done at that clinic. A surprisingly large percentage of their tests results indicate pregnancy. A consumer reporter in New York sent out a number of young women to have pregnancy tests at the clinics. They were certified by a physician as not pregnant before they began their investigation. In three out of four clinics visited, the tests were positive and the young women were recommended for abortion.

If you are dealing with an abortion clinic, it would be best to have tests done by an independent person, your own physician, a hospital clinic, or other trustworthy source.

The opposition over abortion appears to be divided into three camps. A segment of abortion opponents argue against it since women can avoid responsibility for the fruits of their promiscuity. In point of fact, many married women with children have abortions to keep down the size of their families. Another segment says the fetus has an immortal soul. By destroying the infant, the woman and doctor are destroying an immortal soul. This religious argument should certainly be honored among the people who believe it to be true, but these believers are imposing on the rights of others when they attempt to make a law of their religious philosophy. The third segment merely wants to save the babies. This argument, though emotional, certainly stems from a fine purpose. However, these people are not going to be the ones who raise the unwanted children.

On the other hand, medical science can now tell us when genetically defective children have been conceived. These tests can detect mongolism, Tay-Sachs disease, and other genetically caused illnesses. If the mother has a choice, she may not desire the heartache and burden of caring for such a child. More prosperous women could go abroad to have defective fetuses aborted, but a poor woman would not be able to bear the expense. Abortion does help put a woman in control of her own life. It is not an easy choice under the best circumstances, and most women prefer to use birth control to avoid ever having to decide to have an abortion.

The breakthrough in abortion cases is much more significant than the abortion issue itself. The abortion cases are a warning to legislatures that they now must have a compelling interest when passing legislation which interferes with freedoms which the court considers to be implicit in the Bill of Rights. Reasonable justification by the legislature is no longer adequate if the bills restrict individual freedoms.

In recent years the courts have been more and more reluctant to make highly controversial civil rights decisions. Some of this has to do with a more conservative Supreme Court, but the primary reason for the court's drawing back from civil rights decisions is the behavior of the legislature. At the time *Brown* v. *Board of Education* was decided in 1954, the federal and state legislatures had totally abandoned their responsibilities to protect the civil rights of our citizens. The court felt that it was the only governmental body able to make decisions in this area. It maintained its authority to make social change until the legislatures were able to act in this area free of political harm. Civil rights is now a political issue of some consequence and the courts are not the only ones bearing the standard of the individual's freedom.

Under the Constitution "Congress shall have the power to enforce . . . by appropriate legislation." The Congress has the right to draw legislation which somewhat modifies judicial decisions. However, Congress cannot interfere with rights the court has declared are protected by the Constitution. Therefore, the court will decide what personal rights are constitutionally protected. The Congress may then use any rational means to enforce the standard. Voting rights are an example of the difference. The courts decided that certain types of voter registration had the effect of depriving certain citizens of their right to vote. It was left to the Congress to decide precisely how voter registration was to be conducted. The courts will not make decisions on absolutely every problem, or as the Supreme Court has stated, "the Constitution does not provide judicial remedies for every social and economic ill." Social and economic ills are the responsibility of the legislatures and, ultimately, ourselves.

There are a great many civil rights which are not discussed in this chapter. No treatment of racial discrimination, the right to travel, voting rights, private discrimination, could be adequately treated within the space allotted. Some civil rights issues are picked up in other chapters where they are appropriate.

If the Constitution is the mother of law, civil rights is the mother of justice. We are fortunate that our Constitution is flexible enough to allow the incorporation of changing social attitudes, no matter how unwelcome these attitudes might be to certain segments of the population. Societies have a choice: to change and grow, or to stay the same and die. People, not governments, cause change, and people need civil rights to be able to cause change. Civil rights are both our fortress and our freedom. Guard them.

Chapter 18
RAPE

I've learned now that certain laws are different from what I'd imagined them to be; but I can't accept that such laws can be right.
—*A Doll's House,* Act Three, Henrik Ibsen, Michael Meyer, translator.

The contents of this chapter may make you angry. What you will read represents the prosecution of rape as it stands today.

Rape generally must satisfy the following:
1. Unlawful
2. Sexual intercourse
3. With a woman
4. Against her will
5. By force or threat of immediate force.

RULE: A HUSBAND CANNOT RAPE HIS WIFE.

Under the common-law principles of rape, it is not possible for a man to rape his wife. After a couple has married, sexual intercourse between spouses can never be unlawful. The states in which a woman cannot bring charges of rape against her husband are: Arizona, California, Colorado, Connecticut, Delaware, Illinois, Kentucky, Minnesota, Montana, New Mexico, Oklahoma, Pennsylvania, South Dakota, Texas, Utah, Vermont, Washington, West Virginia, and Wyoming. Since 1967 some states have begun to allow a charge of rape if the couple are legally separated or living apart. The requirements of the statutes vary from state to state, but some version of the statute is available in: Louisiana, Maine, New Hampshire, New York, North Dakota, Ohio, Oregon, and Wisconsin.

Research for this book uncovered some extraordinary information. Whether by legislative oversight or design, the statutes of many states do not exclude a man's wife from the definition of rape victims. Since wives are not excluded from the definition, these women could theoretically charge their husbands. However, there are no cases in any of these states showing that a wife had brought rape charges against her husband. The states which seem to allow rape charges brought by wives against husbands are: Alabama, Alaska, Arkansas, Florida, Georgia, Hawaii, Idaho, Indiana, Iowa, Kansas, Maryland, Massachusetts, Michigan, Mississippi, Missouri, Nebraska, Nevada, New Jersey, Rhode Island, South Carolina, Tennessee, and Virginia; the District of Columbia also seems to allow such charges.

Possibly the prosecutors in these states have refused to pursue a wife's charges against her husband. The Rideout case in Oregon may be an example of the difficulties involved in a rape charge against a husband. Mrs. Rideout charged her estranged husband with rape, and he was acquitted. Shortly after the end of the trial, Mr. and Mrs. Rideout were reconciled. This puzzling turnabout astounded everyone, and many took it as confirmation that a wife should not be able to press rape charges against her husband. However, one woman's inconsistencies should not limit the rest of us.

RULE: SEXUAL INTERCOURSE IS ONLY PENILE-VAGINAL CONTACT.

The common-law rule restricted rape to penile-vaginal contact alone, and did not include any other type of contact. This is the law in most states. The penile penetration need not be more than superficial.

Rape does not include sodomy. The law defines sodomy as sexual contact with any body cavity other than the vagina. Homosexual rape or the woman's rape of a man is not rape in the common-law sense. Also no other contact with a vagina would be rape. It is not unusual for a rapist to be impotent, and other body parts and instruments have been used to perform an act which the law would refuse to recognize as a rape. In this instance the rapist could be charged with sodomy or aggravated sexual assault.

The model penal code is now beginning to recognize sodomy as a type of rape. Homosexual rape is also becoming a crime. Some state statutes are being enlarged to allow a woman to be charged with rape.

One case pointed out a woman who had forced a man to have sex with her at gunpoint. This occurrence falls into the strange-but-true category.

RULE: THE LAW REQUIRES YOU TO RESIST.

Because the definition of rape includes that the sexual act be contrary to the woman's will, the woman must put up a fight if she is to charge rape. The woman must substantially resist. Words such as "No! Leave me alone," etc., will not suffice. However, if the woman is so physically boxed in that her escape might cause her death, serious bodily injury, or continually being recaptured, she is free to use this fact as the reason why she did not offer greater resistance.

RULE: HE HAS TO THINK HE'S RAPING YOU.

If he has any cause to believe that you have given your consent, the law believes that it would be impossible for him to form the intent to commit rape. For this reason the law has long been hard on women out late at night alone, prostitutes, women who go to men's apartments, and other women whose actions might indicate a certain willingness to be seduced. In other words, a woman is expected to actively guard her virtue. If she does not, forced use of her body will not be rape.

RULE: THE FORCE MUST BE STRONGER THAN YOUR RESISTANCE.

Just how much force is needed to make a rape forcible is a matter for the jury's interpretation in each case. If a woman tries to run away and her assailant grabs her, it is probably forcible. Guns and knives are also an obvious form of force. Recently in New York City, two rapists were killed by their chosen victims. In one instance, the woman took the man's knife away and used it on him. In the second incident, the victim was an off-duty female police officer who crushed her attacker's windpipe.

RULE: THERE IS NO EXCUSE FOR STATUTORY RAPE.

Statutory rape is intercourse with a female under a particular age. The age varies from state to state, but 16 is the average age. The man need have no idea that the girl was under age. The fact that the girl represented herself to be 18 when she was actually 15 will not protect the male offender.

Sometimes statutory rape is restricted to girls under 13. If the state has this particular type of statute, it probably has an additional crime called carnal knowledge of a child. Although this is a less serious offense, it will still protect the underage girl. The statutes concerning carnal knowledge of a child cover girls who are a bit older, in some states as old as 18.

This description of rape you have just read is the standard common-law definition of a particular sexual abuse. It obviously does not cover other types of sexual abuse. Two additional types of sexual abuse are common under criminal-law statutes. These are sodomy and aggravated sexual assault, which may be incorporated into a rape statute or stand on their own as individual offenses. Sodomy is sexual contact with any orifice of the body other than the vagina. Aggravated sexual assault is a rape with an instrument such as a screwdriver which is used to violate the woman. The penalties for these statutory offenses are the same as for rape.

Different types of sex offenses carry different penalties. Rape, sodomy, and aggravated sexual assault are considered very serious crimes. In some states they carry the death penalty. In most states they have the second-longest sentence, after murder. Statutory rape is less serious, and the penalty for it is sometimes avoided if the male is under age as well. Carnal knowledge of a child is less serious yet.

Particular evidence is required for the successful prosecution of a rape case. This evidence is called "physical evidence" or "hard evidence." Physical evidence is things like fingerprints, a murder weapon, etc. In a rape case, the physical evidence would be semen samples, torn clothing, samples of the assailant's hair and skin, or a weapon. However, the law requires that physical evidence be protected by a "chain of custody," an orderly possession of the evidence from the time it is collected until the time it is offered as evidence in court. Each possessor along the line must be able to swear that the evidence could not have been mixed up or that some other evidence was not substituted for the original.

Until recently, much of the physical evidence of a rape was destroyed when the victim was taken to the hospital. Typically, a rape victim would be treated and her damaged clothing destroyed. Semen samples might not be taken and the required chain of custody might be ignored.

The Houston plan was formulated to protect the physical evidence of a rape. Under the Houston plan, emergency room personnel are trained to collect evidence. Semen samples are required. These samples are analyzed to determine the assailant's blood type, which can serve as support for identification by the victim. Clothing is carefully preserved so that police technicians can search for samples of the attacker's hair and skin, another identification technique. The torn clothing can also be used at the trial to illustrate the violence of the attack. The evidence is sealed by hospital personnel and passed to the police in an orderly fashion. Sealing the evidence protects the chain of custody.

The Houston plan greatly aids in rape prosecutions. If your local hospital is not currently using this plan, you should encourage it to do so.

Probably the most dramatized part of rapes is the problems involved in prosecuting these cases. About half of the women raped are purely innocent victims. Unfortunately, some women press rape charges out of revenge or to protect their reputation. In New York City, police detectives estimate that fully one half of rape charges are made on the basis of social necessity. (The rate of false charges is lower elsewhere.) For example, a teen-age girl will often allege that she became pregnant due to a rape. She didn't inform her parents at the time because she was so embarrassed. This type of case sometimes turns out to be fallacious. The girl was sleeping with her boy friend and was hiding this fact from her family.

Some very strange mental aberrations on the woman's part can bring on the charge of rape. One college girl had an excessive crush on a professor. She followed him around the halls and haunted his classroom. When her admiration was not returned, she charged him with rape. Fortunately good detective work uncovered her particular craziness.

When the state prosecutor is faced with the practicalities of pursuing a rape charge, she has many prejudices of the society and legal problems of proof to deal with. After you finish this particular section, you may be amazed that there are any rape convictions at all.

If the victim is a child, her age will sometimes stand in the way of any prosecution whatsoever. Under the age of 12, children must be questioned to discover whether or not they understand the seriousness of the trial before them. If the child is too young, or not bright, no charge can be brought unless someone witnessed the rape of the child. The court may also have a difficult time explaining to the child the concept of penetration.

If the rape victim does not protest immediately, the medical evidence which would corroborate her story will be destroyed. This situation is quite typical when a child or a separated wife has been raped. This "lack of recent outcry" will also be indicative to the jury which hears the case that this may be a put-up job. Juries rarely believe charges which are raised weeks after the event was supposed to have happened.

The relationship between the parties will also modify the rape charge. If the man and woman were out on a date, and he insisted on intercourse, she may not be able to charge him with rape unless she is injured to such a degree that the amount of resistance she showed is obvious. Intercourse under these circumstances, even if some force is used, is more properly defined as seduction. Seduction may also be criminal, but not of the same magnitude as rape. The so-called "Saturday Night Fever" forced intercourse is never taken as seriously by juries as a rape would be.

If the woman is reluctant to have a physical examination, the rape charge can probably not be pursued. Refusal of an examination is typical if the victim is young. She simply can't face another intrusion into her body.

And then there is the problem of identification. Most women are not calm while being raped. They have a very hard time identifying the man later. There is also a great reluctance on the part of the families of the victim to allow the young woman to face the vigorous cross-examination in court. This cross-examination is necessary in any criminal case to protect the rights of the accused, but can be a truly awful experience, as you will see in a moment.

Additionally, criminal defendants are rarely convicted on the testimony of one person alone. Obviously there are few cases where there are any witnesses to the act besides the female herself.

Rape is often confused with seduction by deception. The man and woman met in a bar, at a party, or any one of a number of places where people congregate. An invitation up to his apartment to see etchings, etc., is an old story to most jurors. They really don't believe that the man is guilty of rape. Seduction differs from rape in that some consent, either implied or explicit, has been procured by artifice, deception, flattery, fraud, or promise. Obviously many events of unwanted intercourse fall into this category. If a woman is in compromising circumstances, her consent may be implied by the man. Since one of the requirements of rape is his intent to commit rape, the charge of rape will fail.

The jurors who find the facts in the case often have their own private beliefs as to what constitutes behavior which would invite seduction. Such things as scanty clothing, being alone in a bar, or having a profession such as prostitution or nude dancing indicate to the jury that the woman, at the very least, was inviting seduction. Sometimes actions will cause the jury to disbelieve the woman's charge. Inviting strangers to her apartment makes a charge of rape less than believable.

Depending on the state where the woman charges rape, her history of sexual activity may be admitted to impeach her testimony. If a woman is shown to be promiscuous, the jury will disbelieve her somewhat, and dismiss the charge on the basis of their opinion that "What's one more man?" Even the states which do not allow general testimony regarding the victim's sexual history will probably allow testimony regarding prior sexual relationships the victim had with this particular defendant.

We now get to the ugliest problem of them all. Victims of rape frequently seek psychiatric help to handle the problems activated by the rape. The defense attorney will have to be told about the victim's psychiatric history as part of preparation for the case. The defense attorney will then use the psychiatric history created by the rape to imply that the victim is too crazy to be a good witness. Juries often agree. Any incidence of mental aberration will also put the victim on trial, instead of the rapist. Any psychiatric history, retardation, or drug use will cause the jury to disbelieve the victim.

That's the way it works. Damned sad.

Chapter 19
BATTERED WOMEN

When women were a possession of their husbands, justice abstained from dealing with the problem of violence between the spouses. The wife was more important than an ox but less important than farmland. A woman's position sprouted from very practical reasoning. The likelihood of a woman surviving childbirth was low. A man could always get a new wife, but land was scarce. Additionally, under Anglo-Saxon law, the family is a patriarchy. The father is king, and his word is final. Male jurists were uncomfortable messing with another patriarch. Wife beating was "a family matter," so judges refused to make law about it. And for eight centuries wife beating was ignored.

Now times have changed, and democracy has entered the family structure. Suddenly, women refuse the concept that wife beating is outside of the law. We discovered we could enforce assault laws against physically cruel husbands. But law enforcement officials, just like the ancient judges, are loath to interfere.

Let's back up for a moment and take a look at the nature of the problem. One million women in the United States are habitually abused by their husbands. The reason for the wife beating is occasionally cultural—the husband's mother was beaten. Job and money tensions often contribute—the man's frustration vents against the nearest target, his wife. Drug use is the catalyst, as 75 per cent of these violent incidents involve alcohol. So the typical wife beater is a frustrated man who drinks.

Although wife beating is not restricted to a particular social class, it is most pathetic when it happens to an uneducated woman with children. She finds she has no practical alternative to staying with her husband, since she has no way to feed herself or her children. Nor has society taught her that she has the duty to protect her integrity.

The problems of battered women can't be solved solely by use of the law. A battered woman must also consider the psychic and economic survival of herself and her children. Most of the decisions a battered woman has to make are not legal in nature.

The first decision is whether she wishes to stay with her husband and work the problem out. However, if she makes this decision she may remain in physical danger for an extended period. She may decide to leave the home temporarily. She may decide to divorce. She may even go so far as pressing criminal assault charges.

If a woman has no children, these decisions are simplified. But if children are involved, she must also consider their security. Obviously this is an individual problem with no clear-cut answer.

The rules in this chapter are guidelines based on the experience of experts in the field. The rules are not always legal in nature since the point is the woman's survival, not her legal sophistication.

RULE: LEAVE HIM IF HE STRIKES YOU.

Many battered women were beaten for the first time on their honeymoon. Pregnancy may also initiate physical abuse. Experience shows that beatings tend to accelerate rather than diminish.

The first few times a man beats his wife, he's likely to be careful. She may not even be bruised. She may say to herself, "Well, I'm only a little sore. I'll just forget it this time." But this attitude gives a man permission to continue and the beatings are likely to become more severe. In fact, they may eventually result in the woman's death.

The only simple thing for a woman to do is to leave before the responsibility of children ties her to the home.

RULE: TELL SOMEBODY WHY YOU LEFT HIM.

In nearly all states (except New York and North Carolina), if a woman leaves her home, she has abandoned the marriage. She then becomes the guilty party in a divorce. In the case of abuse, she should take steps to protect herself. When she gets to her mother's or friend's house, she should come out with the truth: "I've been beaten." Emotional statements made to family or close friends immediately after an incident will have a ring of truth.

Any decent lawyer can defeat abandonment in a divorce action if the woman has evidence that she was beaten. Statements made just after the incidents are one type of proof. See the chapter on divorce.

A woman's first line of defense against violence at home is the police. Many women assume that the police will be able to help with the problem. But the interests of the police are somewhat different. First of all, the officer will have a hard time deciding if any real harm is likely to come to the woman. He doesn't want to spend a whole night writing reports if the couple are going to kiss and make up after he leaves. His background may not have prepared him to mediate in a family dispute. And then there is some chance that the police officer will be either wounded or killed for his efforts. Nationwide, some fifteen officers a year lose their lives during family dispute calls. Many police departments have been training their officers to handle family disputes. However, the primary purpose of the training is to keep the officers from being killed.

RULE: IF YOU CAN'T LEAVE HOME,
CALL THE POLICE.

In spite of the police officer's shortcomings, the woman will need a police report to back her up for any of the legal steps which might end the violence problem. Family court counseling, civil or criminal assault, cease and desist orders, or citizen's arrest will all be enhanced by the existence of a police report. As it is unlikely that the woman will be able to call the police during a violent incident, she may make arrangements for a neighbor to call for her. She can put a neighbor on alert to call the police if the neighbor hears a disturbance.

RULE: DON'T HIDE THE PROBLEM JUST
BECAUSE YOU HAVE CHILDREN.

Many battered woman say that they've not left home because they wanted family stability for their children. But for children living in a brutal home, the effects of abuse can negate stability and cripple the course of their whole lives.

In fact, the children try to find an explanation for the brutality. Since it is not rational that Daddy would beat Mommy, most children decide that Mommy is bad and that Daddy is right to beat her. The children grow to hate Mommy, and in their eyes not only is she so weak as to allow the beatings, she must also be evil.

Woman who value their own relationship with their children will find it improved by getting the children out of the home. Battered women

must break the pattern or they may be condemning their own grandchildren to the same misery. The sons of such marriages often grow up
to beat their own wives; the daughters choose husbands who will beat
them.

RULE: REMOVE YOUR DAUGHTERS IF YOUR
HUSBAND DESIRES THEM.

Incest is a hidden crime. It is far more prevalent than one might expect. Jim Post, a woman's prison chaplain in Kansas, says he is astounded when one of the prisoners has *not* been sexually assaulted by
her father or stepfather. The percentage of female felons who have
been in incestuous relationships may be as high as 95 per cent.

One woman told me that her husband had seduced each of their
daughters as they reached puberty. When she saw him starting on the
youngest of the three girls, she couldn't stand it anymore. She moved
all of them out.

Few mothers are willing to bring incest charges for fear of stigmatiz-
ing their daughters. The only resolution for the incest problem may be
to break up the family.

Incest is defined as intercourse between any blood or half-blood relative with a relationship closer than a cousin. Some states include first
cousins. Illinois permits incest charges only for intercourse between a
brother and sister, never between a father and daughter. Many statutes
never mention stepfathers, the most common offender. Of course, a
stepfather could be charged with statutory rape.

The penalty for incest runs between one to twenty-one years in
prison. Five years is average. Some states also impose fines or years at
hard labor. However, a prison term will not solve the woman's problem.
She'll have to kick him out of the house and probably divorce him.
She shouldn't wait a moment to do this.

RULE: IF YOUR FAMILY ALREADY
HAS A HISTORY OF ABUSE,
SEEK HELP.

Many groups are forming all over the country with the specific purpose of counseling battered families. They provide shelter and services
to women and children, and sometimes these services are granted to the
man of the family as well. Many women find that the centers' understanding of their problems is more practical and remedial than the services of psychologists with less experience in the field. The local chapters
of the National Organization for Women (N.O.W.), your church, a so-

cial agency, or the police department may be able to provide you with the location of centers in your area.

These centers also have information to help guide a battered woman through the legal processes in her state. There are a number of different remedies available. Which one a woman chooses depends on her own situation. There is a choice of five remedies. She may use one or all of them.

FAMILY COURT COUNSELING: Family courts are informal courts which can grant a separation and support agreement while the couple tries to lick the problem. Many family courts have social workers on their payrolls, and often the cost of their services is very low. One of the purposes of the family court is to salvage the marital relationship.

Family courts also grant divorces if the woman so decides.

A RESTRAINING ORDER: A restraining order, also called a cease and desist order, is issued by a civil or family court. It requires either that the husband stay out of the home or that he stop doing particular offensive acts. Although it is usually part of a divorce proceeding, it is also available for those who are trying to cure a sick marriage. The petitioner must be able to show the court that the order is necessary and that she will be further damaged if it is not issued. If her husband beats her after that, he will be held in contempt of court and may go to jail for a few days or pay a small fine. This remedy is preferred because it does not require lengthy jail sentences and is unlikely to cause financial damage to the family.

There are two other types of orders a court may grant. One is an order to vacate. In this case the judge orders the husband out of the home. The other is a peace bond. A man swears to the court that he will leave his family free from harm. He posts a bond, say $500, to guarantee this. Then if he violates his word, he forfeits the bond to the court. It's not done very often, because courts don't like the bookkeeping. A restraining order is just as effective.

CITIZEN'S ARREST: If her husband has beaten her, a woman may arrest him herself. She notifies the police about whom she will arrest and what crime she will charge him with. Then the police will come and collect the wrongdoer. Either she may hold him herself until they arrive or she may point him out to a police officer, depending on the statute of her city. Check with the local police.

If she has a restraining order, either she, the police, or a marshal of the court can arrest her husband for contempt of court. The court will explain this when the restraining order is granted.

If a woman arrests her husband for criminal assault, she must provide the district attorney with certain facts. The district attorney will need "probable cause" that her husband beat her. Four things will help her establish probable cause: police reports on file, a history or diary of previous attacks, evidence of injuries, and witnesses. Then the district attorney will be able to charge criminal assault. She later has the option of dropping the charges or diminishing them to a misdemeanor such as disturbing the peace.

CIVIL ASSAULT: Civil assault itself is a pointless remedy for a battered spouse. Although it seems very attractive at first, women universally drop the suit because they have little to gain from it, except a bill from a lawyer. Additionally, some states will not allow a person to sue his or her spouse for damages. Such a rule is called interspousal tort immunity. But sometimes a battered woman has to sue for civil assault in order to get a restraining order.

The rare woman who completes the civil assault suit has to assume responsibility for the whole action. She will have to pay an attorney. She may receive money damages. Many jurisdictions limit assault suits between a husband and wife to a family court. In this case the husband may also receive a short jail term, usually with probation. The courts are reluctant to send a man to jail, since he would be unable to work and his wife and children may end up on welfare.

CRIMINAL ASSAULT: Criminal assault is a felony and could put a brutal husband in prison for over a year. He will probably lose his job, and he may be unable to get another, if he has a prison record. He won't be able to pay child support. Though he is surely as guilty of criminal assault if he beats his wife as if he beat a stranger in a bar, the woman must keep the financial interests of her family in mind.

In a criminal assault case the woman prefers charges against her husband. The district attorney in her county prosecutes the case. She doesn't have to pay a lawyer. But a woman shouldn't be surprised if the police and the district attorney try to talk her out of the charge. She may be justifiably angry, but putting the old man away can be counterproductive to the family's financial interests.

RULE: RAPE AND ABUSE MAY BE A
DEFENSE FOR MURDER.

Although charges of rape brought against a husband, especially if he is living in the house, are nearly impossible to pursue, the woman does not lose the right to defend herself. Her defense must be against extraordinary acts. Rough love play may not be enough to qualify as abuse, but abusive husbands aren't merely rough. More often they force oral or anal intercourse upon their wives.

The state of Michigan charged Mrs. Hartwell with murder after she fatally stabbed her husband. Mr. Hartwell had a history of wife abuse. On the night of his death, he came home drunk and threatened her with anal intercourse. She knifed him. Her attorney argued that the killing was self-defense. The jury agreed.

The Hartwell case represents a victory for married women. Violence and abuse by husbands can be defended against, even if it involves a killing. Additionally, a woman can even up her physical disadvantage, especially if she's defending against a rape. Though Mrs. Hartwell might well have lived through the sodomy, she was not required to submit—even to her husband.

One of the important elements in this case is that Mr. Hartwell had a documentable history of wife abuse. If this history had not existed, Mrs. Hartwell would probably have been convicted. Husbandly rape and abuse are flimsy defenses, and the police will investigate thoroughly.

Fortunately the law is changing for married women. New York passed a modification of its rape statute which now allows a woman who is separated from her husband under a decree of judgment of separation, or an order requiring living apart, or a written agreement of separation, to charge her husband with rape, even though they are legally married. This exception for separated couples is a break, since sexual abuse can occur during this trying period of adjustment. Indeed, part of the reason for the separation may have been the man's abusive practices. Statutes of this kind will probably become common before too long, as they are eminently fair.

The law regarding battered women is developing very quickly. Many women's groups are writing legislation to simplify a battered woman's problems. Nearly every month another state amends its statutes in this area. Consult a shelter in your area for the most recent information.

Chapter 20
PERSONAL INJURIES

Since the thirteenth century, records have been kept of the whole human drama. Man's foibles, errors, and disasters are all immortalized in a series of judges' decisions. Very little law having to do with personal injury comes from legislatures. Most personal injury law originates with cases written by judges.

The legal classification of personal injuries is called by many names, such as civil wrongs, to distinguish them from criminal wrongs. The most legally descriptive name is the one used by the Normans. They call it torts, from the Latin *tortus,* meaning twisted. Personal injuries is also called the law of negligence. All these terms mean more or less the same thing—injury to a person, her property, or her reputation.

RULE: PERSONAL INJURIES ARE SUED
FOR IN CIVIL COURT.

Civil courts do not try crimes, and a jail penalty is used only if a witness knowingly lies during testimony in a civil trial. The absence of the jail penalty distinguishes civil courts from criminal courts. Much of the procedure in a civil court resembles a criminal court. In a civil court the plaintiff will be the damaged party and the defendant will be the party who is purported to have done the damaging. In a criminal court the plaintiff is the state and the defendant is the accused criminal. (In less populated areas, civil and criminal actions may be tried in the same courtroom, but the judge will use different standards, depending on what type of case he is trying.) Occasionally civil and criminal jurisdiction will overlap, particularly in drunken driving cases. Normally, the drunken driver will first be tried on the criminal charge, and the negligence case will be tried in a civil court to determine the damages. Courts will rarely allow the criminal conviction to be mentioned during the civil suit.

Additionally, the level of proof required in a civil court is different from that required in a criminal court. Since less is at stake, the proof need not be as overwhelming. A civil trial requires a "preponderance of the evidence," meaning that the judge or jury decides if the fact the plaintiff asserts is more probable than not. "Preponderance" simply means having better evidence than the other party. In criminal courts, the standard of proof required is "beyond a reasonable doubt." This standard does not indicate that the jury could not err, only that the jurors feel that the facts presented have pushed any reasonable doubt from their minds. In criminal trials, "moral certainty" is used as an even higher standard of proof which is required when some important piece of evidence is missing, such as the body in a homicide. A juror has reached moral certainty when he or she would "act in reliance upon its truth in matters of the greatest importance to himself."

RULE: CIVIL COURTS AWARD DAMAGES.

You have probably read newspaper accounts of spectacular damages for a personal injury. These judgments were entered in a civil court. The civil court may be a trial by jury, or it may have a judge adjudicating the facts, but guilt is not an issue in a civil trial. The emphasis in a civil trial is on the injured, and recompensing him for the injuries suffered through the irresponsible or wrongful action of another.

RULE: YOU MUST PROVE A DEGREE OF LEGAL RESPONSIBILITY.

The degree of legal responsibility between the injured and injurer is the first decision to be made at the trial. If the defendant has no responsibility to the injured party, the injured party cannot win. For example, a burglar sneaking into someone's house in the dead of night who falls and slips on the faulty basement stairs, breaking a leg, could sue. However, the court will laugh in his face, since the homeowner had no degree of legal responsibility for the damages the burglar might acquire. It would be quite a different story if a repairman was invited into the home only to break his leg on the basement steps.

RULE: YOU TAKE THE PLAINTIFF AS YOU FIND HIM.

If you injure someone, you will be held responsible even though the harm is entirely out of proportion to your irresponsible act. A barge owner neglected to clean the oil residue out of his barge. He tied it up to a wharf. A lightning bolt hit the barge, and the petroleum residue in the barge exploded, killing two workmen in a neighboring warehouse. The barge owner was held responsible.

Let's say you stop your car for a light, edging just over the white crosswalk line. Your car bumper delivers a minuscule blow to someone's knee. If you bumped a normal person with normal knees, you might not create any damage since the blow was so light. But if you hit one of Joe Namath's fragile, million-dollar knees, you will be held responsible for the damage.

> RULE: YOU MUST HAVE SOME CONTROL
>   OVER THE LOCATION IN WHICH
>   THE INJURY OCCURRED IN
>   ORDER TO BE LIABLE.

An example will illustrate this rule better than anything else. A man set up a homemade teeter-totter in a vacant lot next to his house. The neighborhood children were welcome to play on it any time they wished. One little boy fell off and required stitches in his head. The man was not held liable. He had no responsibility for the supervision of the teeter-totter next door. He would have been held responsible if he had set it up in his own backyard.

In this case a teeter-totter is a normally safe toy for a child to be attracted to. If instead of building such a mild toy, the man had built a star-gazing platform ten feet high, the man might have been held liable for falls from that platform, whether or not he had included guardrails. Some "Pied Piper" cases also hold that ice cream vendors have a responsibility to keep children out of the street while selling them ice cream. It's clear that care and common sense must be applied to any situation which threatens harm.

> RULE: YOUR DUTY TO PROTECT SOMEONE
>   FROM HARM DIMINISHES WITH THE
>   LEVEL OF RELATIONSHIP.

If a guest of an airline is injured, the airline is totally responsible, since the airline promises to deliver us at the other end, and in good shape. Any public carriers, all the way down to the local taxi, have similar responsibilities to their riders. Any more ordinary sort of business must exercise reasonable care and actually inspect the premises on a regular basis to minimize any chance of accident. For example, let's say there had been an earthquake. The restaurant seems to have survived in fine shape. You as a patron toddle off to the powder room, start to open the door, and the whole door, jamb and all, falls on you. There had been no indication prior to this that anything was amiss with the door. A restaurant owner has the responsibility to protect you since you are paying him to be on his property. After the earthquake, he should have invited in an engineer to thoroughly inspect the premises for damage. A homeowner has less responsibility since people come to her house as guests. She must notice things that might injure people and have them repaired, but she only has to use common sense. If there is a loose board on the porch, it's up to her to fix it. But she would not be held responsible for a well-maintained gas stove which explodes.

By the same token a homeowner is responsible for the actions of her dog. If her dog harms another, she will have to pay damages. She knows the dog better than anybody else and should take precautions if the dog is too protective of her property. Such dogs bite.

Most people are invited onto a person's property and are called invitees. Invitees include guests, repairmen, your children's friends, your neighbor coming for coffee, etc. Other people have the right to come onto someone else's property; these people are called licensees. These are police, firemen, the mailman, the gas man, and other service people. You owe very much the same responsibility to licensees as you do to invitees, except that you are not responsible for injuries received in the line of duty. For example, there's a fire at your house. One fireman gets scorched. Another one falls through your rotten front porch. You are liable only to the one who fell through the porch.

RULE: YOU WILL BE HELD RESPONSIBLE FOR INJURIES TO CHILDREN.

If a child is injured on your property, chances are a judgment will be entered against you. Children are fond of exotic playthings. Your swimming pool, duck blind, construction site, windmill, tree, or even your garage roof can be unbearably seductive to an adventurous child. Unfortunately children can get hurt. If the property is in your control, you will be held responsible. It's up to you to supervise any attractive nuisance beyond all normal precautions. Children just don't think.

RULE: YOU MUST PROVE DAMAGES.

Once legal responsibility is proven, and you can show that the responsibility was breached, you must show the extent of the injury. If the injury is minor and unlikely to be troublesome in the future, the damages may be nothing more than lost salary and doctor's bills. If the damage is severe, the award may be very high. Personal injury trials usually contain a lengthy presentation of the exact nature of the injury and its ramifications. Since the jury awards money based on earnings lost, pain, and suffering, and likely medical bills in the future, this information is necessary for its decision.

RULE: YOU MAY NOT RECOVER WHEN
IT'S YOUR FAULT TOO.

Sometimes cases arrive in court so tangled up that it's impossible to assign guilt. For example, a woman backing out of her driveway is hit by a man driving down the street. She should have looked and he should have seen her car. Who created the accident? They both did. If there are no major injuries, the insurance companies will just settle. In fact, the only auto accident with absolutely no contributory negligence is the parking accident in which a moving car hits a properly parked car.

Contributory negligence is defined as an injury that is partially caused by the injured person. Persons who might be injured must also exercise reasonable care to avoid injury. They shouldn't jump off trains before they stop, wander around in dangerous areas, or take other actions that could bring them trouble.

Under common-law contributory negligence, a horribly injured plaintiff can sometimes be denied recovery. Because denial of recovery may be unfair, more and more states are adopting the concept of comparative negligence as a replacement for contributory negligence. Under comparative negligence, the jury makes two decisions: the amount of damages and the relative percentage of fault. For example, the jury might decide that the damages are $300,000 and the injured plaintiff was 10 per cent at fault. (The defendant caused 90 per cent of the injury.) The damages are then reduced by 10 per cent so that the injured party collects $270,000.

If you do have an automobile accident, it's best to follow certain steps starting right after the accident. But that may not be as easy as it sounds. First of all, you're upset and so is the other guy. Both cars will have to be fixed and the police will want to know if either party was doing anything reckless. Injuries from auto accidents can show up days after the accident, and be quite legitimate. The only way to keep yourself from suffering continued aggravation is to handle the situation correctly.

All these rules apply to any sort of accident you may have, whether it's in a private car, on public transportation, or slipping on a wet floor.

RULE: YOU NEED A POLICE REPORT
ON ANY AUTO ACCIDENT.

Most states require that you report all auto accidents to the police. A police report will protect you from wild claims the other guy might make to his insurance company. If he's injured and brings suit, the jury is more likely to believe him than you, so it's best to have an official report to back up your facts.

When the police come to the scene of an accident, they will take note of the physical evidence at the scene. They notice the position of the cars, the skid marks, look for open bottles of alcohol in the cars, possibly take breath samples, and gather other evidence. Their investigation can be very helpful to you if you have to defend yourself.

Most insurance companies require police reports. You may find the insurance company unwilling to honor your claim if you don't have such a report to back it up.

If you're injured in a building, on a sidewalk, etc., report it immediately to the property owner, janitor, etc. Also take the names and addresses of anyone who saw the accident happen.

RULE: ASSUME THE WORST AND
PREPARE FOR IT.

Six girls were coming back from college in a station wagon. The rear tires weren't strong enough for such a heavy car. The tires blew simultaneously and the car ended up in a ditch. The girls seemed to be all right, but they went to the local hospital for a checkup anyway. Two days later one of the girls developed numbness in her right arm. A hairline fracture in her neck had not appeared on the first set of X rays, but was clearly apparent on the second set. She went into the hospital and was there for ten weeks. Fortunately for everyone involved, the police and insurance company had been notified immediately. They never questioned paying her hospital bill. If they had not been notified immediately or if the girl had endured the numbness for several weeks before it was diagnosed, the cause of the fracture would have been open to question, and possibly no damages would have been paid.

RULE: SEE A DOCTOR RIGHT AWAY.

Occasionally people who have been in accidents will put off seeking medical treatment. The further from the date of the accident that the doctor sees you, the more difficult it is to prove that the accident caused the injury. The girl with the broken neck might not have seen a doctor unless the people she was staying with had been very alert. In fact, she had not said anything about the numbness to them. She dropped a glass, they asked her if she was all right, and then she mentioned that her arm was numb.

Another woman slipped on an icy sidewalk. Unbeknownst to her, she had broken her hip. She walked on the hip for several years before it started to give way. After twenty years this injury to her hip totally crippled her, but she is unable to sue for damages. Additionally, her medical insurance does not cover her hip, since the injury occurred before she obtained the policy.

Many people survive accidents with little or no injury, but it is always best to take every precaution.

RULE: TAKE PICTURES.

Often the best proof of an accident is a photograph. If you have a camera in your car, it would be a very good idea to take pictures both from a long distance and close up. These can be used later either to settle the claim or as evidence in a lawsuit. Grotesque as it sounds, it is also a good idea to have pictures taken of your injuries. The cost is very small, but it can help a jury later on. Often personal injury cases are not heard by a court for four or more years. In four years, much if not all of the trauma will heal. The jury will be less inclined to take a suit seriously. For example, a young woman went through the windshield of a car. She broke her nose, her jaw, and several teeth and was seriously cut. The surgeons went to work and did a fine job of restoring her features. Four years later she looked very nice, even beautiful. However, the face she now had was not the one she was born with. There was a three-year period when she could barely leave the house for fear of people's stares. Without photographs, the jury might have found this impossible to believe.

RULE: NEVER MINIMIZE YOUR INJURIES.

Don't make statements such as "It's not so bad," "It's nothing really," or "I'll be all right in a few days." Insurance claims adjusters have the job of settling your claim. If you minimize your injury to the adjuster or to other persons, you may find your statement coming back as the reason why they're giving you less money. The more you talk about an injury, the more it's likely to hurt. But if you want full recompense for your injury, you'll have to either talk about it or refer the claims adjuster to your attorney.

Attorneys would rather handle the claims adjuster themselves than have you do it. The attorney is less likely to concede points which may help you later.

RULE: FIND YOUR OWN ATTORNEY.

Some hospital personnel are on an informal retainer to a certain unethical portion of the legal profession. You may find a nurse, an orderly, or even a physician trying to talk you into suing. Somehow, they just happen to know the best attorney for your case. The attorney may very well be excellent. However, having hospital personnel on retainer is only a more refined version of ambulance chasing. Referrals by retainer are strictly forbidden in the Canon of Ethics of the American Bar Association. Very carefully avoid any attorney recommended by hospital personnel, since the attorney could turn out to be dishonest in other ways. He may also put undue pressure on you to sue, so he can earn his fee. You may not want to sue anybody at all.

Many people are puzzled about whether a suit should be settled rather than sued for. Insurance companies frequently offer settlements to pay for the damages incurred. However, once you've accepted the settlement and signed the paper, your suit is gone for good.

RULE: REFUSE ALL SETTLEMENTS WITHIN
TWO WEEKS OF THE ACCIDENT.

The reason for this delay is that you may not know the extent of your personal injuries until days, even weeks later. If you settle before all the injuries have had time to be diagnosed, you may receive far less than you deserve. However, you may certainly go ahead and have your car fixed in the meantime.

RULE: MAKE A CAREFUL ACCOUNTING
OF YOUR ACTUAL DAMAGES.

Accidents are never pleasant and they can put you behind in ways you might never have anticipated. Everyone can anticipate the hospital expenses, but if the injury is serious it may require care for the rest of your life. Follow-up medical expenses should be amply allowed for. The salary you lose is also obvious, but you have also lost pension contributions, Social Security payments, and other items which could affect your future. Pain and suffering are the damages paid because you hurt. A value must also be assigned to pain and suffering, especially if the injury is likely to bother you in the future. Then there are additional expenses such as child care, practical nursing care, taxis, or even special transportation you may require in the future. The accident may also have shortened the person's life span. All these financial losses can add up to a great deal of money, and consequently large cases are rarely settled quickly. The real damage takes time to assess.

The actual damages to you are weighed against how much money is available. If the fellow who hit you only carries $10,000 in liability insurance and hasn't a penny more in the world, $10,000 may be as much as you can recover.

RULE: THE LAST THING YOU DO IS SUE.

Bringing suit is very costly and will take years to complete. No attorney ever recommends a lawsuit lightly. He or she would far rather settle the case than try it. Trial preparation takes a lot of time and can be very expensive. The attorney may have to bear much of the trial preparation costs himself. He also can't develop other sources of income while he is preparing a big trial. On top of this, the jury may decide against his client. If the attorney is paid by a contingency fee, as is common in personal injury cases, he has lost a great deal of time and money. Settling a case will also benefit the client, since the client doesn't have to take the chance that the jury will decide against her. However, the attorney may have to bring a formal suit as a matter of form. In fact, the insurance company may expect it. A huge majority of these cases are settled before they ever reach trial.

The best chance that you and the attorney have of avoiding trial is to build a good case. If your case is good, settlement at near the amount you want is very likely. So even if you think you'd never sue, go ahead and build a case using the steps of the police report, pictures, and a physical examination, as outlined earlier in this chapter. It's the best protection you have.

Personal injuries are by far the most common sort of torts. There are a variety of others for special situations. Libel and slander have to do with one person besmirching the good name of another. Civil assault is a verbal attack on another person which leads him to believe he will be physically harmed. "I'll kill you, you son of a bitch," is one example of a civil assault. Battery is the second half of assault. That's when one guy actually punches the other. Products liability is very much like a personal injury suit, but it's a product, rather than a person, that causes the injury. Civil fraud is charged when one person lies to another in order to extract money. False arrest is charged when you are held against your will without good reason.

RULE: TRUE STATEMENTS ARE NOT LIBEL.

Libel is an untrue written statement. Slander is an untrue spoken statement. In order for harm to occur the untrue statement must be published, that is, spoken or written to another person. If someone makes a statement to you about yourself which you know to be untrue, no harm has been done. If he says it to another person, there is harm. The person who publishes the untrue item must know it is untrue and must intend for the statement to harm you. One of the difficulties with libel is that it is possible for a news article to tell only part of the truth, thereby slanting the story to create a falsehood. Unfortunately, this is not libel, it's just bad journalism.

There's a little-used modification of slander which can be very useful. It's called slander of credit. If a merchant refuses to admit to other creditors that you've paid your bill, just mention that he is slandering your credit. He'll shape up.

The other type of injury which may be caused by words is called the intentional infliction of mental distress. The defendant has done something so outrageous as to shock a decent person. These outrages are extreme, such as loudly cursing a corpse laid out in a funeral home, spreading rumors of suicide, lynching threats by a mob, and on and on. The emotional distress caused must be severe, and physical illness following the occurrence will be evidence of the mental distress.

RULE: NOBODY CAN TALK MEAN TO YOU.

Assault is merely angry words. If someone is persistently assaulting you, you may want to bring suit. This type of suit is fairly rare, since the damages are unlikely to cover the cost of the suit.

The second half of assault is battery, the action of striking another. This suit is more common since harm to the body may result. You'll find more about this topic in the chapter on battered women.

RULE: YOU CAN RECOVER DAMAGES
FROM HARMFUL PRODUCTS.

Cars with defective steering wheels, dye which turns your hair green, and a mouse in your soft-drink bottle are all examples of products liability. This subject is covered more fully in the chapter on products liability. Suffice it to say that you should keep the mouse or the hair dye as evidence. Nearly every large manufacturing concern has lawyers to handle products liability and you may find them willing to make a settlement you consider satisfactory. For example, if you have a strong stomach, you may be quite willing to take a case of soft drinks to make up for the mouse in the bottle.

RULE: LYING TO GET MONEY IS FRAUD.

Anyone who sells a product while misrepresenting its value and state of repair can be guilty of fraud. But there's a fine distinction between fraud and enthusiasm. Used-car salesmen are masters at making non-fraudulent statements while at the same time not telling the whole truth. However, if they make any specific statements which you can prove to be untrue, it's fraud. For example, you are in the used-car lot and you say, "How many miles has this car got?" He could say either "The speedometer only shows 27,000 miles; you're getting a real bargain," or "Just look at the speedometer—only 27,000 miles." Neither of these statements is fraud, in spite of the fact that he may have turned the speedometer back from 80,000 or 100,000 miles. (Most states have laws prohibiting changing the mileage reading, but that is not civil fraud.) However, if he had said, "I know the former owner myself; he just used it back and forth to the railroad station," and if it's a lie, the salesman has committed fraud. It's up to you to prove it.

RULE: THEY CANNOT HOLD YOU
AGAINST YOUR WILL.

The most common incidents of false arrest and imprisonment arise because of a shoplifting accusation. Store detectives will occasionally take someone into custody who is innocent of any crime. In such a case the store may have to pay damages to the person who was held.

False imprisonment is slightly different in that it can be equated with the civil side of kidnapping. Of course, it's not nearly as serious. False imprisonment cases arise in numerous ways, like the fellow who worked late and couldn't get out of the office, or the female restaurant patron who got locked into a ladies' room. False imprisonment is another one of those suits in which the assignment of damages is difficult and these are consequently relatively rare.

The rule "The last thing you do is sue" is even more applicable for injuries to the psyche than injuries to the body. Unless the harm is very serious, the courts and jury may take your case lightly. You can count on paying attorney's fees which may possibly exceed the damages you recover. It might be wiser to investigate the small claims court. You can usually sue for consumer fraud in these courts, and you can avoid attorney's fees by presenting your own evidence.

You can also settle cases out of court by talking to the person who has injured you. He may be willing to settle with you. Large corporations often have departments specially set up to handle these settlements.

Part VI
DEALING WITH GOVERNMENTS

Chapter 21
ADMINISTRATIVE LAW

Administrative agencies are responsible for the vast majority of legal decisions in the United States. You may be more familiar with the term "bureaucracy" than administrative agency, but they mean the same thing. An agency can be any governmental administrative body, from your local sewer district to the big federal agencies like Housing and Urban Development. Social Security, the Internal Revenue Service, and the Treasury Department are all federal agencies. Welfare, motor vehicles, unemployment, and Workmen's Compensation are usually state agencies. The marriage license bureau, fishing license bureau, or real estate tax assessor may be either a state or a county agency. Although you may not be aware of institutions as government agencies, you would be far more likely to run afoul of one of these lawmaking institutions than you would a regular court of law.

These agencies spend the bulk of government budgets, and are responsible for disbursing transfer payments—income paid to a person who is not working. Social Security and welfare are the leading transfer payments.

As you will see in this chapter, agencies make a lot of legal decisions. The IRS decides how much tax you owe, the motor vehicle department decides if you will be allowed to drive a car, and so on. The legal decisions an agency makes cannot send you directly to jail, but they can cost you money, sometimes a lot. Most people will never see the inside of a court, but everyone will deal with an agency.

Our civics teachers in high school uniformly pointed out that our government is divided into three branches: judicial, executive, and legislative. Today, however, more and more functions of our government are being taken over by agencies. This "take-over" has in effect created a fourth branch of government—the administrative branch.

The administrative branch is the workhorse of government. Though it belongs in the executive branch, it might as well be considered its own branch, since on the federal level anyway, the President merely "reigns" over agencies. He really can't do much to control them. His only recourse is firing the agency boss.

The three original branches of our government are part of a check-and-balance system. Each branch limits the power of the other branches. Agencies are internally exempt from the check and balance, and do not comply with this theory of government. Agencies are set up in such a way that each agency may have all three functions of government. They may make the law, enforce the law, and hear any arguments that involve their law. You are probably most familiar with the functions of the IRS. Congress gave the right to the IRS to collect federal taxes. Congress then sets certain boundaries within which the IRS is to exercise its power. The IRS takes the law that Congress gives it and makes rules to supplement the law. People are audited as part of a fact-finding process to see whether or not a particular taxpayer is in violation of the law (rule) and the regulations that the IRS has set up. The person who does the audit is the investigator, the prosecutor, and the judge rolled into one.

Although putting the legislative, judicial, and administrative powers in one agency is contrary to our political theory, courts are willing to accept the collapse of all governmental powers into one agency because an agency has limited powers over the citizenry. It is felt that it is important for the government to be able to move forward efficiently, so uniting these powers in one governmental body for efficiency's sake is allowed by the courts.

You may wonder what prevents agencies from getting out of hand, since there is seemingly no control on their conduct. As agency law is set up, the agency will make a law, charge someone with its violation, and then try the case. The courts don't enter the picture unless the agency exceeds its power under the congressional act which brought it into existence.

So we come to the subject of political control. Since the law really doesn't control the agency, politics must. The primary source of control is the power of the purse string. If the agency offends politicians or their constituents, it may find its budget cut back severely. Regardless of the legal independence of the agency, the agency executive must please the politician. The unfortunate aspect of this situation is that politicians may have powers over the agency which may wrongfully modify how it does its job. Therefore, the fellow who runs such an agency must walk a fine line between independence and currying political favor with the legislative or executive branch. Political ability is especially important for the heads of the large regulatory agencies such as the Federal Communications Commission or the Federal Trade Commission and, to a lesser extent, in well-established public-aid agencies such as Social Security or unemployment. These smaller agencies have much less discretion on how they will be administered, and consequently a much higher degree of certainty about what is an acceptable use of their power. There is also an organization called the Administrative Conference, which is a watchdog over the conduct of federal agencies. It gathers information on the procedures of agencies to see if too much injustice is occurring in a particular agency.

RULE: AGENCIES CANNOT SEND YOU TO JAIL.

Although agencies are allowed to make the law, to hold hearings, and to fine you, they can never impose the penalty of prison. Imprisoning a person is far more serious than fining him. It would be considered a denial of due process to assign a prison term outside the regular court system. It is within the ability of some agencies to bring criminal charges, but the case must be tried in a regular court of law. For example, the IRS would handle many of the stages of a regular audit within its own administrative procedure. However, if it is charging someone with tax fraud (really a very rare charge), it will have to go into the federal district courts to bring the case.

RULE: THEY HAVE TO GIVE
YOU A HEARING.

The Constitution states that a person may not be deprived of life, liberty, or property without due process of law. Although agencies can very rarely affect a person's liberty, and can almost never affect a person's life, they can often affect a person's property and, indeed, usually do. They can levy fines, allow you to marry, or exercise other sanctions over your daily life. But they cannot do this without giving you some type of hearing.

The amount of due process which is required depends on the interest which is involved. Also, the due process must be appropriate to the circumstances. If you are paying a $2.50 parking ticket, you are obviously not entitled to as formal and expensive a hearing as you would be entitled to if there were several thousand dollars at stake.

If you have been denied a driver's license because you flunked the driving test, your level of interest would call for another driving test within a specified period of time. The hearing need not meet any particular procedural requirements. The hearing must only be one which is practical under the circumstances, fair to the parties involved, and allows for some order or decision to be made in light of the evidence which the citizen presents. There is also no requirement that the procedure be the ideal procedure. It only need be appropriate to the circumstances. We'll spend a great deal of time later in this chapter on the exact specifications of a hearing.

Agencies have particular functions which they fulfill. These functions will be more or less important, depending on the job assigned to the agency. Investigation is one function which is very important in areas like motor vehicles, health and safety, and the census. There is also a role called informal actions. These informal proceedings cover a wide range of activities, such as testing skills for granting a driver's license, supervision of corporations (such as bank examinations), processing applications for various privileges (such as radio transmission or the privilege to immigrate). This area also includes claims against the government, such as income tax refunds or Social Security benefits. The administrators also negotiate and settle cases, and render informal opinions on what they think the law is. The administrators may also participate in publicity campaigns to inform or change the public's mind on a particular issue.

Agencies also make rules through a formal process called "rule making."

First we will explore these informal actions of agencies, and then go on to look at the formal process of hearings.

One of the primary roles of administrative agencies is the gathering of information. This information is necessary to them in order to develop economic statistics for forecasting; to protect health, safety, the environment, and other public interests; to regulate industry; and to collect taxes. This information may be used strictly to gather facts, or it may also be a preliminary step in bringing further action through a hearing.

RULE: YOU HAVE A LIMITED
RIGHT TO PRIVACY.

The Fourth Amendment prohibition against unreasonable search and seizure only partially protects you from the curiosity of administrative officials. An official can't ask you absolutely anything, but as a broad general principle he is entitled to ask you almost anything, if he does so in a lawful manner and within his lawful delegated powers.

He is given the authority to investigate in order to fulfill his function. His investigative power will depend on what his end product must be. For example, when the Securities and Exchange Commission is investigating what may be a fraudulent stock deal, it will have very broad powers of investigation, since the end product would be the protection of the public from fraudulent stock dealings. On the other hand, if a person is making a claim for retirement benefits under the Social Security Commission, the administrator could only ask questions directly relevant to approving the benefit.

Information is also gathered in the interest of national security. The government is entitled to go poking around if you seem to be a threat, or even prominent. J. Edgar Hoover was famous for this. Anyone active in the peace movement of the 1960s probably has a file. I'll probably have one after this book is published, if I don't already. You can get copies of your files through the Freedom of Information Act, if you're willing to work hard enough. You'll find more information on this in the chapter on civil rights.

The government must operate within certain boundaries. The investigation must be lawful, the information must be relevant to a lawful investigation, the demand made for information must be reasonable, and privileged information need not be disclosed. Any requests for information which fall outside of these boundaries can be refused. The agency is then forced to get a judicial order requiring the person to come forth with the information. The hearing will give the citizen an opportunity to question the court on the "reasonableness" of the information which the agency seeks.

If you want to fight some governmental request for information, it's best for you to hire an attorney. You might find yourself bound up in a grinding of government machinery far beyond your comprehension. You may find government attorneys granting you immunity from criminal prosecution when you had no idea you were doing anything wrong. This could be especially true of corporate employees. It's not the agency hearing itself which you or the other person may fear, but criminal charges which might grow out of the agency proceeding. Of course, this is involved with the Fifth Amendment privilege against self-incrimination.

RULE: THE AGENCY CAN MAKE
PHYSICAL INSPECTIONS.

The right to make a physical inspection is very important for local agencies such as motor vehicle safety inspectors, health department inspectors, and safety inspectors for both homes and factories. The right to physical inspection is unlimited when the object of the inspection is a public or commercial enterprise such as a large apartment building, a restaurant, a store, or a factory. In this instance public health factors outweigh individual rights to privacy. Businesses don't really have a right to privacy anyway.

People's homes require a different type of authority if health or fire inspections are to be made. A 1967 decision seems to indicate that even routine health inspections may require a court-ordered search warrant.

One of the reasons for the necessity of a court-ordered warrant is that fire and health codes violations often bear criminal penalties. These search warrants are quite different from the highly specific search warrant which is issued when searching for a criminal or contraband. The public health search warrant may be issued to a general area as opposed to a specific dwelling, if the administrator has a reasonable standard for conducting a search of the area. For example, in big cities public health officials carry on a routine rat inspection. In such a case they are searching for a condition, not in any particular dwelling, but within a large but still defined area.

The individual is still protected even if the warrant is issued without a detailed judicial inquiry. The warrant would not be legal to seize evidence of some criminal wrongdoing other than health or fire violations. If the evidence were seized, it would not be admissible in a criminal prosecution.

RULE: ADMINISTRATIVE PUBLICITY
CAN BE ABUSED.

There are two basic areas of publicity which concern the average individual. One aspect of this is the confidentiality of the information the individual might give as a witness to the investigation. The other side it, which is far more destructive, is the publicity which an administrator may use as an informal sanction against an offending company. Both powers can be used to abuse or punish.

The confidentiality issue can strongly affect a witness, since the agency personnel leaking the material to the press may cause the person to lose his job, get thrown out of his union, or possibly utter words which another person might consider to be defamatory or intimidating. If this witness is forced to give public testimony, the effect on his life could be quite disastrous. Therefore, agencies practically always allow a witness to give private testimony if he or she requests it. If a criminal trial later results, the witness will have to make the statement publicly.

The problem with private testimony is that it can float around in government files for half a century, even if it is not true. The person discussed in the testimony may never be informed that the testimony was given or have a chance to challenge its validity. The Freedom of Information Act described in the chapter on civil rights has helped to make private testimony fairer to the accused.

The other part of publicity which is frequently abused is the agency's power of the press release. Perhaps you remember the cranberry crop scare of 1959, which was caused by an ill-advised press release issued by the Secretary of HEW. The press release almost put the cranberry growers out of business. Corporations have been bankrupted on bad publicity. The Securities and Exchange Commission is very sensitive to its public statements regarding the strength of a stock, since adverse publicity from the SEC can drive the price of a stock so low that the company's very existence is in danger. Recently a New Jersey gambling license hearing caused a loss of millions of dollars on the stock market, since it looked like Atlantic City might not turn out to be the gambling gold mine investors had previously assumed.

Unfortunately there are almost no legal controls on administrative use of publicity. Any administrator who makes a statement in good faith cannot be sued for any type of defamation, whether it be libel or slander. Probably the only remedy for this abuse would be an act of Congress allowing individuals and corporations to sue administrative officials for irresponsible remarks. Incidentally, the cranberry industry had enough political clout to get a big subsidy from the Congress to make up for the HEW Secretary's error.

RULE: AGENCIES CAN TEST
AND INSPECT.

One example of a test is a driver's license examination. In this case an examiner is trained to recognize the degree of skill which the motor vehicles department requires from a driver. In all likelihood the agency itself decided on qualifications under a state statute which gave it this authority. There is no reason why a trial should be held to determine whether or not a person should have a license to drive, as this would be a waste of everybody's time, so an examiner is given the authority. This examiner's performance is checked on in a variety of ways in order to keep him current in the profession and relatively honest in judgment. The fellow is unlikely to write more than a cursory report or gather evidence. He simply administers a standard test. This example is more or less true of any government employee who tests.

Inspections can be used to prevent dangerous products or services from reaching the market. An example of this would be testing food to see that it is pure. If a problem is found, the food is usually seized. For example, if botulism is found in canned goods, the whole shipment would be seized and destroyed immediately. This procedure is also used for drug inspections. The agency must be able to rely on the expertise of the inspector, since he may be the only person in a position to test for impurities before the goods are shipped to consumers.

Another area of inspection has to do with general safety inspections. Your state motor vehicles bureau may require a yearly inspection of your automobile. Other vehicles which are inspected regularly are airplanes (Civil Aeronautics Board), trains (Interstate Commerce Commission), and boats (the Coast Guard). If any of these means of conveyance have mechanical flaws, they are dangerous to persons other than the owner.

RULE: AGENCIES SUPERVISE.

Although supervision does not affect the individual directly, this aspect of agency procedure can be very important to us in a secondary way, since it is used primarily in the regulation of money and financial markets. The Federal Reserve Board and the Federal Deposit Insurance Corporation carry on regular announced or surprise bank examinations to ensure that a bank is operating within conservative limits. The purpose of these inspections is to stabilize banks throughout the country and to minimize losses to depositors. Since a finding of misconduct against a bank seriously threatens its survival, the primary regulatory tool of these organizations is supervision. If the administrator of one of these agencies announces that a bank is mismanaged, the expected life span of that bank is negligible. Therefore, we seldom hear banks criticized by supervising agencies. The offending bank is sure to adhere to the supervisory suggestions given by the agency administrator, because it knows it will be out of business if it doesn't.

The supervisory power is used by other agencies besides banking ones, but this is less evident to the public. For example, the FCC uses supervision as the technique for regulating interstate telephone rates. In the first twenty-nine years this supervision enabled the FCC to negotiate twenty-two rate reductions and one rate increase. Constant supervision and better technology have made our long-distance calls cheaper.

RULE: EVERYONE CAN GO TO FINLAND
BUT NO ONE CAN GO TO CUBA.

When we get right down to it, the primary job of most agencies is to handle applications and claims. The IRS processes about 130 million tax returns a year. There are about five million Social Security claims made. Also countless requests for passports, immigration visas, CB radio licenses, fishing and hunting licenses, and marriage licenses. Almost all of these applications are approved after a cursory inspection. The standard of processing applications (over a billion a year) requires that it be swift, simple, and fair. The swift requirement is often ignored and rarely enforced. If you've ever wanted anything from the government and had to fill out a form, you may doubt that simplicity is much of a standard either.

Fairness is by far the most important administrative standard. Two famous passport cases are the basis for this strange rule you see above. Two young men applied for passports for the purpose of going to Communist youth festivals. One young man wanted to go to a meeting in Finland; the other wanted to go to Cuba. Both passports were denied, but when the cases were appealed, the fellow seeking a passport for Finland won. The Cuban passport case lost. Though each decision was many pages long, the Supreme Court's thinking boiled down to the pithy rule above. At the time of the cases, all American citizens could travel to Finland, but there was a complete U.S. embargo on travel to Cuba. The fairness standard is very straightforward—the agency must use the same rules for everybody, regardless of whether the purpose of the travel is a vacation or a Communist youth festival. The fairness doctrine applies to every agency, regardless of the type of decision it makes.

RULE: AGENCIES HAVE TO CONSIDER SETTLEMENT.

The Administrative Procedure Act requires that a federal agency offer a citizen or a corporation an opportunity to settle the matter prior to the hearing, similar to an out-of-court legal settlement. This opportunity must be provided by the agency when urgency, the public interest, and the nature of the proceeding would permit it.

Agency settlements do not generally imply either guilt or innocence because the person or corporation charged may wish to settle merely to avoid large legal fees. The settlement will usually be negotiated by an attorney, and if the agency's case is good, the person charged may even pay a fine, just to avoid a legal battle with a better-financed federal agency.

The requirement for administrative settlement is especially true for licenses and applications. If you don't fill out the forms correctly, they can't deny the license on that basis. They have to tell you what you did wrong and give you a chance to correct it.

RULE: IT'S BETTER TO HAVE BAD
INTERPRETATION THAN NO
INTERPRETATION AT ALL.

Often the citizen is baffled by the regulations of an agency. Or the citizen may think that his or her own situation is halfway between one rule and another and doesn't know which rule to apply. In this case the citizen can call upon the agency to interpret its own rules.

The courts don't make the agencies stand behind these interpretations. An agency can give you an interpretation and then back out of it later. The IRS is famous for this. At first glance this seems very unfair. Many citizens have argued that if the agency has given them advice, the agency ought to stand behind its opinion. The courts think otherwise. They appreciate that the head administrator can only do so much and that these interpretations must often come from less experienced personnel. In some cases the interpretations will be dead wrong.

The courts think that any dialogue between the agency and the citizen, whether it be good, bad, or indifferent, is superior to the total lack of dialogue which would result from the agency being held accountable for every word it utters. Suppose you go to the IRS for help with your tax return. When you talk to the person who helps with these things, she says that acupuncture is a legitimate medical expense for your tax return. (Medical expenses are deductible if that particular medical practice is legal in the state in which you received the service.) Later you are audited and the IRS says it won't accept the acupuncture expenses because the procedure is illegal in the state where you received it. If you had gone across the river to another state where acupuncture was legal, you could have claimed the deduction. The IRS representative who told you that you could deduct the acupuncture simply didn't have the right information. But she probably had good information for a lot of other people. Since it's better that taxpayers get some assistance than none at all, the citizen cannot use "bad information" as a defense against the IRS for collecting the tax due.

Agencies also make laws and regulations which have the effect of legislative statutes. You have to follow these laws just as though they were acts of the legislature. These laws are called rules, not to be confused with the rule in this book, although they are pretty much the same thing —both are general principles of conduct. Rules come in three different varieties. Procedural rules determine how an agency is organized, how it operates, and how it will go about making rules. The agency can't change its own procedural rules. It has to abide most especially by its rules on how it will make rules.

Interpretative rules are the rules by which the agency will decide what it is within its power to do. For example, an interpretative rule would state that the FTC is of the opinion that a particular business practice is monopolistic and within the responsibility of the FTC to control.

Legislative rules are the meat and potatoes of agency rules. These specific regulations tell the citizenry what rules will be enforced in the future. The IRS acupuncture rule is an example of a legislative rule, called so because it might as well be an act of Congress.

Any legislative rule can be changed, but the agency has to follow specific steps to do so. The process of changing a rule or making a new one is called rule making. The first step is giving advance notice that rule-making hearings will be held. This notice must appear in the Federal Register. The agency must then allow interested persons to state their opinion. The agency can control whether the opinions will be given by letter, in open hearings, or both.

The agency must publish the rule it finally makes at least thirty days before the rule goes into effect. The agency is sometimes required to hold a trial-like proceeding to hear evidence—for instance, when an agency is trying to set standards for food. Evidence is admitted and cross-examination is allowed. This hearing is called "rule making on a record."

The Food and Drug Administration has just completed a nine-year-long session of rule making on a record. The subject of this lengthy hearing was just how many peanuts have to be in peanut butter. Some manufacturers of peanut butter insisted it should be 87.5 per cent peanuts. The FDA wanted 90 per cent peanuts. When the FDA insisted on 90 per cent peanuts, two manufacturers appealed. At last look the matter was still not settled. I hate to think how many millions of dollars in legal fees that 2.5 per cent peanuts will cost us.

Administrative law varies markedly from the common law. In the common law, possible approaches are tested in many cases to discover their workability. The most workable approach then gains wide acceptance. This procedure takes time. Administrative law is faster than common law, but administrative tribunals often act without the practical experience of the courts. Actually, a federal agency can't try out cases. It might be a deprivation of due process for an agency to prosecute a number of different persons under different rules to find out which rule works best without having made a prior pronouncement about what the law will be. And so we get peanut butter fiascos.

RULE: YOUR RIGHT TO DUE PROCESS
IS NOT ABSOLUTE.

The due process clause of the Constitution says that a person may not be deprived of life, liberty, or property without due process of law. There is no particular requirement that this be ideal procedure, simply that it be some procedure. Obviously, there is no need for any procedure at all unless someone loses a right or money.

One example of constitutionally required hearings is property taxes. After property taxes are levied, some hearing process must be available for the property owner to bring evidence to show why his property taxes should be reduced from the amount he was billed. Two cases in this area hold that any type of hearing is all right as long as some hearing is available prior to the time the fellow must pay. If only one person is being affected, a hearing will be required. If large numbers are affected, it's possible that a general hearing or rule-making hearing will be appropriate.

Sometimes the statute setting up the agency will require particular types of hearings in particular types of situations. In this case the agency must do exactly what its statute instructs.

Additionally, it is largely within the power of the agency to decide whether it will hold a general hearing or individual hearings. The courts feel that the agency has a much better grasp of which method will be more efficient for the agency. Therefore, the courts will generally give the agency the choice, rather than the individual.

RULE: GETTING ANY HEARING
MAY BE UP TO YOU.

Most property owners just pay up on the tax bill, without demanding a hearing. Other persons want a hearing. Consequently, administrators are allowed the shortcut of making hearings available in general, but without having to hear every case unless a hearing is requested. This is a very normal way for administrators to proceed.

Before you can ask for a hearing, the administrator must issue an order (or a tax bill). Sometimes this document is called a provisional order. You must have the opportunity to request a hearing before the order becomes final. The length of time you have will be printed on the bill. For example, if it says, "Pay within thirty days," you can bet that you have thirty days to request a hearing. A few agencies even require that you show cause of why you need a hearing.

RULE: AGENCIES CANNOT STEP
ON YOUR RIGHTS.

The government cannot condition a job or public aid on an unconstitutional ground. For example, a policeman cannot be fired for political involvement. No one has a right to be a policeman, and it cannot be used as a club to limit a constitutional right, such as free speech. Welfare recipients and government workers have used this rule a lot. The welfare recipients have won the right to a hearing prior to cancellation of welfare benefits. They have also won a freedom from unwarranted searches of their homes. The welfare worker can enter a welfare recipient's home, but he or she may not search it.

Government workers are protected by due process as well. The employee is entitled to a hearing before being fired. The employee must first receive notice of termination and then he or she must have an opportunity to be heard. Additionally, if a government employee is being dismissed, the government is required to reveal the evidence it will use against the individual. This procedure gives the individual a chance to prove that the evidence is untrue.

Administrative hearing procedure varies widely depending on the agency. There are certain basic principles you can count on but the agency is entitled to modify these principles within certain limitations. The agency must inform you of its particular procedural requirements and the level of proof you will need.

RULE: ALL PARTIES MUST BE NOTIFIED.

Any person who will be affected by the hearing is entitled to notice of that hearing, because his freedom or economic interests are at stake. In an unemployment claim, for example, the employer is entitled to appeal if he wishes to contest the claim. He has higher insurance costs at stake.

Sometimes interested citizens' groups will also have the right to appear as interveners. These parties do not have a significant monetary interest, but may have a demonstrable civic interest. The right to intervene is especially important to consumer action groups and conservation groups. These groups have recently won wider powers to intervene in their areas of interest.

The service of notice is usually done by mail, and most agencies consider this adequate. An ironic exception is the U. S. Postal Service. The parties to be notified are usually those directly involved, the main parties in the proceeding. If someone is not given notice, the hearing has no legal hold over the unnotified party's interests, and he must be given an additional hearing.

Agencies are trying to work out better ways to notify the general public of hearings. For example, if the FCC wants to know more about children's television, and it holds a hearing, it doubtless wants to talk to some mothers and children. The Federal Register is widely accepted as a method of giving notice, but this publication may not reach the public that the agency wants to notify. The Atomic Energy Commission has been trying to deal with this problem, and has even gone so far as buying television advertising to publicize hearings. More development is expected.

RULE: THE HEARING OFFICER
IS AN EXPERT.

Hearing officers in state administrative agencies may be political appointees, but federal hearing officers are professionals. The federal government has made a great effort to raise the competency of hearing officers. These individuals are often experts in their field, and may or may not be lawyers, depending on the agency.

The legislation which controls the agency probably gives the head of the agency final word over all hearing decisions. This power was once more important than it is now. The number of cases has multiplied so greatly that the agency head can no longer take all the responsibility. The reality of the matter now is that the fellow sitting before you in your tax audit will make what is probably the final decision on your case. Agencies have not been in the habit of overruling these so-called preliminary findings. Unless the opinion varies widely from the norm, it is likely to stand.

An administrative judge is much noisier in a courtroom than a judicial judge. The judicial officer is really more like a referee between two sides of an argument (the adversary procedure). The administrative judge is charged with the additional responsibility of developing a record (making sure all relevant facts are brought out). He asks far more questions than a judicial judge. He is the finder of fact, as well as the tryer of the law. He is charged with trying the case within the policies and rules which the agency has established.

Just about any evidence is admissible in an administrative proceeding which could conceivably open up and illuminate any part of the questions involved. The evidence merely must be reliable, tending to prove or disprove the case at hand, and relevant to the case at large. Evidence obtained by illegal means is never admissible.

RULE: THE HEARING OFFICER EVALUATES
THE EVIDENCE.

Whether it be a judicial or an administrative court, all evidence has different values. For example, the fact that an armed robber drove a beige Ford is not as important as the fact that he carried a gun. In a judicial court the jury weighs these facts and puts them in their own perspective. The administrative officer does the same thing. He weighs all of the evidence presented, and decides the outcome of the case from a common-sense point of view. The legal standard to which he is held is best summed up from a decision by Judge Learned Hand. Examiners must make findings "supported by the kind of evidence on which responsible persons are accustomed to rely in serious affairs." One thinker on the topic, Ernest Gellhorn, has pointed out that hearing officers have worked out fairly accurate ways to deal with evidence.

RULE: THE PARTY WHO WANTS SOMETHING
HAS THE BURDEN OF PROOF.

The burden of proof is how much evidence is necessary before the case is decided in one way or another. Parties who sue and then lose have not satisfied their burden of proof. The burden of proof isn't uniformly on the agency or the citizen. In an agency proceeding, the burden of proof rests with the party who wants something to change, and he has to prove the need for the change.

The size of the burden of proof will change depending on the type of case before a court. For example, the burden of proof in a criminal case is "beyond a reasonable doubt." If one seeks to reform a contract, the evidence must be "clear and convincing."

In agency hearings two different standards are used. If a person's liberty is at stake, for example in immigration cases, the standard of proof is higher—"clear, unequivocal, and convincing" evidence is required. When less than personal liberty is involved, the standard of proof changes. The person or the agency who has the burden of proof must bring in evidence which is better in quality, not quantity, than their opponent's. Requiring better evidence is essentially the "preponderance" of evidence rule used so frequently in personal injury cases. "Preponderance" refers to how convincing the evidence is.

RULE: YOU MAY CROSS-EXAMINE WITNESSES.

Cross-examination is asking questions of the other side's witness. One would cross-examine to bring out evidence in support of your side or to show that the witness is less than reliable. Cross-examination is not usually "Perry Mason" style; rather it is simply one person asking questions of another, to clarify facts. For example, in a Workmen's Compensation case the employer may appear to state that the harmful substance which the plaintiff claims injured her had not harmed anyone else in the factory. The plaintiff or her attorney might ask questions about how long the harmful substance had been present in the factory and what the plaintiff's contact had been with that substance. Questions might also be asked which could indicate that the plaintiff had a closer working relationship with the harmful substance than other employees.

One of the exceptional aspects of agency proceedings is that much of the case may be based on written evidence which one side or the other brings in. Written evidence can help things move along very swiftly, and it is also cheaper, since the experts or witnesses themselves do not have to be present, lose work time, pay travel expenses, etc. The only difficulty with written evidence is that the person who gave the evidence prior to the hearing might not be available for cross-examination. If the truth of the witness's statement is an issue, the witness must appear so that he or she can be cross-examined. If the witness's written statements are merely matters of opinion, or if she is an expert, she probably does not have to appear, since experts are generally unshakable on cross-examination. The opposing party is likely to get nothing additional out of the expert witness anyway.

There are certain things about administrative hearings which enter the nether world of the law. These areas are as difficult to evaluate as they are delicate to discuss.

One of these areas is the hearing officer's use of facts which are not on the record as it is developed during the hearing. The hearing officer may rely on these pieces of evidence when making his decision. Admission of such evidence into the decision could be a very dangerous practice, since the parties to the hearing would have no chance to challenge the validity of the data. Therefore, a particular way of dealing with this so-called non-record evidence has been established. The procedure usually works like this. The agency's own experts develop a particular fact which it insists judges use as part of their decision-making process. An example of this procedure might be a presumption on the part of a Workmen's Compensation agency that bladder cancer among asbestos workers is primarily caused by the asbestos. If the hearing officer is to use this information, he must give official notice to the parties that this particular item will be used as part of his decision. The parties then have the opportunity to rebut the facts the hearing officer is assuming. In this case, the employer might wish to rebut the likelihood of this particular employee's getting bladder cancer in his factory. Maybe the employee didn't work there long enough.

The examining officer can search many sources for facts as long as they are relevant, and he maintains a fairness in his selection of the facts. This particular latitude being granted to hearing examiners may not be trustworthy because commonly accepted myth can often be confused with fact. A myth about heroin users, for example, is that they are capable of wild, depraved, and criminal conduct. Actual research tends to indicate that heroin users, while under its influence, are passive in the extreme and may even be incapable, in some cases, of as minor an act of will as cooking dinner. (See *Agency of Fear* by Edward Jay Epstein, published by G. P. Putnam's Sons, 1977.) Government officials have used the myth surrounding heroin usage to set up many administrative policies which turn out to be not backed by fact. This experience indicates that much care must be taken if the hearing officer is to assume (call official notice to) any particular set of facts. It seems hearing officers can be just as subject to rumor as the rest of us.

The other element of administrative law which might be somewhat sub rosa is the area of bias and influence—the concept that judges in agencies may be too tied up with the forward movement of their agencies, and therefore may be partial to one side or the other. There is an absolutely remarkable quote from Justice Jackson of the U. S. Supreme Court: "Men are more often bribed by their loyalties and ambitions than by money." This statement brings into focus the essential problem of an agency hearing officer. The law requires that he be an impartial judge and yet promotions and higher salary may rest on how he finds the facts in his cases. A liberal administrator may block the efforts of a conservative officer, or vice versa. At the very least, having your decisions questioned is professionally demeaning.

The administrative system seems to have settled for a standard of judicial fairness under which hearing officers must have no personal relationship to the parties involved; nor should they have any financial interest in the outcome of the case. If it is even remotely possible that the hearing officer could not be entirely fair, he is expected to excuse himself.

The hearing officer is required to give you a written statement of findings and conclusions, the reasoning used to arrive at the conclusion, and a summary of the issues which were involved. The statement must be thorough, articulate, and in no way mysterious. If you cannot understand the statement of findings, you can probably complain and get a clearer statement.

If you are dissatisfied with the outcome of an agency proceeding, you have a number of alternatives. If the agency is large enough, it probably has an appellate procedure of its own. You may also appeal to the courts from almost every agency, but your appeal will probably be limited to questions of the law. The court is unlikely to retry the facts in your case. If you wish to appeal through the agency, it is required to tell you how you go about doing this. You will probably have to bring the subject up. If you are appealing to the courts, you need an attorney. She'll know what to do.

RULE: YOU CAN'T FIGHT
CITY HALL.

This maxim, though old, is as true as the day it was coined. You may not be able to fight it, but you can work along with it. In trying to deal with the government, the first principle is to use their method of doing things, regardless of how wasteful of time and energy it may seem. The minute you step outside of their way of doing things, you are inviting disaster. You don't have to agree with their method. Just use it.

The first standard operating policy in dealing with any government worker is: get his name. Don't enter into any serious discussion of your problem until you've asked his name and written the name down. You will thereby put the worker on notice that he will be responsible for whatever rudeness or misinformation he throws your way.

Additionally, you should always keep copies of every form you fill out as well as copies of all supporting documents you send in. Also keep a master sheet which contains dates and names and summaries of each contact you make. If your forms are lost or your requests are ignored, you will be able to place blame. If any documents have to be filed by a particular date, either send them by registered mail or ask for a receipt for the documents if you deliver them in person. You will thereby keep the agency from denying your request on the grounds that you filed too late.

If you've tried to work within the rules of the agency, you always have the alternative of taking the matter to a judicial court. However, if you do this, you will have to find an attorney to help. The pleadings in such cases are rather complicated. Chances are you won't have to go this far if you've tried to work with city hall, instead of fighting it.

Chapter 22
SOCIAL SECURITY

The Social Security Act went into effect in 1935. The original purpose of this act was to provide a worker with a pension. The act has grown substantially over the years and now covers many classifications of individuals. The types of workers which are covered are now practically universal, and even young Americans are covered through dependent and disability benefits.

There is no doubt that Social Security is very expensive. From time to time there is talk that the system will be bankrupt before younger citizens ever have an opportunity to collect it. Fortunately for all of us, people are living longer and they are continuing to collect Social Security benefits. There are now far more older people in proportion to the rest of the population than there ever have been before. Additionally, the type of services currently rendered are far more extensive and expensive than the original plan allowed for.

I will not discuss the actual dollar benefits which the different classes of Social Security recipients receive. These amounts change from time to time and are calculated using a large number of mathematical variables. In my experience the Social Security Administration is helpful, kind, and even patient when dealing with the public's questions. If you're curious as to the exact benefits, Social Security will be able to help you. If you're planning for insurance and need Social Security information, the insurance agent will be able to provide it.

RULE: EVERYONE NEEDS A SOCIAL
SECURITY NUMBER.

All persons obtain a Social Security card from a nearby Social Security office. They require evidence of your age, identity, and citizenship or alien status. Birth and baptismal certificates are preferred. If these are unavailable, evidence of your age and citizenship can come from school, church, marriage, military, draft, and census records. You may also present a U.S. passport as proof. You have to give them the original copy of the record. They return your papers to you in about four weeks. You must also present evidence of your identity. This could be a driver's license, a voter's registration, a work or draft card, passport, library card, credit card, and any document which has either your photograph or your signature. Immigrants have special rules. They should consult Social Security.

Parents may obtain Social Security numbers for their very young children. Usually the purpose of this is to put savings accounts under the Social Security number of the child, so the parent can avoid paying income tax on the interest. The child must also file a tax return in this instance, but the tax is at a much lower rate, since the child usually has no other income. One four-year-old had his own tax return, reporting $1,700 in interest. He was very precocious and insisted on signing the return.

RULE: YOU CAN RETIRE AT 62.

The first age at which any able worker can collect Social Security is age 62. In the future, workers will have to accumulate ten years of work before they can receive benefits. Fewer work years are required for workers who become 62 years old before 1983.

If you start to collect benefits at 62, you get a smaller monthly check than you would get if you wait until 65 to claim. However, some people are encouraged to start receiving checks at 62, since they will get more money in the long run.

If you continue to work past age 65, you will receive slightly higher benefits. If you continue to work you have an opportunity to put in years of work with possibly higher Social Security contributions than the years before you were 65. Another bonus for continuing to work is that your benefit increases 1 per cent for every year you work. The Social Security bonus for continuing to work may not be enough to keep you working, but it may be enough to not penalize you if you want to keep working.

If you have worked and meet the above requirements, you will receive benefits equal to the benefits earned or equal to your wife's benefit calculated on your husband's benefit. You can choose the arrangement that will pay you the most.

RULE: WIVES GET BENEFITS.

If the husband is collecting Social Security benefits, the wife is entitled to a wife's share, which is one half of her husband's check. At age 65, however, if the wife is currently working, she may be earning too much money for benefits to be payable to her. However, if a wife is still working, her earnings don't affect her husband's benefit.

If you are caring for a child who is under 18 or disabled, and your husband is collecting benefits, you can collect benefits as well, regardless of your age. The child must also be entitled to collect Social Security benefits. If you are not caring for a child, you'll have to be 62 before you can collect your share. Medicare benefits do not begin until you are 65.

RULE: WIDOWS GET BENEFITS.

Widows of two classifications are entitled to Social Security benefits. Regardless of her age, a woman can collect the widow's benefits if she is taking care of children who are collecting benefits. The widow's benefit will cease when the youngest child reaches 18. However, the children's benefits will continue until they are 22, as long as they remain in school and do not marry.

Widows can start to collect benefits at age 60, but benefits are smaller if claimed at 60. The widow's benefit is the husband's benefit reduced by a factor, depending on what age you are when you claim the benefit. You will get 100 per cent of his benefit if you wait until 65 to claim. You get 71.5 per cent of his benefit if you claim at age 60. Disabled widows can claim as early as age 50, but the benefit is even further reduced. Don't put off claiming just because you'll get a larger benefit if you wait until 65. You may actually get more money by claiming early. If you're working you must wait to claim.

Widows normally lose Social Security benefits if they remarry before the age of 60. If a widow remarries after 60, her benefits will not be reduced if she claims early, but that would be true of any person.

RULE: DIVORCE BEFORE TEN YEARS
OF MARRIAGE CANCELS
SOCIAL SECURITY.

As of January 1979, a woman who has been married ten years before she divorces will be entitled to any regular benefits a wife would receive. If you are getting a divorce, an investigation trip to the Social Security office will be well worth your time.

RULE: DISABILITY BENEFITS ARE AVAILABLE.

If you have a disability which is likely to keep you out of work for more than a year, disability benefits are available from Social Security. These benefits can be paid to workers, persons disabled before age 22, or disabled widows and sometimes widowers. The disability benefit is based on the amount earned during a particular period. The period depends on the worker's age when disabled. The younger the person is when disabled, the fewer years of work he needs in order to qualify. This law is written so that a maximum number of persons are covered. Almost all retarded or physically handicapped persons can be aided under one of the Social Security disability programs.

Disability is defined as any physical or mental impairment which would keep you from performing any substantial gainful work for at least twelve months. It will also be covered if the disability is expected to cause the beneficiary's death. When deciding whether or not the claimant can do any substantial gainful work, the Social Security Administration will look at the person's usual work, and then his education, age, and work experience. For example, a steelworker has heart surgery. Because his work is strenuous, his doctor recommends that he not return to work for at least a year. The doctor does say that after six months the man can work a few hours a day in a simple job, such as a security guard. The steelworker would be entitled to collect disability benefits.

Blind workers are also covered under the Social Security disability benefit. The person need not be totally blind in order to qualify, but sight impairment of a severe degree is required. There are also special provisions for persons whose sight has worsened so that they are no longer able to hold down the same job they once did. If you know a person whose income is diminishing because of sight loss, you should talk to him about the disability freeze. If he discusses this with Social Security, he can protect the amount of his benefits when he claims them at a later date.

In addition to special benefits for blind persons, Social Security through the Medicare program also covers persons with chronic kidney disease and the medical expenses of disabled workers, dependents, and widows and widowers. The age for qualification varies depending on the person's benefit classification. Disabled workers of any age are covered.

RULE: THE CREDITS REMAIN ON YOUR RECORD.

Each year that you work you get an additional year of credit toward your benefits. You can leave your job to take care of the children and then return to work much later with your Social Security benefits more or less intact. The only difficulty here is that the years when you do not work may reduce the benefits you receive. For example, if several years with no earnings have to be included in the computation, you will receive lower benefits.

A year is composed of four calendar quarters of three months each. In order to be eligible for coverage in a quarter, you must be paid wages of at least $260 during the year. To establish credit for all four quarters in a year, you must earn $1,040 at any time during the year. Social Security can modify this amount as needed to protect the system. It is not changed for individuals. Under the general ten-year rule of thumb, you would need 40 quarters in order to be covered. If you turn 62 before 1983, you will need fewer quarters.

RULE: BENEFITS INCREASE WITH INFLATION.

There is a provision in Social Security legislation which allows for automatic increases in benefits for any year when the cost of living increases 3 per cent or more. The increase occurs in July unless Congress has already acted to increase everybody's benefit.

RULE: DEATH BENEFITS ARE AVAILABLE.

There are also death benefits available under Social Security. This benefit of $255 helps pay burial expenses, although there is some talk of abolishing this benefit.

RULE: YOU PROTECT YOUR HOUSEHOLD WORKERS.

Household workers are covered under Social Security too. These are people who actually work in your home. This could include a cleaning woman, a baby-sitter, or a handyman. If you pay them more than $50 in a three-month calendar quarter, you are required to pay Social Security for them. There is a special form to fill out called the Employer's Quarterly Tax Return for Household Employees, IRS Form 942. You can get it from an IRS office. You can also get a booklet from the Social Security office called *Social Security and Your Household Employee*.

My mother did this for our baby-sitter, Auntie Full, allowing Mrs. Fuller to collect her Social Security. Auntie Full was a professional baby-sitter, and never did anything except love us all. Without my mother's consistent efforts in this direction, there is some doubt that Auntie Full would have been able to receive either Social Security or Medicare benefits. Both have been valuable to her. Incidentally, Auntie Full was still baby-sitting me when I was 23 years old. My mother wanted to be sure that she would get maximum Social Security.

RULE: TELL SOCIAL SECURITY
OF NAME CHANGES.

Social Security gets very confused when people change their names. The payment reports come in and are checked both against Social Security number and the person's name. If the name doesn't match its record for that number, Social Security is not sure it has given credit to the right person. Of course, there is no requirement that you change your name if you marry; however, if you wish to do this, you must notify Social Security so that your new name can be put on the record for your old number. You'll want to do this in order to protect your benefits. If you don't, you won't necessarily lose benefits, but Social Security may have a difficult time tracking down the benefits you are entitled to. It has a simple form to fill out to handle this.

RULE: CHECK YOUR RECORDS
FROM TIME TO TIME.

Occasionally an individual doesn't get credit for the Social Security withholding she put in. This mistake can happen for a number of different reasons. Your employer can forget to send in your Social Security payments, he can make an error when reporting it, you can make a mistake when giving an employer your Social Security number, or Social Security itself can make an error. For these reasons it is best to request a copy of your record. Every three years is often enough, in most cases. If you tend to move from one employer to another, as some waitresses do, or you do temporary work, you may want to check your status more often. Protection of your Social Security is also a good reason for keeping pay stubs. After you've checked the record to make sure that it is accurate, you can throw the pay stubs away. You may also check your Social Security records against W-2 tax information forms, which also contain some Social Security information.

It's especially important to check Social Security if your employer has been in financial trouble or has gone out of business. Occasionally employers in serious financial trouble will cheat by not paying the benefits to the government that they are withholding from their employees' paychecks. Although the regulations on failing to pay unemployment insurance vary from state to state, it is an absolute rule that the IRS is charged with the responsibility to collect payroll withholding for federal income taxes and Social Security. If the IRS fails to collect this money on your behalf, you are still entitled to credit for it. The most effective way to make this claim is giving the IRS copies of your pay stubs. Another method is reconstructing the payroll and withholding. This method requires an expert, and the result is only approximate.

Another benefit is available, called Supplemental Security Income (SSI). SSI is for persons in financial need who are 65 years or older, blind, or disabled. State health care programs called Medicaid may also be available through a local social-aid office. If you know an older person in financial need, you may refer her to Social Security to investigate these benefits. She need not qualify for Social Security to collect SSI.

Some retired persons live on Social Security, others are fortunate enough that Social Security pays for the groceries or golf games. Social Security by itself is not adequate to maintain the standard of living we have while we are working. Other benefits must be added to this to ensure a comfortable standard, but at least with Social Security we can be sure that our older and disabled citizens will not be in grave need.

Part VII
CONSUMERISM

Chapter 23
CONTRACTS AND SALES

A consumer is a person who buys something for her own use or for the use of her family. The most basic element in consumerism is a contract. When you hear of Ralph Nader talking about expanding warranties on goods, he is actually advocating increasing a seller's contractual obligation. When you buy a newspaper, there is a contract. The same is true when you buy groceries, a fur coat, or a house. Knowing about contracts can make you a better consumer, or a better businesswoman.

RULE: A CONTRACT IS A TWO-SIDED PROMISE.

It is as simple as that. Most of the rest of this chapter defines what is necessary (in legal terms) to make a promise. The promise can be that you will sell me goods and I will pay you money for them. This is the most common type of consumer contract. We could also promise to exchange services, so that I will tend your garden and you will paint my house. Obviously a contract has at least two sides.

Although a contract is always a promise, a promise is different from a contract. A promise is one-sided, such as "I'll help you hang wallpaper." A contract is legally enforceable; a simple promise is not.

RULE: A CONTRACT REQUIRES AN OFFER.

An offer is some sort of indication that someone is willing to enter into a contract. Putting a note up on the bulletin board that you are willing to perform baby-sitting services at a particular price is an offer.

Putting an ad in a newspaper might be an offer, as is any definite language or action which would lead a person to believe that you are willing to perform as you have stated. When one makes an offer, it is the start of making a contract, but no one is obligated yet. The only requirement of an offer is that it be definite. When I offer to sell you my dining-room table if you pay me $500 within ten days, the offer would be considered definite. I've named a price and a definite date when the offer will terminate. Had I said, "I *may* sell you the table if you can come up with $500," it becomes just talk and not an offer at all. I named a definite price, but I used qualifying language: "I *may* sell you the table." The willingness to make a deal is the important issue.

RULE: THE OFFER MUST BE ACCEPTED.

Acceptance is the second step in forming a contract—that is, the statement of the other party of her willingness to become obligated. So now we have a willing seller who offered and a willing buyer who accepted. In the midst of the offering and the accepting, they have come to an agreement regarding the terms of the contract, though not all terms must be agreed upon. Many terms can be left up to common business practice or fair play. In consumer transactions the acceptance usually includes precisely what merchandise or service is to be delivered, as well as the price for the merchandise, etc. The delivery dates and other items can be worked out later. Commercial acceptances may only describe the goods the seller is sending to the merchant.

RULE: CONSIDERATION MAKES IT A CONTRACT.

Consideration is a general term for some exchange. Consideration could be money changing hands or a service being rendered. It must be something of value. Until consideration changes hands the promises made are not binding. When consideration is paid or performed, the promise becomes a contract.

One of the funny things about consideration is that no particular amount of money or service is required before there is consideration. It just has to be *some* exchange for the promises to turn into a contract. For example, if I left a $25 deposit with Alexander the Fur Merchant for my $3,000 mink coat, that would be enough consideration as far as the law is concerned. Alexander might not consent to such a small deposit, in which case I would have to give him more money or the deal would be off.

These are the elements of almost all contracts, whether they be written or oral.

RULE: INTENT IS MOST IMPORTANT.

These elements of offer-acceptance-consideration will mean nothing unless you and the seller actually intend to make a deal. In contracts, intent is everything. The intent to be bound separates a contract from a promise.

Intent is somewhat less important in common-law contracts than it is in consumer contracts, which are governed by the Uniform Commercial Code. Common-law contracts are very rarely formed by everyday people. Corporations will sometimes write a common-law contract with another corporation—perhaps to form a temporary partnership or for some other esoteric purpose. In the common-law contract, the requirements of contract will be very formal—with a formal offer, a formal acceptance, and formal consideration. Intent will be less important.

Even more common is the UCC contract. Probably 99 per cent of all contracts made fall into this category. *All* of your contracts will probably be UCC contracts. In this case, the formal steps are unimportant in comparison to what you and the seller intended to have happen.

Now that you know the basic elements of a contract and how they fit together, we can talk about offer-acceptance-consideration in more detail.

RULE: AN OFFER MUST BE SPECIFIC.

An offer must be more than simple negotiations. A statement must arouse the idea in the mind of a reasonable person that the person making the offer is willing to form a contract. The terms must be reasonably certain, but every detail need not be worked out. If it's a common-law contract, more details are required than for a contract under the Uniform Commercial Code (UCC). Most sales and service contracts fall under the UCC. The UCC governs almost every consumer deal, not just business deals, and is the law in every state. (Louisiana has adopted only part of the UCC, and it does not have the sales section, which is the most important to customers.) Under the common law certain terms of the contract must be definite, such as price, quantity, delivery date, etc. Under the UCC the parties must have had an intention to make a contract. Under the common law, if there were not enough terms that were specific, and the contract developed problems, a court would find that there was no contract. Under the Uniform Commercial Code the court would first decide if the parties had actually intended to form a contract. If the court finds that they did, it would then look to see if there is a solution to fix up the contract so that it would actually work. Under the UCC both parties would be placed in a position where they could act on the other guy's promise without injury to himself.

The intention is decided from what the average reasonable man or woman would decide if he or she had received the actual communication. Let's say you received a letter saying, "Ms. Jones, I hear from a friend that you need a new typewriter. I am selling Smith-Corona typewriters at 30 per cent below the manufacturer's suggested retail price. I'd like to sell you one. Please come in and pick out a model." Every reasonable person would consider this to be an offer.

Intention to make a deal is decided on the overall effect of the communication, whether it be a letter, telegram, or phone call. If the contract develops irresolvable problems, the court or jury will look at how definite the proposal is; the more definite, the more likely it is to be an offer. If the proposal is addressed to a number of different individuals, such as a mailed advertisement, it may not be an offer. If the buyer asks for price quotes and the seller responds, this will be considered an offer. If the buyer and seller have a history of transactions, any communication is likely to be an offer. Advertising is not an offer. It is merely an invitation to the buyer to make an offer.

You might be surprised that an advertisement is merely an invitation to make an offer. An offer is not restricted to the seller alone. Either a buyer or a seller can make an offer. A seller could offer a typewriter at $250. As the buyer, I could make the seller an offer that I would buy the typewriter for $230. We would offer back and forth until one of us accepts the offer, or until it is clear that we can't make a contract.

RULE: MAKE SURE THE OFFER IS SPECIFIC.

The primary reason people run into trouble when fulfilling a contract is some inaccuracy present in the contract itself—the purchase order is wrong or it doesn't say enough about the goods. For example, the salesman could write down the wrong model number, or the delivery date might not be on the sales slip. There is quite a bit of law in this area, but all a consumer needs to do is check the sales slip for accuracy at the time of the purchase. (The delivery date need not be part of the contract, but it usually is. The seller has to deliver sometime, but only as quickly as circumstances will allow.)

Offers have to be sent directly from the offerer to the other person. For example, Margaret might send an offer through the mail to sell her farm to Joseph. Margaret's friend Thelma calls up Joseph and says, "Margaret's gonna sell you her farm." The phone call isn't an offer, since it's not the way Margaret intended the offer to be made. If

Thelma had been acting under Margaret's instructions (as real estate agents do), the offer would have been binding.

Offers last for a reasonable period of time or as long as the offer says it lasts. The reasonable period of time could be two hours or two months depending on the nature of the deal offered. If the offer is rejected, it ceases to exist. If the offer says it expires on December 20, it expires on that date.

RULE: YOU CAN TAKE BACK AN OFFER.

The person who makes an offer can take it back at any time prior to its acceptance by the other party. In other words, the offerer can revoke his offer. Offers can be revoked directly, or through a third party, or by selling the goods which were the subject of the offer. Practically any type of language which shows second thoughts will be adequate to revoke. Examples of direct revocation include statements like: "I've changed my mind," "I'm having second thoughts," "I've got an immediate buyer." A third-party revocation can be very informal, sometimes even hazy. If the person to whom the offer was made receives gossip revoking the offer, the offer may be considered to have been revoked, depending on the nature of the gossip. (You notice that the offer is a more serious event than its revocation.) And obviously, if you've sold out the supply of goods, you have revoked the offer.

Ideally, you should revoke an offer in the same way the offer was originally made. So, if you offered over the telephone, revoke over the telephone. If you offered by letter, revoke by letter. Although it's all right to revoke by telephone, better judgment would recommend that you revoke by telephone and also send a letter revoking the offer.

RULE: ACCEPTANCE DEPENDS ON THE
TYPE OF CONTRACT.

There are two types of contracts: unilateral (one-sided) and bilateral (two-sided). In a unilateral contract, only one side need promise anything. In a bilateral contract, both sides promise. In a unilateral contract, the party making the offer does not require acceptance prior to performing the contract. In a bilateral contract, there must be an acceptance.

A unilateral contract happens like this: Susan Jones sends a note to Ace Air Conditioner Repair which says, "My air conditioner is broken again. Could you come by and take a look?" Ace comes in and fixes the air conditioner. Susan has to pay the bill, even if she thinks the price is too high. If she had said, "Could you come by and give me an estimate for repair?" Ace would have been obligated to wait before they repaired. The request for an estimate would have made this a bilateral contract.

At law a bilateral contract must be accepted in precisely the form in which it was offered. Any changes in the offer will not constitute acceptance. So if one said, "I accept, please acknowledge my acceptance," a contract results. On the other hand, if one said, "I accept if you deliver in five days instead of ten days," there has been no acceptance. Instead a counter-offer has been made. In common law any definite words such as "It's a deal," or "I'll send you a check in the morning," may constitute acceptance.

The Uniform Commercial Code maintains an exception to this common-law rule that the acceptance must be a mirror image of the offer, but this applies only to the sale of goods and services. The UCC allows an acceptance even though it may state a new term. If you said, "I accept, but you have to deliver in five days," the UCC would consider this a valid contract. Consumers use the UCC type of acceptance.

Once again the acceptance should generally be in the same manner as the offer, but written acceptances are preferred. The acceptance is timely and valid if it is made while the offer is still open.

RULE: CONSIDERATION REQUIRES A CHANGE IN POSITION.

Consideration is normally money that changes hands, but other things can also be consideration. The main attribute of consideration is that both parties must be in a slightly different position after the contract has been signed than before it. Money could change hands or more subtle things could be exchanged. These things are usually services. For instance, I could promise to drive both your children and mine to the roller-skating rink if you would promise to pick them up. In this case, both persons are required to do an action they would not have had to do without the contract.

Sometimes a contract will ask a person to give up a right he currently has in exchange for either another act or a payment. This exchange is very common in performers' contracts: "We promise to let you be on 'Search for Tomorrow' and to pay you, but you must give up doing television commercials." Giving up the television commercials is a type of consideration, and is the legal detriment concept. The parties must have a greater obligation after the contract is signed than before it. They must either acquire rights or give up rights they already have.

The law does not decide what amount of consideration is adequate. It will only decide whether or not some level of consideration existed. If I promise to sell you the Mona Lisa for $75, there is no question about consideration, although there may be some question about my mental capacity when making the contract. The Uniform Commercial Code allows modifications to be made in a contract without new consideration being paid. The contract, if it is unsatisfactory to the parties, can also be rescinded and a whole new contract put in its place.

Modification of a contract without consideration is important if the contract is revised. It usually doesn't happen, but you may have already acted on the portion of the old contract which was your part of the consideration. You may have paid your money or performed your service, only to discover that when a new contract is formed, you can't collect, since you have no consideration in it. Under the old method of law, if you and I had formed a contract to buy a Model 243 dishwasher and I paid my money, that would be it. Under the strict letter of the law, it was a Model 243 or nothing. You as the merchant couldn't substitute a newer model. Of course, you as the merchant would have to return my money. But legally we have no contract, since my money really can't go on a new model. Under the Uniform Commercial Code we could substitute goods without losing our contract, as long as they were the same general price and quality. The UCC view is more sensible than the common-law view.

A problem can arise if you try to reform contracts under the old common-law contract and someone has already performed his duty under the first contract. This situation is called a pre-existing duty. It's something someone has already done, or already agreed to do. For example, I am a roofer and have agreed to put a new roof on your house if you, a plumber, will install a new bathroom in my house. You install the new bathroom and I break a leg, preventing me from roofing your house. If we were using a pre-existing duty theory for consideration, your work of putting in my bathroom could not be found as consideration under the old contract theory. Under modern UCC contracts, the work you did would be consideration and there would be no problem for you to enforce the contract or to have me pay you. Of course, honor and my good name would prevent me from letting you down, so it is obvious that in most cases this whole matter has much more theoretical than practical significance.

The exchange element is most important in consideration. If one party is getting something for nothing, it will not be considered a bargain exchange. For example, if someone told a derelict to walk over to the church hall to get his supper, the derelict's action of walking over for his supper is not a legal detriment, nor is it performance of a contract. The bum is getting something for nothing and just walking to collect it is not his consideration.

Contracts can arise from other sources, in which case offer-acceptance-consideration will never be used. This type of contract is usually the outgrowth of a lawsuit. The most typical of these cases is a physician who performs lifesaving services while the patient was too ill to accept the doctor's offer of services. In such an instance a court would say that the patient had a quasi-contract. Quasi means "as if," so the court would decide that the patient had to pay "as if" there were a contract. This exception to the general pattern of contracts would prevent one party from gaining a substantial advantage without a fair exchange.

In addition to quasi-contracts there is another type of judicially made-up contract called promissory estoppel. This exception will enforce a contract when someone has made a promise which he could reasonably expect would produce either an action or a forebearance of action. The person who promised gets the result performed, and then he backs out on the promise. If injustice can be avoided only by enforcing such a promise, even though it was not really a contract, the court will use the idea of promissory estoppel as a substitute for consideration. So the guy who promised is said to have been "estopped" from claiming there is no contract. He allowed the other person to rely on the promise. The most typical case in this area is the retiring employee who has stuck with the company because he thought he had a pension, only to discover upon retirement that there was no such contract. The employer had allowed the employee to rely on the pension the employer had promised. The employer cannot argue that there was no contract.

Both quasi-contracts and promissory estoppel are far more a matter for the courts than they are for a consumer. Consumers rarely, if ever, need to know about these concepts. However, they are part of the law of contracts and might come in handy if one had to sue. Neither of them is much used in the marketplace. There it's plain offer-acceptance-consideration.

RULE: CONTRACTS ARE NOT COMPLICATED.

The most normal contract, a sale, has very simple requirements. It should contain the names and addresses of both buyer and seller, a description of the goods, the quantity, and the price. The most common contract is a sales receipt. If more things are to be done about the goods, the contract should also state this. For example, the delivery date and specific warranties might also be included.

More complicated contracts will contain this information and probably much more. If you follow the old newspaperman's rule of who, what, where, when, and add how much, you can succeed at writing your own contract. You need not use any special or technical language in your contract. In fact, I recommend against it. If you're not sure what you're talking about, everyone else will be even more confused. Just use language which is simple so everyone understands. Make sure that all your oral agreements from the negotiation are covered by the contract.

Complicated contractual provisions, like highly detailed delivery arrangements, will only cause you difficulty in the enforcement. So once again, simpler is better. Many professional draftsmen (contract writers) also include a provision that if there is a difference of opinion about the contract, it will be taken to the American Arbitration Association for solution. Many courts are years behind in their cases. The American Arbitration Association may be able to settle the matter very quickly, perhaps even in days, if there is some need for rush. If there is a branch of this organization near you, it would be best to include it in the contract as a means of settlement. Not only is it faster, but it is also less costly than a trial.

RULE: KNOW WHAT THE CONTRACT MEANS.

Sometimes even a well-educated person will not be able to read a contract and understand what it means. Somehow the meanings of the words don't reach the person's mind. The words get altered, even though they may be clear to others. The person who doesn't understand may stubbornly refuse to acknowledge that a particular provision of the contract exists. If you are dealing with a person who doesn't seem to comprehend part of a contract you are negotiating, it is best to discuss fully all provisions before the signing. If you are the one who doesn't understand, you should ask questions until you do understand. If a party misunderstands one of the provisions, the contract is likely to end up in difficulty. There is no rational reason for this, but misunderstandings and difficulties seem to go hand in hand.

RULE: ORAL CONTRACTS ARE O.K.,
BUT NOT DESIRABLE.

There's nothing basically wrong with an oral contract. If it can be completed within a year, the law will not ignore the contract, and you can bring suit if you have to. The problems with oral contracts are more practical than legal. The requirement that an oral contract be performed in less time than a year grows out of the Statute of Frauds discussed next in this chapter. The problem with oral contracts and the reason for their lack of popularity is twofold. First, you may not be able to get the other party to admit to saying what he said. If you have a written contract you have evidence that there was an agreement. Most attorneys refuse to take on cases involving an oral contract since they are so hard to prove. The general legal maxim is: "no writing, no contract." The second and subtler problem is that people tend to remember only what is beneficial to them and nothing else. Even if the other person is honorable and has many sterling qualities and owns up to the fact that she did make a contract, she might literally forget inconvenient portions of the contract. So even though there is nothing to prevent short-term oral contracts from being enforced, they are not recommended. As a very wise man said, "If it ain't in writing, it ain't true."

RULE: GET A RECEIPT FOR SALES OVER $30.

If you develop difficulties regarding something you buy, you must have some record of the sale. States require records of sale for sales over different amounts of money. If more than $30 changes hands, Missouri and Arkansas require a receipt, or the buyer will not have standing to enforce the contract. This receipt is the contract. Other states require a written contract only for much larger amounts. Many require a written contract only if more than $500 will change hands. But since $30 is the minimum in any state, you can use this as a basic rule. Of course, all rules have exceptions. North Carolina requires that all sales in excess of $10 which are made to an Indian must be in writing unless the Indian can write and speak English.

This rule about minimum amounts came about through the passage of Statutes of Fraud throughout the country. The Statutes of Fraud require that contracts be written under particular circumstances. If the contract isn't written, the buyer has no standing to sue the seller. The Statutes of Fraud also require a written contract if the contract will take longer than one year to perform, or if it is a lease for longer than a year. (A few states allow three years.) Some states also require that every agreement concerning land also be in writing.

RULE: BOTH PARTIES MUST BE COMPETENT
TO SIGN THE CONTRACT.

Both parties to a contract must have enough knowledge and basic intelligence to know what the contract entails. They can be incompetent due to being under age (in most states under 18 years old), retarded, senile, or mentally deranged.

RULE: THE CONTRACT MUST HAVE
A LEGAL PURPOSE.

Sometimes the contracts themselves are illegal. The most obvious of the illegal contracts are ones which have a criminal purpose, such as dealing narcotics or contracting a murder. These acts are illegal all by themselves. Others are prohibited on matters of public policy, often public health reasons. For example, it might be illegal to sell fish caught in Canadian waters. The supplier delivers the Canadian fish, and the buyer resells them. Once the illegality is discovered the seller could sell no more Canadian fish, but could collect on fish already sold. The crime would be balanced out with the loss and how strongly the contract violates the public policy.

Duress or undue influence can also overcome a contract. When threats are used to force the signing of a contract, duress is charged. Undue influence is slightly different in that the threat may not have been obvious, but one party to the contract may have had a weakened mind upon which another person operated. Widows, orphans, and manic-depressives could plead undue influence if the result of the contract is outrageous.

Contracts will also be canceled because of fraud or misrepresentation. Some types of fraud are intentional and will become a defense against the enforcement of the contract. The minute the buyer discovers the fraud or misrepresentation, she must start action to cancel the contract. After weighing the cost, she should either hire a lawyer or start a letter campaign of her own. If she waits, the contract, even though fraudulent, may be enforced against her. Innocent misrepresentation is not fraud, but a mistake. The court will be more lenient with innocent misrepresentations and will treat them as honest contractual promises which have failed.

RULE: ALL CONTRACTS HAVE WARRANTIES.

Regardless of the nature of the contract, it carries with it certain warranties. A warranty is a promise that certain things will be true of the product or service which is sold. The warranties of goods and services are governed by the Uniform Commercial Code in all states except Louisiana. Warranties fall into three categories: express warranties, implied warranties of merchantability, and implied warranties of fitness. ("Implied" means unspoken but still understood.) Among these, the warranty of merchantability is most important to the consumer.

An express warranty is a specific, overt statement made about a product. Auto manufacturers often make express warranties in writing to repair or replace certain parts of a car should these prove faulty. Express warranties can also include oral statements made by the seller to the buyer. For example, if the seller represents that the product is new, it had better be new. If the buyer asks for #2 grade fuel oil, the seller can sell her only that grade. In short, the express warranty must be part of the basis of the bargain, according to the UCC. Therefore, any statements made about defects in the goods must come before the sale is closed.

RULE: ALL CONSUMERS GET IMPLIED WARRANTIES.

The implied warranty of merchantability is useful, inescapable, and part of every sale made by a merchant. The merchant warrants that the goods are "fit for the ordinary purposes for which such goods are used." This warranty is absolutely dandy in that the goods sold must actually do what they are supposed to. Your swimsuit cannot fade when exposed to chlorine, the dye cannot turn your hair green, the seam in your dress cannot come out after your second wearing, and the refrigerator must cool your food. If the goods are unsatisfactory, the merchant has to replace the goods or refund your money. In turn, the manufacturer of the goods will have to make a refund to the merchant, so don't feel sorry for the merchant when you ask for your money back.

The warranty of fitness is a little bit more particular than the warranty of merchantability. Under the warranty of fitness the seller promises that the goods are suitable for a particular purpose the buyer has described. (The seller doesn't have to be a merchant.) For example, if I went to a typewriter store and told the merchant that I wanted a portable typewriter which was strong enough for heavy use, and then relied upon the merchant's judgment as to which typewriter could take the heavy use, the merchant is responsible for his opinion when selecting the goods. There are two elements which must be satisfied: the buyer must rely on the seller's judgment and the merchant must know the particular circumstances under which the goods will be used. Occasionally warranties of fitness will be waived by the buyer. For example, if a restaurant owner buys dishes of standard household quality, a warranty of fitness would not apply, for these dishes are not made to be strong enough to take the pounding they would receive in a restaurant.

Warranties extend to the buyer's family, household, and house guests. Any injury suffered by any of these persons can be sued on and any of those persons might sue to recover for those injuries. Generally, breaches (breaking) of warranty can be handled informally directly with the seller. The contract can be canceled and any payments recovered.

All implied warranties can be eliminated if there is language in the contract stating this. Disclaimers of the warranty of merchantability must be in writing and must actually mention merchantability in the sentence. Disclaimers of warranties of fitness must be in writing but need not mention fitness. General disclaimers such as "as is" or "demonstrator model" will call the buyer's attention to the faults of the goods. These statements would operate as a disclaimer of the warranties. However, if a seller has made specific oral or written statements (express warranties) about the goods, he cannot nullify them by disclaiming them in the sales agreement.

Warranties may also be limited by language in the contract. Normally this would be a guarantee to replace or repair equipment which is not satisfactory. This provision is very commonplace. But even if a contract contained such provisions, the item must end up working properly. If it doesn't, the buyer can sue. Suppose a new-car buyer has made every attempt to get his car working properly. Every effort to correct his lemon has failed. The seller in the end must deliver him a new car which works properly, since it would be unfair for a warranty provision to bar him from getting a car which would live up to the essential purpose of the transaction (a car which operates as a new car should).

RULE: SELLERS MUST GIVE WRITTEN WARRANTIES.

An act of Congress in 1975, called the Magnuson-Moss Warranty Act, prevents the use of deceptive written warranties. The Magnuson-Moss Act requires that the language used in the warranty be readily understandable. If the goods cost more than $10, the warranty must state whether it is "full or limited." In order to be a full warranty, the warrantor, who can be both the manufacturer and the dealer, must repair an item which does not work properly. It must be repaired within a reasonable time and without charge. If it cannot be properly repaired after every effort has been made to do so, it must be replaced. A typical limited warranty would be a guarantee of parts and labor for ninety days, parts for one year, and no warranty whatsoever after that.

Under the Magnuson-Moss Act, when the seller writes the required warranty it becomes an express warranty. If the seller makes the express warranty, he cannot disclaim implied warranties of fitness or merchantability. This requirement gives one the best of both worlds. Not only does the contract state that the goods will be repaired, but it also gives you the right to return the goods if they don't work as they should.

If you are having a problem which is covered by a warranty, the Magnuson-Moss Act requires that you first try to settle your dispute with the warrantor under the procedures he has set up. That will handle almost every case. If every attempt you've made to have your goods fixed has failed, you may take your matter to either a state or federal court and sue under the warranty. Suing on a warranty is generally a waste of time for a consumer, since the cost of the suit may be higher than simply buying a replacement for your lemon.

Advertising has no real home in the law. It's not really a contract issue, nor is it really a consumer credit or sales issue. But there are some things you should know about it.

RULE: ADVERTISERS MUST TELL THE TRUTH.

Several different elements go into the laws of truth in advertising. The most prominent of these is the Federal Trade Commission's truth-in-advertising regulations. Examples of these are the requirements that celebrities actually use products for which they are the spokespersons, some TV commercials with the word "dramatization" flashed on the screen, or the recent FTC ruling that some Listerine commercials mis-leadingly stated that the product prevented colds. As a penalty, Listerine was required to run ads for two years which withdrew this statement. The FTC has within its power the ability to bring cease and desist or-ders against commercials, ads, or other business practices which offend FTC regulations. The manufacturer or merchant advertises first, and then if the FTC finds the ad misleading, it can bring the cease and desist order to stop advertising of that nature. The FTC can also nego-tiate and impose some type of penalty such as the one Listerine is fulfilling.

Truth in advertising is separated into two basic categories: opinion and fact. Opinion is restricted to general statements such as "Best car on the market for this price." This claim is largely a matter of puffery (enhancing goods through statements of high opinion). Such state-ments are immune from truth in advertising, since fair men might all hold differing opinions regarding the suitability of a range of items. For example, one man might say that a Pinto is the best buy for the money; another might think a Chevette has better features for the price. It would all depend on what each man considered to be important in a car purchase.

Misstatements of fact are quite different. If an advertiser makes a claim as to the special workability of goods, he'd better have sound scientific studies to back up his claim. If the manufacturer says its washer has three cycles, it had better have just that. If Listerine says it prevents the common cold, there'd better be research to prove it. These positive assertions are differentiated from opinion in that they make a claim regarding how a particular product works. Incidentally, the FTC encourages ads which illustrate competitive differences between products. The Zest commercials showing no soap film are examples. However, you notice that Zest makes no particular claims about whether it cleans better than another soap, only that it does not leave a soap film.

If an advertiser makes certain specifications in his ads, he will be held contractually liable for these claims. The claims become part of the warranties in the contract. For example, if a Sears catalogue advertises a power drill with a one-third horsepower motor which is self-cooling, they must deliver exactly that product or renegotiate the contract so that the consumer understands precisely what goods are being delivered. This rule is an express warranty under the UCC.

RULE: THE MERCHANT MUST HAVE THE GOODS HE ADVERTISES.

There are a series of rules formulated by the FTC on the subject of bait-and-switch advertising. Bait-and-switch advertising is probably the clearest example of a deceptive practice. Bait-and-switch advertising operates like this: A seller advertises goods or services at an unbelievably low price. When the buyer appears in the store, the salesmen steer the buyer from the advertised goods or service to a more expensive item. The bait is the ad and the switch is putting the consumer's attention on the more expensive item. The primary standard in a bait-and-switch decision is how many sales of the bait item were actually made. In one case involving an optician, bait advertising was found when only 10 pairs of glasses out of 1,400 were sold at the bait price of $7.50. This optician's salesmen certainly belong in some hall of infamy. Other symptoms of bait advertising are refusal to show the advertised product, the salesman's advice against buying the advertised item, failure to have the advertised item in stock and in reasonable quantities, or refusal to deliver within a reasonable time.

If you meet with any of these tactics when trying to buy something which is advertised, mention to the salesman that this certainly sounds like it is a bait-and-switch ad. You may find him selling you the advertised item for delivery tomorrow. If this tactic doesn't work, write the FTC to complain about the merchant. Whatever you do, don't buy from him unless you can buy the advertised item.

Certain states and municipalities have their own laws prohibiting bait-and-switch advertising. In New York City when a supermarket runs out of an advertised item, it must give you a rain check to buy that item at the advertised price when it is next in stock, if you demand it. Check with consumer groups in your area to determine if your town or county has such a regulation.

RULE: CONTRACTS MUST BE PERFORMED UPON.

The contracts which are performed upon never see the inside of an attorney's office. You are absolutely required to perform on a contract, or pay the price of not doing so. However, you may not have to perform your part of the contract until the other person has done his part. This rule is called a dependent promise. If you do not have to pay the local grass cutter until he cuts your lawn, that is a dependent promise. Other contracts for exactly the same purpose might not be dependent. For example, you may have a contract with a lawn maintenance firm at $40 a month with the agreement that the firm will cut your grass as often as needed. Some months it is cut twice; others, three times. Your price is still $40 per month.

Almost all law in the area of contract performance has nothing to do with performance and everything to do with the lack of performance. The following is a survey of "excuses" which will call off a contract. If you tried to perform and the other party wouldn't allow you to, you are excused. If you substantially fulfill the contract, but one item was off, you will be excused unless you made a knowing or bad faith departure from the requirements of the contract. If the other fellow didn't do some job you needed in order to fulfill the contract, you will also be excused. For example, if the other party was to inform you of where you were to deliver the goods and he never did so, you are excused. Before any performance is started, the other party may call the whole thing off and you will be excused from your part of the bargain. By the same token, if the other guy does something which would not allow him to perform, such as selling the goods to somebody else, you will be excused from your bargain. There are several other minor bases for excuse. If something doesn't seem fair to you, chances are it is a valid excuse.

The other half of performance is "breach" of contract. There are two basic types of breaches. The anticipatory breach is a breaking of the performance of the contract prior to the time any real performance has actually occurred. If you're an innocent party, and it looks like the other fellow is not willing or able to keep up his part of the bargain, you may cease your preparation of your performance. You may even be required to cease your preparation in order to keep the damages down. Anticipatory breach of contract is used only when there is a

CONSUMERISM

pressing reason to find one, as when damage may result to the innocent party.

Breach of contract can also be sued upon if the contract is partially or fully performed. Most of these suits seem to involve home construction contracts where the homeowner does not feel that the contractor has lived up to his bargain. The court then rules how substantial the breach is. The contractor almost always gets paid, even though the house is in the wrong spot, the wrong pipe was installed, or the wiring was inadequate. He may not get paid the whole amount if the fault is rectifiable. Wiring or pipe can be replaced, but it's rare that a house can be moved.

RULE: BUYERS MAY REJECT THE GOODS.

The Uniform Commercial Code allows a buyer to reject goods on their delivery if the goods fail in any respect to conform to the contract. The failure must be judged in good faith by the buyer. He must look at the goods in a fair way to see if they do or do not meet the contractual obligation. Obviously the wrong air conditioner is the wrong air conditioner. For most consumers the good faith provision will never be a problem. However, if the air conditioner is banged up or scratched upon delivery, it's best to complain at once. A sealed carton is no assurance that the goods are new. It's best to demand that the carton be opened and the appliance plugged in and working before the deliverymen leave. This immediate inspection is not important from a legal point of view. But from a convenience point of view, it will save the trucker a trip. Of course, if goods do not meet the contractual provisions, let the merchant know immediately.

RULE: CONTRACTS END.

Nothing goes on forever and neither does a contract. When a contract ends, it is said to be discharged. The most common type of discharge is performance. Almost all contracts are discharged this way. Another type of discharge is the method called accord and satisfaction. The seller is unable to perform the original contract. The buyer and the seller come to an agreement for a substitute. The agreement is the accord. When the parties satisfy the accord, the contract is ended. Rescission is another method of discharge. Under rescission the parties decide to call off, or rescind, the contract. Rescission should be in writing if the contract would be required to be in writing, such as a land deal or the sale of goods in excess of $30. When you return a dress to the store, you have rescinded a contract. The store gives you a credit receipt, the written rescission.

Impossibility of performance is another type of discharge. The impossibility must be some unforeseeable event which would make performance impossible for just about anybody. Death or major illness of one of the parties to the contract would be a basis for impossibility of performance. Inadequate finance would not be something which would allow discharge. I might be inadequately financed to continue business, but that's my problem and not the problem of the other party. Destruction of highly individual goods through no fault of the seller would also discharge the contract. For example, destruction of a work of art before it can be delivered to the buyer would call the deal off. Destruction of an item which could be replaced, such as any typical consumer item, would not cause the contract to be discharged.

If between the time the contract is signed and the time it is to be performed upon, somebody passes a law making the contract illegal, performance is not required. For example, you contracted with a builder to drill a well in your backyard. After you sign the contract, your town outlaws private wells and requires all houses to link up to city water. The contract will be rescinded. If the new law just makes the job more difficult, the contract stands. In this case, you and the building contractor have an agreement to build a three-family house. A new fire regulation requires expensive fireproofing which had not been anticipated. The contract stands.

If the purpose of the contract is frustrated, the contract can be canceled. In frustration of purpose, the parties can still perform but performance would be absolutely worthless to one of them. The event which frustrates their purpose must be unforeseeable. An auto dealer used this defense when suing to have the lease for his showroom canceled. World War II had broken out and steel rationing had ended the production of new cars. He had no cars to sell. The lease was not canceled since he could have sold used cars.

RULE: TITLE PASSES WITH DELIVERY.

Normally, title passes when the goods are physically delivered, if you and the seller don't make an explicit agreement to the contrary. Your actual intent is the important factor. The court, if your problem goes that far, will decide what you intended to have happen. Most people intend for title to pass when delivery is made.

If the merchant is responsible for delivery, any damage that occurs up until the time the goods enter your home is the merchant's responsibility. In local transactions this is not a problem. However, you may order the goods from someone at a distance from you. In such a case, if the order is marked FOB (Free on Board), the merchant's responsibility ends when the goods are delivered to the carrier (like UPS). Sometimes FOB will include a city, such as FOB Peoria. FOB Peoria is a fast way of saying that the seller will bear the cost of delivery of the goods until they reach the carrier in Peoria who will then bring them to you, wherever you are. You pay for shipment from Peoria to your home and you are responsible for damage during shipment. For this reason it is mandatory to carry insurance to cover cost of damages during shipping. Almost all shippers (such as UPS, Greyhound, or trucking companies) arrange for insurance right along with the delivery. Another term of shipment is FAS (Free Along Side). This term is used primarily when goods are purchased abroad. FAS includes the cost of shipment to the dock but does not include the cost of loading the goods onto the ship. The seller maintains responsibility for the goods until they reach the dock. CIF means Cost, Insurance, and Freight. CIF is always accompanied by the name of a city, such as CIF New York or CIF Houston. The seller pays cost, insurance, and freight to that city. You may be responsible for shipment from that city to your own location.

COD is probably the most common of all terms in commerce. COD stands for Collect On Delivery. Title generally passes on a COD sale at the time the seller delivers the goods to the shipper. COD has nothing to do with delivery, but is merely a payment method for the buyer's convenience.

Sales are always contracts. Because sales are such an important element of commerce, all states (except Louisiana) adhere to the sales section of the UCC. It would be utter chaos if each different state had different laws regarding sales. In a sale the primary element is who has risk of loss. Risk of loss is important, since the contract is not complete until both parties have what they are supposed to have. In a sale the merchant has his money and the consumer has the goods.

RULE: YOU OWN DELIVERED GOODS.

Even if you have not paid for them, goods which have been delivered to you are your responsibility. Let's say I buy a lampshade at Gimbels. On the way out of the store I catch the lampshade in a revolving door and crush it. Although Gimbels might be nice and give me a new lampshade, they have no responsibility to do so. However, if I asked them to deliver the lampshade to me and it is crushed while being delivered by their own deliverymen, they must replace the lampshade.

The rule about delivery is a practical rule which is generally followed. However, remember that you and the seller can agree that the transfer of title will occur at a time other than delivery, depending on the customs of the business in which you are dealing, what type of merchandise you're buying, your intent of when title will pass, or any number of other items. It may be that special-order items such as a sofa, made and upholstered to your specific instructions, might be delivered directly from the factory to you. In such a case the title may pass directly from the manufacturer to you without title ever passing to the merchant. This kind of transfer is rare in domestic sales, but not so unusual if the item is to be delivered overseas.

Passage of title can also be deferred by agreement while the merchant waits for payment in full. These contracts are called conditional sales. Major appliances are often sold in this way. In such a case the seller would record his title with the county seat. You would have possession of the goods, but would not have title until you fulfilled your part of the contract by paying off all the installments. However, conditional sales contracts will not modify your risk of loss if goods have been delivered to you. If the washer and dryer are destroyed by fire, you will still be responsible for paying off the sales contract. A conditional sale is more a matter of credit than it is the risk of loss in a sale.

Of all of the different kinds of law that there are, contracts is probably the one you'll use the most. You can't go shopping without making a contract. The area of contracts is also probably the least abused area of the law. Most sellers want everything to go right, and most buyers just naturally use a good faith standard when appraising goods they have purchased. The area of contracts is broader and more convoluted than this chapter presents it to be, but the emphasis here has been on the consumer's use of a contract, just as the next three chapters will all emphasize the consumer instead of the commercial person. Robert J. Ringer, as he said in *Winning Through Intimidation,* always writes his own contracts, since he doesn't trust a lawyer to do it. Many businessmen feel the same way and only a very small percentage of contracts are actually drafted by a professional.

Chapter 24
PRODUCTS LIABILITY

If a pop bottle blows up in your face, your home permanent causes your hair to fall out, or you find a human toe in a plug of chewing tobacco, you may have just been injured by a product. The product manufacturer may be liable.

Products liability is somewhat distinct from other types of personal injuries, since it basically relies on a contractual relationship between the manufacturer or seller and the buyer. The manufacturer who fails to exercise due care in the making or distributing of his product is held liable to any person who foreseeably could be injured. That the manufacturer's conduct was negligent is more or less assumed, depending on the nature of the injury.

Another area of products liability is something called negligent misrepresentation. This could also be called careless claims. The manufacturer who has not checked the facts he asserts about his product will be held liable if a buyer relies upon these claims and is injured. Automobile steering which proves to be dangerous, shoes that slip because the soles are slick, and hypo-allergenic cosmetics that cause skin break-outs are all examples of products represented as safe but which in fact might be harmful or even dangerous.

Different types of sellers have different responsibilities to a buyer. Manufacturers must follow all government regulations and must also exercise due care in product design. They are charged with a reasonable amount of quality control. The more dangerous the product, the greater is the manufacturer's duty to warn the consumer of the dangers which may be involved.

Retailers have a slightly different standard. In most jurisdictions a retailer is not liable for goods which turn out to be dangerous. Fewer jurisdictions require that a retailer use ordinary care and to inspect goods for dangers which can be seen by the eye, such as a loose refrigerator door. However, if a retailer sells goods of a manufacturer generally unknown to him, he has a higher duty to inspect. For example, a retailer selling a General Electric refrigerator has less duty to the customer than the same retailer selling a "Corsica King" refrigerator. Auto dealers are not required to take a car apart to see if it's all right, but they do have a duty to give the car a thorough check-out before they deliver it. The courts are unsure as to whether a used-car dealer has the same duty. It can be said that a used-car dealer mustn't sell a car which might be dangerous to someone operating it, such as no brakes or doors that come open when the car is rounding curves.

Warranties are also important in the area of products liability, but this subject has been covered in the chapter on contracts. Legal thinkers are split on whether products liability should be a strict personal injury matter or should remain hanging halfway between contracts and personal injuries.

The basic principle of products liability is one of strict tort liability, meaning that if an injury has been suffered and the injury can be directly linked to the product involved, the buyer need not prove negligence on the part of the seller or manufacturer to win the case. This principle is very helpful to an injured person, since proving the negligence of a faraway manufacturer would be difficult, if not impossible.

RULE: HE WHO MADE IT
IS RESPONSIBLE.

If a manufacturer makes goods which are defective because they are improperly crafted, improperly designed, or improperly packaged, the manufacturer will be liable. Although many of these cases in the past have involved a breach of a warranty, this basis of liability is losing popularity. The breach of warranty action generally requires privity of contract, a special contractual relationship between the manufacturer and the injured party. All too often the person injured is merely an innocent bystander, with no privity of contract. To help the innocent bystander, the courts have largely rejected warranties as the basis for products liability, and instead have taken up the banner of strict liability.

Sellers and manufacturers can each be responsible for unreasonably dangerous goods. The manufacturer is responsible if he completes the goods to such a degree that they reach the consumer substantially unchanged. Most consumer goods fall into this category. The seller of the goods can also be held responsible if he did not inspect as required, or if he altered the manufacturer's product. There is no exception, even if the seller exercised all possible care in the preparation of his product. The position just stated is considered the most ideal for law in the United States. All the states adhere to this position to some degree, but there are slight variations among them.

RULE: YOU CHOOSE THE METHOD OF RECOVERY.

The least costly method is seeking redress from the manufacturer before suit is brought. You seek to restore yourself to the same position you were in before the product turned out to be harmful. This course of action is preferred since little cost or effort is required.

If it becomes necessary to bring suit, an injured person will often claim three different bases for the suit. Strict liability favors the injured person. Breach of warranty will also be argued, since no proof of negligence is required. And sometimes negligence is argued. Juries like negligence cases, and are thought to return higher awards when negligence can be shown. However, negligence can get pretty ridiculous in products liability cases, since it may be difficult to connect the manufacturer with the negligent act. In one case a woman actually argued negligence on the part of a dress shop when she was bitten by a spider while trying on a pair of slacks. The jury did not believe that a spider in a pair of slacks was necessarily proof of negligence.

Three types of loss are subject to recovery. Personal injuries can be recovered, but so can economic or pecuniary loss. Pecuniary loss is the loss of money or harm to property. Horses that die as a result of poisoned feed would be a pecuniary loss. Economic losses are more subtle, are almost always between businesses and manufacturers, and involve money one could have made if the manufacturer or seller had not been negligent. Different types of recoveries are allowable through different types of actions, but as a consumer, you need to know only that all of these recoveries are possible.

RULE: RECOVERY REQUIRES A DEFECT.

As a broad general rule, any product which falls short of a consumer's reasonable expectations can be considered to be defective. What is considered "reasonable" is the subject of much discussion. If the ordinary consumer would not contemplate that a certain product might be dangerous, the product may fall into the category of "unreasonably dangerous." One of the tests for this is whether or not the goods were "fit" for the purpose intended.

Foreign objects are one measure of fitness. A fishbone case is an example. A woman got a fishbone lodged in her throat while eating fish chowder in a tearoom in Massachusetts. Two operations were required to remove the fishbone. The fish chowder was judged to be fit for its purpose. The court waxed profound on the subject of fish chowder, calling it one of the "joys of life in New England," and implying that in some instances consumers had to accept the bad along with the good, since a fishbone is a reasonable danger of fish chowder. The woman could not recover for her fishbone misadventure.

Another food case revolved around an olive which still contained its pit. A restaurant patron broke his tooth on the pit and sued because the olive had a hole in one end, leading him to the conclusion that the olive had been pitted. Only the fact that the man with the broken tooth had noticed a hole in the olive allowed him to recover. Otherwise, the broken tooth would have been his own problem, since a pit is not a foreign object in an olive.

The unreasonably dangerous defect is only one element required to prove a case. The injured party must also be able to prove that the defect caused the injury. Between the defect and the cause there is often a wide gap. In order to bridge this gap, the law has invented the "but for" rule, which means if the defect hadn't existed, the injury would not have occurred.

Defects can also exist due to overuse of a product. There is a famous case involving the use of cigarettes. The widow of a man who had died of lung cancer was denied recovery, since the cigarettes were not found to have contained any dangerous or foreign substances other than tobacco.

The user of something potentially dangerous assumes the risk to a certain degree, especially in the use of tobacco and alcohol. Both tobacco and alcohol can be habit-forming. Since the habit-forming aspects are broadly known, the user assumes some amount of risk.

Old products can sometimes fall apart and injure someone. If the deterioration is hard to detect, and the potential for harm is severe, the manufacturer will be held responsible. Tires blowing out after a short period of time fall into this category. If the user had driven the tires far beyond their limit, resulting blowouts would be the user's problem. If a tire blows out well before the end of its normal life span, it is the manufacturer's fault. The jury decides what is an expected life span for a tire. The jury usually decides such questions of "reasonableness" in products liability cases.

Sometimes a purveyor of goods will argue that it is not possible to

discover that a product is faulty through scientific methods. Blood
transfusions carrying hepatitis and pork with trichinosis are two examples of scientifically undiscoverable dangers. Although I find it hard to
believe, there seems to be no technique for discovery of hepatitis germs
in donated blood. Hospitals where such blood has been administered
are held free from fault, usually as a matter of state statute. Dangerous
pork cannot be recovered upon, since trichinosis inspection has proved
difficult. The pork was spoiling before the inspection was completed.
One court reasoned that inspection might create a false sense of security in the public. It is also widely known that pork must be cooked
thoroughly to avoid this danger.

Some products are just plain unsafe. The products might be necessary for use, but somebody somewhere is sure to be injured. The most
common example is prescription drugs. In these cases, the manufacturer is not strictly liable for the side effects which the drugs might
create. Scientific knowledge in this area is judicially recognized as inadequate. The drug products must be well prepared with good quality
control, but that's about it.

In drug cases, a rough line is drawn between the seriousness of the
side effects and the seriousness of the disease. Rabies vaccine can create
spectacular and dangerous side effects, such as shock, convulsions, or
brain damage, but rabies in a human is an absolute death sentence.
Therefore the potentially damaging side effects of the rabies vaccine are
not as abhorrent to juries as blindness caused by a drug used to treat
arthritis.

RULE: DESIGN CAN BE A DEFECT TOO.

Design defects have become more popular as a basis for suit. In a
defective design, either the specifications are inadequate or the materials chosen are inadequate. Design defects are distinguished from the
more common production defects. With production defects, the design
is O.K. but something went wrong on the assembly line.

Defects in design can prompt an automobile recall. Passage of the
National Traffic and Motor Vehicle Safety Act gave rise to a large
number of lawsuits based on defective design. Under this act, the Secretary of Transportation can set safety standards for automobiles. Seat
belts are one example of what's been done. The auto maker also has a
duty to notify purchasers when a defect is discovered.

There are two basic types of design defects: concealed dangers and
missing safety devices. Concealed dangers usually involve inadequate
materials. This classification covers items which fail suddenly—for ex-

ample, steering wheels that break in one's hands and plastic gear-shift knobs which fracture on impact. A woman driving a thirteen-year-old car was involved in an accident. Her body hit the plastic knob on the gear shift, causing it to shatter. The gear-shift rod plunged through her body and severed her spinal cord, causing paralysis. The auto company knew when the car was manufactured in 1949 that the plastic would deteriorate after one year of exposure to direct sunlight. The use of the plastic was found to be negligent.

Other concealed dangers can result from faulty engineering or design. If these defects are concealed, the injured person may recover. Examples of this are aluminum folding chairs which cut off fingers, toys which backfire causing injury to the child, and lawn mowers which go into gear and start moving all by themselves. All of these defects are illustrative of unexpected dangers—things which just don't operate as could be anticipated.

Sometimes a safety feature will be absent which might cause severe injury. Many power lawn mower cases are found in this area. Power lawn mowers are obviously dangerous and the manufacturer would therefore not be liable for hidden dangers. However, injured parties have been successful in cases showing an absence of safety features. The safety features required seem to be some sort of guard around the cutting device. If the mower is being used in a normal fashion and an injury occurs, there is some chance of recovery. The tragedy of these lawn mower cases is that they have almost always involved children playing near the mower. The children fell and were injured, usually losing a hand or foot.

RULE: THE MANUFACTURER MUST FORESEE UNUSUAL USES.

A manufacturer is not allowed to back out of his responsibilities merely because the product was not used exactly as he intended. The manufacturer must foresee all that might occur, instead of what ought to occur. One example is paint dropping off a paintbrush into a painter's eyes, causing blindness. The paint company could certainly foresee such a possibility. Chairs being used as stepladders are another example.

A rather strange exception to the foreseeability requirement is auto collisions. In spite of the fact that a substantial percentage of automobiles are in accidents (perhaps as high as 40 per cent), the courts to this date have considered auto collisions to be unintended and unforeseeable uses of automobiles. Certainly no one intends an auto accident to happen, but they happen with such regularity that the lack of substantial safety features should impose some liability on the manufacturer. This is my personal opinion and not yet the opinion of any court.

RULE: THE SELLER HAS TO TELL YOU HOW TO USE IT.

If there is any danger in the product, it is the responsibility of the manufacturer or seller to explain the proper use. The manufacturer also has a duty to warn of dangers which might result from improper use.

There are two basic types of cases in this area. One involves cosmetics and the other, poisonous substances. For example, with a home permanent, the manufacturer is required, as a matter of good business practice, to give full directions for use. If the consumer's failure to follow directions could cause serious harm, the manufacturer then has the additional duty to warn of the potential harm. If the manufacturer warns of the risk, the warning must be clear and specific. Subtle warnings will not do.

Poisonous substances require a strict duty to warn, since poison is unreasonably dangerous. Poisonous substances are also required by a federal law to be labeled as such. However, accidents can occur. A sixteen-month-old drank a bottle of furniture polish and died. The court allowed recovery, since the bottle should have been labeled. Although the sixteen-month-old could not have read the label, the parent might have prevented the occurrence by putting the bottle in a high place. Since children under three consider everything, including rocks, to be food, the parent had a right to be warned.

Sometimes the risks are simply unknown. Many drug cases fall into this category. If the risk could not be discovered, the manufacturer would not be liable. Then the duty to warn is suspended, since there is no way to discover what you should be warned of. On the other hand, the duty to warn is not suspended in a drug case when the side effects are known to the manufacturer. He has the duty to inform the consumer so that the consumer can assume the risk or not. One example of this is a drug for the treatment of high cholesterol which had an occasional side effect of causing cataracts. Since there are a number of harmless ways to treat high cholesterol, the court found that the user should have been warned so that she could have taken the risk analytically. This point of view developed from the idea that the risk for a known or obvious danger is assumed by the informed user. Therefore the manufacturer must inform, or keep the risk himself.

If the flaw turns up after the goods are made, the manufacturer still has a duty to warn, even though the goods may have long ago left his control. This duty to warn depends on how dangerous the flaw is. Defective airplane parts are dangerous enough, as are adulterated foods. Other flaws might also fit this category, such as dangerous toys or blades which loosen and fly off machinery like power mowers or electric saws. If this happens with a piece of your own equipment, it's a good idea to notify the manufacturer, even if no serious injury has occurred. It may be due to some defect in design. The manufacturer will not be able to act responsibly unless the users of the equipment inform the maker of difficulties.

RULE: ALLERGIC USERS ARE SPECIAL.

One particularly vexing area of the law surrounds persons who are allergic to particular products. The manufacturer has a duty to warn if he knew or should have known that an allergic problem might occur. However, the risk of allergies must be created among a rather large number of the persons who use the product. How large the number must be is very much open to interpretation. One allergy in 5,000,000 users would not require a warning. The Federal Trade Commission has set a standard that if one person out of 10,000 develops an allergic reaction, a warning must be given. If the harm could be very serious, a warning might be required even though far fewer persons could be injured. If one person out of 10,000 had her hair fall out as a result of using a hair dye, a warning would be required. But what if one person out of 1,000,000 might develop a blood disease? Because of the seriousness of the blood disease, a warning would be required even though the relative numbers affected are minuscule.

The product may well be defective, but sometimes the user contributes to her own injury. Manufacturers rejoice at this fact because it is often their best defense in products liability.

The basic principle involved here is this: he who is best able to guard against the risk of harm should be the person responsible for the harm. When the user does something unusual with the goods, the jury must question whether the manufacturer could have foreseen the problem. The fact that a housedress might burn up when brought too near a stove was found to be foreseeable by the dress company. When children might be involved, manufacturers have to foresee more inventive uses of goods. For example, a stove manufacturer was found liable when a child was burned while standing on the oven door to inspect what was cooking. The stove tipped over, so that boiling water spilled on the child. However, the manufacturer will not be responsible for ridiculous misuses by adults.

RULE: THE USER CAN ASSUME THE RISK.

According to the Uniform Commercial Code, the buyer has the responsibility to inspect the goods to discover defects. If he neither inspects nor complains of defects discovered, and then goes ahead and uses the goods, he has taken the responsibility for the risks involved. The assumption of risk consists of voluntarily and unreasonably going ahead with the use in the face of a known danger. What is voluntary and unreasonable depends primarily on the age and experience of the person assuming the risk. Young children are less responsible than teen-agers. Mechanics are more responsible about cars than housewives are. Sometimes a danger is so obvious that recovery is denied. For example, a guy whose foot comes in contact with a moving table saw blade has assumed the risk, since the saw blade was safe, except when someone's foot ran into it.

The assumption of risk on the part of the user can be overcome if the manufacturer or seller gave assurances that the item is safe in spite of the user's protest. The user's own mistakes also might not protect the manufacturer, although these cases seem to shade over into improper safety devices. For example, someone who loses a hand in a momentary lapse of attention might recover, even though she was aware of the danger.

Sometimes a user doesn't assume the risk even though she knows of the danger. If the user can show a strong necessity for continuing to use a defective item, the manufacturer will not be free from responsibility. These cases seem to involve working conditions, though there is no reason for this to be exclusively the case. A woman who slipped and fell into a punch press had not assumed the risk, even though she knew the danger of the punch press. A person who knew her brakes to be defective had an auto accident while driving a sick child to a doctor. Necessity to work and necessity to receive medical treatment are both valid excuses. Necessity to go get groceries might or might not be a good excuse, depending on the number of your children and the size of your larder. Necessity to drive the car to the place where it would be fixed is an excuse.

If a product you have been using proves to be defective, but no injury has occurred, the most efficient way to get your goods fixed will be through the express and implied warranties discussed in the chapter on contracts. If a product or service you have purchased proves to be defective, seek to have the situation rectified immediately. If you don't, you will be assuming the risk.

If a product is very dangerous, you must discontinue use, unless necessity requires the use of that item. Since no amount of money can repay a child for burn scars or an adult for a lost limb, caution in the continued use of dangerous goods is a practical necessity. If you have to buy replacement goods, figure out some way to buy them. If your goods are truly defective, the manufacturer will be responsible for the replacements.

If a product or service proves to be defective and a personal injury occurs, the barn door has been closed too late. You will have to start building a case. You will need to prove that an accident occurred, that the product was involved in the accident, and that there was a relationship between the product and the injury. You will need expert testimony, and may contrast the product you used with similar products to show whether or not the product was safe. Most of all, you will need an attorney to help you through the intricacies of this particular area of the law.

Products liability cases are difficult, time-consuming, filled with emotional strain, expensive, and in every other way a difficult experience for the injured party. Most injured parties would rather accept a settlement than put up with the strain.

To avoid suits and injury, keep your home safe. Follow safety directions, and *do* the patch test on hair dye. Inspect for anything which could be dangerous. Put toxic substances far out of the reach of children, keep tools unplugged, keep children well away from lawn mowers, wear safety glasses, and take every precaution you possibly can. You are your own first line of defense against injuries.

Chapter 25
CREDIT

Practically all of our day-to-day transactions are consumer transactions. A consumer transaction is anything that is purchased for personal use or for the use of the family in a home setting. For example, a refrigerator purchased for the family home is a consumer transaction. The same refrigerator purchased for the same family's restaurant would not be. The sole distinguishing characteristic between the two is whether the item will be used for personal family endeavors or for business.

These consumer transactions can involve credit practices or cash sales. Most of the law in this area deals with credit practices. Consumer credit is relatively new on the scene. Up until 1900 it did not exist at all, since there were so few goods on the market of high enough value to be purchased on credit. The early part of the twentieth century and the availability of home electricity made many goods available which would benefit the family. Loan sharking in the big cities became a major problem. The first of the Consumer Credit Acts were passed around 1912. These acts restricted the price of credit to 3½% per month if the loan was under $300.

RULE: FIVE INSTALLMENTS MAKE IT CREDIT.

If a sale requires more than four payments, all the credit rules discussed in this chapter start to apply. If only four installments are required, the contract is said to be one of "forbearance." Forbearance means that the seller is simply not collecting his money quite so fast. No finance charge need be stated. He is entitled to charge a slightly higher price to pay him for arranging the installment sale. Forbearance is rarely used in consumer contracts, but is often used when purchasing land or commercial goods. For example, wholesalers often will make a deal with a merchant that the full price is $100 if paid in 90 days. If paid in 30 days, the price will be $90 ($100—10%). If the merchant waits 90 days to pay the bill, he pays the wholesaler an extra sum for the forbearance of collection. Forbearance is not interest or a service charge, but merely a higher cost since a longer payment period is allowed.

There has been a quiet revolution in the area of credit. Many credit practices once thought to be above the law have been outlawed or modified by the Consumer Credit Protection Act of 1968. The Fair Credit Reporting Act is part of this movement. For the first time credit-reporting agencies came under some type of legal supervision. Up until this time they could carry erroneous information on their records for years without a consumer ever discovering it. All this has been wiped away.

Credit-reporting agencies fall into two basic categories: credit bureaus and investigative bureaus. Sometimes one company will do both functions. Credit bureaus usually confine their information to financial data, such as bank accounts, charge accounts, debts outstanding, occupation, income, lawsuits, past bankruptcies, marital status, and how quickly the individual pays her bills. Credit bureaus obtain their information from merchants and creditors in the area. They rarely use any other type of investigation.

Investigative bureaus will carry more information which they themselves may have gathered through an actual investigation of a particular individual. Almost anything could be in these records: marital battles, your IQ, drug use, etc. The investigative reports are most often used by potential employers, insurance companies, and landlords.

Credit reporting is a very big business. There are probably 130 million persons' credit histories filed in various credit bureaus. Nearly as many credit reports are issued each year. The Fair Credit Reporting Act was passed to help control this area, since the common law had been totally ineffective in handling it.

> RULE: CREDIT-REPORTING FIRMS MUST
>   TELL YOU WHAT IS IN YOUR
>   CREDIT HISTORY.

If a seller has denied you credit on the basis of your credit history, the reporting firm must tell you what was in the report it sent. There is no charge for this. If you are merely curious about your credit history, you still get the same report but the reporting firm may charge a small fee. Either you must request your report in writing or you may go in person if you have the proper identification. You may also take a friend with you. I'd recommend this, since some people in the credit business have a low reputation.

The report they give you must include the nature and substance of all information in your file. They must tell you where they got the information and who has received the report within a six-month period. If you've applied for a job and the employer asked for your credit history, the reporting firm has to tell you the names of all employers who received it within the last two years. To obtain this report, just call the bank or wherever you made a loan application and ask which credit-reporting firm they use. They'll refer you to the credit firm.

RULE: YOU MAY CORRECT ERRORS
ON YOUR CREDIT HISTORY.

If you think an item on your credit history misrepresents the facts, you can make corrections or enter a protest. This area is now covered by state law, and the procedure varies from state to state. The credit-reporting agency may be able to acquaint you with proper procedure.

If you discover that someone has purposely entered erroneous information on your credit record, you can sue him for "slander of credit." This suit is based on someone's incorrect and damaging statements concerning another's credit.

RULE: INVESTIGATIVE REPORTS MAY
NOT BE PREPARED UNLESS
THE CONSUMER IS NOTIFIED.

Investigative reports are sometimes requested by employers, or by creditors when you make a very large loan request. An investigative report may include information about your character, general reputation, or any other information or rumor the investigator may happen upon.

You are now entitled to see a copy of any reports which are currently in your file. In the future you must be notified before the investigation begins. You can challenge the information in the report if you consider it misleading or inaccurate. If you dispute the accuracy of the report, the reporting firm is required to reinvestigate, and your disagreement must be registered in your file. If the information is changed due to the reinvestigation, you can request that the reporting company notify all those who received the misleading report.

RULE: CREDIT MUST BE REPORTED
IN THE NAMES OF BOTH
HUSBAND AND WIFE.

Credit-reporting agencies can be no better than the creditors who send them the information. Since many creditors report charge accounts and bank loans in the husband's name, the wife may never acquire a credit history, even though she's equally liable for the credit. Creditors must now report transactions in both the husband's and wife's name. But you must ask the creditor to do so on any accounts you opened before 1977.

RULE: SELLERS CAN'T PASS THE
REPORT AROUND.

If a merchant or other creditor requests your credit record, he must protect the confidentiality of the report. If he tells others about your credit history, he becomes a credit-reporting agency himself. If he occasionally tells another merchant of his experience with you, it's O.K., but if he reports what he heard from others, he is subject to the federal credit-reporting regulations.

By the same token, the credit-reporting agency must also protect the confidentiality of its files. If it is dealing with a new creditor, it is its responsibility to check his credentials to be sure he has a bona fide right to your credit history.

Up until 1975, creditors could arbitrarily decide on what basis they would grant credit. That year the U. S. Congress passed the Equal Credit Opportunity Act. The act eliminated discrimination in practically every area of the credit process. This chapter, based on that act, is about the rules *creditors* must follow for granting and maintaining credit, but you as the borrower will have to keep the creditor on his toes.

RULE: STUDY YOUR CREDIT RIGHTS
BEFORE APPLYING FOR CREDIT.

Beginning in 1975, credit law has grown more quickly than inflation. You may have a lot to learn.

If you understand your rights, you may have the unique pleasure of being in the driver's seat when you are applying for credit. At the least you can limit your discussions to the point—whether or not your income and credit rating will support your credit request.

The original purpose of the Equal Credit Opportunity Act of 1975 was to eliminate discrimination based on sex or marital status. A year later the bill was amended to cover all the other elements in the rule below.

RULE: CREDITORS MAY NOT DISCRIMINATE.

Now anyone who can afford to repay the loan must be considered equally with all others. Creditors may not discriminate during any part of a credit transaction on the basis of sex, marital status, age, race, color, religion, or national origin.

A creditor can no longer use any of the outlawed considerations as part of a credit scoring system. Each creditor is likely to have his own scoring system. These systems are used to rate the credit-worthiness of an applicant. In the past, credit scoring assigned point values to considerations of income, neighborhood, marital status, credit rating, age, race, number of children, and sometimes even how well you were dressed. Now creditors have changed their credit scoring system to conform with the law. The creditor may still inquire about your marital status and age, since these may alter the legal title of the credit agreement or your ability to repay, but sex, marital status, age, etc., can no longer be figured into your credit-worthiness.

RULE: SENIOR CITIZENS MAY BE ASKED TO MODIFY LOAN REQUESTS.

The Congress was especially concerned that senior citizens were being denied credit. For example, many older people were refused credit because of age, regardless of their credit history or the amount of their personal assets. Creditors assumed anyone approaching 65 would be retiring and couldn't repay the loan. Now this has changed.

A creditor may still ask about your age, but the way he uses your age as part of his credit decision is significantly changed. Formerly, a 70-year-old man might be denied a loan simply because he was 70. Now the creditor must use actuarial tables to decide if the man, by the law of averages, is likely to live long enough to repay the loan. Let's say the man asks for a four-year auto loan. The creditor refuses a four-year loan since the man has a life expectancy of 72¼. The creditor must show the man these tables as part of his reason for the rejection. The 70-year-old could then say, "All right, I'll take a two-year loan instead." The creditor would have to grant the two-year loan if the man was otherwise credit-worthy.

There is an exception to this age discrimination proviso. All states have laws which protect minors from a natural inclination to acquire debt. This law will *not* be changed by the Equal Credit Opportunity Act. Your 14-year-old will not be able to take out a loan for that moped he's been coveting all summer—unless you co-sign it.

RULE: EVERY CREDITOR HAS TO BE FAIR.

A creditor is any person who *regularly* extends, renews, or continues credit. A creditor is any individual, bank, department store, corporation, charge card company, government, partnership, agency, trust, etc., who maintains a credit system. Practically all creditors in the United States are regulated by the provisions of the Equal Credit Opportunity Act. Don't let anybody tell you that he doesn't have to follow the rules.

RULE: CREDITORS CAN'T DEMEAN YOU.

This is a small rule, but an important one. A creditor may not make discouraging statements to a credit applicant based on the applicant's sex, marital status, age, race, color, religion, or national origin. If you are discouraged from making the application for a loan, you have no proof against the creditor for denying it. Statements like "We never give women mortgages," or "Patagonians make bad risks," would discourage any reasonable person. The Equal Credit Opportunity Act outlaws any statement which would discourage a reasonable person.

If a creditor discourages you, take out a notebook immediately and write down what he said. Read it back, and ask him to sign it. Unless he's stupid, he won't sign it, because his statement gives you grounds for a lawsuit. However, from that point on, you'll be taken very seriously.

RULE: CREDITORS CAN'T ASK ABOUT YOUR SEX LIFE.

Creditors are no longer able to deny your loan on the possibility of your having children. They may not inquire about your childbearing capability and intentions, nor may they ask about your birth-control practices. Some of you may think this is a strange rule, unless you've experienced this kind of questioning.

I've been on the receiving end of the practice this rule is designed to prevent. In 1969 I applied for a loan. When the bank loan officer asked if I had a boy friend, I was embarrassed. I didn't know if it was a friendly inquiry, sexual innuendo, or a comment on my social adjustment. It never occurred to me it was a credit question.

Since banks may no longer discount a woman's income, a couple seeking credit must take greater personal responsibility for how much debt they acquire. If they include both salaries, the couple might be in for a surprise. After all, they could be planning a child, but what if it's triplets?

Your banker can be very helpful to you. He or she can inform you as to what size mortgage or loan is realistic within the plans you have set for yourselves. For example, one young couple were making nearly $40,000 between them when they bought their house five years ago. Although the mortgage formulas said they could afford an $80,000 house, they bought one for $40,000 instead. The $40,000 house was entirely realistic for his salary alone, as she had decided to quit her job to become a full-time mother.

This aspect of the Equal Credit Opportunity Act frees both us and the poor loan officer from speaking about our sexual habits. However, it puts the responsibility on us to examine our own capacity to repay the loan if a child were born.

> RULE: THEY CAN'T USE YOUR HUSBAND'S
> CREDIT RATING IF YOU WANT
> THE LOAN.

If you are applying for a loan in your own name, the creditor cannot go ahead and add your husband's information. This rule keeps a woman financially independent. She no longer has to rely on her husband's judgment or credit rating when she wants to borrow money. She can now have credit to the extent that her own income provides for repayment.

There are three exceptions to this rule: (1) When the husband is liable to pay the account or may use it, his credit is also investigated. (2) In community-property states the husband's credit would be investigated, since he owns half of everything the wife has title to. (3) If a woman uses alimony as part of her income for the credit application, the ex-husband may be investigated too.

> RULE: CREDITORS MUST CONSIDER ANY
> TYPE OF INCOME YOU RECEIVE.

Up until now banks and other creditors have been very particular about whose or what type of income they would consider when you applied for credit.

Creditors often dismissed their least favorite type of income—the wife's salary. The creditor would explain that she might get pregnant or lazy and quit work. If that same couple applying for a loan today ask the creditor to consider her income, he is required to do so.

Under the old credit procedures, alimony and child support were often dismissed as unreliable. After all, the ex-husband wasn't signing the loan. He might run away, lose his job, or stop paying. Then the bank would have no way to collect.

The Equal Credit Opportunity Act modified this rule so that now a divorcee may ask the bank to use her alimony and child support as a source of income. Under these circumstances, the bank has the right to investigate the credit rating of the ex-husband.

Any income, even part-time work or public assistance payments, must be considered, but the loan applicant must request it.

RULE: CREDITORS MUST OPEN SEPARATE
ACCOUNTS FOR BOTH SPOUSES.

If you and your spouse have had joint charge accounts, you may now request that a creditor report credit information in both your names. This provision allows a woman to start her own credit history with the credit-reporting services.

Many widows or divorcees discovered that they had no credit in their own names. As soon as their marital status changed, the creditors felt obligated to terminate their credit accounts. Creditors had created a catch-22. Credit was only carried in the husband's name, regardless of the wife's credit-worthiness. When the husband was no longer around, all accounts had to be closed because the wife had no credit history. The Equal Credit Opportunity Act short-circuits this dastardly practice by keeping the wife's credit history open.

Now any woman may maintain her own credit throughout her life. If she marries, she has the choice of keeping her maiden name on her own charge account or adding her husband's last name to her own. If she divorces, her credit is not modified, unless it was based on her spouse's income.

RULE: CREDITORS MUST CONSIDER YOUR REASONS
WHY A JOINT ACCOUNT SHOULD NOT
REPRESENT YOUR PERSONAL HISTORY.

This rule will probably be most useful to those in the throes of divorce. Frequently one spouse will be more conservative about money than the other. The reliable one can now request that a creditor disregard the joint account, since the spouse is a financial lunatic. Whether or not the creditor listens depends largely on how you present your arguments. The more you can back them up with proof, the more likely you'll be taken seriously.

RULE: CREDITORS MAY NOT REQUIRE
A CO-SIGNER FOR YOUR LOAN.

One of the terrific dodges for creditors has been to require that a totally acceptable individual co-sign along with the not quite so acceptable loan applicant. Many women were denied loans unless their father,
brother, or boy friend would co-sign. Not only was this embarrassing; it
also added nothing to a woman's credit history. Co-signed loans are
never used as proof of credit-worthiness. There's always a suspicion
that the co-signer is actually the one paying the installments.

Co-signers can still be required when an applicant's credit does not
justify the loan. If the creditor asks you to obtain a co-signer, request
an explanation. You may see that he is totally correct due to your slow
payments in the past, or a loan that's too big for your income. He may
also request a co-signer simply because you are new at your job or you
have never borrowed money before. That's all right too. But don't expect this particular loan to build up your credit history.

RULE: CREDITORS MUST GIVE YOU A REASON
IF THEY DENY YOUR LOAN APPLICATION.

If you apply for credit, and your application is denied, the creditor
has to come up with a reason based on only your credit history or your
ability to repay. Many creditors now send out explanations of credit denial as a matter of course. If you haven't received an explanation within
thirty days of your application, either call or write the creditor. Ask
him why your loan has not received approval. You have a right to an
explanation in writing *unless* the creditor receives less than 150 credit
applications in a calendar year. Then the explanation can be verbal.

This practice prevents a creditor from denying a loan for arbitrary or
illegal reasons. He can no longer hide discrimination behind a wall of
silence.

One of the reasons for credit denial is "no credit." This means that
you have no credit history, either good or bad. A creditor can reject
you on the basis of no information. You can remedy this by taking out
a bank loan for a small amount and paying it back quickly. Many people will get such a loan, put the proceeds in a savings account, and pay
the loan out of the savings. It will cost $20 or $30 in interest charges,
but establishing a credit record may be worth it.

There is a beneficial side to this rule about credit denial. If your
credit history is unreliable, you'll be able to see where you went wrong.

You won't be able to change the past, but you can learn to be more mature about your financial affairs in the future.

The following rules need no explanation:

> RULE: CREDITORS MUST KEEP RECORDS OF
>   CREDIT APPLICATIONS FOR FIFTEEN MONTHS
>   AFTER YOU HAVE BEEN NOTIFIED
>   OF THE RESULT.

> RULE: CREDIT APPLICATION FORMS MUST
>   INCLUDE A NOTICE OF YOUR RIGHTS
>   UNDER THE EQUAL CREDIT OPPORTUNITY ACT.

> RULE: STATE LAWS WHICH FORBID SEPARATE
>   CONSUMER CREDIT FOR A HUSBAND AND
>   WIFE ARE ABOLISHED. FEDERAL LAW
>   REQUIRES THAT EACH MARRIAGE PARTNER
>   BE SOLELY RESPONSIBLE FOR HIS OR
>   HER DEBTS.

Creditors who fail to live up to the provisions of the Equal Credit Opportunity Act may be sued by the individual applicant or the applicants may get together to form something called a class-action suit. In a class-action suit, individuals with similar complaints sue as a unit. The damages a creditor will have to pay to the individual are the actual damages incurred, plus punitive damages up to $10,000, plus attorney's fees. For a class-action suit the damages are limited to the lesser of $500,000 or 1 per cent of the creditor's net worth. If you have been injured by a creditor, and you have a good case, your lawyer can ask the United States District Court for an order that the creditor mend his ways.

You have an alternative. You may complain to the federal agency which controls that creditor. For example, if a state-chartered bank arbitrarily denies you credit, you may complain to the Federal Reserve Board. If an airline denies you a credit card, the Civil Aeronautics Board will handle your complaint. To find out which federal agency regulates your creditor, write to the Office of Saver and Consumer Affairs, Federal Reserve Board, Washington, D.C. 20551. These federal agencies won't be able to fine the creditor on your behalf, but they may be able to discipline him. However, they are not required to act on your complaint. In fact, since the beginning of this program, less than one complaint out of a hundred has been pursued by the FTC. If you're really angry and want redress, a private suit is the best way to do it. But you may find the damages you collect are not worth the aggravation. Even though the top limit for punitive damages is $10,000, the court may award you only a few hundred. Talk to your lawyer.

Another part of the Consumer Credit Protection Act of 1968 was the so-called Truth in Lending section. Truth in lending requires that creditors disclose certain elements of the credit contract before the consumer signs it. The Board of Governors of the Federal Reserve Bank were given the responsibility to make additional rules to supplement the act. Their additional regulations are called Regulation Z.

RULE: THE CREDIT MUST BE EXTENDED
FOR PERSONAL USE.

The act specifically says that the transaction must be "for personal, family, household, or agricultural purpose." Commercial or business credit is not governed by the truth in lending provisions. All farm credit of any type seems to be covered, as would almost any item which is used around the house, the family's cars, the house itself, and any repairs or additions to it.

RULE: THE LOAN MUST BE UNDER $25,000,
EXCEPT FOR MORTGAGES.

The Truth in Lending Act specifically exempts home mortgages from the $25,000 limit. Today almost every home, when it is first purchased, will have a mortgage larger than $25,000. Regardless of the person's sophistication, the mortgage can be very substantial. However, if somebody is borrowing $25,000 for his own personal use, the act assumes he's quite a different breed of cat. Someone who can figure out what to do with $25,000 for personal purposes is assumed to be more sophisticated. There's also a tacit assumption that the loan may be for business purposes. Business loans are not covered by the act. Nor does the act cover loans to corporations or partnerships. The act uses the words "natural person" to describe the type of borrower protected.

RULE: ALL CREDITORS ARE COVERED
BY TRUTH IN LENDING.

The basic definition of a creditor for truth in lending is a person who regularly extends or arranges for extensions of credit. It must be in the ordinary course of his business. The term "regularly" is somewhat up for grabs at this point, since no one is really sure just what percentage of business "regularly" applies to, or how often a person must extend credit in order to be covered. Personal business transactions are not necessarily exempt. If a fellow has a sideline of buying and selling land, he may have to conform to truth in lending rules, if he extends credit on at least some of his transactions. One court decision indicates he must disclose the credit terms of the sale.

RULE: A FINANCE CHARGE FORCES DISCLOSURE.

Truth in lending requires that the finance charge be disclosed. The problem is defining the finance charge. In most cases the charge is fairly clear. The creditor is charging some type of interest, but it is less clear when an inflated cash price is used without adding any interest. The advertisement "No Charge for Credit" is probably a credit sale. The merchant has raised the cash price to pay himself interest. The four-installment rule discussed above handles this difficulty. When more than four installments are needed to pay off the agreement, it is a credit sale, whether it says so or not. The exception to this is the debtor who simply decides by himself to pay off the charge in five installments without permission from the creditor.

RULE: DISCLOSURE IS REQUIRED BEFORE THE DEAL IS MADE.

Under the Truth in Lending Act, the creditor must disclose the credit terms prior to the time the debtor becomes bound. When these terms must be disclosed depends on the nature of the credit and the type of contract being signed. If the contract involves a mortgage, the finance charges must be disclosed very early. In fact, finance charges are the primary thing that the consumer shops for when looking for a mortgage. More ordinary consumer credit must be disclosed at the time the papers are signed. Sometimes only a limited amount of disclosure will be possible. For example, credit card agreements must disclose the basic percentage rates, but no actual dollars of finance charge could be disclosed, because the amounts which will be charged on the credit card are not yet available. With ordinary loans and installment purchases, it is within the ability of the creditor to describe the finance charge in dollars as well as in percentages at the time the papers are signed.

Truth in lending sets out two basic types of credit agreements. One is called the open-end agreement. These agreements are charge accounts which have a finance charge levied on them, like Master Charge, Sears, BankAmericard, etc. The other type is officially called "other than open-end" credit, but the legal profession has shortened this to "closed-end" credit. Closed-end credit is a loan or a credit agreement for the purchase of one or two items, like a car, or washer and dryer, which are paid off in monthly installments. First we will discuss disclosure requirements on open-end credit.

RULE: OPEN-END CREDIT MUST HAVE CLEAR STATEMENTS.

Because of the number of transactions which may happen in the future, the creditor is not able to tell the debtor what the actual finance charges are in dollars. However, under truth in lending requirements, he must disclose the basic percentage of the finance charge and other requirements the creditor may have, such as carrying credit insurance. When the debtor actually receives her bill, the dollars of finance charge must be disclosed. The consumer must be billed every time there is a closing balance of more than a dollar, or any time a finance charge is added. Although the bill need not be sent at any particular time, it must be mailed at least fourteen days prior to the time the finance charge is levied. If the creditor fails to do this, he cannot collect the finance charge.

When you sign the credit agreement for a charge account, the creditor must tell you when a finance charge will be imposed, and what free period of time you have before the finance charge becomes payable. You must be informed of what balance the finance charge will be figured on. For example, the finance charge could be figured on the opening balance, the closing balance, or the opening balance with adjustments. The creditor must also tell you the basic amount of the finance charge. For example, 1½ per cent per month and an annual percentage rate of 18 per cent. The monthly finance charge and annual percentage rate are required in every credit contract.

RULE: THE BILL TELLS ALL.

In the open-end credit card transaction, the billing statement takes up the slack of disclosure which the credit agreement simply could not fulfill. Now that the amount of credit is known, the creditor can get specific about the dollars of interest charged. He must state:

1. The amount of the finance charge and any minimum amounts charged for carrying the account.
2. The periodic rate, such as 1½ per cent per month, and the annual percentage rate, such as 18 per cent a year.

3. The outstanding balance at the start of the billing period. The creditor must use the words "previous balance."

4. Amounts subtracted during the billing period. These must be broken into payments and credits. Exactly those words must be used.

5. The unpaid balance on which the interest was figured and some type of statement of how this balance was determined.

6. The closing date of the bill and the outstanding balance due.

7. How long you have to pay the bill before the finance charge comes due.

8. All amounts charged and the date they were charged. Some description of the charge is also required, such as children's shoes or washer.

RULE: CLOSED-END REQUIRES
IMMEDIATE DISCLOSURE.

Closed-end credit is the type of credit agreement you would make when buying a car or a single item on time. A home mortgage is also closed-end. (Mortgages are covered in the chapter on mortgages.) Finance charges are part of your negotiations in any credit agreement. Smart shoppers consider credit terms right along with other terms of the sale. Even though the seller is not required to disclose the amount of finance charge until the papers are signed, you can still walk out if you find the credit agreement unsatisfactory.

The finance charge itself is not as easy to determine as one might think, since it may include more than merely the interest charged. For example, it's not uncommon for merchants to demand a carrying charge, such as $5.00 a month for as long as the account is active. This amount must be included as part of the finance charge. There are other charges which need not be included if they are specifically itemized, such as license fees, registration fees, etc. If the creditor requires that you carry life insurance to cover your debt, the cost of insurance must also be included in the finance charge.

The truth in lending provisions also require disclosure of buried finance charges. In order to circumvent these requirements, some retailers started to inflate the cash price of their service or goods without telling the consumer. This inflated cash price is called a buried finance charge. Health club credit practices have been the subject of suits in this area.

Some health clubs used to inflate their prices to include a finance charge, but the health club didn't tell the consumer that the fee included finance charges. In other words, the health club was not disclosing the finance charge.

Health clubs commonly sell their installment contracts to finance companies. By making this sale, the health club gets some money sooner. For example, the health club might collect only $375 for the sale to the finance company of a $500 membership contract. It's up to the finance company to collect the $500. The finance company makes a $125 profit. Finance companies recognized the profitability of health clubs and began to buy them to generate these big profits. Some health clubs started their own finance companies. Meanwhile, the poor consumer was paying outrageous interest. On top of this, health clubs started to refuse cash payments for memberships, since the real profit was in the installment contract. The health club was no longer in the exercise business; it was in the finance business.

The courts stopped this practice with a number of decisions holding that health clubs must disclose finance charges. The courts also defined the finance charge for these contracts. The finance charge is the face price ($500) less the price obtained when the installment contract is sold ($375). The $375 resale price is called the discount price or rate. The installment sale is said to be a "discounted" contract. When a health club contract is discounted, the health club must disclose that fact, just as though it were selling an appliance on time.

RULE: THE ANNUAL PERCENTAGE RATE IS NOT OBVIOUS.

Our high school mathematics is of little help in determining the annual percentage rate of interest charged, because so many different factors may be included. The Federal Reserve Board has set up tables to standardize the annual percentage rate. After the finance charge is figured out, it is broken down into finance charge per $100 of amount financed. Using the number of payments and the finance charge per $100, the interest rate can then be determined.

There are many other items to be disclosed under truth in lending closed-end consumer credit transactions. A partial list of these details follows:

1. The total dollars of finance charge.
2. The date on which the finance charge will be applied.
3. The number, amount, and due date of payments.
4. The total dollars of payment.
5. The penalty which will be charged if there is a penalty for paying off early.
6. The cash price.
7. A description of the security interest of the creditor.

Whether the closed-end agreement has the form of a credit sale or a loan, most of these elements will be required for each type of agreement.

You can enforce these truth in lending requirements yourself. There are three basic types of actions: the individual action, the criminal action, and the administrative action.

The administrative action is the type of suit the government would bring against someone who has violated truth in lending. This kind of action is not very effective, since the budgets to pursue these prosecutions are very small and the number of creditors is very large, probably in excess of a million. The FTC handles creditors which are not banks; various other governmental bodies supervise banks.

Criminal action is also available through the Department of Justice against a creditor who "willfully and knowingly" cheats the consumer by giving false information. There have been less than a dozen convictions under this provision.

The most effective type of remedy for truth in lending is the individual lawsuit. A consumer must establish that the transaction was subject to truth in lending and that the creditor failed to follow the truth in lending regulations. The consumer may sue for actual damages and for twice the amount of the finance charge. The maximum recovery is $1,000. The consumer may also recover reasonable attorney's fees. If both a husband and wife sign the agreement, a few courts allow each of them to recover full damages.

For the most part, it's a bad idea for a debtor to subtract her damages from the debt without court approval. The consumer must first get a court judgment, and then the court judgment and costs can be subtracted from the debt owed.

RULE: YOU CAN CALL OFF A CREDIT CONTRACT.

You have three days from the time the creditor discloses the terms of the credit to call off (rescind) the contract. Although there is still a great deal of confusion in this area, truth in lending seems to allow contract rescission if the consumer can put the creditor back into his position before the contract was signed. The consumer would have to return the money or the goods to make this stick. This area of the law is so new that it will take time to establish clear rescission guidelines.

RULE: YOU HAVE ONE YEAR TO ACT.

According to truth in lending, the statute of limitations for bringing suit on a violation runs out at one year from the date of the violation.

This time period seems to be fairly clear except when one considers that one of the violations of truth in lending is not disclosing information. Therefore, it's up in the air whether the violation occurs when the lender doesn't disclose or when the consumer discovers the lack of disclosure. So far, the courts have held that the one year starts at the date the credit was actually extended. The one-year statute of limitations may apply to both open-end or closed-end transactions.

Errors the creditor makes in disclosing will be punished only if he does not exercise reasonable care to avoid such errors. So the court recognizes that a mistake is merely a mistake, but the creditor must take steps to prevent them. He is allowed to correct his error within fifteen days of the time he discovers it or before the consumer brings an action. His correction wipes out his error and ends any possibility of a suit. However, if the consumer had sued prior to the creditor's finding the error, his correction will not affect the lawsuit.

RULE: STATES HAVE CONSUMER CREDIT LAWS TOO.

Part of the Federal Reserve Board's Regulation Z was a proviso about state credit laws. State statutes now govern only if they benefit the consumer more than the federal regulation. The state must also provide some type of enforcement. If the state statute also requires disclosure of more items than the federal law does, creditors must comply. However, the finance charge and other basic elements must comply with the federal regulation.

You may find that your own state law is your most effective protection. Each credit agreement in Connecticut, Maine, Massachusetts, Oklahoma, and Wyoming will contain some state regulations. The reason for this is that states can apply for an exemption to Regulation Z. Partial exemptions from truth in lending have been granted to all of the states above. Other states have applied.

In the purest sense, the word "usury" means interest, the extra money that is paid for the privilege of borrowing money. Usury in the modern world has come to mean excessive interest. Usury statutes generally put a top limit on the interest which can be charged for different kinds of loans. For example, mortgages may be limited to 8½ per cent per year. Consumer loans are usually restricted to 18 per cent. Usury laws are almost always state statutes.

Differences between interest rates on different types of loans have to do with the amounts of risk involved. The risk of loss on a mortgage is normally very small, since the loan is secured by the house itself. The consumer loan may not have any security at all. Additionally, the large demand for small loans allows high interest rates. The market can stand the 18 per cent interest. You probably know that consumer loans are normally paid off in installments every month; however, business loans are usually paid in one lump payment.

Usury requires that there be a loan, that there is more than the legal rate of interest, and that the creditor has wrongful intent. This last requirement is most meaningful when an honest man makes a mistake and then rectifies the situation.

The states have a variety of penalties when a usurious transaction has taken place. The creditor may be required to forfeit the interest times a penalty figure (dollars of interest multiplied by 1½). Some states even go so far as to forfeit the whole loan, principal and interest included. If a national bank violates a state usury law, the national bank must forfeit the entire interest and may be liable for a penalty of twice the interest actually received. Usury is more or less a dead issue today. The banks generally have enough power in the state legislatures to raise the interest rate if a usury law is costing them profits.

Sometimes a creditor will give a debtor the option to carry insurance on the debt outstanding. The purpose of the insurance is to pay for the debt if something should happen to the debtor. This insurance can be very beneficial to the debtor's family, since the debt would be paid off in the event of death or mishap. The insurance may be either life insurance or health and accident. Some creditors will also include liability insurance, usually in the case of a mortgage.

RULE: DEBT INSURANCE MUST BE DISCLOSED.

If the creditor requires the insurance, the cost of the insurance must be included in your finance charge. Therefore, the insurance cost would come out of the creditor's pocket.

Most credit insurance covers debts from credit cards. State usury laws generally restrict the credit charge on the first $500 to 18 per cent per year. The creditor cannot charge more than this. Therefore, if the creditor requires that you carry credit insurance, it comes out of the 18 per cent that he would charge you anyway for the use of the credit card.

If the creditor doesn't want to pick up the cost of the credit insurance, he must inform the consumer that the credit insurance is optional. He must send you a statement that fulfills the following requirements: (1) he must state that he does not require the insurance, (2) this statement must be made clearly and conspicuously in writing, and (3) the consumer must sign a separate statement that she desires insurance.

The debtor also must have the option to carry her own credit insurance, although this is rarely done. Liability credit insurance has its own rules, but this is so rare it won't be discussed.

State laws also provide that the creditor may not charge you more for the insurance than he himself pays. Credit insurance is always purchased from the creditor and is part of a group policy for all of his debtors. The fact that it is always a group policy leads to a substantial amount of bad business practice. We will discuss this momentarily.

RULE: CREDIT INSURANCE
COST IS MISLEADING.

Credit insurance is a very big business. Creditors may have thousands or even millions of debtors. Credit insurance itself is an industry exceeding a billion dollars a year. In 1969 it was estimated that Americans were overcharged on their credit insurance by $200,000,000. Ten years later this figure may be twice as high. We are obviously talking about a lot of money.

This area is misused, but in such a complex way that it eludes most consumers. This overcharge scam occurs because the creditors may get a rebate from the insurance company, or they may even own the insurance company which they encourage their debtors to use. Over 90 per cent of debtors consent to credit insurance.

Although credit insurance rebates are outlawed by state law, the same result can be had in at least two different ways. In one case, the creditor may own part of the insurance company with which his debtors are insured. He receives part of your premium back as a corporate dividend. He may also get something called a retrospective rate credit. The amount of this refund depends on the rates charged and the experiences the insurance company has with that particular creditor's group of debtors. In either case, it is not in the best interest of the creditor to keep the debtor's insurance rates down, since this would lower his dividend or retrospective rate credit. The creditor is most likely to pick an expensive insurance company, in the hope of finding a greater profit.

There is another way to skim profit from credit insurance. This method is called reinsurance or fronting. This whole hustle begins with the creditor setting up his own insurance company in a state with favorable laws—Arizona, for example. He then goes to an established insurance company and makes a deal with the insurance company to insure his debtors in exchange for reinsuring with the creditor's own company. The established insurer may or may not know that that little insurance company out in Arizona is actually the property of the creditor himself.

The established insurance company will pay the bulk of the premiums to the creditor's own insurance company. The insurance goes into effect and the debtor receives an insurance statement under the name of the established company. To the debtor the insurance looks fine. The established company's statement gives the debtor the choice of carrying his own credit insurance or paying for this company's credit insurance through his charge card, etc. The choice is not of much practical use, since the debtor is hardly likely to find insurance for such a small outstanding amount. On top of that, the replacement insurance the debtor might find would not be group insurance and might be more expensive. So the debtor signs up for the insurance.

Thus the creditor ends up with most of your insurance money. He is not likely to encourage collection on insurance that will come out of his own pocket. The debtor may think that his inability to collect on a claim is the fault of the established insurance company.

The law is not totally helpless in this area. The state insurance boards may limit the creditor's cut to 30 or 40 per cent of the premium charged. If you have millions of debtors, like some of the big charge card companies, this 30 or 40 per cent could be quite a large amount of money, and most of it would be profit. The law sometimes requires that the insurance rates be cut if the loss incurred is less the 50 per cent of the total premiums charged. However, this doesn't always work. Because the insurance companies compete with each other to get the creditor's business, the costs are likely to remain high.

Every area has a little series of rules that are important but belong in no logical order. Credit is no exception. What follows is a potpourri of the rest of credit law for the consumer.

RULE: CREDIT ADVERTISERS MUST TELL ALL,
        OR NOTHING.

Credit advertising has a very peculiar requirement. The advertiser must tell everything about a credit deal that he offers or must say nothing at all. This advertising standard is called the all-or-nothing rule. The ad must be something of this nature: "We have low, low rates. Come see us," or it must be very, very specific. The minute one specific detail is included in the ad, all other details of the credit must also be included. For example, if an appliance store advertises a washer and dryer for only $25 a month, the ad must also include the number of months of payment, the cash price for the washer and dryer, the amount of down payment required, and the annual percentage rate of interest which will be charged. The same holds true for ads of any type which discuss the extension of credit. All of the terms must be given so that the consumer will not be misled by the ad. As in the example above, if the washer and dryer ad didn't include the information that the payments ran for 48 months (48 months at $25 is $1,700), the purchase price might seem low. If the full price of $1,700 were given, the consumer would be a lot less interested. This rule bridges the gap between truth in advertising laws and fair credit practice regulations.

RULE: ADVERTISED CREDIT MUST BE AVAILABLE.

One sneaky practice outlawed by truth in lending is so-called bait advertising. The advertiser quotes credit terms which he rarely grants. For example, if he said, "No down payment," but would only grant this to persons making more than $100,000 a year, or the third customer who comes in on Tuesday, the ad would be considered to be bait advertising. If a creditor is to advertise a particular credit arrangement, he must usually and customarily grant credit on the terms he advertises. It does not mean he must grant those terms to everyone, but he must grant the terms to a significant portion of his customers. Bait advertising is a form of the bait-and-switch sale, discussed in the chapter on contracts.

RULE: YOU CAN CANCEL A CONTRACT WITH A DOOR-TO-DOOR SALESMAN.

The door-to-door salesman tends to travel around quite a bit. The consumer may have a hard time finding him if something goes wrong with the goods delivered. Additionally, the salesman is likely to sell his credit contract to another party who also has no idea of the salesman's whereabouts. When discussing these door-to-door salesmen, the Avon and Fuller Brush ladies are really not an issue. Their companies are well established and rarely use credit. The state statutes governing door-to-door salesmen are far more concerned with itinerant aluminum siding, roofing, blacktop, and furnace salespeople. These areas have been abused.

Door-to-door sales are split into two basic categories, emergency sales and other sales. Emergency sales are normally outside the provisions we discuss here. The emergency sale is an exception since the buyer may request the seller to provide goods or services quickly because of an emergency, such as the roof having blown off the house.

Non-emergency situations generally allow for a cooling-off period prior to the time the workmen start to perform on the contract. These cooling-off periods are available in forty states. The contract may be canceled if the sale was solicited in the consumer's home. The statutes may provide for a cancellation fee or penalty for cancellation, usually applying to credit sales. The consumer normally has 72 hours to change his mind. The 72 hours begin when the consumer is given notice that she has the right to cancel the contract. The consumer can be asked why she changed her mind, but she need not state any reason.

The Federal Trade Commission also has a nationwide regulation about door-to-door salesmen. This regulation applies to both cash and credit transactions. Under the FTC regulation any door-to-door sales contract can be canceled within three days. It is a deceptive trade practice for the seller not to disclose the three-day cancellation period. The notification must be in Spanish if the deal is negotiated in Spanish. The FTC does not allow any cancellation fee. If the FTC rule and the state statute differ, the FTC provides that it will take the back seat if the state statute is more beneficial to the consumer.

RULE: REFERRAL SALES ARE ILLEGAL.

A referral sale is a type of arrangement a merchant makes in which he promises a discount *after* the sale if the buyer brings in customers. For example, the merchant could say, "I will sell you this couch worth $600 for $1,200 on credit, and for each customer you bring in who buys a $1,200 couch, I will take $50 off the price. If you bring in 24 buyers, you'll get the couch for nothing." This seems like a terrific deal, but the merchant is probably making the same deal with everybody. The buyer will have a hard time finding anyone else willing to pay $1,200 for the medium-priced couch. For example, if you submit 25 names in one of these schemes and each one of the 25 names submits 25 names who each submit 25 names, etc. after the seventh round of referrals, the pyramid would consist of 6.1 *trillion* persons. This is obviously a deal which is going to stick somebody with a very high price for the goods. Referral sales are usually used as a way to sweeten an unfairly high price.

If the credit contract requires an event to occur after the time the consumer buys or leases, the deal is illegal. This regulation does not affect discounts which the consumer gets at the time of sale in exchange for a list of possible clients. For example, a merchant could quite legally give a discount in exchange for a list of names not already on his records. The discount would have to occur at the time of sale, and not later.

The merchant's penalty for a referral contract is that the consumer gets to keep the goods without paying for them. The credit purchase is simply canceled. If you are offered the illegal type of referral credit

sales contract, take it and then report it. You may help to put fraudulent merchants out of business.

RULE: BALLOON PAYMENTS MUST BE DISCLOSED.

A balloon payment is used in the extension of business credit. The
interest may be paid monthly or semiannually, with big chunks (balloon) of the principal due periodically, such as once a year or at the
end of the loan. Businessmen are used to balloon payments and there is
nothing wrong with them.

Consumers are not as used to balloon payments as businessmen are.
Truth in lending protects consumers by requiring disclosure of the
balloon payment. As far as truth in lending is concerned, a balloon
payment is any installment which is more than twice a normal installment. In consumer contracts, the balloon payment is almost always at
the end of the installment contract. For example, the contract may
require payments of $50 a month for eleven months and $200 for the
twelfth and last month of the agreement. Balloon payments may be
used, but the consumer can force the creditor to refinance the amount
of the balloon payment—at the time it is due. There is no penalty for
this, except for extra interest. The operative phrase above is "at the
time it is due." If you are unable to meet the balloon payment, you
are required to talk to the creditor promptly.

RULE: DON'T AGREE TO A FLOATING LIEN.

A floating lien is a general lien against all of your personal property.
"Floating" means that the lien can attach to any property you own, or
the amount of the lien can increase or decrease, depending on how
much you owe. A floating lien is essentially a security agreement which
floats around until you miss a payment and the creditor decides to exercise it. You may have used the money to buy a washer, only to discover
that it is within the creditor's rights to repossess your car.

This floating lien need not be disclosed in any particular way, although you will find a description of it in the fine print. The law limits
the goods the creditor can take. Goods acquired more than ten days
after the loan are not subject to a floating security agreement *unless it is
specifically stated in the contract*. You can pretty well bet that the contract will include all your property, whenever acquired, in the floating
lien clause.

As a consumer you should examine the contract to see if there is anything called a continuing general lien or a floating lien. Never borrow
money from someone who insists on such a provision. It is quite all

right to borrow under a "purchase money security interest." This type of security restricts the creditor to the item or items actually purchased with the money borrowed.

RULE: NEVER SIGN A WAGE ASSIGNMENT.

Always check your consumer contract to see if it contains a wage assignment. Many consumer contracts have a clause allowing a creditor to present a bill to your employer and to have your wages routed to him to pay your debt. The wage assignment can be done without a court order. The creditor merely presents a copy of the contract. If the employer refuses to pay, the creditor can get a court order forcing payment. The debtor has no notice that this transaction is going on. The wage assignment can be used to scoop up all earnings, past, present, and future. The courts and the law do not control the wage assignments, although some states prohibit wage assignments altogether. The area of wage assignment and garnishment is fully covered in the chapter on debts and bankruptcy.

There are other elements which deal with consumer credit transactions. One of them is the unconscionability (unfairness) of high prices as part of a consumer contract. One case found an unconscionable price when a $300 freezer went for the total price of $1,092.96. This transaction was considered fraudulent. There is a lot of difficulty in this area, since judges are unwilling to decide what is crooked and what is merely high interest.

Another area is the concept of cash discounts. When the big bank credit cards were getting started, some credit card companies asked subscribing merchants to promise that the merchants would not give discounts for cash. You see, credit card companies charge 3 to 5 per cent of the face value of the charge amount as a service charge to the merchant. So the merchant could give a small discount for cash, and still have the same amount of profit. The Fair Credit Billing Act outlaws this particular credit card company-merchant agreement. The merchant need not offer a cash discount, but the credit card company cannot forbid cash discounts.

Warranties also strongly affect consumer credit transactions. This area of credit was covered in the chapter on sales and contracts, where it more properly belongs. Suffice it to say here that the merchant's ability to get out of the warranty must be in bold print on the consumer contract. Certain warranties cannot be disclaimed under any circumstances.

Chapter 26
DEBTS AND BANKRUPTCY

As soon as the papers are signed, your new washer and dryer become yours to use and enjoy. However, in the world of finance and personal budgets, these items become simply one more debt. This chapter picks up at the point the goods become yours to talk about problems which occur after the papers have been signed.

These problems can be simple, such as disagreeing with the bill which Master Charge has sent you, or they can be serious, where the debtor is unable to keep up with her debt load.

The basis of credit is trust. If a person's credit starts to go awry and the creditors no longer have faith that they will receive their money, they have a wide range of things they can do to recover their money. They can start collection proceedings through a bill collector, they can place a legal claim on the property they loaned the money for, or they can force you, the debtor, into receivership or bankruptcy. Receivership is a state action in which the court preserves a debtor's property so that it can be sold and the proceeds distributed among the people to whom money is owed. Bankruptcy is usually a federal action which corresponds to state receivership.

RULE: HANDLE YOUR CREDIT PROBLEMS PROMPTLY.

Credit problems fall into two basic categories: billing errors and too much credit outstanding. Billing errors are by far the easier to correct. These usually involve credit card or charge account transactions of some sort. Either the amount charged is incorrect or the description of the goods is insufficient to jog the debtor's memory of having charged it. If you've ever tried to carry on correspondence with a computer, you'll understand how important the Fair Credit Billing Act is. This law went into effect in 1975, and it provides a procedure for people to complain regarding their charge accounts and credit cards.

Your monthly statement must have an address where you can send questions or complaints about your bill. These questions can cover: charges you think you never made, amounts charged for goods, a need for explanation or a copy of the charge receipt, complaints about undelivered goods or services which have been charged but not performed upon, returns of items which should have wiped out the charge, and clerical errors.

It's a good idea to send a letter separate from your payment. It costs you an extra stamp, but the company may require it. Whatever you do, don't write on the payment stub. It's a sure way to get no action at all. If you complain, it must be in writing. You have to send it to the address the creditor provides you with. You must also include the following information: your name and account number, your belief that there is a billing error, the amount of the billing error, and the reason you think it's wrong.

The creditor has thirty days to tell you he received your letter. He has ninety days to answer the letter specifically. The creditor's answer must be specific as to whether the account was correct as stated and why, or, if there was an error, he must state the specific amount of the error. If he differs from your correction, he must explain. He must also adjust the finance charge.

He cannot collect on a disputed amount until he replies. If you receive a second notice stating that your bill is overdue, the best thing to do is to send a copy of that second notice along with a copy of your letter. Simply write on the letter that under the Fair Credit Billing Act of 1975 no amount of money can be collected until the dispute is settled. These second and third notices are probably just computer oversights, but they can be maddening and mess up your credit rating.

The creditor can't stop your use of the account. However, if the disputed amount brings the consumer up to the credit limit granted, no more charges may be made until the dispute is resolved. If you don't agree with the creditor's response to your letter, you have ten days from the *postmark* on the letter to tell him in writing that the dispute continues. Be sure to keep copies of all correspondence until the dispute is settled.

The unfortunate part of what is an otherwise fair act is that the penalty paid to you for the business's failing to respond is only a maximum of $50 per occurrence. This penalty may not be great enough to force the creditor to comply with the Fair Credit Billing Act. It may cost him more to reply to you than to pay you the penalty for not replying. If you write and the creditor doesn't respond, he will forfeit up to $50 for each item which was in error. That money is taken off your bill. However, you may have to hire a lawyer to force recognition of the $50 penalty, so once again, the cost is likely to be greater than the reward.

RULE: THEY MUST SEND THE BILL PROMPTLY.

There is no requirement that a creditor must offer you a period during which you can pay off your charge free of interest. However, most creditors do offer what is called a free-ride period. The free-ride period can be from 10 to 30 days, and usually starts on the date the billing cycle ends. For example, if your billing cycle closes on the 20th of the month, and you have 10 days in which to pay, interest-free, the creditor could preclude you from interest-free payment by merely sending the bill out late. Although there is no requirement that a free-ride period be offered, the bill must be sent out at least 14 days before the last day you could take advantage of the free ride. (In our example, by the 16th of the previous month.) If the creditor doesn't do this, he cannot collect his finance charge, even though the consumer does not pay until long after the free-ride period is over. The free-ride period is one thing to shop for when opening a credit account.

RULE: KNOW THEIR BILLING SYSTEM.

The finance charges you pay can vary to an amazing degree, depending on what figure the company uses to compute the interest. There are five basic types of credit billing. The following five paragraphs explain each system, from the most expensive system to the cheapest.

The worst type is the ending balance method, under which the finance charge is computed on the ending balance of last month's bill. This method is the most costly—five times more costly than the cheapest.

The next most expensive is the average daily balance method including current charges. Under this method all previous amounts and amounts charged this month will have a finance charge imposed upon them. This method is three times as costly as the cheapest method.

The previous balance method starts to get reasonable. The charge is levied unless paid in full in a certain amount of time, such as thirty days. This method is twice as expensive as the cheapest method.

The average daily balance excluding current charges is the next method. Interest is charged on amounts that were in the account, but this month's charges are not included until next month. This method is also about twice as expensive.

By far the cheapest is the adjusted balance method. The payments you make this month are deducted from previous charges. If you are going to buy something very expensive, such as a stove or refrigerator, it would be a very good idea to shop among the big retail merchants and credit card companies as to what method they will use. The cost of the refrigerator might be lower at Macy's, but Gimbels might turn out to be cheaper in the long run because of a different billing system.

RULE: BEWARE OF THE RULE OF 78.

The Rule of 78 is the rule by which many banks and loan companies compute how much interest they get to charge if you pay off a loan early. Yes, you read it right, and it's perfectly legal for a creditor to fix a penalty if the loan is paid off early. The Rule of 78 is the most typical of these and is widely used. If you have a familiarity with accounting, you may have struggled through sum-of-the-digits depreciation. The Rule of 78 is a type of sum-of-the-digits computation. (The number 78 comes from the total of the months in a year. $1+2+3 \ldots +12=78$.) In highly simplified form, if a one-year loan were paid off in the second month, the creditor would be entitled to 23/78 of the total interest, 12/78 for the first month plus 11/78 for the second month's use of the principal. In other words, the interest is not evenly divided over the total period of the loan. The greater part of the interest is loaded into the early period of the loan, before the loan payments have decreased the principal. The Rule of 78 favors the creditors substantially. I once paid off a $4,000 loan early, only to discover that the prepayment penalty was almost $300. I don't think I will ever again agree to a loan using the Rule of 78 to compute the penalty for prepayment.

Fortunately, much consumer credit legislation protects consumers from prepayment penalties. If you pay off early, the finance company will have to return to you the interest they haven't earned because of the prepayment. However, if you borrow money from a bank, you may find the Rule of 78 lurking down in the small print. The bank must disclose only what method will be used to compute the penalty or how much money the penalty will be. There is no requirement that any particular type of penalty be used.

Unfortunately, many credit problems are not billing errors or surprises in the contract. Often the debtor simply has too many bills and can't keep up. It is possible that you may be able to personally negotiate new terms with your creditors. Or you may hire an attorney to help do this. There have been some very remarkable negotiations during which a debtor was able to handle her creditors and save her business from going under. However, this instance is far more the exception than the rule. Many debtors buckle under emotionally and physically as well as financially when the debt load gets too high.

Consumers can find help with an organization called Consumer Credit Counseling Service. This not-for-profit organization now has several hundred offices in many cities. Either consult your telephone directory or write: National Foundation for Consumer Credit, Inc., Federal Bar Building West, 1819 H Street, N.W., Washington, D.C. 20006.

CCCS works with the debtor and her creditors, arriving at a budget and payments which all will find acceptable. What CCCS does is put the family on a budget and pay off creditors from the debtor's current income. This process can be very lengthy, lasting two years or more; however, the debtor will probably end up with more knowledge about finances and a far better credit rating that she began with. CCCS also does budget planning to keep consumers out of trouble in the first place.

If you've gotten in over your head, avoiding your difficulties is a serious mistake. Although it will be very difficult, the only way that you will recover is to confront your creditors and try to make arrangements. If you can't do this yourself, you must find someone, either an attorney or Consumer Credit Counseling Service, who will handle it for you. If you don't, you're in for a lot of aggravation, time in court, and possibly either receivership or bankruptcy forced on you by your creditors.

When a debtor doesn't pay her bill, the creditor will start some type of collection procedure. He may write letters or call, using these simple methods to encourage the debtor to pay up. If this doesn't work, the creditor may be able to take the property back. This is called repossession. If repossession fails for one reason or another, the creditor may be forced to take the action to court. These are the basic steps in any credit collection procedure.

RULE: BILL COLLECTORS MUST BEHAVE THEMSELVES.

Bill collectors have been known to pull some dirty tricks during their efforts to collect. These people get paid a percentage of the amount they collect for the creditor. The less they collect, the less money they make. Hostile letters are not considered to be fraudulent or abusive, nor are visits to the house at certain times, nor are threats of a lawsuit. However, courts will allow recovery for defamation of character if the bill collector publishes the debtor's name and debt in a newspaper, calls the debtor's neighbors, makes repeated calls on her employer, or uses other overwhelming tactics. Nor can the creditor invade the debtor's privacy beyond all bounds of decency. The creditor cannot, for example, make late-night phone calls, prowl around the house, or do anything that is considered outrageous conduct. If the debtor can establish that the creditor's conduct caused him serious mental distress, or resulted in a physical injury or illness, most courts will allow a recovery. However, the law in this area remains woefully inadequate.

RULE: THE CREDITOR CAN TAKE IT BACK.

Whether you borrow money to buy a car or ask a retailer to finance your purchase of a refrigerator, the company which made your purchase possible has certain rights to your property. It is required that you and the creditor have an agreement that you give him money for the purchase and that you acquire title to the property. This agreement is called a security interest. Under the security interest agreement the creditor is entitled to regular payments and you are entitled to use the goods.

As a rule, this agreement goes through without a hitch, but occasionally the debtor will not be able to keep up with her payments. When the payments fall behind, the debt is said to be in default. This default can arise either from common error, such as failing to make the payments on time, or from some specialized agreement such as an obligation to insure, to keep the creditor posted of current addresses, and in some cases even to keep union dues paid up when it is the union's credit association which made the loan. Obviously it is a good idea to read the fine print in your agreement to find out if there are any peculiar rules you must adhere to. As you can see, this type of agreement works just like a contract.

Creditors with such agreements can repossess the goods without judicial process as long as there is no breach of the peace. Breach of peace in this particular instance requires that the repossessors break off the repossession if the owner makes a strong protest while they are attempting to take the goods back. By the same token, they are not allowed to break into garages or houses to repossess the goods.

If goods have been repossessed, the owner of the goods will have to pay the entire balance of the loan plus repossession costs, attorney's fees, and any other costs in order to get her property back. If the owner of the property can't pay up, the creditor has the right to keep the goods or sell them. The creditor is not required to give you prior notice of repossession. Generally, the debtor knows very well that repossession is likely to occur.

Consumer goods have special rules. The creditor who has repossessed consumer goods may not keep them for personal use, but the debtor must object within thirty days of the creditor's written notice that the creditor intends to keep whatever was repossessed. If a sale is forced by the debtor, the debtor must have notice of the date and place of the sale and may bid in to buy the goods back. If the price paid at the sale does not cover the debt, the debtor will still have to pay the balance. If the sale price is in excess of the debt, the debtor receives the surplus.

Repossession is sometimes called self-help. The creditor is entitled to try to repossess the goods without a court order. If the debtor thwarts the creditor's attempt at repossession, the creditor will have to go to court to get an order that the goods be surrendered.

RULE: SOME CREDITORS HAVE A
RIGHT TO YOUR PROPERTY
WITHOUT ANY AGREEMENT.

Many states have statutes giving certain classes of business people rights to goods because of some service they have performed. These rights in property are called liens. A lien is not a right to ownership; it's simply a right to have a debt satisfied. Many different classifications of services are entitled to liens. The most common of these are the mechanic's and artisan's liens. If you take your television set to be repaired, the TV repairman is quite within his rights to refuse to hand it over until you have paid your bill. The garage owner who fixes your car can do the same thing, as can a plumber or an electrician who makes repairs to your home. In the case of the plumber or electrician, he can register his claim with the county and collect his money before your house is sold. To be absolutely proper, a mechanic's lien refers to unpaid repairs made to real estate. An artisan's lien means the right which repairmen have in personal property, such as a TV set or a car. Hotelkeepers and landlords also have a lien against a person's personal property if a person is unable to pay her bill. This lien is called an innkeeper's lien. It's established by common law and need not be agreed to beforehand. It is thought to be widely understood that if you don't pay your bill he can keep your property until you do. However, innkeepers do have some responsibility to hold the property in a safe place where it will be free from harm, from water, and from other destructive elements. The person whose goods are impounded by a landlord or innkeeper may find that she has to pay an additional fee for the rental on the place where her goods are stored. After a certain passage of time (sixty to ninety days), the property may be sold to satisfy the debt.

If the creditor is unable to collect his money using one of the methods just discussed, he may be forced to take the issue to court. When he does this, he presents his evidence of the debt. The debtor may or may not be present, as you will see. The court then gives the creditor a judgment lien.

RULE: JUDGMENTS DEFINE THE DEBT.

For a creditor to act to collect the debt owed to him, he usually needs a judgment. The creditor presents the claim and the court finds just how much is owed. The judgment gives the creditor the right to collect.

One type of judgment is called a judgment by confession or cognovit judgment. In this case the creditor's attorney swears that a particular amount is due. He presents the agreement which created the debt and shows what portion remains unpaid. Various legal fees and charges are added to the debt and the creditor is then ready to collect. The debtor is usually unaware that this process has occurred.

A default judgment is entered when the debtor does not appear at the hearing. Many states allow private individuals to serve the process which notifies the debtor of the judgment hearing. The process servers are usually paid when they complete the service of process. When they can't find the debtor, they often throw away the process and say that they served it. This action is called sewer service, since the process was served to the sewer and not to the debtor. For this reason, more default judgments are entered simply because the debtor was never notified.

The federal government can institute a civil action against process servers if they deprived the debtor of the due process of law. The fines can put the process server, and the merchant who employs him, out of business. Sewer service is primarily restricted to ghetto areas, although there is nothing to prevent this from happening in an affluent area as well.

RULE: A JUDGMENT CREATES A LIEN.

A lien is a creditor's claim upon the debtor's property. It is not ownership of the property, merely a right in the property, so that the debt will be paid before the property is sold. We've already discussed the liens created by statutes, such as mechanic's and innkeeper's liens. Liens are also created by contracts, called security interests or consensual liens. An example is the voluntary lien that is created when you borrow money to buy a car. A security interest is usually registered with a county official. Liens can also be created by a court judgment.

The mechanic's lien, the security interest lien, or the innkeeper's lien affects only a limited amount of property. Only the personal property already subject to the lien can be reached to satisfy the debt. However, a judgment lien is a general lien against all of the person's real estate. A judgment lien is serious, because the creditor can take your house. Alabama, Georgia, and Mississippi let the creditor also take the debtor's personal property.

The person with the lien has only a right in the property of the lien. He can't get the property or sell it until he has obtained a writ of execution. This writ allows the sheriff or marshal to take the property into the sheriff's possession. This taking into possession is called a levy. The sheriff then arranges for the sale. The real estate is appraised and a minimum price is placed on it. The sale takes place and the debtor recovers the value of his property in excess of the total of the debt, court costs, and the expense of the sale. This procedure is ideal, but not all states adhere to the idea of having appraisals made prior to the sale. If a lien has been placed on your house, you'd better pay up immediately—or hire an attorney. You could possibly lose your home.

Prices brought at such sales are generally very low, because the person who buys the property may be deprived of the title to his purchase. After the sale, faults may turn up in the debtor's title to the property. In such a case, the fellow who bought the property cannot recover the creditor's share of the sale price. Few people are willing to take such a risk, and this fact forces down the prices at an execution sale.

RULE: A CREDITOR MAY TAKE YOUR SALARY.

There are two ways he may do this. The first way is a wage assignment, which might arise out of the consumer credit agreement if such a clause was in that agreement. You as the debtor might sign a contract with this provision when you take out the loan or buy the goods. The creditor with a wage assignment will not require a court order to collect against your salary. The second type is a garnishment. Garnishment is an action through the courts and is somewhat controlled by the law. Either assignment or garnishment can be described by the wider category of wage attachment.

Employers object to any type of wage attachment, since it will require some effort and expense on their part. Therefore, it is not unusual for employers to fire employees whose wages are attached. As you read in the chapter on credit, it is very undesirable to sign an agreement allowing wage assignment. Under a wage assignment the creditor presents the contract to the employer. If the employer does not honor it, the creditor can get a court order forcing the employer's cooperation. The debtor does not find out about this prior to the time the creditor presents the contract. He may not even find out about it then. His first notice may be a smaller paycheck or a pink slip.

Wage assignment is allowed in most states as long as certain requirements are met, such as consent of the employer or spouse prior to the time the agreement is signed. This consent protects spouses since they can refuse to sign if they feel the assignment is contrary to their interests. Sometimes the loan with the wage assignment has to be under a specified amount. Alabama, the District of Columbia, Florida, New Jersey, Idaho, Kansas, Nevada, and Ohio outlaw wage assignment altogether. Connecticut, Puerto Rico, and Utah allow it only under very special circumstances (in Utah the debtor can call it off) or only to a special class of creditors, such as hospitals (Puerto Rico) or unions and children receiving child support (Connecticut).

The other type of wage attachment is called a garnishment. Garnishment is not a result of the contract, but is a remedy creditors have by law for past due loans or other credit extensions. Garnishment is far more of a judicial process than is a wage assignment. The garnishment may occur either before or after an actual suit. Before the suit the creditor notifies the employer to hold wages owed to the debtor. The creditor could also get a garnishment against the debtor's bank accounts. Garnishment requires that the person withholding payment to the debtor appear before the court and state the amount he owes the debtor. In this case the debtor almost always has notice, since the employer or bank is sure to let him know prior to the hearing. Persons holding the debtor's money do this in order to prevent the debtor from suing for a violation of a trust. The money is left with the employer or bank until a final judgment is issued. (In the case of assignment, the money is turned over to the creditor, prior to any suit.)

The primary difference between wage assignment and garnishment is that federal law controls garnishment. The Consumer Credit Protection Act limits collection to not more than 25 per cent of each net paycheck of the debtor regardless of the number of creditors. The net paycheck is salary less taxes and Social Security withheld. There is also an hourly wage limitation. Even a person making as little as $80 a week can receive no less than a $63 paycheck. The creditors can reach the hourly wage limitation or the 25 per cent limitation, whichever results in the creditor getting less money. This total limitation is applied to all creditors seeking a garnishment. They can only have up to 25 per cent all put together. Some states do not allow any type of garnishment. When this is true the state statute overrides this federal limitation. The federal statute also prohibits the firing of an employee if only one creditor asks for a garnishment. If two or more creditors ask for garnishment, this rule does not apply. The Secretary of Labor enforces this rule against firing.

Many states also have statutes which prohibit an employer from firing an employee because of garnishment of the employee's salary. The following flatly prohibit firing: Colorado, Delaware, the District of Columbia, Idaho, Louisiana, Michigan, Minnesota, New Jersey, New York, Oregon, Texas, Utah, and Wisconsin. Other states prohibit firing if a limited number of creditors have sought garnishment. The parentheses following the states listed below show the number of creditors allowed to seek garnishment without the employee being fired: California (1), Connecticut (7 in one year), Georgia (1), Illinois (1), Kansas (3), Kentucky (1), Missouri (1), Ohio (1), Vermont (5), Washington (3). Once again, if the state law is more beneficial to the employee than the federal law, the state law will take precedence. The states not listed are governed by the federal law described above.

If credit gets to be simply too much for the debtor to handle, bankruptcy proceedings can be sought. Once the bankruptcy proceedings have started, the court takes all of the creditors together, examines their claims, sells the debtor's property, and distributes the proceeds proportionately among the creditors. Bankruptcy is a federal law. There are also state insolvency proceedings used for more limited sorts of actions. The federal bankruptcy statute has recently been reformed. What you read below conforms to the old law, but if you decide to declare bankruptcy you *must* have an attorney. He should be current with the revisions that affect you.

RULE: BANKRUPTCY IS THE INABILITY
TO PAY DEBTS AS THEY COME DUE.

Very often a debtor will have assets insufficient to pay her bills if they all come due at the same time. This debtor is not bankrupt, merely over her head. If she continues to work, chances are she can pay off the loans. Bankruptcy is defined as the inability of the debtor to pay his bills as they become due.

The most normal type of bankruptcy proceeding is called straight bankruptcy, although it is usually referred to simply as bankruptcy. This procedure is not complex. It merely involves liquidating the debtor's assets and paying off the creditors proportionately. A bankruptcy can be started by the debtor himself, called a voluntary bankruptcy, or by his creditors, an involuntary bankruptcy. Voluntary bankruptcy is by far the more popular, occurring a hundred times more often than involuntary bankruptcy.

Bankruptcy is begun by the debtor's petitioning the federal district court. The form to be filed is Official Form 1. The debtor is declared bankrupt, the court appoints a trustee who will conduct the bankruptcy, and the trustee notifies the creditors to attend a meeting. The debtor turns over his property, the creditors present their claims, the property is sold, and the creditors are paid off by a proportion. The proportion is arrived at by determining what amount is owed to the particular creditor in relationship to all amounts owed. For example, if the creditor was owed $2,500 out of a total debt of $10,000, the creditor would be entitled to 25 per cent of the assets. If only $8,000 were available to pay off the creditors, this creditor would get 25 per cent of the $8,000, or $2,000. Normally creditors do not do this well.

At the end of the bankruptcy proceedings the debtor is usually discharged—that is, made free of all the debts he owes in the United States. However, bankruptcy does not wipe out federal income taxes which are due. The bankrupt will have to pay the taxes on his own.

The costs of bankruptcy is rather low, usually under $500 for a simple bankruptcy proceeding. The largest part of this cost is attorney's fees. The bankrupt can usually dig up the fees someplace, or pay them off from his much increased expendable income, since he's no longer paying off debts.

RULE: WAGE EARNERS ARE ENTITLED
TO A SPECIAL BANKRUPTCY.

The primary purpose of bankruptcy in general is to rehabilitate and reorganize the debtor, so that he can earn his living free from the constant harassment of creditors. Chapter 8 of the Bankruptcy Act is called the Wage Earner Plan. The Wage Earner Plan is for persons whose primary source of income is salary, wages, or commissions. It allows the debtor to put together a plan to extend his debts over a longer period of time. The Wage Earner Plan is not used as much as regular bankruptcy but can be of significant help to a beleaguered family. The Wage Earner Plan is substantially the same sort of service that is provided by the Consumer Credit Counseling Service. If you don't have a Consumer Credit Counseling Service in your city, the Wage Earner Plan is a fair alternative. You will not suffer from the dishonor usually equated with the bankrupt. Your creditors will be happy because they will eventually receive all their money. Your salary may be tied up for a substantial period of time, but at the end you will understand finance better and be free of all debts.

RULE: THEY CAN'T HAVE ALL
OF YOUR PROPERTY.

The Bankruptcy Act exempts certain property from the reach of creditors. Although there is no federal law determining exactly which property is exempt, the federal district courts use the exempt property statutes of the state in which the debtor resides. Some states exempt the family home and almost all exempt necessary household goods, such as beds, school books, family pictures, the dog, and clothing. The creditors may not take the family's food, but may take practically anything else that they think has any resale value. Some states exempt one car, others do not. New York does not exempt the family car. The legislatures will not allow a family to become totally destitute and unable to maintain their daily life. If a professional person goes bankrupt, such as a doctor or lawyer, he will probably be allowed to keep the tools of his trade, like medical instruments or a law library.

However, if a creditor already has a lien on the property, he will be able to take possession of this property regardless of whether it falls into the exemption of your state. For example, your state may exempt a cooking stove. If you bought the stove on credit, the creditor could get it regardless of the fact that it is exempt property.

Although the information in this chapter may seem orderly and fairly straightforward, much has been left out due to space limitations. Creditors have many more remedies available than are outlined here. Nor can a few simple words about the legal process describe the anguish a family must confront if their credit load becomes too heavy.

As one of the rules in this chapter states, credit problems must be confronted. The creditors will not allow the money owed to them to be dismissed or swept under a rug. If you feel that your family's monthly debt load is too high, the best thing to do is to cut up all your credit cards and throw them away. Make no further purchases until the debt is reduced to a minor amount. Consumer debts owed at any one time, such as to Master Charge, Sears, or the local department store, should not exceed more than one third of the family's yearly salary. If your family's debt load exceeds this, you may work it down yourself or seek the help of CCCS, your union, or perhaps even the local banker.

Part VIII
CRIME AND PUNISHMENT

Chapter 27
GETTING A TICKET

The greatest annoyance of modern transportation is the ever alert traffic cop and his citation book. Whether it's a parking ticket or a moving violation, the insult is nearly of the same magnitude. By the way, the legal phrase for getting a ticket is "being arrested."

RULE: MOST PARKING TICKETS
CAN BE PAID BY MAIL.

Although there is very little statutory reference for this, every city which has ever issued me a parking summons has allowed it to be paid by mail. Most cities have low parking fines. Whether guilty or not, the best use of your time may be simply to pay it off. However, every time you get a parking ticket, check to make sure that your auto license number is stated correctly. Someone may have moved the ticket from his car to yours. Also check to see if the location on the ticket is correct. It may say that you were parked in the 300 block of 55th Street, when you were actually in violation on the 200 block. These details will allow you to overcome the ticket if you decide to fight it.

Parking violations will not affect your license to drive a car, but if you have too many unpaid violations, the state may refuse to re-register your automobile. The statutes governing unpaid parking tickets are called scofflaw statutes. Under the scofflaw statutes, the local police may have the right to arrest you and hold you until the violations are paid up.

RULE: LOOK UP THE LAW.

Tickets, whether they be parking tickets or moving violations, will usually cite only a code number which represents the ordinance you are charged with. For example, you may be charged with Section 80A of the New York City parking code. Unless you research what Section 80A is, you can't very well state that you are not guilty. The clerk in the traffic court will be able to show you the code section that you are charged with.

RULE: PLEAD NOT GUILTY.

If you decide to argue your parking ticket, you must plead not guilty if the traffic court judge is to wipe out your fine. If you plead guilty or guilty with an excuse, the best he can do is diminish your fine.

When you get a parking ticket, read it carefully. It will have all the instructions you need if you wish to appear and argue your case. When you arrive to argue your case, you are likely to find that the traffic court is conducted very swiftly and informally. You are required to take an oath that the testimony you give will be true and accurate. Some traffic courts tape their proceedings for the record should you appeal your traffic ticket. Chances are you will be called in along with a group of many other people. If you want to be among the first to be heard, you'll have to get there early.

RULE: BRING YOUR EVIDENCE.

If you received a parking violation because there was no sign visible, photographs will help you prove to the judge that the no-parking sign was missing. If at all possible the photographs should be taken in such a way that street signs are visible. The photographs, taken from different angles, will prove that the area is indeed the area in which you received the ticket and that all "No Parking" signs were missing.

RULE: APPEAR FOR ALL MOVING VIOLATIONS.

If you have more than two moving violations in a year, your auto insurance may go up. If you appear and have the violations overturned, you may save on the cost of insurance as well as the ticket. You can follow the procedure outlined for parking tickets. You'll need evidence, but the court procedure will be informal. And there's always the chance that your arresting officer won't show up. If he doesn't, your case will be "dismissed," which means the court will judge you innocent of the violation.

Many states have laws which require the suspension of a driver's license if the driver has had three moving violations in a one-year period. If you've had two moving violations in one year, it's safest to hire an attorney to represent you on the second violation. If you wait until the third one, you may have done something so awful that he can't help you. In big cities you may even find clusters of storefront attorneys' offices around the traffic court. These people won't charge you much, since they're at the traffic court anyway and won't have to make a special trip. You may also find attorneys in the hallways of the traffic court. Just walk up to anyone carrying a briefcase, find out if he's an attorney, and ask him to represent you. Have cash on hand for the purpose.

If you've been attracting moving violations, whether they've been speeding tickets or turns in the wrong places, you'd better slow down and be more careful. You might even have your glasses checked. Most states send a multiple offender back to driving school anyway. It might be best to send yourself back to school before the court makes you.

Chapter 28
THE CRIMINAL

Although few of the readers of this book are likely to be involved in criminal activity, newspapers, TV, and films often use crime as their central theme. Crime is also a substantial political issue. This chapter is included to aid the reader in understanding these things she sees around her. Besides the informational value, criminal law is interesting and contains some clues about legal reasoning. The penalties the criminal pays are very real. The effects the criminal creates on those around him are at the least disturbing and at the most terrifying.

Incidentally, the crimes discussed in this chapter are generally the common-law definitions. Many states have modified one or all of these crimes by acts of their legislatures.

Death was the uniform penalty for any crime under the ancient common law. The most depraved murderer suffered no greater penalty than a pickpocket. Recent societies have found this standard too harsh and have continually modified death penalty offenses, leaving the criminal law itself in a complex state. Under the common law, even a murder with extenuating circumstances would be punished by the death penalty, and so the judges had to invent less serious forms of homicide. Therefore, the law ended up with many different types of homicide. The same principle applied to other types of criminal activity, including theft.

Of all the crimes, larceny is the most prevalent. "Larceny" is an old English word which covers all the different types of unlawful taking. Last year there were 36 million reported cases of larcenous offenses in the United States. Larceny is slightly less repulsive than other crimes, since larceny is a crime against property and not against people.

Larceny is the unlawful taking of another's property. All larceny, whatever the form, requires that the taking be unlawful. This principle is not quite as clear-cut as it might seem. Trespass is one of the requirements of an unlawful taking. The thief must take possession of property without the rightful possessor's consent. For example, if thief A steals property which thief B has stolen, thief A is guilty of larceny, since he committed a trespass on thief B's property. By the same token, if Charlie's boss gives him a diamond ring and tells him to deliver it to Sam, and Charlie fails to deliver it, Charlie is not guilty of larceny because he had the right to possess the diamond ring. Charlie would be guilty of embezzlement if he fails to deliver the ring or return it to the boss.

In order to prove that there has been an unlawful taking, the criminal prosecutor must also show that there has been an asportation. Asportation means carrying away. This carrying away can be a very small one, such as the shoplifter who gets stopped a foot outside the store entrance. By the same token, the police always let the pickpocket remove the wallet from the victim's pocket before arresting him, since the pickpocket's hand in the man's pocket is no evidence that there will be a carrying away.

Larceny is committed against personal property. Real estate is never the subject of larceny. For example, you can't steal a tree. If a fellow chops down a tree on your land and then carries it away, he converted your real estate into personal property and then carried it away. If a fellow manages to steal land by tricking someone, it's not larceny, but embezzlement or fraud.

Larceny is taking the property of another. Normally, it's very easy to determine exactly what "another" means. However, there is some confusion between husbands and wives. Under the old common law, husband and wife were the same person and therefore could not steal from one another. This view is considered outdated and the criminal law in some states is beginning to recognize the difference between the husband's property and the wife's property. Under the modern view, a husband can commit a theft against his wife's money, personal goods, or possibly even the title to her house. The Model Penal Code distinguishes between household goods, in which case no theft would be allowed, and purely personal items which are solely the property of one or the other. If both own the property, a joint bank account for example, theft could also be charged, since a partner has no right to carry away the property of the partnership.

Surprisingly, it is possible for a person to steal from herself, as sometimes happens in credit cases. The credit company forecloses on the refrigerator and notifies the person that the refrigerator will be repossessed. The person then removes the refrigerator so that it can't be taken by the creditor. The person has in effect stolen her own refrigerator, since the statutory lien of the creditor is legally superior to the person's possession.

Larceny requires an intent to permanently deprive of possession. Larceny is not unauthorized borrowing of property. For example, the act of walking into your neighbor's garage and taking away his lawn mower has all of the elements of larceny except one—your intent to permanently deprive your neighbor of possession.

Joyriding also fails as larceny, since there's no intent to permanently deprive the person of possession. Many states have passed statutes to cover this particular exception so that joyriding is a criminal offense, but it is not larceny. Someone can also mistake someone else's property for his own. An example of this mistake is the drunk who gets in somebody else's car, turns it on, and drives away. He had no intention of depriving the owner of the property because he thought it was his own. Our drunken friend could be charged with drunk driving, but he clearly has made an honest mistake, although an unreasonable one, and larceny could not be properly charged against him.

There are lots of different types of larceny. Many of them depend on the person's right to be in possession of the goods. Larceny is divided into: larceny by stealth, larceny by an employee, larceny by a finder, larceny by a bailee, and larceny by trick. (Embezzlement is not larceny because of rightful possession by the taker, but is often grouped with other types of stealing.) Many states assign different penalties to different kinds of larceny. The most basic division is between grand larceny and petit larceny. The state statutes vary widely as to where petit ends and grand begins. It ranges anywhere between $20 and $500. However, it is not relevant that the thief know the value of the items he is stealing. He may think the item to be of minor value and think himself guilty of petit larceny. If it turns out that the item is valued at an amount making his crime grand larceny, he will be charged with grand larceny. The practical difference between grand and petit larceny is the length of sentence, and someone found guilty of grand larceny is considered a felon. A felon loses his civil rights and cannot hold many jobs which require a license.

Larceny by stealth is the most typical larceny. The thief carries away goods without the knowledge of the victim. Burglary is one type of larceny by stealth, as are shoplifting, pickpocketing, and other sneaky activities. Robbery is not larceny by stealth, since it implies a forcible stealing from the person. In a robbery the victim is aware that he is being deprived of his property, and violence or threats of violence are used. Mugging is a type of robbery. Many statutes have heavier penalties for armed robbery (threatening the use of a gun, knife, etc.). The likelihood of the person being killed or maimed in an armed robbery is much greater than in simple robbery, where only the threat of physical force is used. Burglary is distinguished from larceny in general by the requirement of an unlawful entry into a building. Actually, at common law burglary was restricted to the actual breaking into a home during the nighttime with intent to commit a felony. Modern statutes rarely confine burglary to either homes or the nighttime, nor do they require a forcible entry. Just remaining in a building after normal closing with the intent to steal usually will qualify as a burglary.

Larceny by an employee occurs when someone has been given custody of the goods which he eventually steals. The moment that the employee converts the property to his own purposes he qualifies under all of the requirements of larceny. The differences between larceny by an employee and embezzlement depend primarily on the statutes of the state where the taking occurs. The same facts would satisfy an embezzlement charge in one state and a larceny charge in another state. Some types of workers could never be charged with embezzlement because the statute of their state restricts embezzlement to certain occupations. For example, the majority of statutes limit embezzlement to attorneys, accountants, public officials, and agents of the employer. An agent is a person who acts with the consent of his employer.

If a person finds property on the street, and then keeps it, she could be guilty of larceny. The finder must have the intention to keep it for herself at the moment she finds it. For example, if you find a $100 bill right in front of you, and you say, "Terrific, there's the school shoes for the kids," you are guilty of larceny. If you thought, "A hundred dollars. I'd better pick it up, but how will I ever find the owner?" you are not guilty of larceny. Most states require that you register what you found with some designated official, such as the town clerk or the police department. You may also have to advertise what you found in the newspaper. If you don't, it's a criminal offense. On the other hand, it's difficult to prosecute on this law, since it's hard to determine who has found lost property.

Larceny by bailee is a very old-fashioned type of crime. A bailment is the property which a bailee is responsible for. The bailee holds property in trust and may or may not take any action with the property. For example, the bank is the bailee of your safe-deposit box. They'd better not let anybody else in there. Delivering goods to a warehouse will also create a bailment in that the bailee stores the goods until they are delivered to a third party, for example the trucking company. If the bailee breaks the bulk of what you delivered to him and then takes part of the goods, he is guilty of larceny. Modern statutes vary on whether the bailee must break open the package in order to be guilty of larceny, but he will be guilty of either larceny or embezzlement, depending on the local statute.

Larceny by trick is not quite as much fun as it sounds. In this instance a person obtains possession of the property with an obligation to dispose of it in one way, but he intends at the time that he acquires the possession to do something quite different with it. A modern example of this would be the guy who rents a car from a car-rental company with the intention of selling the car as though it were his own. The fellow who rents the car is called a trickster. Larceny by trick does not cover the instance when one misapplies the goods, such as taking the car to a different location than you had originally said. All of the other qualifications of larceny must also be met.

There is a large group of other crimes against property which are best described by the general classification of criminal fraud. Criminal fraud usually consists of a "misrepresentation, concealment, or non-disclosure of a material fact, or at least misleading conduct, devices, or contrivance." As this definition applies to crimes against property, there must also be an intention to deprive another of the property in question. Any number of con games and illegal takings are covered under this umbrella.

Forgery is a type of crime against property, but is far different from larceny in that there is an intent to defraud rather than to steal. Checks are the most common targets of forgers. They may alter a check so that it reads a greater amount than you intended, or they may write somebody else's check and even sign that person's name. If you sign a check for an amount greater than you have in your bank account, you would not be guilty of forgery, since you are entitled to write checks. However, you would violate the bad-check statutes in practically every state. If you are signing your own name, you're not guilty of forgery.

Receiving stolen goods is a crime quite similar to larceny in that the fellow who takes stolen goods becomes an accessory to the crime itself. The receiver must believe that the goods were stolen and take them anyway. He also has to take them for a dishonest purpose, such as reselling them. However, if he receives them in order to return them to the owner, he has no dishonest purpose and is guilty of no crime.

Extortion is similar to robbery in that threats are used to obtain money or property. The difference between extortion and robbery is that the threat used in extortion may be more subtle than the robbery threat of immediate physical harm. What is threatened need not be unlawful. An extortionist could threaten to tell one's spouse about an affair unless he receives money for keeping silent. The more common form of extortion is protection money. A gang extracts payments from a store owner in exchange for refraining from breaking up the place. The most subtle form of extortion is the type which public officials exercise. It is the building inspector who forgoes issuing violations in exchange for payments from the landlord, or the policeman who forgets an arrest in exchange for money or property.

Arson is another crime against property which originated in the common-law principle of an intentional or outrageously reckless burning of another person's home. Modern statutes have expanded this law to include any type of building which is burned. Rather colorfully, the common law would not allow scorching as arson, nor would it allow blowing up of a building, unless it then caught fire. Even more ludicrous, the house had to be still a house when it burned. If the explosion had so fragmented the house that what burned were mere splinters, arson had not occurred. Modern legislation punishes any person who starts a fire with the intention of destroying property or blows up a building. A person will also be guilty of arson if he burns down his own property with intent to defraud an insurance company.

Homicide is a general term which means the killing of one person by another. Homicide does not necessarily constitute a crime. "Justifiable" homicide will occur when a police officer shoots a civilian with proper cause, when a person is executed, or when a killing was done in self-defense.

In homicide, two different elements must be considered. The first is the charge itself, such as murder or manslaughter. The other element is the degree, the seriousness of the crime within the general description of murder or manslaughter.

Murder is the most serious of the homicides. Murder must contain what the judges call "malice aforethought." "Malice aforethought" is called a term of art. In other words, it doesn't really mean what it sounds like. "Malice," in the law, requires a willful or wanton disregard for the consequences. "Aforethought" has an element of premeditation, but doesn't necessarily imply a plan to murder. The murderer's dangerous mental state is what distinguishes murder from the lesser charge of manslaughter.

Murder in the first degree always includes premeditation. All murders are considered to be second degree until the prosecutor can show that premeditation was present. Intentional murders are the most outstanding example of premeditation, although the premeditation (planning) can take place in just a moment of time. Another type of first-degree murder is felony murder. An example of a felony murder is the store owner who dies of a heart attack during an armed robbery. In some states, if one of the armed robbers is killed by the police, the other armed robber can be charged with felony murder, even though he did not pull the trigger which killed his criminal cohort. The element of premeditation is present in a felony murder since the criminals took on the responsibility of creating mayhem and must have anticipated the consequences. "Outrageously reckless" homicide has been invented to cover bizarre events such as dropping bricks off buildings and shooting guns into crowds. Outrageously reckless homicide could be first-degree murder or first-degree manslaughter, depending on the statutes of the state.

Second-degree murder is assigned to homicides which do not have an element of premeditation. The reckless state of mind is present but not the element of planning. Second-degree murder would include any intentional act threatening serious bodily harm during which a death occurred, more or less by accident. Second-degree murder would generally be characterized by beating deaths, as opposed to killing with weapons. In wife- or child-beating deaths, the husband is often charged with second-degree murder.

Manslaughter is differentiated from murder in that the perpetrator's mind does not contain malice aforethought. Manslaughter includes: homicides committed in the heat of passion; homicides due to the negligent operation of an automobile; and homicides occurring during the commission of a minor crime, known as a misdemeanor. Manslaughter would also include self-defense killings which occurred under circumstances which would not justify the means of self-defense used.

First-degree manslaughter is sometimes called voluntary manslaughter. The most normal example of first-degree manslaughter is the barroom fight when the victim has so provoked the assailant that the assailant's passion gets out of hand and he takes the provoker's life. Sufficient provocation can include admissions of adultery, mutual combat, fear, and assault. The difficulty with first-degree manslaughter is that most states will not allow words to reduce a homicide to a manslaughter charge. Even outrageous statements such as "I just raped your wife" may not be enough. Whichever of these provocations is used as a defense, the law requires that there not be a sufficient cooling-off period between the time of a provocation and the time that the homicide occurs. In other words, "I just raped your wife" would not be sufficient provocation for a homicide which occurs hours later. That homicide would be a murder.

Second-degree manslaughter is also called involuntary manslaughter. Many states use this to charge persons who have caused a death by the negligent use of an automobile. The degree of negligence required is very high and is more than ordinary negligence—for example, drunken driving, drag racing, or exceptionally high speeds. It requires a conscious disregard of a substantial and unjustifiable risk with a gross deviation from law-abiding conduct.

Another form of involuntary manslaughter is called misdemeanor manslaughter, a charge carrying a very light compulsory sentence. For example, a teen-ager steals a candy bar and the store owner runs after him, falls into an open manhole, and dies of concussion. This is officially misdemeanor manslaughter since stealing a candy bar caused the concussion and the child is guilty of causing the death of the owner. However, juries are unwilling to strongly punish a person whose insignificant criminal act accidentally caused such a serious consequence as death. Since most states have compulsory sentences for each different grade of homicide, misdemeanor manslaughter was added to prosecute for deaths which occur because of petty thefts and other misdemeanors.

There are additional classifications of violent crimes against a person's body. Most of these have a corresponding suit in civil law. For example, assault and battery can be either a criminal charge or a basis for a civil suit. Mayhem could possibly fall into the negligence category on the civil side. Rape and other sexual offenses can be both criminal and civil. Kidnapping is the criminal version of civil false imprisonment.

A person who is the subject of one of these crimes may also sue the felon for damages. Normally, the state insists on bringing the criminal charge first. The state's interest in protecting the society is considered to be superior to the individual's right to damages. After the criminal prosecution is completed, the person injured can then bring an action in a civil court. Most jurisdictions do not allow the criminal conviction at the first trial to become evidence at the civil trial. The problem with the civil suit for injuries is that the felon rarely has any assets with which to pay damages to the plaintiff.

Assault and battery are normally tied together in criminal statutes. Assault is the *threat* of striking a blow. Assault is sometimes considered to be an attempted battery. In other words, the guy tried to hit the other person but couldn't land his punch. Assault will also be charged when a criminal intentionally causes fear of physical abuse. Battery is best remembered if you think of it in terms of battering. Battery is the intentional offensive touching or harming of another. A man who won't take his hands off a woman is guilty of battery. If a woman hits the man over the head with her umbrella, she has committed battery, unless she is striking in self-defense. You'll read about self-defense further on in this chapter. Some states have now dropped the use of the word "battery" and have substituted the word "assault" for both elements in this crime—the threat and the striking.

Aggravated assault and battery is a more serious type of assault, as when a criminal has been thwarted while in the act of rape, murder, or mayhem. Aggravated assault is also charged when a deadly weapon is used or serious bodily injury results from the battery.

Mayhem is used by most states as a separate criminal offense when the attack results in loss of a limb, eyesight, or other disabling injury. Loss of a sex organ may also be considered mayhem, but some states have invented a special charge called malicious castration. The law requires that the batterer had an intent to maim or kill his victim.

Rape is, of course, a specialized crime against a female person. It can be defined as "unlawful sexual intercourse with a woman against her will by force or threat of immediate force." Rape and other sexual offenses are covered extensively in their own chapter in this book.

Kidnapping requires that a person be captured and carried away against her will. The capture can be physical or it can be based on fraud. Kidnapping can be charged if a person was carried to another place for what she thought was a legitimate purpose. When she and the kidnapper arrived at the location, and she discovered that his only intentions were sexual, kidnapping has occurred. The law requires that the kidnapper have the intent to act outside the law. If the fellow feels, however wrongly, that he has the legal right to carry her away, he is not guilty of kidnapping.

A carrying away is also required. This carrying away can be either to a neighboring house or across a state line. The FBI can investigate all kidnappings in which there is a possibility that the victim has been carried across the state line. The FBI is entitled to make this assumption when the victim has been missing for twenty-four hours. As a rule, the FBI is immediately notified of all kidnapping cases.

The kidnapping must also occur without the victim's consent. If the victim feels that she is being taken to a place for some purpose other than the one intended by the kidnapper, consent has not been granted. If a child is carried away, the consent of the parents is required. Because of parental consent, many states refuse to indict a parent for kidnapping when he has whisked away his natural child who is in the custody of another person. The parent may be in contempt of the divorce court, but criminal charges are not applicable.

In spite of the occasionally frightening newspaper articles which report a crime victim being prosecuted for an act committed in self-defense, every crime victim may defend herself against a criminal. The rules vary, depending on the type of crime that is being committed.

RULE: NEVER USE DEADLY FORCE.

A crime victim can do anything short of killing her assailant. Deadly force is defined as a force likely to inflict death or serious bodily injury. The victim may not use deadly force to prevent simple injury to herself, but may use it when death or serious personal injury appears to be immediate. In other words, if a burglar is holding a gun on you, you may knife him, shoot him, or anything else. If there is no gun or other weapon, you're out of luck. Deadly weapons may also be used when a serious felony is being committed, such as murder or armed robbery. A woman may argue that she had to use some weapon because of the superior physical strength of a male attacker. She must be cautious about the use of weapons, since she might kill somebody.

If you use a deadly weapon, it will be up to you to prove that your use of the weapon was justified. If you cannot prove this, you will fall into the category of "imperfect" self-defense. Manslaughter charges may be brought against you.

RULE: RETREAT, IF POSSIBLE.

If you are being threatened, nearly half of the states require that you retreat before resorting to the use of deadly force. Of course, you still may not use deadly force unless threatened with death. Some states modify this rule so that the victim must know that he can retreat in complete safety, with absolutely no risk of injury to himself. The retreat rule is very rarely applied when a person is attacked in his own home.

RULE: SHOOT IN YOUR OWN HOME.

Use of deadly force is allowed when the homeowner comes upon a burglar or other person in the act of a felony, such as kidnap or rape. This rule is modified in that the felony must actually be dangerous. Burglars are dangerous, since one doesn't know whether they have a gun or not. However, people who come into your home for a short period, even if you are not there, are not considered burglars. They may have come in because it was raining outside or their car broke down and they needed a phone. If you arrive home and find someone standing in your foyer, first ask what he's doing there.

If you think you hear burglars downstairs, call the police, wait five minutes, and then turn on the lights and your radio and start yelling at your husband. Many burglars don't want any trouble and they may walk out of the house straight into the arms of the policemen you called. If nothing else, the lights and radio will keep the guys out of the bedrooms. It's really very foolish to run around a dark house with a pistol. You could end up shooting your Uncle Harry, yourself, the dog, or your teen-aged son who was raiding the refrigerator.

Punishments for any crime are determined by the state or federal statute which governs the particular criminal act. These statutes vary widely, and a discussion of them is not germane to this book. However, there are constitutional limitations on punishment.

RULE: PUNISHMENT MAY NOT BE
CRUEL OR UNUSUAL.

The Eighth Amendment to the U. S. Constitution forbids punishment which is disproportionate to the crime committed. Although this area of the law is yet to be fully developed, the idea of disproportionality seems to be a sound one. There are two standards for judging when the punishment is disproportionate to the crime. Common sense is one standard. The crime itself is weighed with the penalty of other similarly serious crimes. For example, stealing a loaf of bread could require a year in prison under the statute of the state, but this punishment would certainly be cruelly disproportionate to the crime. Another standard is the punishment which other states exact for a particular crime. If the state in which the person is found guilty has a penalty extraordinarily higher than the punishment by other states, the punishment may be called cruel and unusual.

Implicit in the standards for punishment is the degree of violence which the crime contains. For example, a man could be found guilty of statutory rape (having intercourse with a female too young to be capable of mature judgment). The fellow may have used absolutely no violence and yet be found guilty of rape. In some states rape might be punishable by the death penalty. The death penalty would certainly be disproportionate, since violence was not involved in the act. Parenthetically, the statutes of many states indicate different penalties for rape and statutory rape. This subject is covered more fully in the chapter on rape.

RULE: THE DEATH PENALTY IS CONSTITUTIONAL.

The Supreme Court has *never* found the death penalty unconstitutional. It has, however, ruled that its application can be cruel and unusual. Application was the problem when *Furman* v. *Georgia* appeared in 1972. Four years passed while thirty-five states formed new death penalty legislation. In 1976 the Supreme Court reviewed a number of new death penalty statutes, and approved three: Florida, Texas, and Georgia. Similar legislation is likely to be constitutional.

Imposing the death penalty requires two stages. First, the jury decides whether the defendant is guilty or not guilty. If the defendant is guilty, there must be a separate decision about the imposition of the death penalty. In order to prevent an arbitrary and capricious penalty, evidence must be presented concerning the murderer's background and any aggravating or mitigating circumstances. Appellate courts are also warned to apply the most rigorous standards when reviewing cases in which the death penalty has been imposed.

The Supreme Court will not allow absolute imposition of the death penalty. For example, New York's law requiring the death penalty for murder of a police officer was unconstitutional. Death penalties for lesser crimes than murder may also be unconstitutional. The death penalty for rape might not pass muster.

The Supreme Court said that the death penalty is "an extreme sanction suitable for the most extreme crimes." This may imply that the death penalty should be imposed only for the most shocking crimes.

One of the great dissatisfactions of the citizenry is that punishment of criminals has little or no relationship to the crime itself. As Arnold Loewy, a criminal law professor, puts it, punishment has three R's and a D. The basic reasons for punishment are reformation, restraint, retribution, and deterrence. None of these singly provides any sound basis for imprisonment.

The most liberal current view of imprisonment is that it affords the criminal an opportunity for reform. There are a few exceptional examples of persons who use prison time to become outstanding experts in some field and redeem their lives by making valuable contributions to the society. The Birdman of Alcatraz is one such example. Unfortunately these cases are by far the exception. The difficulty with reform in prison is that it simply doesn't work. Some people are sent to prison for a crime they are unlikely ever to repeat, like the man who kills his wife after putting up with fifteen years of her infidelity. Prison has no chance of reforming this particular man, since he is unlikely ever to murder again. On the other hand, a burglar who is sent to prison will be around a lot of other burglars. The chance of reforming anyone when he is among his peers is very limited. In fact, 85 per cent of felons return to prison. The 15 per cent who never go back could easily belong to the group of one-time murderers, reckless drivers, etc. Reform through punishment seems to be a false hope.

Restraint is also argued as a reason for imprisonment. The fellow needs to be restrained from committing further crimes so that the experts can have a chance to reform him. But reform rarely works, so we are left with retribution.

Retribution is the idea that the criminal has committed acts for which the society cannot be repaid. Prison is substituted as pure and simple punishment for criminal misdeeds. Experts argue that retribution has no place in our society, since it is not helpful to the criminal. The other side of this coin is that the state takes on retribution in order to prevent the citizenry from exacting a personal retribution of its own—for example, forming lynch mobs. Expiation is the criminal's version of retribution, and the criminal can atone for his sins through serving time in prison. The society is able to make atonement to the victim of the crime by sending the criminal to jail. From a philosophical point of view, retribution is interesting, but criminals don't seem to pay much heed to philosophy.

The last reason given for punishment is deterrence. It is argued that if there were no punishment for crime, people would commit much more of it. The most commonly argued deterrent is the death penalty. Some think that people will not commit murder in order to avoid having their own lives taken. Of course, this argument has nothing to do with reform or rehabilitation. One study concluded that since most criminals are not aware of the actual penalty for any particular crime, deterrence cannot be claimed as an appropriate basis for punishment. However, these penologists used the incarcerated person's prior knowledge of the length of sentence that he would serve for that crime as a measure. Whether the inmate knew he would be punished was not surveyed. Deterrence seems to have more effect on the sane, law-abiding population than it does on the criminal population. You or I might not commit crimes merely to avoid prison. The criminal doesn't seem to consider his loss of freedom as important as you or I might. The rational conclusion to this dilemma is that the criminal has a far different standard of survival than the rest of us, and that standard of survival may look crazy to the law-abiding population.

The criminal isn't exactly a champion when it comes to dealing with himself and the world. The basic idea of acts of larceny is to get something for nothing. The fellow who holds up a liquor store is trying to take the owner's profits without paying for them, through either money or labor. If the criminal is trying to get something for nothing, society might change its tack and make sure the criminal puts in his effort as his exchange for his misdeeds. He must also put in enough work to support himself. Living free in prison is much like stealing from the liquor store, except that now he is stealing from the taxpayer.

Besides getting something for nothing, the criminal act may include attempts to handle problems for which the criminal has no rational solution. For example, a man may murder his wife because he knows no other way to make her stop sleeping with other lovers. An armed robber may kill the store owner the moment the robber sees that the theft may not be successful.

All psychological mumbo jumbo aside, the criminal is mostly an inadequate citizen with no ability to think about tomorrow. He's probably illiterate, drug-addicted, non-communicative, unemployed, and puzzled by the world. A solution might be to break his drug habit, teach him to read well, get him talking, get him to take responsibility for his destructive acts, and have him examine ways he could survive without criminality. He'll get less and less puzzled. The guy is also going to have to have a good job, or he'll have to go back to crime to support himself. Part of this approach is being used successfully in Arizona prisons by a group called Narcanon.

Narcanon was founded in 1966 by Willie Benitez, who was an inmate of the Arizona State Prison at the time. Narcanon is now available in prisons in nine states and as many foreign countries. It is a voluntary drug treatment program which has the effect of rehabilitating the criminal right along with his drug habit.

A recent New York prison survey showed that 63 per cent of the prison population abused drugs—even while in prison—but the survey didn't include marijuana or alcohol in the drug list. Narcanon officials estimate that if these two drugs had been included in the survey, the statistic would have been virtually 100 per cent.

Eighty-five per cent of all offenders go back to prison. This return to prison is called the recidivism rate. Narcanon has managed to entirely turn around this rate—85 per cent of the Narcanon members stay out of prison. Of the 15 per cent that return to prison, practically all are parole violators. Narcanon also operates residential drug-abuse treatment facilities with similar success. Narcanon's method includes what it calls environmental orientation, vitamins, and a study course. Because of the voluntary nature of the Narcanon program, the success rate may be better than it would be if the same program were forced upon the inmates, but it is the most successful prison program which research brought to light. For more information on Narcanon, write: Narcanon —U.S., 6425 Hollywood Boulevard, Suite 206, Hollywood, California 90028.

Narcanon represents a small ray of light in the criminal darkness. Prisons don't work, and most prisoners go back to prison. Violent crime continues to increase in spite of, and possibly because of, attempts at prison reform. One of the difficulties in the area is that many decisions made about crime and punishment are based on theory and myth rather than hard fact. The leading book in the area of prosecution and punishment is *Criminal Violence, Criminal Justice* by Charles E. Silberman (Random House, 1978). It may help to take the cobwebs out of thinking in this area. This book is fascinating to a lay person and is highly recommended by leading criminal attorneys.

Part IX
ADVOCACY

Chapter 29
HOW TO MANAGE AN ATTORNEY

This book has discussed the details of law you need to know to settle things for yourself, and has attempted to explain the things that nobody explains to you, even if you do have an attorney. The day could come when you won't be able to handle something yourself and will therefore have to hire someone to do it for you. Sometimes accountants can handle these matters, but usually one hires an attorney.

This chapter is about the things you need to know to manage your attorney. Remember that he or she works for you, though the attorney might try to make it seem otherwise.

A lot of people prefer to find an attorney long before they need any help. When a family moves to a new community, the pediatrician is usually the first professional selected, then the dentist, then the tax person, and then the attorney. If they've bought a house, the attorney may be moved up to first place.

What is an attorney? An attorney is a person who practices law and belongs to a bar association. A lawyer is a person who has been trained in the law, but does not necessarily practice or belong to a bar association. A dictionary will document this difference, but in common usage, attorneys are often called lawyers. Attorneys will often insist on being called just that—attorneys.

There are about twice as many people who are trained in the law as actually end up practicing on a regular basis. These "lawyers" use their knowledge in other fields. They may become publishers, sell, manage companies, work in personnel departments, or like this author, write.

The reason for this broad spectrum of occupations is that law school is like the liberal arts course of graduate schools. One gains skills which might not be available in any other type of training. The primary of these skills is learning how to read. Of course we know how to read, sort of, but in law school one learns that every comma and semicolon has a meaning. One also learns how to reason, a skill missing in many other educational disciplines. One also learns a great deal of the history of philosophy and how it affects our thinking. The traditional law schools commit a great deal of their students' time to the study of ancient law cases. The more practical schools tend to concentrate on what the law is today. The law student studies the relationship between facts and the outcome of any particular case.

All of these elements in the attorney's education will be present when you interview him to discuss your problem. Depending on his educational background and personal bent, he will be more or less interested in the philosophy of the matter. Unless he regularly practices in the particular area of your problem, he will probably not have the answers to all of your questions. So he will take the facts from you. He will have a fairly good idea of the general area of the law which covers your problem. He will then look up the answer. After all, the true mark of the educated person is not the facts that she carries in her head, but the ability to find out the answer to a question.

Attorneys come in as wide a range of personalities as the rest of the general public. Some are paragons of virtue and others are crooks. One's ethical stand has very little to do with the intelligence and cash needed to graduate from law school. When you choose an attorney, you may think that intelligence or style or convenience or similarity of ethnic background is most important to you. These qualities are strictly a matter of personal choice. Just remember that the most important asset in an attorney is the ability to do the job and to do it quickly. Attorneys have been known to put off handling their cases. In the profession this is called being "dilatory."

Your first step in hiring an attorney is to find recommendations. You'll want two or three of these. You can find attorneys through your union, a friend who had a similar problem, or a nearby law school. Also, a directory of attorneys, called *Martindale-Hubbell,* is published in most big cities. This directory lists attorneys both alphabetically and by specialty, such as estates, patent, corporate, etc. Local bar associations also run referral services which allow you to talk over a problem with an attorney in exchange for a small fee. In New York the bar association sets the consultation fee at $20 for a half-hour consultation.

RULE: YOU INTERVIEW THEM.

Remember that the attorney works for you. If you were hiring an employee, you probably wouldn't hire the very first person who came along, unless she met your specifications precisely. The same thing is true of attorneys, except that you go to them instead of them coming to you.

Interview at least two or three attorneys for whom you receive recommendations. You have no requirement to retain any of these fellows, and they have no requirement to take you on as a client. Most of them won't even charge you if you tell them you're only trying to hire someone, not discuss the whole case.

The conversation would run something like this:

YOU: My new stove blew up and burned out my kitchen. I think the stove company ought to pay for my repairs.

ATT.: That wouldn't be unusual.

YOU: Have you ever handled a case like this?

ATT.: I haven't handled a stove-blowing-up case, but I have handled a number of cases in this warranty area you're discussing.

YOU: How did you do on those cases?

ATT.: All but one was settled out of court, and the one that went to court eventually lost. It wasn't a good case anyway or else the company would have settled.

YOU: What do you think of my case?

ATT.: Well, we'd have to have a fire expert examine your kitchen to see if the stove was really the cause of the fire. If it was, a fair settlement shouldn't be a problem.

YOU: Is that what you'd do first?

ATT.: Yes, and depending on the expert's report, I'd write a letter to the company and let them know of your problem.

YOU: How much is this going to cost?

ATT.: That depends on the amount of work involved. I charge an hourly fee of $60, and my experience is that I settle these cases in four or five hours. You'll also have to pay the expert—about $75.

YOU: When would you get started?

ATT.: Right away, if you retain me.

Now you know the answers to these pertinent questions:

1. The attorney's experience in the field and the outcome of his cases.
2. His opinion of your chance of success.
3. What steps the attorney will take in handling your case and how long each of these will take.

4.   Approximately how much this is going to cost you.

5.   How quickly he will act in your behalf.

You'll need to get all of this information from each attorney you interview. You can then look at your notes and decide which one is the most appropriate for your particular case. If you are hiring an attorney for general purposes, your requirements will be slightly modified. In this case, how much you like him will also have something to do with your decision.

RULE: EXAMINE THE FEE STRUCTURE
CAREFULLY.

How much each case costs may vary slightly depending on the fee structure the attorney has. One fee structure may appear to be cheaper and turn out to be more expensive in the long run.

Many attorneys charge a flat set fee for a service, especially for types of legal services which take a predictable amount of time. Wills, tax returns, SEC filings, and incorporations are usually charged on a flat-fee basis. The attorney knows just how much it will cost.

If the attorney is less sure of the amount of work involved, he may insist on an hourly rate. This hourly rate varies widely depending on the location, the experience of the attorney, and the type of work involved. Attorneys in small towns may charge $30 or $40 an hour. In New York quality legal work of a general nature costs about $75 an hour. Trial attorneys and highly sophisticated corporate attorneys may charge $150 an hour. When you receive an hourly-rate quote, you must also find out how many hours the attorney estimates your case will take. You should also ask what other charges he will pass on to you. For example, he may charge you for the paralegal fees for research, or for just plain running around. He may also charge you for phone calls or special mailings.

People who generate a lot of legal work—businessmen, for example, or real estate owners—will often put an attorney on a retainer basis. The attorney agrees to work within a certain range of services for a set monthly fee. Very rich people may also have an attorney on retainer. An attorney can also ask for an advance payment before he or she starts working on your case. The attorney may also call this a retainer. If your retainer is really an advance payment for your case, you will want to ask the attorney how much you can get back if the case is settled early.

Sometimes an attorney will consent to represent you on a contingency basis, if there is a likelihood of your receiving a substantial settlement or award from the jury. This kind of payment is used frequently in personal injury cases. The attorney will collect a percentage of the money you receive. Thirty per cent is normal. The attorney initially receives nothing but a small down payment or filing costs. Many people feel that an attorney's willingness to represent them on a contingency basis is some indication of the attorney's faith in the strength of their case. Contingency fees are never used in criminal cases and are rarely used in domestic relations cases.

In some cases—probate, Workman's Compensation, bankruptcy—the court may set the fees on the attorney's behalf. Sometimes the local bar association will set the fee, and then it will be confirmed by the court. For example, probate fees are set on a sliding scale. The attorney gets a percentage of the estate. The percentage decreases as the estate gets larger, but the larger estate always ends up paying a higher amount of probate fees.

Many attorneys will charge you for the costs of filing suit. These costs are the court's charges, filing fees, and sometimes clerical fees. The attorney may charge for long-distance phone calls, or for staff hired to handle your case. Attorneys can hire paralegals through temporary agencies to do special research. The cost need not be overwhelming. Local associations once set mandatory minimum fees for its members, but these minimum fees were found illegal in 1975 by the U. S. Supreme Court. The attorney now has the latitude to charge as little as he likes.

There has been a rapid growth in recent years of legal clinics, like legal aid. These clinics restrict their clientele to particular salary classifications. Some require that their clients have income under $8,500 a year. Others take cases from people who are making up to $20,000. For the most part these clinics are high-volume operations and handle simple repetitive cases such as divorces, adoptions, house sales, and will writing. If you have a simple matter to handle, and qualify to use these clinics, you can get good standard service.

The legal business has been changing substantially over the past five years. Besides legal clinics, three other types of legal help have sprung up.

Prepaid legal services are sometimes available through a union or employer. These services are often paid through payroll deductions and may cost you only $12 to $200 a year, depending on the level of service they offer. Many unions and employers also may arrange for legal help through a reduced-fee group which gives breaks on the prices to its participating public. There are 4,800 reduced-fee groups such as these. The average cost of help from reduced-fee groups is $30 to $40. Legal supermarkets are also growing up since the ban has been lifted on professional advertising.

Prepaid legal services are probably the most ideal arrangement from a theoretical perspective. It may be one of the few ways that inexpensive preventative law can be practiced. The consumer may get a very wide range of services, such as someone to look at consumer contracts before they are signed, criminal defense, consumer complaints, housing problems, traffic violations, and even civil suits, all paid for by the payroll deduction. Of course, the more services offered, the higher the yearly price will be. The attorneys can also rely on a stable, though not extraordinary, income.

Legal supermarkets are the free-enterprise equivalent of prepaid legal services. These groups of attorneys may offer a low-cost first visit to get acquainted. You can bring up problems and receive advice in exchange for your $10 or $15. They also may have low set fees for handling particular repetitive operations, such as house closings or no-fault divorces. Of course, the quality of the service you receive depends mostly on how much the guy sitting across the desk from you cares about himself and his reputation.

A lot of people are unsure about when they should get a lawyer. Some of that depends on you and how well you think you can handle things. The more sophisticated you are, the less likely you are to need one. Regardless of sophistication, anybody in a big jam needs an attorney. Here is a list you may find helpful:

1. Criminal—always get an attorney.
2. Speeding ticket—get an attorney on the second offense.
3. Wills—very simple, do it yourself; complex, get an attorney.
4. Probate—simple, yourself; complex, attorney.
5. Adoption—always get an attorney.
6. Contested divorce—always get an attorney.
7. No-fault divorce—do it yourself.
8. Real estate—get an attorney (the state may require this).
9. Civil suit—always get an attorney.
10. Small claims—do it yourself.

This list is incomplete, but includes most situations. If your liberty is at stake, you always get an attorney. If money is at stake, most people prefer to try to handle it themselves, and most do a very good job. If you decide to handle it yourself, it's mandatory to keep records of all correspondence you send or receive so that an attorney can help you if the matter gets too big.

RULE: SUE WHEN THREATENED.

Many persons are unsure about when they should sue. The decision to sue is a personal one. You should not undertake a lawsuit at someone else's urging. You are the person who will be suffering from the emotional drain, so you must decide.

The issue to look at most closely is how serious the problem is. If your life, reputation, or livelihood is threatened, you must sue. You have no choice because your survivial is at stake.

Of course, you must decide what is the right kind of survival for you. Your own good feelings about yourself can be just as necessary to survival as more complex, material issues such as ownership of real estate.

You can call off a lawsuit at any time. You may have to start up a suit so the other person notices that the matter is quite serious. It's unfortunate when someone doesn't listen to your point of view early enough to correct the problem, but it does happen. Additionally, sometimes suits will have to be started merely as a matter of form, as in personal injury cases.

The success of your relationship with the attorney and the outcome of your case depends as much on your conduct as it does on his. Attorneys are far from being gods, and they need all the help they can get.

There are four basic ways to ensure that you get good service. They are: (1) presenting your case well, (2) doing your own legwork, (3) communicating, and (4) staying cool.

You may have been harmed in an obscure way. When you present this to the attorney, you may muddle up the facts. He may simply not understand what you're talking about. If you present your facts in order of occurrence, you're going to get better help right from the start. The attorney will be able to grasp the situation more readily.

If the attorney has to do more work, it's going to cost you more money to pursue the case. Also remember that you are the person who is most interested in the outcome. There are many things that you can do to help yourself, including searching out documents, finding witnesses, and researching newspaper files. You may also have some special skill which you can add to the case. For example, an engineer might be able to do much of the research work in his own patent infringement case. Your research will add a great deal to the case, since you are likely to show great enterprise in your legwork. It also gives you something to do, and a way to affect the outcome of the proceedings.

Nobody lives in a vacuum, and attorneys are no different. You have to talk to them if you want action. An attorney will normally send you copies of all the letters he writes in your behalf. If he is not sending you letters dealing with the subject matter, he may be sleeping on the job. He needs a wake-up call. He can also get wake-up letters from you asking about his progress. Above all, he needs a lot of communication to help him understand the action of the parties, their personalities, and their interests in the outcome.

Above all, you must stay cool. Attorneys don't like to deal with excited, upset people any more than you do. On top of that, the excited client may mess up her own case. The attorney also spends so much time handling the uncool client that she may not have time to work on the case. If you are paying an hourly fee, it will profit you to remember that the lawyer makes the same money for consoling you as she does for handling your case.

Students in law school do not specialize in any particular area. They study the whole law and may take one additional course in their field of interest, although this is no indication that the student will grow up to be an attorney specializing in that particular field. Specialties in the law are developed by doing them rather than by being educated in them. Don't expect any particular expertise in any particular area from a guy who is essentially a general practitioner. The most important thing in law school is learning how to find what you need to know. The attorney is sure to be able to do this.

If you have an odd case, or there is an especially large amount of money involved, you may wish to seek out a specialist. The general practitioner attorney you talk to may be able to point you in the right direction. He may also continue to work with you and the specialist. For example, it is not unusual for a general practitioner attorney to suggest that you also hire on an attorney who specializes in trial work. Your attorney may prepare the case, but the trial attorney will argue it. They will work out some fee-splitting arrangement between them.

Every once in a while the relationship between attorney and client will go bad. The most common sort of problem is the dilatory attorney. The dilatory attorney fools around and doesn't handle your case. She could also be working on your case but just look dilatory, since she isn't telling you about her efforts. If you haven't heard from your attorney recently, call her up and tell her point-blank that you're not sure she's working because she hasn't been talking to you or sending you letters. Tell her that the two of you seem to have a communication problem. It could be that she's just been rushed, or has a very big case pending. She'll be able to tell you what's been going on and can give you an estimate of how much time she'll have in the near future to devote to your case. If she hasn't got enough time for you, tell her that you're sorry, but you'll have to find someone else. The attorney is honor bound to turn over the files to the new attorney, who may work out better for you.

Only very rarely are excessive fees charged. If this should happen to you, you can complain to your local bar association. In all likelihood they will handle the fee arbitration on your behalf.

One trick attorneys use to collect their bills is refusing to continue or complete work until the fee has been paid. This practice is most common in divorce cases and is forbidden by the American Bar Association Code of Responsibility. Refusing to work on a case is neglect of duty on the part of the attorney. Neglect of duty is grounds for a malpractice suit.

The two biggest types of malpractice are caused by the dilatory attorney and by the attorney who refuses to continue working on the case. The client can sue for malpractice in a civil court and recover damages for the harm caused her.

If you think that your attorney has been guilty of malpractice, or has lied or cheated in your case, you can call the local bar association or the highest court in your area. Both organizations run ethics committees to investigate such accusations and to discipline those operating on less than the highest ethical standard.

When dealing with an attorney keep in mind that he is subject to all of the same failings as the rest of humankind. Sloth, pride, lust, anger, gluttony, envy, and covetousness are no strangers to the ranks at the bar. Keep copies of all documents you give to the attorney, and *never* give him any money unless you have receipts to back it up. A lot of attorneys wouldn't abscond, but some might.

BIBLIOGRAPHY

Barret, Edward L., Jr., Bruton, Paul W., and Honnold, John. *Constitutional Law*. 2nd. ed. New York: The Foundation Press, 1963.

Bernhardt, Robert. *Real Property in a Nutshell*. St. Paul: West Publishing Co., 1975.

Blaine, William L., and Bishop, John. *Practical Guide for the Unmarried Couple*. New York: Two Continents Publishing Group, 1976.

Clark, Homer H., Jr. *The Law of Domestic Relations*. St. Paul: West Publishing Co., 1968.

Epstein, David G. *Debtor-Creditor Law in a Nutshell*. St. Paul: West Publishing Co., 1973.

————. *Consumer Protection in a Nutshell*. St. Paul: West Publishing Co., 1976.

Friedman, Milton. *Capitalism and Freedom*. Chicago: University of Chicago Press, 1962.

Gellhorn, Ernest. *Administrative Law and Process in a Nutshell*. St. Paul: West Publishing Co., 1972.

Hallman, G. Victor, and Rosenbloom, Jerry S. *Personal Financial Planning*. New York: McGraw-Hill Book Company, 1975.

Hubbard, L. Ron. *The Volunteer Minister's Handbook*. Los Angeles: Church of Scientology Publications Organization United States, 1976. (The quote from this book on page 28 is copyrighted © 1959, 1976 by L. Ron Hubbard.)

Loewy, Arnold H. *Criminal Law in a Nutshell*. St. Paul: West Publishing Co., 1975.

Lynn, Robert J. *Introduction to Estate Planning in a Nutshell*. 2nd. ed. St. Paul: West Publishing Co., 1978.

Noel, Dix W., and Phillips, Jerry J. *Products Liability in a Nutshell*. St. Paul: West Publishing Co., 1974.

Player, Mack A. *Federal Law of Employment Discrimination in a Nutshell*. St. Paul: West Publishing Co., 1976.

Prosser, William L. *Handbook of the Law of Torts*. 2nd. ed. St. Paul: West Publishing Co., 1971.

Schaber, Gordon D., and Rohwer, Claude D. *Contracts in a Nutshell*. St. Paul: West Publishing Co., 1975.

Silberman, Charles E. *Criminal Violence, Criminal Justice*. New York: Random House, 1978.

Simes, Lewis M., and Fratcher, William F. *Cases and Materials on the Law of Fiduciary Administration*. 2nd. ed. Chicago: Callaghan and Company, 1956.

Stone, Bradford. *Uniform Commercial Code in a Nutshell*. St. Paul: West Publishing Co., 1975.

Striker, John M., and Shapiro, Andrew O. *Super Tenant*. Rev. ed. New York: Holt, Rinehart and Winston, 1978.

Viera, Norman. *Civil Rights in a Nutshell*. St. Paul: West Publishing Co., 1978.

Index

Debs, Eugene, 226
Debts, 352–64 (*see also* Credit);
   couples and responsibility for,
   11–12, 122; in estate, 206
Declaration of Independence, 226
Decree nisi, 50
Deeds, 130–32
Defamation of character, 356–57
Default decrees, 51
Default judgment, 359
Delaware, and divorce on refusal of
   sexual intercourse, 35; and
   garnishment, 362; and
   incompatibility, 38; and no-fault
   divorce, 39; and parties to
   divorce, 44; and rape, 244;
   venereal disease and divorce, 40;
   and wife's right to sue husband, 13
"Dependent" children, 67
Dependent promise, 313
Deportation, 239
Depositions, 47
Desertion, 35–36
Design defects, 322–23
Dilatory attorneys, 385, 391–92
Disability, pregnancy and, 87–88,
   90; and Social Security, 292, 293,
   296
Discovery, in divorce cases, 47
Discrimination. *See* specific areas
Disinheritance, 192–93, 201
Dispossess, 110, 111
District of Columbia (Washington),
   building codes, 103–4; and
   common-law marriage, 3, 116;
   and fornication, 118 and
   garnishment, 362; and
   incompatibility, 38; and no-fault
   divorce, 39; and parties to
   divorce, 44; and rape, 245; and
   wage assignment, 361; and wife's
   right to sue husband, 13
Dividends, insurance, 173
Divorce, 27–73, 115–16 (*see also*
   Alimony; Child custody; Child
   support; Credit; specific grounds);
   attorneys and fees, 392; and

health insurance, 180; shoe-box,
   115; and marriage license, 5; and
   physical abuse, 252–53, 255; and
   Social Security, 292–93
Doctors, and accidents, 263–64; and
   quasi-contracts, 305. *See also*
   Abortion
Doe v. *Bolton,* 240
Dogs, responsibility for, 261
Do-it-yourself divorce, 73
Door-to-door salesmen, 348–49
Dower, 9–10, 200
Driving. *See* Automobiles
Drugs, and battered women, 251;
   and divorce, 40; heroin, 288;
   prison and, 382; and products
   liability, 322, 324
Drunkenness. *See* Alcohol
Due process, 224, 233, 239, 274,
   283, 284. *See also* specific
   situations
Duress, contracts and, 308

Earnest money, 125
Education (*see also* College and
   university; School), and first
   books, 225
Effective tax rate, 147–48
Elkton, Maryland, 4
Emancipation, doctrine of, 26
Embalming, 76
Embezzlement, 184; 370ff.
Employment. *See* Working
Employment agencies, 83
Encounters, marriage, 28
Encumbrances, real estate, 126, 127
Endowment insurance, 168, 173
Engagement ring, 2–3
England, 225–26, 229, 230; and
   alimony, 51–52; Bill of Rights,
   223; and cruelty, 37; and divorce,
   34; and equity, 44; and fire
   insurance, 162
"Enoch Arden" divorce, 36
Epstein, Edward Jay, 288
Equal Credit Opportunity Act, 142,
   331ff.